S0-ALC-532

To Brother Jim Welsh,

A little something to read on an airplane or a rain tarnished day. I hope you find something in it of help in your work, your career and your future. Please share it with my nephews before they become completely educated in the conventional wisdom.

Best wishes,

John A. Welch

Administering
the
Closely Held Company

Administering
the
Closely Held Company

John A. Welsh
and
Jerry F. White

Prentice-Hall, Inc.   **Englewood Cliffs, New Jersey**

Prentice-Hall International, Inc., *London*
Prentice-Hall of Australia, Pty. Ltd., *Sydney*
Prentice-Hall of Canada, Ltd., *Toronto*
Prentice-Hall of India Private Ltd., *New Delhi*
Prentice-Hall of Japan, Inc., *Tokyo*
Prentice-Hall of Southeast Asia Pte. Ltd., *Singapore*
Whitehall Books, Ltd., *Wellington, New Zealand*

© 1980 by
Prentice-Hall, Inc.
Englewood Cliffs, N.J.

*All rights reserved. No part of this book
may be reproduced in any form or by
any means without permission in
writing from the publisher.*

Library of Congress Cataloging in Publication Data

Welsh, John A
    Administrating the closely held company.

    Includes index.
    1. Close corporations—Management. 2. Business.
3. Management. I. White, Jerry F., joint author.
II. Title.
HD2741.W37   658'.045   79-25489
ISBN 0-13-004887-9

Printed in the United States of America

This book is dedicated to
W.W. CARUTH, JR.,
and the Caruth Institute
of
Owner-Managed Business
at the Edwin L. Cox School of Business,
Southern Methodist University.

About the Authors

JOHN A. WELSH

John A. Welsh is the director of the Caruth Institute of Owner-Managed Business at the Edwin L. Cox School of Business, Southern Methodist University. He was a member of the founding team of the energy conversion firm, Thermo Electron, Inc. serving as its treasurer for four years. He was president of the high technology engineering firm Joseph Kaye & Co. of Cambridge, Massachusetts.

In 1961 he founded Flow Laboratories, Inc., a company which after several mergers is now listed on the American Stock Exchange as Flow General Corporation and headquartered in McLean, Virginia. During his tenure as president of Flow, he founded Flow Laboratories, Ltd. in Scotland to serve Europe; Flow Research Animals in Dublin, Virginia; and Flow Pharmaceuticals, Inc. in Palo Alto, California to provide quality prescription and over-the-counter drugs. During his earlier career he taught at the Massachusetts Institute of Technology.

JERRY F. WHITE

Jerry F. White is a founder and senior partner of Welsh, White, Wood and Associates, Inc., a management consulting firm specializing in fast-growth businesses. He is also a founder and chairman of the Owner-Managed Business Center, Inc. in Dallas, Texas which produces and markets innovative management development programs for owner-managers. The author is affiliated with the Edwin L. Cox School of Business, Southern Methodist University, as associate director of the Caruth Institute of Owner-Managed Business.

Mr. White has presented more than 200 seminars on Profit and Cash Flow Management throughout the United States and Canada to more than 5,000 owner-managers. As author of numerous publications on management of the closely held business, his works have appeared in professional journals including the *Journal of Small Business Management, Administrative Management* and the *Advanced Management Journal.* During his earlier career he was associated with Westinghouse, IBM and Collins Radio.

What This Book Will Do for You

This book is written by individuals who have devoted their professional careers to the challenges of administering the closely held business. While principles and techniques discussed in this book are specifically directed at the closely held company, they are applicable to businesses of any size that want to boost bottom line figures. Dramatically. Consistently.

If you are a manager who has ever felt the "concern" of meeting the payroll, or if you have ever felt like you know you're making money but there is no cash in the bank, this book is for you. This book will demonstrate how to become more effective in dealing with people challenges, money challenges, selling challenges, and production challenges associated with administering the closely held company.

Why do you need this book? What will it do for you? A few answers to these questions are given in the following checklist.

- This book completely spells out tested ways to calculate PROFIT and CASH FLOW. Examples covering manufacturing, retail and service businesses are used to demonstrate key principles. A procedure is outlined for determining how fast you can grow without falling into the deadly "rapid growth" pitfall. See Chapter 1.

- The book reveals the ACCOUNTS RECEIVABLE pitfall and how to avoid it. It points out 14 techniques for getting your customers' money faster. Pros and Cons of different collection techniques are presented and the most effective techniques are identified. See Chapter 2.

- It explains how to improve profit and cash flow through effective management of INVENTORY. How to avoid the stockpiling pitfall is described. The "red flags" associated with quantity discounts, long lead times and minimum order quantities are identified. See Chapter 3.

- The book shows you how to decide whether or not to take CASH DISCOUNTS. Improving financial performance through ACCOUNTS PAYABLE management is accented. The authors show you how to formulate a reverse discount strategy and how to change the cost of supplier financing. They provide a working chart to help you determine the *real* cost of your bank financing. A method is outlined for determining if late payment penalties are a bargain. See Chapter 4.

- The book demonstrates how DEPRECIATION and the INVESTMENT TAX CREDIT represent powerful profit and cash flow management techniques. Understanding and dealing with recapture are discussed. How to select the best depreciation method is outlined. See Chapter 5.

- It gives you the ABC's of smart use of LIFO and FIFO inventory costing techniques. How LIFO and FIFO impact profit, cash flow and balance sheet ratios is demonstrated with specific examples. See Chapter 6.

- The book tells you how to play and WIN THE PROFIT AND CASH FLOW GAME. It tells you how to use the CRDM approach to improving cash flow and bank balances. It shows you how to "play the game" for a contracting business, a service business, and a retail business. See Chapter 7.

- The book describes three major game plans for MINIMIZING TAXES. It points out five strategies for reducing the amount subjected to the income tax calculation. It suggests seven ways to postpone income taxes. It shows you how to develop your own tax estimating and planning chart. How to use ACCOUNTING MANEUVERS to minimize taxes is revealed along with five cautions. See Chapter 8.

- It shows you why A BUSINESS MUST GROW. The eight places where profit goes in a business are identified. See Chapter 9.

- The book provides you with a convenient list of common RETURN ON INVESTMENT formulas useful in measuring the effectiveness with which you manage the company's financial resources. It tells you how to use ROI and points out the owner-manager's special perspective. It gives you a methodology for comparing future dollars and present dollars. How the TIME VALUE OF MONEY is used in analyzing potential investments is revealed. Compounding and discounting as decision tools are investigated. See Chapter 10.

- The book identifies five RECURRING REASONS why closely held businesses fail. It explains the 100-days blindspot built into timely financial statments and suggests how the smart manager deals with this dilemma. See Chapter 11.

- It reveals how the BALANCE SHEET, the CASH FLOW STATEMENT and the INCOME STATEMENT are derived. It tells you how to avoid the superficiality pitfall. See Chapter 12.

- The book provides an intelligent approach to SELECTING A BANK and a banker. It provides a checklist for making a loan application. It reveals why banks turn down loan requests. What the U.S. SMALL BUSINESS ADMINIS- TRATION (SBA) can do for you is outlined. How to locate formal and informal sources of VENTURE CAPITAL is discussed. The pros and cons of GOING PUBLIC are investigated. See Chapter 13.

- The book tells you how the LEARNING CURVE and the EXPERIENCE CURVE suggest an approach for dominating the competition. It shows you how to identify your Experience Curve. A tested methodology is revealed for planning an effective EXPANSION STRATEGY and evolving a competitive PRICING POLICY. See Chapter 14.

- It suggests a way to measure PRODUCTIVITY. The financial impact of productivity on PROFIT, RETURN ON INVESTMENT and CASH FLOW is examined. It tells you how the SCANLON PLAN works, and why. See Chapter 15.

• The book tells you how to find a buyer for your company. It reveals how to VALUE A BUSINESS. It examines the pros and cons of KEEPING, SELLING and MERGING. The authors provide insights regarding WHEN is the best time TO SELL. How to use PRICE EARNINGS RATIO is outlined. See Chapter 16.

Each chapter is fully supported with commentary, charts, graphs and tabular exhibits. A major goal is not only to point out unique techniques and working aids but to do so in a way that the owner-manager can grasp and implement them quickly.

How This Book is Organized

Administering the Closely Held Company is organized under four major topics that are at the heart of the owner-manager's operating concerns. These four major areas arise from examination of what a business is in the first place.

A business is a group of people working together to satisfy their individual needs, goals, and aspirations.

This group includes not only

- Employees

  but also,

- Customers
- Suppliers
- Regulatory Agencies
- Employees' Families
- Institutions
- Independent Professionals

It seems rather clear that,

A BUSINESS IS A PEOPLE PROPOSITION.

The value of each person's contribution as well as the value of the ultimate product or service must be measured. Money is the measuring mechanism. It is obvious that,

A BUSINESS IS A MONEY PROPOSITION.

Businesses operate in an environment in which others are competing to satisfy the customers' needs. Competitive selling results. Logically,

A BUSINESS IS A SELLING PROPOSITION.

To satisfy their own needs, goals and aspirations, some of the group (employees) band together to produce a product or a service that satisfies the needs, goals, and aspirations of other individuals. Fundamentally,

A BUSINESS IS A PRODUCING PROPOSITION.

Focusing on these four major management areas, this book is organized so that

PEOPLE are the major focus of Chapters 9, 11.

MONEY is the major focus of Chapters 1, 2, 3, 4, 5, 6, 7, 8, 10, 12, 13, 16.

SELLING is the major focus of Chapter 14.

PRODUCING is the major focus of Chapter 15.

The authors' approach is to take the time to convey, in pragmatic, down-to-earth language (and frequently in a unique manner), understanding of how a fundamental principle or technique works. Examples, checklists, cautions, and other working aids are then utilized to demonstrate how the manager of a closely held business can effectively take advantage of the principle or technique.

How to Use This Book

The preceding pages told you what this book will do for you and how this book is organized. Now consider the following possible uses of this book:

Specific Challenges: If you are interested in a specific decision, such as whether or not to offer a discount when trying to better manage Accounts Receivable, turn to the Table of Contents to locate the chapter in which that topic is discussed. In this case, it is Chapter 2. An explanation is given of the various aspects of the topic. Pitfalls are pointed out and recommended strategies are presented. Use them for effective problem solving.

General Challenges: If you can identify most of your challenges as falling in one of the following four general areas:

- People
- Money
- Selling
- Producing

you can direct your initial reading toward one of the following groups of chapters:

General Problem	Relevant Chapters
People	9, 11
Money	1, 2, 3, 4, 5, 6, 7, 8, 10, 12, 13, 16
Selling	14
Producing	15

For across-the-board types of challenges in one of these four major areas, go to the indicated chapters. Study the points of each chapter one at a time until you've mastered the relevant principle or technique. Utilize the "how to's" and recommended strategies to improve performance in that particular area.

The Owner-Manager Perspective: This book emphasizes problems and solutions from the perspective of the person at the top, the owner-manager. Though the techniques, strategies and tactics discussed are directed at that individual, those who deal intimately with the chief executive of a closely held company will also find this book invaluable. Your effectiveness can be dramatically increased by turning to the chapters containing topics that relate to your particular dealings with a specific owner-manager. Take the time to understand the problem from the owner-manager's point of view. Finally, use the recommended techniques to arrive at a practical and acceptable solution.

John A. Welsh

Jerry F. White

Acknowledgments

The authors would like to acknowledge the contribution of various individuals who helped make this book possible. We are particularly grateful to Lois E. Adams for administration and editing, and Lee D. Breeden for statistics and research. We are especially grateful to Larry S. Barnett for his graphic illustrations and artwork.

We would also like to acknowledge the helpful suggestions and professional critique provided by William W. Wood (Management Consultant), Wally J. Boyer (Banker), Craig E. Felber (Management Consultant), W.R. (Bob) Wilson (Merger/Acquisitions Specialist), C. Charles Bahr (Manager), and Vicki S. Downing (Business Consultant).

Business Acknowledgments

We are deeply grateful to the following firms for allowing us to use selected information in this book.

Specific references appear in the Chapter Notes.

Arthur Andersen & Co.

Dow Jones-Irwin

Journal of Small Business Management

Matthew Bender & Company, Inc.

Prentice-Hall, Inc.

Table of Contents

Table of Exhibits

Chapter 3

Inventory Management - Key to Financial Prosperity in the Closely Held Firm

Chapter 4

Administering Accounts Payable - Making Money in the Way You Pay Your Bills

Chapter 5

Powerful Profit and Cash Flow Techniques Using Depreciation and the Investment Tax Credit

Chapter 6

Smart Administration with LIFO and FIFO Inventory Costing Techniques

Chapter 7

A Special Approach for Boosting Cash Flow and Bank Balances for Closely Held Enterprises

Chapter 8

Approaches to Cutting the Company's Taxes Versus the Owner-Manager's Taxes

Chapter 9

Eight Ratholes Where Profits Go in the Closely Held Firm

Chapter 10

Return on Investment or Liquidity: Solving a Dilemma for the Closely Held Manager

Chapter 11

Five Recurring Reasons Why Owner-Managed Businesses Fail: Lining Up the Defenses

Chapter 12

How to Get a Fix on the Numbers of Your Closely Held Business

Chapter 14

Blueprinting and Administering Lucrative Expansion Strategies and Beat-the-Competition Policies

Chapter 15

Improving Productivity in Your Closely Held Organization

1

Administering Profit, Cash Flow and Growth in the Closely Held Enterprise

This book focuses on the closely held company even though many of the principles, concepts, strategies and techniques to be discussed apply to all businesses. There are a variety of ways to define what is meant by closely held company. What the authors are referring to are companies that are not publicly owned, that is companies not traded on the New York Stock Exchange, American Stock Exchange or any Over the Counter Market. The phrase owner-managed company is used here interchangeably with closely held company.

The examples, working aids and practices discussed are directed at owner-managers. The authors like to think of these individuals as persons responsible for running the day to day operations of a business and ones who own enough of the company that they feel a genuine concern for meeting the payroll.

Many closely held businesses struggle for long periods of time, under adverse conditions to achieve success. It is difficult for some individuals to comprehend how success usually creates a potentially fatal set of circumstances for the business. To understand how this can occur, and subsequently how you can deal with the problem, it is crucial to understand in detail two fundamental but frequently confused concepts, profit and cash flow.

PROFIT AND CASH FLOW: CRUCIAL MEASURES OF COMPANY PERFORMANCE

Profit and cash flow are precise but distinctly different approaches to viewing a company's operations. These two concepts are at most only indirectly related. Many management problems result from attempts to draw conclusions about one based on information about the other.

The Concept of Profit

Profit is the difference between revenues and expenses, that is, profit equals revenues minus expenses. One needn't try to state it any more simply and there is no need to try to state it more meaningfully. Such efforts only cloud the issue.

The essence of the profit concept then depends upon what is meant by revenues and what is meant by expenses.[1]

REVENUES

The problem of recognizing revenues centers around when to write down the number representing a sale. Is it when the order was received? Is it when the goods were shipped? Is it when the bill was sent? Is it when payment was received from the customer?[2]

The question is generally settled by asking when the customer becomes obligated to pay. If one has not yet filled an order, then the customer does not yet owe for it. When one ships the goods or performs the services ordered, then the customer owes for the goods or services. That is when the obligation to pay begins.[3]

Revenue is recorded as of the date a business completes its part of a transaction which will result in payment to the business for a product shipped or a service performed.[4]

EXPENSES

Expenses refer to what was consumed, or used up, (materials, labor, etc.) during a given period of time to get the revenues recorded during that particular period of time. It does not matter when the item consumed was bought, received or paid for. What is crucial is what was consumed and how much of it, during a given time period to get the revenues in that same time period. (For example, $850 in office rent could have been consumed in July in the process of generating the sales for July.)[5]

CALCULATING PROFIT

Somewhat different formats are used for calculating and reporting profit in different businesses. Manufacturing businesses and retail businesses provide examples of two common formats.

Example of a Manufacturing Business

The income statement (sometimes referred to as a profit and loss statement, P & L statement, or simply operating statement) shown in Exhibit 1-1 illustrates the basic format for a manufacturing business.[6]

EXHIBIT 1-1
Income Statement
Basic Format for a Manufacturing Business

REVENUES	$1,000
EXPENSES	
Direct Material	400
Direct Labor	100
Overhead	50
Cost of Goods Sold	550
Gross Profit	450
General & Administrative	150
Marketing	200
Total Expenses	900
Pre-Tax Profit	100
Income Tax	17
Net Profit	$ 83

The Direct Material referred to in Exhibit 1-1 pertains to materials actually ending up in the products that were sold for the period in question. Direct Labor refers to the labor actually consumed in producing the products which were sold during the time frame in question. Overhead refers to those indirect costs associated with getting the product in a condition ready to be sold. This overhead might include such items as storage cost for the direct materials or the direct labor supervisor's salary. Also, fringe benefits for the direct laborers, utilities in the manufacturing area, quality control, manufacturing, engineering and other such indirect costs would be included in this category.

Cost of Goods Sold represents the sum of all the direct costs, that is Direct Material, Direct Labor and Manufacturing Overhead. Gross Profit is merely the difference between total Revenues of a period and the total Cost of Goods Sold for that same period.

General and Administrative expenses have to do with the administration of the business. Frequently referred to as G & A, these expenses include the president's salary, the president's secretary's salary, legal fees, accounting costs, the cost of stationery and other office supplies, company insurance coverages, telephone, postage and other such expenses. Marketing expenses refer to those costs incurred in an effort to get the customer to buy the product. Advertising, salespeople's salaries, brochures and market surveys are expenses that could logically be included in this category.

Pre-Tax Profit is obtained by subtracting the Total of all Expenses from the total Revenues for a given time period. Income Tax refers to Federal income tax. For this basic example an effective income tax rate of 17% is assumed. Net Profit, often referred to as "the bottom line" is calculated by subtracting the Income Tax liability from the Pre-Tax Profit.

Income statements represent one of the most common finanacial statements. Since they list what was "used up" to make the sales, we humorously refer to them as "Use 'em up reports." They are prepared for a particular period of time, such as for the month of June or for the last fiscal year.

Example of a Retail Business

An example of a slightly different format utilized to calculate profit is presented in Exhibit 1-2. This Exhibit portrays the basic format for an income statement of a retail business.

EXHIBIT 1-2
Income Statement
Basic Format for a Retail Business

REVENUES		$1,000
EXPENSES		
Cost of Goods Sold		
Beginning Inventory	$3,000	
plus Purchases	500	
less Ending Inventory	2,900	
Cost of Goods Sold		600
Gross Profit		400
General & Administrative		150
Marketing		160
Total Expenses		910
Pre-Tax Profit		90
Income Tax		15
Net Profit		$ 75

The principal difference between the retail business format and that of the manufacturing company occurs in the area of Cost of Goods Sold. In a manufacturing business, laborers work on materials to produce units which are then sold. In a retail business, units are purchased in a form ready to be sold. The manufacturing business income statement, consequently, focuses on identifying what were the materials cost, the labor cost and the overhead cost related to the goods actually shipped in a given time period. The retail business income statement, on the other hand, typically analyzes the inventory of merchandise. What was on hand at the beginning of a period is added to how much was received during the period of time in question and Ending Inventory is subtracted from the sum of these two. This allows calculation of the cost of the goods which were actually sold during the time period under consideration. General and Administrative expenses as well as Marketing expenses have essentially the same meanings for a retail business as for a manufacturing business. Once the Total Expenses of a period are identified and subtracted from the Total Revenues of that same period, the method for calculating Pre-Tax Profit, Income Tax and Net Profit is the same for all businesses.

The Concept of Cash Flow

Cash flow is a net concept. During a particular period of time, like a month, cash will be deposited to the bank account of a business. During the same period, cash will be withdrawn, usually by writing checks. The difference between the deposits and the checks is the net of what went into the bank. If one adds up all of the deposits and then subtracts all of the checks withdrawn, the result is the net cash flow into the bank account. Cash flow is calculated for a given period of time by finding the difference between receipts and disbursements of cash.[7]

RECEIPTS

Receipts refer to bank deposits. One of the reasons for using this word is to emphasize the difference between revenues and receipts. They are not interchangeable words. Many managers would like to think of them as such, but that can lead to disaster. Revenues result from obligations of customers to pay a business as a result of goods shipped and services provided. Receipts appear when those obligations are fulfilled.[8]

There are, however, other sources of receipts. When investors buy common stock in a company, there is a receipt by the business of the cash paid for that stock. When a business borrows from the bank, there is likewise a receipt of cash. Neither of these receipts is in any way related to revenues.[9]

DISBURSEMENTS

Disbursements refer to cash withdrawn from the bank account of the business. The word disbursements is no more interchangeable with the word expenses than receipts is with revenues. Disbursements are the movement of real cash from a business. Expenses are an obligation to move cash at some time generally in the future. Furthermore, the size of disbursements and their timing can be and usually is very different from that of expenses.[10]

There are some disbursements that do not represent payment of expenses. Repaying the principal on a bank loan constitutes a disbursement unrelated to an expense (nothing was used up, only borrowed and then given back). Payment for the purchase of a long-life asset represents a current disbursement that materializes as an expense only a little bit at a time over the useful life of the asset, through the mechanism of depreciation.

CALCULATING CASH FLOW

Calculating cash flow is rather straightforward. For a given time period, an orderly listing of the disbursements subtracted from a list of the receipts yields the cash flow. [11] If this cash flow is added to the beginning bank balance, the bank balance at the end of the period can be computed.

Example of a Manufacturing Business

The basic format for the cash flow statement of a manufacturing business is shown in Exhibit 1-3.[12]

EXHIBIT 1-3
Cash Flow Statement
Basic Format for a Manufacturing Business

RECEIPTS	
From Sales	$ 980
Paid In Capital	125
Loans Received	-0-
Total Receipts	1,105
DISBURSEMENTS	
Direct Material	600
Direct Labor	100
Overhead	52
General & Administrative	141
Marketing	204
Capital Equipment Purchased	300
Tax Deposits	60
Loan Principal Repayments	35
Total Disbursements	1,492
Cash Flow	$ (387)
Beginning Bank Balance	$ 800
Ending Bank Balance	$ 413

When this cash flow statement (that is like a summary of the company's checkbook) is viewed in light of the income statement shown in Exhibit 1-1, a number of differences become evident. First of all, the basic nomenclature is different; revenues and expenses on the income statement and receipts and disbursements on the cash flow statement. Receipts include cash coming into the company from sources such as Paid In Capital or Loans Received, as well as from sales. It is also important to observe that in this illustrative example $1,000 in revenues was recognized but only $980 was actually collected in cash. Direct Material, Direct Labor, Overhead, General and Administrative and Marketing represent categories that are common between the two statements. It is interesting to note, however, that the amount recognized as an expense of the period is not necessarily the amount of cash that was actually disbursed in that category for that period. Capital Equipment, Tax Deposits and Loan Repayments represent items that are unique to the cash flow statement.

It is common that the total disbursed will be greater than the total received. In this case the cash flow is negative as evidenced by the total being enclosed in brackets. It is interesting to note that in this example there is a positive net profit but a negative cash flow.

Since the main purpose of Exhibit 1-3 is to demonstrate the basic format of the cash flow statement for a manufacturing business, no attempt is made to derive extensive logic relating this to the income statement of Exhibit 1-1. The detailed interactions between the income statement and the cash flow statement will be discussed in a subsequent example.

Example of a Retail Business

To illustrate a slightly different cash flow statement, the basic format for a retail business is presented in Exhibit 1-4.

EXHIBIT 1-4
Cash Flow Statement
Basic Format for a Retail Business

RECEIPTS	
From Sales	$1,000
Paid In Capital	-0-
Loans Received	225
Total Receipts	1,225
DISBURSEMENTS	
Merchandise (Payments for)	550
General & Administrative	140
Marketing	158
Capital Equipment Purchased	20
Tax Deposits	45
Loan Repayments	15
Total Disbursements	928
Cash Flow	$ 297
Beginning Bank Balance	$ 800
Ending Bank Balance	$1,097

This cash flow statement resembles the one for a manufacturing business shown in Exhibit 1-3. Perhaps the most significant difference occurs in the disbursements category entitled merchandise. For the retail business, the goods sold are purchased in a form ready to be sold. In the manufacturing business, materials that go into the product, labor that then works on the materials and overhead that is related to both materials and labor must be considered individually.

When the cash flow statement for a simple retail business is viewed in light of the basic format for the income statement of a retail business shown in Exhibit 1-2, several differences are apparent. Perhaps the most significant occurs in the area relating to the goods that were sold. On the income statement, an analysis of changes in inventory permits deduction of the cost of the goods sold. On the cash flow statement, payments for merchandise—checks written to the suppliers of the merchandise—are all that appear. Categories of expenses being different from counterpart categories of disbursements are typical in that the expenses recognized may not be the ones actually paid for in a given time period. Since many retail businesses sell only on a cash basis, it would not be uncommon to see the revenue recognized on the income statement being identical to the receipts from sales shown on the cash flow statement.

In this example both the net profit and cash flow were positive. Under a slightly different set of circumstances, this could have been a very different situation.

Once again, the cash flow statement of Exhibit 1-4 is primarily a demonstration of the basic format for a retail business. Logical interactions between the income statement and the cash flow statement will be further examined later in this chapter.

Profit Is Not Cash Flow

The phenomenon of cash flow being very unlike profit (suggested by the illustrations of Exhibits 1-1, 1-2, 1-3 and 1-4) is generally the result of two things. First, there is the lapse of time between obtaining raw materials and employing labor to prepare a product for sale and the time of the actual sale of the product. Second, there is the influence of credit. Cash is not necessarily paid for labor and materials at the time the labor is employed or the materials are purchased. Likewise, cash may or may not be paid at the time a sale is made.[13]

Profit is a mathematical concept representing the difference between two numerical sums. One is the price which the customer agrees to pay. The other is the total of prices the business commits to pay for all of the goods and services used in the preparation of the product or service for sale. Profit is the difference between agreed upon prices to be paid.[14]

Cash flow is best described as the money deposited to the bank account of the business less the cash withdrawals from that account. Most deposits result from customers paying for products previously sold. Disbursements generally result from the business' paying for goods or services previously purchased. Cash flow is not a mathematical concept; it is the money put in the bank less the money taken out of the bank. The size of the cash flow and its direction, positive or negative, depends every bit as much upon when the money is deposited or withdrawn as upon how much is deposited or withdrawn.[15]

Profit is not cash flow. To illustrate this point in detail, consider the example of Intercity Assembly Company, Inc. The president of Intercity prepared a forecasted income statement for the next seven months of operations as seen in Exhibit 1-5.[16]

EXHIBIT 1-5
INTERCITY ASSEMBLY COMPANY, INC.
PRO FORMA INCOME STATEMENT

Month	1	2	3	4	5	6	7
REVENUE							
Units Sold	40,000	42,000	44,000	47,000	50,000	53,000	55,000
Sales	$ 80,000	84,000	88,000	94,000	100,000	106,000	110,000
EXPENSES							
Direct Materials	40,000	42,000	44,000	47,000	50,000	53,000	55,000
Direct Labor	4,000	4,200	4,400	4,700	5,000	5,300	5,500
Overhead	4,000	4,000	4,000	4,000	4,000	4,000	4,000
Cost of Goods Sold	48,000	50,200	52,400	55,700	59,000	62,300	64,500
Gross Profit	32,000	33,800	35,600	38,300	41,000	43,700	45,500
General & Administrative							
Salaries	6,900	7,450	7,500	8,350	8,350	9,000	9,000
Rent	2,000	2,000	2,000	2,000	2,000	2,000	2,000
Insurance	500	500	500	500	500	500	500
Depreciation	170	170	170	170	170	170	170
Other G&A	3,000	4,100	4,550	5,500	6,600	7,050	7,850
Marketing							
Advertising	9,750	9,800	10,200	11,000	11,600	12,500	13,000
Brochures	450	450	450	450	450	450	450
Total Expense	70,770	74,670	77,770	83,670	88,670	93,970	97,470
Taxable Income	9,230	9,330	10,230	10,330	11,330	12,030	12,530
Income Taxes	2,769	2,799	3,069	3,099	3,399	3,609	3,759
Net Profit	$ 6,461	6,531	7,161	7,231	7,931	8,421	8,771

The units in this example sell for $2.00 each. The cost of Direct Materials is averaging $1.00 per unit. Direct Labor is averaging $.10 per unit. Manufacturing Overhead consists of indirect costs associated with the materials and the labor. In this example it includes $2,700 in depreciation each month, based on the purchase of a $180,000 asset (manufacturing equipment used to produce the product) in Month 1, that is depreciated straight line over a five-year period with a 10% salvage value. In addition, there is $1,300 per month in other miscellaneous manufacturing overhead costs for a total fixed monthly overhead of $4,000.

The Cost of Goods Sold is the sum of all of the direct expenses each month that include Direct Materials, Direct Labor and Manufacturing Overhead. Gross Profit is obtained by subtracting the Cost of Goods Sold in a given month from the Sales of that month. Salaries refer to the portion of the payroll that goes to administrative employees, including the president and several clerical persons. Rent is related to the building in which Intercity resides. It is medium quality warehouse space near the edge of the city limits. The annual insurance premium is $6,000. Spreading this cost out over the 12 months of the coming year results in $500 per month in insurance costs. Depreciation on equipment utilized in an administrative capacity in the company is based on a total of $10,200 in used equipment purchased and depreciated on the straight-line basis over a period of five years with a zero salvage value. Of this $10,200 in equipment, $3,000 is to be acquired in Month 1. The remainder was acquired during prior periods. Other G & A includes an allowance for general and administrative expenses including postage, telephone, legal, accounting, office supplies, etc.

Advertising includes an allowance for promotion costs related to several different media. Brochures include an allocation of the cost of a relatively inexpensive information piece. A 12-month supply costs $5,400. Spreading this out equally over 12 months yields $450 per month.

Taxable Income is calculated by subtracting the Total Expenses each month from the Sales of that month. Income Taxes refer to Federal income taxes for a corporation. For this example an effective income tax rate of 30% is assumed. The corporate income tax is a progressive tax charging a higher rate at higher income levels. For the business being discussed, an average rate of 30% for the year is reasonable. The latest corporate tax rate may be obtained by requesting a copy of Bulletin 334, "Tax Guide for Small Business." The Bulletin is free from the Internal Revenue Service.

Net Profit is calculated by subtracting income taxes in a given month from the pre-tax profit or taxable income of that month. It is assumed that Month 1 is the first month of the company's fiscal year and that none of the equipment acquired that month qualifies for investment tax credit (to be discussed later).

In addition to the forecasted income statement shown in Exhibit 1-5, the president of Intercity Assembly Company prepared its cash flow counterpart as seen in Exhibit 1-6.[17]

A private placement of common stock totaling $175,000 will be completed in Month 2. Payments from customers for sales are received in an average of 60 days after the sale is recorded. On the forecast this is shown as a two-month delay in the cash received from sales revenues.

Direct Materials are acquired and paid for as outlined in the inventory schedule of Exhibit 1-7. Direct Materials are purchased such that the Ending Inventory will be sufficient to cover the following month's sales. Orders for materials must be in multiples of 5,000 units with 5,000 units being the minimum order. Payment is 30 days after receipt of goods. Direct Materials cost $1.00 per unit.

The Direct Labor is paid in the month that the expense is incurred. Manufacturing Overhead consists of $2,700 per month that is a non-cash expense in the form of depreciation and $1,300 that is a cash outlay in that month. Only the $1,300 actual cash outlay portion is shown on the cash flow forecast. Salaries for the administrative personnel are paid in the month

EXHIBIT 1-6
INTERCITY ASSEMBLY COMPANY, INC.
PRO FORMA CASH FLOW STATEMENT

Month	1	2	3	4	5	6	7
RECEIPTS							
Sales Receipts	74,000*	77,000*	80,000	84,000	88,000	94,000	100,000
Common Stock	—	175,000	—	—	—	—	—
Total Received	$ 74,000	252,000	80,000	84,000	88,000	94,000	100,000
DISBURSEMENTS							
Direct Materials	40,000*	40,000	45,000	45,000	50,000	55,000	55,000
Direct Labor	4,000	4,200	4,400	4,700	5,000	5,300	5,500
Overhead	1,300	1,300	1,300	1,300	1,300	1,300	1,300
Manufacturing Equip.	—	180,000	—	—	—	—	—
Salaries	6,900	7,450	7,500	8,350	8,350	9,000	9,000
Rent	2,000	2,000	2,000	2,000	2,000	2,000	2,000
Insurance	6,000	—	—	—	—	—	—
Office Equipment	—	3,000	—	—	—	—	—
Other G&A	2,800*	3,000	4,100	4,550	5,500	6,600	7,050
Advertising	9,000*	9,750	9,800	10,200	11,000	11,600	12,500
Brochures	—	5,400	—	—	—	—	—
Taxes	11,000*	—	—	8,637	—	—	10,107
Total Disbursed	83,000	256,100	74,100	84,737	83,150	90,800	102,457
Total Cash Flow	$ (9,000)	(4,100)	5,900	(737)	4,850	3,200	(2,457)
Beginning Balance	$ 1,100	(7,900)	(12,000)	(6,100)	(6,837)	(1,987)	1,213
Ending Balance	$ (7,900)	(12,000)	(6,100)	(6,837)	(1,987)	1,213	(1,244)

*From operations during prior periods.

EXHIBIT 1-7
MATERIALS INVENTORY SCHEDULE (CALCULATED IN UNITS)
AND PURCHASES OVERVIEW

Month	1	2	3	4	5	6	7
Beginning Inventory	43,500	43,500	46,500	47,500	50,500	55,500	57,500
–Shipments (Out)	40,000	42,000	44,000	47,000	50,000	53,000	55,000
+Purchases (Received)	40,000	45,000	45,000	50,000	55,000	55,000	55,000
Ending Inventory	43,500	46,500	47,500	50,500	55,500	57,500	57,500
Purchases Overview							
Value of Purchases (Received)	$ 40,000	45,000	45,000	50,000	55,000	55,000	55,000
Cash Disbursements (Net 30)	$ 40,000*	40,000	45,000	45,000	50,000	55,000	55,000

*Due to a transaction of a prior period.

of the expense. Rent is paid in the month of the expense. Insurance is paid for the entire year in advance to save interest charged by the insurance company for the right to pay on a monthly basis. Capital Equipment consists of a $180,000 asset utilized in manufacturing and $3,000 in used office equipment. Both assets are acquired in Month 1 and are paid for on a net 30-day basis. Other G & A is paid in an average of 30 days. Advertising is also paid in 30 days. A year's supply of Brochures purchased in Month 1 is paid for on a net 30-day basis.

Federal income taxes must be deposited on a quarterly basis. The first quarter's accrued tax liability is forecasted by the president of Intercity to be actually disbursed at the beginning of Month 4. This would be the accrued income taxes indicated for Months 1, 2 and 3 in the forecasted income statement. The second quarter's estimated tax liability is forecasted to be made in Month 7. The accrued tax liability for the fourth quarter of the preceding fiscal year is estimated to be disbursed at the beginning of next month, Month 1, on the cash flow forecast.

The Cash Flow is computed by subtracting the Total Disbursed from the Total Received each month. The Ending Bank Balance for each month of the next seven months of the company's operations is calculated by adding the Cash Flow to the Beginning Balance for that month. The Beginning Balance for one month is identical to the Ending Balance of the preceding month. At midnight on the last day of the month, the bank balance does not change.

Brackets around cash flow numbers indicate negative cash flow. In those months disbursements exceed receipts. Brackets around bank balances indicate forecasted overdrafts in those months.

As may be seen from Exhibits 1-5 and 1-6 for Intercity, there is not a single month out of the next seven in which profit is equal to cash flow. Furthermore, there is no simple relationship between the two. There is a cliche that circulates among elements of the financial and managerial communities that holds that cash flow may be approximated by taking net profit and adding back depreciation. If this is done for Intercity Assembly Company, the presentation of Exhibit 1-8 results. This Exhibit shows a comparison of cash flow calculated on the receipts and disbursements method versus cash flow approximated by taking net profit after tax and adding back depreciation.

EXHIBIT 1-8
Comparison of Estimated Cash Flow with Actual Cash Flow

Month	Net Profit (from Income Statement)	Total Deprecia-tion (from Income Statement)	Estimated Cash Flow (Net Profit & Depreciation)	Actual Cash Flow (From Cash Flow Statement)
1	$6,461	$(2,700 + 170)	$ 9,331	$ (9,000)
2	6,531	"	9,401	(4,100)
3	7,161	"	10,031	5,900
4	7,231	"	10,101	(737)
5	7,931	"	10,801	4,850
6	8,421	"	11,291	3,200
7	8,771	"	11,641	(2,457)
		Cumulative	$72,597	$ (2,344)

The contrast between the estimated cash flow based on net profit plus depreciation and the actual cash flow based on receipts and disbursements in the company's bank account is dramatically shown in the last two columns of Exhibit 1-8. The difference is so significant that the prudent owner-manager should think twice about estimating cash flow of the business from a cliché.

Cash flow is often confused with what the accountants refer to as funds flow. The concept of funds results from a technique of analyzing changes in a company's balance sheet between two periods of time. There is a tremendous difference between the concept of cash flow as determined from the statement of receipts and disbursements of cash and funds flow as determined from changes in two different balance sheets. The cash flow calculated here is directly related to items owner-managers can identify and get their hands on in day-to-day operations.

One significant benefit of forecasting a company's cash flow is that the amount of financing required to carry out an anticipated series of operations is determined.[18] The ending bank balances for each month of the forecast are allowed to go overdraft as long as we are forecasting with pencil and paper. These overdrafts represent anticipated cash shortfalls. The amount of the calculated overdraft each month is the amount of additional, outside financing that must be procured prior to the actual occurrence of each projected overdraft.

GROWTH CAN PUT YOU OUT OF BUSINESS

Now that two precise measures of a company's performance have been described, profit and cash flow, consider the phenomenon of growth in sales. Many owner-managers feel that all of their problems would be solved if their businesses were just larger. Whether the need is felt for larger quantity purchasing, more sophisticated plant and equipment, access to sources of financing or merely the need for more and better personnel there is frequently an irresistible urge, a self-imposed mandate to grow. Even this book makes a strong case in Chapter 9 that a business must grow.

It is the instinctive urge to grow that unwittingly walks many owner-managers down the path of business suicide. Unenlightened management all too frequently finds itself a victim of the "growth trap."

How Growth Can Put a Manufacturing Company Out of Business

To illustrate what can happen to a typical manufacturing business, consider Intercity Assembly Company, Inc., whose future operations were portrayed in Exhibits 1-5 and 1-6. If sales began to grow faster than expected beginning in Month 4 of the forecast, the improved performance indicated in Exhibit 1-9 could easily result.[19]

With this faster rate of growth, sales would be 65,000 units in Month 7 instead of the originally forecast 55,000 units shipped in that month. Monthly profit would grow from $8,771 in Month 7 to $15,071 in that same month. The projected profits for Months 4 through 7 would be dramatically increased by the forecasted increase in sales for those four months.

It is interesting to note what happens to the company's cash flow and future bank balance if this extra growth in sales should materialize. The projected cash flow indicated in Exhibit 1-10 paints an interesting picture.[20] While sales and profits improve, cash flow takes a turn for the worse. Instead of Month 7 having a projected overdraft of $1,244 as originally forecast, an overdraft totaling $16,794 would result from the faster growth in sales. One of the significant changes in operations is indicated in Exhibit 1-11 with regard to the new materials purchasing schedule. Materials are purchased so that the ending inventory will be sufficient to cover the following month's sales. As with the original forecast, orders must be in multiples of 5,000 with 5,000 units constituting a minimum order. Payment is due 30 days after receipt of goods.

The difference in company performance between the original forecast and the forecast based on faster growth in sales is illustrated in Exhibit 1-12. As may be seen, the faster growth in sales produces an attractive increase in profits. What happens down at the bank, however, is a

EXHIBIT 1-9

INTERCITY ASSEMBLY COMPANY, INC.
PRO FORMA INCOME STATEMENT
WITH GROWTH IN SALES

Month	1	2	3	4	5	6	7
REVENUES							
Units Sold	40,000	42,000	44,000	50,000	55,000	60,000	65,000
Sales	$ 80,000	84,000	88,000	100,000	110,000	120,000	130,000
EXPENSES							
Direct Materials	40,000	42,000	44,000	50,000	55,000	60,000	65,000
Direct Labor	4,000	4,200	4,400	5,000	5,500	6,000	6,500
Overhead	4,000	4,000	4,000	4,000	4,000	4,000	4,000
Cost of Goods Sold	48,000	50,200	52,400	59,000	64,500	70,000	75,500
Gross Profit	32,000	33,800	35,600	41,000	45,500	50,000	54,500
General & Administrative							
Salaries	6,900	7,450	7,500	8,350	8,350	9,000	9,000
Rent	2,000	2,000	2,000	2,000	2,000	2,000	2,000
Insurance	500	500	500	500	500	500	500
Depreciation	170	170	170	170	170	170	170
Other G&A	3,000	4,100	4,550	5,500	6,600	7,050	7,850
Marketing							
Advertising	9,750	9,800	10,200	11,000	11,600	12,500	13,000
Brochures	450	450	450	450	450	450	450
Total Expense	70,770	74,670	77,770	86,970	94,170	101,670	108,470
Taxable Income	9,230	9,330	10,230	13,030	15,830	18,330	21,530
Income Taxes	2,769	2,799	3,069	3,909	4,749	5,499	6,459
Net Profit	$ 6,461	6,531	7,161	9,121	11,081	12,831	15,071

EXHIBIT 1-10

INTERCITY ASSEMBLY COMPANY, INC.
PRO FORMA CASH FLOW STATEMENT
WITH GROWTH IN SALES

Month	1	2	3	4	5	6	7
RECEIPTS							
Sales Receipts	$ 74,000*	77,000*	80,000	84,000	88,000	100,000	110,000
Common Stock	—	175,000	—	—	—	—	—
Total Received	74,000	252,000	80,000	84,000	88,000	100,000	110,000
DISBURSEMENTS							
Direct Materials	40,000*	40,000	45,000	50,000	55,000	60,000	65,000
Direct Labor	4,000	4,200	4,400	5,000	5,500	6,000	6,500
Overhead	1,300	1,300	1,300	1,300	1,300	1,300	1,300
Manufacturing Equip.	—	180,000	—	—	—	—	—
Salaries	6,900	7,450	7,500	8,350	8,350	9,000	9,000
Rent	2,000	2,000	2,000	2,000	2,000	2,000	2,000
Insurance	6,000	—	—	—	—	—	—
Office Equipment	—	3,000	—	—	—	—	—
Other G&A	2,800*	3,000	4,100	4,550	5,500	6,600	7,050
Advertising	9,000*	9,750	9,800	10,200	11,000	11,600	12,500
Brochures	—	5,400	—	—	—	—	—
Taxes	11,000*	—	—	8,637	—	—	14,157
Total Disbursed	83,000	256,100	74,100	90,037	88,650	96,500	117,507
Total Cash Flow	$ (9,000)	(4,100)	5,900	(6,037)	(650)	3,500	(7,507)
Beginning Balance	$ 1,100	(7,900)	(12,000)	(6,100)	(12,137)	(12,787)	(9,287)
Ending Balance	$ (7,900)	(12,000)	(6,100)	(12,137)	(12,787)	(9,287)	(16,794)

*From operations during prior periods.

EXHIBIT 1-11

MATERIALS INVENTORY SCHEDULE (CALCULATED IN UNITS)
AND PURCHASES OVERVIEW
WITH GROWTH IN SALES

Month	1	2	3	4	5	6	7
Beginning Inventory	43,500	43,500	46,500	52,500	57,500	62,500	67,500
−Shipments (Out)	40,000	42,000	44,000	50,000	55,000	60,000	65,000
+Purchases (Received)	40,000	45,000	50,000	55,000	60,000	65,000	70,000
Ending Inventory	43,500	46,500	52,500	57,500	62,500	67,500	72,500
Purchases Overview							
Value of Purchases (Received)	$ 40,000	45,000	50,000	55,000	60,000	65,000	70,000
Cash Disbursements (Net 30)	$ 40,000*	40,000	45,000	50,000	55,000	60,000	65,000

*Due to a transaction of a prior period.

EXHIBIT 1-12

COMPARISON OF PROFIT AND BANK BUSINESS
FOR INTERCITY ASSEMBLY COMPANY, INC.
WITH DIFFERENT RATES OF GROWTH IN SALES

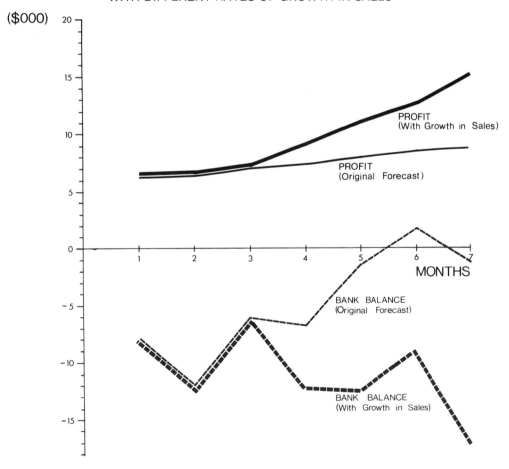

very different story. In month 7 the net profit increases by $6,300, but the overdraft (indicated by negative bank balance) in the company's bank account increases by $15,550. If the president of Intercity Assembly Company is unable to find an additional $15,550 in financing by Month 7, this rate of growth could create a liquidity bind of such magnitude that a crucial payment such as payroll or a payment to the materials supplier would be missed. That's called "out of business."

How Growth Can Put a Service Company Out of Business

Service companies are usually thought of as being very different from manufacturing companies. They don't have warehouses full of goods and manufacturing facilities teeming with assembly workers.

Consider Consulting Company, Inc., a slightly modified version of an existing company. The firm has been in business for several years and has gained an excellent reputation in its field. Recently the corporation found that it has more business available than it can accept. Management has decided to expand the professional staff to permit the acquisition of this additional business.[21]

Knowing the possible consequences of growth, an enlightened chief executive decided to forecast the operations of the firm for the next six months, a period in which sales are expected to grow by 50%. The forecasted income statement for this service business is shown in Exhibit 1-13.[22]

EXHIBIT 1-13
CONSULTING CO., INC.
PRO FORMA INCOME STATEMENT

Month	1	2	3	4	5	6
REVENUES						
Sales Invoiced	$ 30,000	32,000	35,000	40,000	42,000	45,000
Total Revenue	30,000	32,000	35,000	40,000	42,000	45,000
EXPENSES						
Salaries	19,500	19,500	22,300	25,100	25,100	25,100
Payroll Taxes & Fringe	1,450	1,450	1,650	1,800	1,800	1,800
Rent	900	900	900	900	900	900
Utilities & Phone	600	600	700	800	850	900
Office Supplies	300	300	350	400	400	450
Postage	33	33	34	33	33	34
Business Development	900	950	1,000	1,200	1,300	1,350
Travel & Meetings	2,300	2,400	2,800	3,200	3,400	3,600
Depreciation	600	600	700	800	800	800
Interest	100	100	100	100	100	100
Professional Services	900	950	1,050	1,200	1,250	1,350
Legal & Audit	250	—	—	—	—	—
Profit Sharing & Bonus	1,700	1,800	1,950	2,250	2,350	2,500
Total Expense	29,533	29,583	33,534	37,783	38,283	38,884
Taxable Income	467	2,417	1,466	2,217	3,717	6,116
Income Taxes	140	725	440	665	1,115	1,835
Net Profit	$ 327	1,692	1,026	1,552	2,602	4,281

With the addition of two new consultants in Month 3 and two more consultants in Month 4, a substantial increase in sales volume is possible. The increase in net profit after tax is truly impressive. It appears that over the next six months the mere addition of four new professionals will permit the company to increase its profits by approximately 13 times. (Federal income tax is calculated at an average annual rate of 30%.)

The counterpart cash flow forecast was developed by management and is portrayed in Exhibit 1-14.[23]

Payments from the customers are received in an average of 60 days after the invoice is sent. Utilities and Phone, Business Development, Travel and Meetings, Equipment and Legal and Audit Costs are paid for on a net 30-day basis. Office supplies are paid for on a net 60-day basis. Postage is paid for in cash in advance for a 3-month supply. Income Taxes are deposited each quarter in the month following the end of the quarter and Profit Sharing and Bonuses are paid quarterly in the last month of a given quarter. All other disbursements are paid in the month of the expense. A loan totaling $10,000 is scheduled for repayment in Month 6.

EXHIBIT 1-14
CONSULTING CO., INC.
PRO FORMA CASH FLOW STATEMENT

Month	1	2	3	4	5	6
RECEIPTS						
Sales Receipts	$ 30,000*	30,000*	30,000	32,000	35,000	40,000
Loans (Repayment)	—	—	—	—	—	(10,000)
Total Received	30,000	30,000	30,000	32,000	35,000	30,000
DISBURSEMENTS						
Salaries	19,500	19,500	22,300	25,100	25,100	25,100
Payroll Taxes & Fringe	1,450	1,450	1,650	1,800	1,800	1,800
Rent	900	900	900	900	900	900
Utilities & Phone	600*	600	600	700	800	850
Office Supplies	300*	300*	300	300	350	400
Postage	100	—	—	100	—	—
Business Development	900*	900	950	1,000	1,200	1,300
Travel & Meetings	2,300*	2,300	2,400	2,800	3,200	3,400
Equipment Purchases	—	—	3,600	3,600	—	—
Interest	100	100	100	100	100	100
Professional Services	900	950	1,050	1,200	1,250	1,350
Legal & Audit	—	250	—	—	—	—
Taxes	285*	—	—	1,305	—	—
Profit Sharing & Bonus	—	—	5,450	—	—	7,100
Total Disbursed	27,335	27,250	39,300	38,905	34,700	42,300
Total Cash Flow	2,665	2,750	(9,300)	(6,905)	300	(12,300)
Beginning Balance	2,000	4,665	7,415	(1,885)	(8,790)	(8,490)
Ending Balance	$ 4,665	7,415	(1,885)	(8,790)	(8,490)	(20,790)

*From operations during prior periods.

As may be seen, the attractive bank balance at the end of Month 1 has completely disappeared by the end of Month 6, with an overdraft totaling $20,790 forecasted that month. Even without the repayment of the $10,000 loan which comes due in Month 6, the company would have been overdrawn by more than $10,000 during the time period in which profits increased 13-fold.

The extremely dissimilar behavior of profit and cash flow for this service company is demonstrated in the graph in Exhibit 1-15. With profit generally trending upward, cash flow is

EXHIBIT 1-15
COMPARISON OF PROFIT AND CASH FLOW
IN A GROWING SERVICE COMPANY

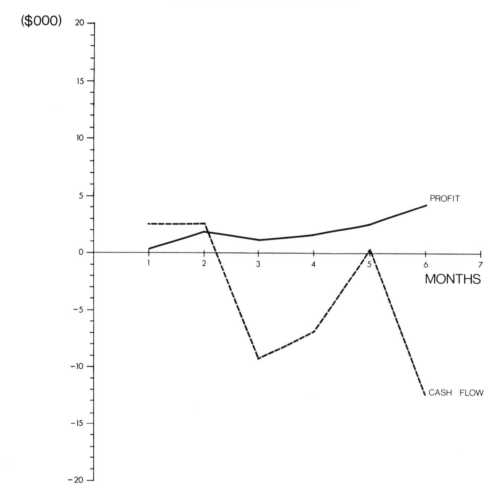

behaving in a typical erratic fashion but generally trending downward. The impact on the company's bank account is even more dramatic, as indicated in Exhibit 1-16 (negative balances indicate forecasted overdrafts).

EXHIBIT 1-16
FORECASTED BANK BALANCE FOR CONSULTING COMPANY, INC.,
A GROWING SERVICE COMPANY

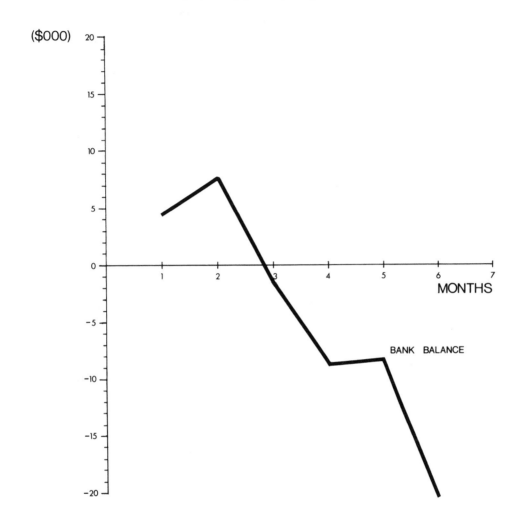

When comparing the behavior of Intercity Assembly Company, Inc. with Consulting Company, Inc., it becomes evident that under similar circumstances of growth in sales, these two strikingly different kinds of businesses behaved in a similar fashion.

The General Principle

The behavior of the preceding manufacturing business (Intercity Assembly Company, Inc.) and the preceding service business (Consulting Company, Inc.) is generally true for most businesses. It is not easy for most owner-managers to accept that a company can be experiencing impressive growth in sales with equally impressive growth in earnings, and at the same time be in a severe financial condition. It goes against one's natural instincts and yet it is one of the most common traps an owner-manager walks into.

The way most businesses operate, growth in sales consumes cash. Cash is needed to purchase items such as raw materials, labor, services and merchandise while preparing to make the sales. Growth in sales requires that greater quantities of these types of items be purchased in anticipation of future sales. Cash is also needed to support the business at its now larger size while awaiting payment from customers for larger sales. Consequently, during periods of rapid growth, the cash flow is characteristically negative. It is perfectly normal to find that a business is growing profitably while going broke down at the bank.

Since there are so many different kinds of businesses—each with its own operating characteristics—it is difficult to generalize. Nevertheless, so many businesses have the traits previously alluded to that it is beneficial to examine this common behavior. Exhibit 1-17 attempts to subjectively illustrate this common characteristic graphically.

EXHIBIT 1-17
TYPICAL RELATIONSHIPS BETWEEN SALES, PROFIT, CASH FLOW AND
BANK BALANCE IN A FAST-GROWTH BUSINESS

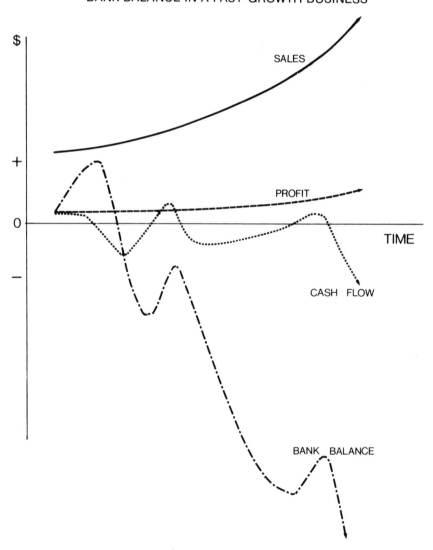

Growth in sales, even though accompanied by growth in profits, usually results in negative cash flow that can cause a significant drain on cash resources in the company's bank account. The graph in Exhibit 1-17 assumes no external financing. The magnitude of the projected negative bank balance is indicative of the amount of external cash that must be infused into the business. Obviously, a bank will not permit the continued presence of a negative balance.

How To Determine How Fast You Can Grow

There is no simple answer to the question, "How fast can I grow without having a liquidity problem down at the bank?" The growth rate that can be sustained with internally generated cash, however, is usually much smaller than one would expect.

The authors suggest a very straightforward, down-to-earth approach in identifying what this maximum growth rate is for your business. The recommended approach is to develop (for your business) a detailed monthly income and cash flow forecast of the variety demonstrated in Exhibits 1-9, 1-10, 1-13 and 1-14. Now vary the anticipated sales. Revise the income and cash flow forecast to determine what the cash needs will be for that new level of sales.

Next, assume a different level of sales and once again revise the income and cash flow forecast to reflect that sales level. The amount of cash required to support each new sales level will then be determined. By experimenting several times with a variety of different rates of growth in sales, the rate of growth that your business can sustain without the need for external cash can be determined.

This systematic approach may seem a bit tedious but the payoff for not exceeding the limits of one's financial resources is worth the effort.

TWO CAUTIONS: SUBTLE DIFFERENCES BETWEEN LARGER AND SMALLER COMPANIES

Larger businesses usually grow at slower rates than smaller businesses. It is possible to double sales in one year if what is being doubled is small. It is nearly impossible to double sales in one year if annual sales are already a billion dollars. Because of this, smaller businesses are more likely to have a continuous and urgent need for proportionally more money to overcome negative cash flow than their larger counterparts.[24]

Larger businesses frequently have less difficulty obtaining additional money under conditions of fast growth. They have long-established relationships, good reputations and historical evidence of their abilities to survive. Lenders and investors feel reasonably comfortable entrusting their money to large businesses that are growing profitably.[25]

Smaller businesses, on the other hand, usually find that the additional money needed is difficult to obtain. They seldom have long-established relationships, they may have little or no reputation and they have meager evidence of their ability to manage the larger business they hope to become. Therefore, lenders and investors find it difficult to entrust their money to smaller businesses. Consequently, money that is made available to smaller businesses often takes longer to procure, costs more and has conditions of control over management attached to it.[26]

One major difference between managing a smaller business and managing a larger business lies in these two problem areas. Smaller businesses need proportionally more external financing and typically have much more difficulty obtaining external financing.[27]

NOTES FOR CHAPTER 1

[1]*Financing Growth*, THAT'S BUSINESS™ Educational Films, Produced by John A. Welsh and Jerry F. White, The Owner-Managed Business Center, Inc., Dallas, 1978.

[2]Ibid.

[3]Ibid.

[4]Ibid.

[5]Ibid.

[6]*Investing in the Entrepreneur*, Proceedings of the Second Annual Seminar, Staff of the Caruth Institute of Owner-Managed Business at Southern Methodist University, Dallas, 1974.

[7]*Financing Growth*.

[8]Ibid.

[9]Ibid.

[10]Ibid.

[11]John A. Welsh and Jerry F. White, "Cash Flow—What's Yours?" *Southwest Home Furnishings News*, Summer 1976, p. 10.

[12]*Investing in the Entrepreneur*, p. 75.

[13]John A. Welsh, "Profit and Cash Flow to Small Businesses and Managers," International Symposium on Small Business, Washington, D.C., 15 Nov. 1976.

[14]Ibid., p. 2.

[15]Ibid.

[16]*Profit Forecasting*, THAT'S BUSINESS™ Educational Films, Produced by John A. Welsh and Jerry F. White, The Owner-Managed Business Center, Inc., Dallas, 1978.

[17]*Cash Flow Forecasting*, THAT'S BUSINESS™ Educational Films, Produced by John A. Welsh and Jerry F. White, The Owner-Managed Business Center, Dallas, 1978.

[18]John A. Welsh and Jerry F. White, "Cash Flow Forecasting: One Solution to Inadequate Financing," *Journal of Small Business Management*, Jan., 1975, Vol. 13, No. 1.

[19]*Financing Growth*.

[20]Ibid.

[21]John A. Welsh and Jerry F. White, *Profit and Cash Flow Management for Non-Financial Managers*, School of Business Administration, Southern Methodist University, Dallas, 1974, p. 9.

[22]Ibid., p. 10.

[23]Ibid., p. 12.

[24]Ibid., p. 3

[25]Ibid., p. 2.

[26]Ibid., p. 3.

[27]Ibid.

2

Administering Accounts Receivable -
Avoiding the Most Deadly Pitfall of All

Businesses may own a variety of assets. Among the most valuable are accounts receivable. They represent the completion of a valid sale and signify that goods have been shipped to or services have been performed for the customer. Among the current assets (those that will turn into cash in less than a year), accounts receivable are usually ranked second—next to cash. Although not cash, accounts receivable are "near cash."

These thoughts indicate why accounts receivable might be considered as friends. How could they be anything else?

Suppose a business has only one sale in its entire history, and that sale totals $1,000. After the cost of goods sold, general and administrative, as well as marketing expenses, are accounted for, assume that a respectable 12% pre-tax profit results as shown in the following simplified income statement:

REVENUES	$1,000
EXPENSES	
Cost of Goods Sold	500
General and Administrative	200
Marketing	180
Total Expenses	$ 880
Pre-Tax Profit	$ 120

In different time periods, varying from a few days to perhaps a couple of months, the suppliers of those items included in the list of expenses will demand to be paid. If the $1,000 in revenues (that is adequate to cover this business' expenses as well as provide a profit) is not collected by the time the suppliers begin demanding payment, a severe financial crisis could result. When not collected promptly, accounts receivable can become a business' worst enemy.

WHAT DIFFERENT COLLECTION SCHEDULES
CAN DO FOR A COMPANY

To illustrate the situation that frequently develops, consider Intercity Assembly Company, Inc., an example of a typical owner-managed business. The forecasted operations for Intercity were portrayed in Exhibits 1-5[1] and 1-6.[2] A summary of the pro forma income statement is presented in Exhibit 2-1 and a summary of the pro forma cash flow statement is presented in Exhibit 2-2.[3]

EXHIBIT 2-1
SUMMARY OF ORIGINAL
PRO FORMA INCOME STATEMENT
FOR
INTERCITY ASSEMBLY COMPANY, INC.

Month	1	2	3	4	5	6	7
REVENUES	$ 80,000	84,000	88,000	94,000	100,000	106,000	110,000
EXPENSES	70,770	74,670	77,770	83,670	88,670	93,970	97,470
Pre-Tax Profit	9,230	9,330	10,230	10,330	11,330	12,030	12,530
Income Taxes	2,769	2,799	3,069	3,099	3,399	3,609	3,759
Net Profit	$ 6,461	6,531	7,161	7,231	7,931	8,421	8,771

EXHIBIT 2-2
SUMMARY OF ORIGINAL
PRO FORMA CASH FLOW STATEMENT
FOR
INTERCITY ASSEMBLY COMPANY, INC.

Month	1	2	3	4	5	6	7
RECEIPTS	$ 74,000	252,000	80,000	84,000	88,000	94,000	100,000
DISBURSEMENTS	83,000	256,100	74,100	84,737	83,150	90,800	102,457
Cash Flow	(9,000)	(4,100)	5,900	(737)	4,850	3,200	(2,457)
Beginning Balance	1,100	(7,900)	(12,000)	(6,100)	(6,837)	(1,987)	1,213
Ending Balance	$ (7,900)	(12,000)	(6,100)	(6,837)	(1,987)	1,213	(1,244)

The Typical Situation

Intercity Assembly Company sells to its customers on a net 30-day basis. As is common, many are not paying on time. The customers are paying in an average of 60 days. While very attractive profits are anticipated as shown in Exhibit 2-1, this collections schedule is producing a cash flow that is marginal at best. Exhibit 2-2 also indicates a number of projected overdrafts in the bank account.

How the Deadly Accounts Receivable Pitfall Develops

In an effort to be prepared for any eventuality, management of Intercity Assembly Company decided to review the impact on company operations if collections occurred somewhat slower than originally anticipated. Instead of collecting accounts receivable in an average of 60 days as had been true historically, management considered what would happen if 10% of the sales of a given month were received in 30 days; 20% in 60 days; and 70% in 90 days; beginning with the sales of next month, Month 1 of the forecast. The collections schedule shown in Exhibit 2-3 was prepared to help determine future receipts from sales.[4]

EXHIBIT 2-3

Schedule of Slower Accounts Receivable Collections

(10% in 30 days; 20% in 60 days; 70% in 90 days)

SALES	Month	1	2	3	4	5	6	7
$ 74,000 in Month −2		$74,000*						
77,000 in Month −1			77,000*					
80,000 in Month 1			8,000	16,000	56,000			
84,000 in Month 2				8,400	16,800	58,800		
88,000 in Month 3					8,800	17,600	61,600	
94,000 in Month 4						9,400	18,800	65,800
100,000 in Month 5							10,000	20,000
106,000 in Month 6								10,600
110,000 in Month 7								
Total Collections		$74,000	85,000	24,400	81,600	85,800	90,400	96,400

*Collections from transactions of a prior period

This collections schedule assumes that the sales of the last two months, that is, the two months prior to Month 1, will continue to be received in an average of 60 days from the date of sale. The new collections schedule would begin next month, Month 1.

When this new schedule is reflected in the detailed cash flow forecast for Intercity, the results shown in Exhibit 2-4 emerge.[5] The projected ending bank balances indicate that a disaster will occur in the company's bank account if this new collections schedule becomes effective. Maximum projected overdrafts increase from $12,000 to more than $60,000. Without even considering bad debts, a mere delay in collections could create a financial catastrophe.

One Solution to Financial Worries

Since slower collections portend a bleak future for the company's bank account, management examined the possibilities of accelerating collections. If, by utilizing a variety of tactics, collections could be accelerated to the point where 70% of the sales of a given month were collected in 30 days; 20% in 60 days; and 10% in 90 days, a very different picture of company operations would emerge. Management of Intercity Assembly Company developed a new schedule of accounts receivable collections based on this assumption. It is shown in Exhibit 2-5.[6]

EXHIBIT 2-4

INTERCITY ASSEMBLY COMPANY, INC.

PRO FORMA CASH FLOW STATEMENT

with collections of

(10% in 30 days; 20% in 60 days; 70% in 90 days)

Month	1	2	3	4	5	6	7
RECEIPTS							
Sales Receipts	$ 74,000*	85,000*	24,400	81,600	85,800	90,400	96,400
Common Stock	—	175,000	—	—	—	—	—
Total Received	74,000	260,000	24,400	81,600	85,800	90,400	96,400
DISBURSEMENTS							
Direct Materials	40,000*	40,000	45,000	45,000	50,000	55,000	55,000
Direct Labor	4,000	4,200	4,400	4,700	5,000	5,300	5,500
Overhead	1,300	1,300	1,300	1,300	1,300	1,300	1,300
Manufacturing Equip.	—	180,000	—	—	—	—	—
Salaries	6,900	7,450	7,500	8,350	8,350	9,000	9,000
Rent	2,000	2,000	2,000	2,000	2,000	2,000	2,000
Insurance	6,000	—	—	—	—	—	—
Office Equipment	—	3,000	—	—	—	—	—
Other G&A	2,800*	3,000	4,100	4,550	5,500	6,600	7,050
Advertising	9,000*	9,750	9,800	10,200	11,000	11,600	12,500
Brochures	—	5,400	—	—	—	—	—
Taxes	11,000*	—	—	8,637	—	—	10,107
Total Disbursed	83,000	256,100	74,100	84,737	83,150	90,800	102,457
Total Cash Flow	$ (9,000)	3,900	(49,700)	(3,137)	2,650	(400)	(6,057)
Beginning Balance	$ 1,100	(7,900)	(4,000)	(53,700)	(56,837)	(54,187)	(54,587)
Ending Balance	$ (7,900)	(4,000)	(53,700)	(56,837)	(54,187)	(54,587)	(60,644)

*From operations during prior periods.

EXHIBIT 2-5

Schedule of Accelerated Accounts Receivable Collections

(70% in 30 days; 20% in 60 days; 10% in 90 days)

SALES	Month	1	2	3	4	5	6	7
$ 74,000 in Month −2		$74,000*						
77,000 in Month −1			77,000*					
80,000 in Month 1			56,000	16,000	8,000			
84,000 in Month 2				58,800	16,800	8,400		
88,000 in Month 3					61,600	17,600	8,800	
94,000 in Month 4						65,800	18,800	9,400
100,000 in Month 5							70,000	20,000
106,000 in Month 6								74,200
110,000 in Month 7								
Total Collections		$74,000	133,000	74,800	86,400	91,800	97,600	103,600

*Collections from transactions of a prior period.

When this accelerated schedule of collections is reflected in the detailed cash flow forecast for Intercity, the results shown in Exhibit 2-6 emerge.[7] Beginning in Month 2, the company has comfortable five-figure balances (at certain points greater than $60,000) every month in its bank account.

Attractive balances may in turn be utilized to improve the company's performance still further. For example, they may be invested in productivity-improving equipment, quantity discounts, etc.

EXHIBIT 2-6

INTERCITY ASSEMBLY COMPANY, INC.
PRO FORMA CASH FLOW STATEMENT
with collections of
(70% in 30 days; 20% in 60 days; 10% in 90 days)

Month	1	2	3	4	5	6	7
RECEIPTS							
Sales Receipts	$ 74,000*	133,000*	74,800	86,400	91,800	97,600	103,600
Common Stock	—	175,000	—	—	—	—	—
Total Received	74,000	308,000	74,800	86,400	91,800	97,600	103,600
DISBURSEMENTS							
Direct Materials	40,000*	40,000	45,000	45,000	50,000	55,000	55,000
Direct Labor	4,000	4,200	4,400	4,700	5,000	5,300	5,500
Overhead	1,300	1,300	1,300	1,300	1,300	1,300	1,300
Manufacturing Equip.	—	180,000	—	—	—	—	—
Salaries	6,900	7,450	7,500	8,350	8,350	9,000	9,000
Rent	2,000	2,000	2,000	2,000	2,000	2,000	2,000
Insurance	6,000	—	—	—	—	—	—
Office Equipment	—	3,000	—	—	—	—	—
Other G&A	2,800*	3,000	4,100	4,550	5,500	6,600	7,050
Advertising	9,000*	9,750	9,800	10,200	11,000	11,600	12,500
Brochures	—	5,400	—	—	—	—	—
Taxes	11,000*	—	—	8,637	—	—	10,107
Total Disbursed	83,000	256,100	74,100	84,737	83,150	90,800	102,457
Total Cash Flow	$ (9,000)	51,900	700	1,663	8,650	6,800	1,143
Beginning Balance	$ 1,100	(7,900)	44,000	44,700	46,363	55,013	61,813
Ending Balance	$ (7,900)	44,000	44,700	46,363	55,013	61,813	62,956

*From operations during prior periods.

Comparison of Operating Results

A comparison of the company's operating results under the three preceding collections schedules is summarized in Exhibit 2-7.[8]

A glance at this table yields a couple of interesting observations. First, the difference between the bank balance in Month 7 for the slower collections example and that of the accelerated collections example represents a favorable cash swing of more than $120,000. Another way of viewing this is if the company can move its sales receipts from the slower collections schedule to the accelerated collections schedule, it can realize, in effect, more than $120,000 of interest-free financing.

EXHIBIT 2-7

SUMMARY OF OPERATING RESULTS
FOR A COMPANY UNDER THREE DIFFERENT
COLLECTIONS SCHEDULES

	Profit for 7 Months	Bank Balance Month 7
Original Forecast (60 days)	$ 52,507	$ (1,244)
Slower Collections (10%-20%-70%)	52,507	(60,644)
Accelerated Collections (70%-20%-10%)	52,507	62,956

A second significant observation is that while the bank balances in Month 7 were varying from a $60,000 overdraft to a positive balance of more than $60,000, the profit for the seven months, indicated in the left-hand column, remained unchanged. Imagine the plight of the manager who receives only an income statement. This company could easily be "marching off a cliff" down at the bank and the income statement would give no indication whatsoever.

A month-by-month picture of operating results is portrayed graphically in Exhibit 2-8.

EXHIBIT 2-8
GRAPH COMPARING PROFIT AND BANK BALANCE FOR A COMPANY
UNDER THREE DIFFERENT COLLECTIONS SCHEDULES

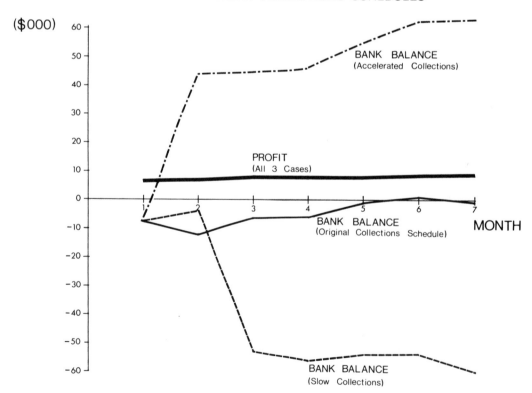

While profit is identical for all three collections schedules, cash in the bank fluctuates all the way from disastrous overdrafts to attractive balances. This graph provides another convincing piece of evidence that profit is not cash flow. Furthermore, the two are not readily related by some general rule of thumb.

Another interesting observation can be made if the level of accounts receivable is compared monthly to the bank balance for Intercity Assembly Company for the three preceding collections schedules. This comparison is shown in Exhibit 2-9. The accounts receivable level portrayed each month is as of the end of the month. The bank balance that is plotted is also at the end of each respective month. There is a conspicuous and inverse relationship between the accounts receivable level and the company's cash in the bank. As the level of accounts receivable increases, the company's bank balance in general decreases.

Exhibits 2-7, 2-8 and 2-9 lead to an inevitable conclusion—delays in collections consume cash. While profit and the income statement may be unaffected, a business could experience a lethal liquidity squeeze if its accounts receivable collection period begins increasing.

EXHIBIT 2-9
COMPARISON OF ACCOUNTS RECEIVABLE (A/R) LEVEL AND BANK
BALANCE FOR A TYPICAL OPERATING COMPANY

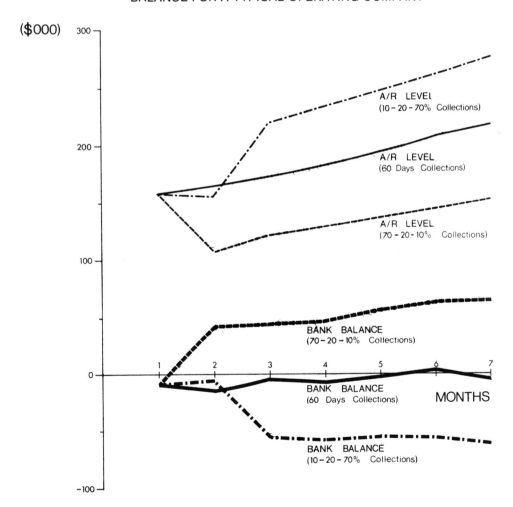

HOW TO GET YOUR CUSTOMERS' MONEY FASTER

As demonstrated in the preceding examples, slower collections tend to create liquidity problems while faster collections tend to create attractive bank balances. An obvious management objective for a business desiring to improve its cash flow is to collect the receivables sooner. As a practical matter, this is much easier said than done. A great deal of time and effort can be expended with little productive results if management is not selective in the choice of collections tactics and skillful in their execution.

Perhaps the first place to start is to develop a method for knowing the current status of the company's accounts receivable. A common management tool used for determining this is the accounts receivable aging schedule. An example of this practical tool is presented in Exhibit 2-10.[9]

EXHIBIT 2-10
ACCOUNTS RECEIVABLE AGING SCHEDULE

Customer	Total Amount Receivable	Current (not past due)	1-30 days (past due)	31-60 days (past due)	61-90 days (past due)	91-120 days (past due)	Over 120 days (past due)
ABC Corp	$1,994.94	$1,256.14	$ 628.30	$110.50			
Continental Ind.	1,651.89	986.40				$122.64	$542.85
Dorall, Inc.	1,607.08	500.26	487.90	510.52	$108.40		
Fraisher & Assoc.	908.42	621.10	287.32				
The Game Room	322.02	189.40	85.26		47.36		
M & F Enterprises	154.80	42.50	112.30				
Nidro, Inc.	168.50						168.50
Norden, B.T.	112.09	65.22	46.87				
Nu-clean	755.30				261.50	493.80	
Oasis Industries	799.59	456.20	232.10	111.29			
Total	$8,474.63	$4,117.22	$1,880.05	$732.31	$417.26	$616.44	$711.35
Percent of Total	100%	49%	22%	9%	5%	7%	8%

This form reviews the status of each unpaid company invoice as of a certain date. Information is presented for each customer. The customer list is organized alphabetically. Those customer accounts that are current are so indicated. Those that are past due are indicated and classified according to how long they are past due. Accounts more than 90 days past due have a high probability of not being collected at all.[10] In the example portrayed in Exhibit 2-10, 15% of the uncollected sales are more than 90 days past due. This may be a higher percentage of the sales than that represented by profit.

There is research that suggests possibly 70% of those closely held businesses with annual sales over $400,000 regularly use an aging schedule.[11] In most reasonably well-managed businesses, an accounts receivable aging schedule will be prepared at least once a month. In extremely well-managed businesses, it is not uncommon to prepare a new aging schedule every week.

It becomes obvious in accounts receivable management that timing is everything.

Common Techniques

There are a variety of techniques that the owner-manager may utilize in an effort to improve collections. Some of these techniques are generally effective; some are generally ineffective. Most have distinct advantages as well as disadvantages. These techniques are discussed from the perspective of the owner-manager and the closely held company. They may differ from those procedures used by members of the Fortune 500.

Screening New Accounts

One effective method for getting your customer's money faster is to restrict those who are granted credit in the first place. The process of extending credit to new customers might be thought of as occurring in three phases: application, investigation and granting or denial.

The application phase consists of having the new customer provide extensive written information that will aid in the credit granting decision. It is common to request a copy of the latest income statement and balance sheet, audited if possible. Other data that should be included in the credit application are the names and addresses of principal suppliers and banks. Additional data might include: the amount the customer is liable for as an endorser, guarantor, or surety; the amount of current assets pledged; the amount of taxes past due; monthly payments on equipment leases or conditional sales contracts; date of latest physical inventory; date of latest audit; date the business was established. If premises are leased, state the annual rental and the expiration date of the lease.

After acquisition of the credit application information, the investigation phase begins. When evaluating the credit applicant, three common sources are utilized: credit reporting agencies, bank references and major trade creditors. Credit reporting agencies include organizations such as Dun & Bradstreet, Inc. and the National Association of Credit Management. There are also specific trade credit reporting agencies such as the Lumberman's Credit Association. Reference to the telephone yellow pages will provide a list of local agencies. A city of 1.3 million inhabitants recently listed 14 different credit reporting agencies in its yellow pages.

The credit applicant's bank references also represent an excellent source of credit information. A letter directed to the customer's bank should clearly state the customer's name and address, the exact amount of credit being requested by the customer together with the specific terms of the sale. The basic request itself might utilize verbiage similar to that suggested in the *Credit Management Handbook.*

> We would appreciate your giving us in the enclosed envelope, the benefit of your experience with our new customer, together with whatever credit and financial information you are free to pass along.
>
> Many thanks for your reply which we assure you will be held in the strictest confidence.[12]

A third important source of information regarding the credit applicant is that provided by major trade creditors. A letter addressed to the credit manager of one of the customer's major creditors should include a precise description of the amount of credit being requested by the customer and the proposed terms of sale.

The body of the letter requesting credit information might include language similar to the following:

> In connection with our investigation, Mr. Brown has given you as a credit reference, and, accordingly, we would very much appreciate your giving us in the

enclosed envelope the benefit of your experience with him. The information you give us will be held in confidence and we shall be glad to reciprocate at any time.[13]

For most closely held companies, it is suggested that as a minimum, one credit reporting agency should be contacted, one bank reference and three major trade creditors. One recent study indicated that among small businesses, older firms were more likely than newer ones to use varied sources of credit information.[14] This may suggest one of the reasons they got to be older firms.

There are two principles that dominate the professional exchange of credit information, confidentiality and consideration. Credit information is confidential and should be treated accordingly. It is intended solely to assist an actual or bona fide prospective creditor in reaching a decision on a genuine credit problem.[15] With regard to consideration, an inquiry should clearly describe the subject, state its object and scope and show that it is made responsibly. Name and address of the subject should be completely and correctly stated. The reason for the requested information and the amount involved are essential. The identity of the inquirer should be established in letter inquiries by manual, not facsimile, signature. It is an acknowledged basic courtesy to enclose a stamped, self-addressed envelope.[16]

The final phase is the actual granting or denial of credit. The granting of credit will depend on numerous considerations of the individual case at hand. Many experienced owner-managers approve credit for new customers with a very conservative credit limit. If this credit arrangement is satisfactory over a period of several months, then the limit is often increased.

In the event that the investigation indicates credit should not be granted, there are a few good practices that may still salvage the applicant as a customer. First of all, the customer should be encouraged to do business on special terms for the present with the prospect of open account terms at a later date. The suggestion of C.O.D. may very well add insult to injury. It is better to suggest that some mutually agreeable cash arrangement be utilized. It is a good idea to welcome the business of your customer and to resell the product, prices and services of your company. Reassure the customer that these temporary terms are subject to revision.[17]

If an employee conducts the investigation, it is a wise idea to have top management make the final decision regarding the granting of credit to a new customer.

Advantages

One of the major advantages of screening new accounts is the reduced bad debt record. Requiring the formal credit application and the investigation procedure also establishes you as a more professional and well-managed supplier.

Disadvantages

One of the disadvantages of screening new accounts carefully is the time delay involved. Instead of shipping the goods or providing services immediately, there is the introduction of a delay that may result in the new customers changing their minds as to where to buy. Also, there is a cost associated with conducting the credit investigation. An individual's time plus the cost of phone calls and correspondence can be substantial. An additional disadvantage is the resulting loss of some business. Marginal credit risks may be readily serviced by competitors.

Diversification and Consolidation of Customers

Diversification here means not permitting one big customer to dominate your business. It is a sad but frequently told story that one customer was allowed to acquire perhaps 80 or 90% of a company's business. At some point, the dominant customer began delaying payments, that resulted in severe financial trauma or insolvency for the supplier. Many owner-managers feel vulnerable if one customer represents, on a continuing basis, more than 25% of the company's business.

Consolidation refers to examining your customer base with a view to identifying those who pay in an attractive manner and discouraging the business of those who do not. Building your business with a smaller number of higher quality customers is at the heart of what is meant here by the term consolidation. One way of doing this is to impose a stricter payment criterion that will, in essence, "shape them up" or get rid of them. Implementing a policy that stops shipment to all customers having an invoice more than two weeks past due is an example of one such criterion.

Discounts

Discounts refer to the common practice of offering the customer an incentive for quick payment. Discounts are effected by reducing the invoice amount by some percent for payment within a specified period of time. For example, if a company sells its products or services with payment due in 30 days, it might offer to reduce the invoice amount by 1% for those customers paying within 10 days. These terms of sale would be stated 1% 10; net 30.

Discounts are among the first tactics discussed when considering ways to get the customers' money sooner. The important point is whether discounts are effective when used by owner-managers. In discussions with several thousand owner-managers, the authors have determined that slightly more than half are basically dissatisfied with the results produced by offering discounts. Many of those owner-managers who are dissatisfied also report that they do not consistently and strictly enforce the discount policy with the customers. The result is discouragement and frustration when customers take the discount and continue to pay late.

There is an obvious but frequently overlooked characteristic of discounts. They fundamentally assume that the customer has the money to take the discount. If the customer is not paying because the customer does not have the money, then it makes little difference whether a 1% discount, a 10% discount or a 50% discount is offered. If they don't have the money, they simply cannot take any discount. Other techniques should be utilized for this type of customer. It is important to analyze why a customer is not paying on time.

An interesting phenomenon reported by a substantial number of owner-managers is the psychological impact that a relatively large discount makes on a customer. For example, while a customer may not respond to a 1% discount, a 10% discount can bring an immediate and positive response. Of course, such a large discount could not be offered unless the profit margin in the product or service would permit it.

Advantages

Perhaps the main advantage of discounts for quick pay is the dramatic improvement that is made on the company's cash flow if the customers take the discount in the manner specified. When receipts from sales arrive in 10 days instead of 30 days, the company's need for external financing is dramatically reduced.

Disadvantages

One obvious disadvantage of discounts is that they erode profit margins. With a 2% discount, a $100 sale yields only $98. Also, keeping track of discounts means some additional record keeping.

Perhaps the most common and persistent disadvantage is customers taking discounts after the discount period has expired. The marketplace is very sophisticated in finding any number of reasons for taking a discount for payment in 10 days, but actually paying in 30, 40, 50 days or more. While a grace period of 2 to 5 extra days is common[18], many customers abuse the discount privilege by paying much later. If discounts are to work effectively, they must be coupled with rigorous enforcement. This represents an additional disadvantage of discounts, the time and money associated with enforcement.

Late Penalties

Late payment penalties refer to charges made to the customer for failure to pay within the specified terms of sale. A late payment penalty of 1% or 1½% per month on all past due balances is common. Most of the owner-managers with whom the authors interact report that for them the late payment penalty is relatively ineffective in bringing the customer's money in sooner. Good results are reported by these owner-managers, however, when the late penalty is a negotiated part of a written contract of sale. There appears to be a consensus among these owner-managers that, in general, late payment penalties are less effective than discounts.

Advantages

If the late penalty technique can be successfully implemented, customers will be discouraged from allowing their accounts to go past due. Since the customer's failure to pay on time causes a business to have to seek additional external working capital, the late penalty represents an additional source of cash useful in defraying the cost of outside capital.

Disadvantages

Unlike discounts that are an incentive for quick pay, late payment penalties represent a punitive action against slow paying accounts. The chance of ill will among customers is increased.

One potential pitfall of implementing the late penalty is a change in the customers' feelings of obligation. Before implementation of the late penalty, a customer commonly feels a sense of urgency to pay as much as possible and as soon as possible. After implementation of the late penalty, a customer may view you as a lender. The feeling is that by paying interest one doesn't have to pay the principal in the short run.

In addition, late penalties are difficult to enforce in some states. In certain regions, one must cope with obstacles presented by local usury laws.

Late payment penalties also result in additional bookkeeping. An account that sends in the payment without the late penalty is an account that is still open on the company's books.

Most owner-managers report that unless rigorously enforced, late penalties are ignored by the marketplace. Consequently, there is the disadvantage of additional costs of enforcement.

Form Letters

Form letters can include both individual pieces of correspondence or a series of consecutive letters that urge the customer to pay the account that is past due. In a series of consecutive letters, each successive one becomes more firm and more insistent upon payment. The first one may only indirectly allude to the need for payment and the last in the series may warn of forthcoming legal proceedings. Discussions with a wide variety of owner-managers indicate that, in general, the use of form letters does not really motivate customers to pay.

If form letters are to be used, they should maintain an attitude of common business courtesy.[19] This is true whether the first collection letter, an intermediate one, or a final stage letter is in question. A variety of psychological appeals is worth trying. You may appeal to the customer's spirit of cooperation and fairness. You may also stress the idea of maintaining a good credit record.[20]

In general, form letters should demonstrate patience and dignity. They should be written in a clear, simple style and revised frequently.

Advantages

Form letters represent a technique that is relatively inexpensive when compared with alternative collection techniques. Also, very little time is involved in sending a form letter. They represent a viable collection technique in the very early stages of collection. They also represent a valid approach when there is a large volume of small accounts.

Disadvantages

One of the main complaints against form letters is that they are detectible as such and, consequently, tend to make the entire collection effort ineffective. Form letters have a way of getting on the top of someone's stack of papers, moving to the bottom of the stack, moving to the next stack, moving to the next desk and then moving to the trash can. They are just too easily misplaced and then dismissed. In addition, the effectiveness of form letters seems to be in inverse proportion to the seriousness of the collection problem.

Sales Personnel as Collectors

Among owner-managers, there is a lively debate as to whether or not sales personnel should be instrumental in the collection of accounts receivable. Two major schools of thought are illustrated in the charts in Exhibit 2-11.

Some take the position that since the salesperson knows the customer better than anyone else in the company, the salesperson is in the best position to communicate with the customer regarding payment. The other school holds that collections represent financial management and are best carried out under the auspices of the financial officer or treasurer of the company. The authors have observed that the two strategies are equally effective. They merely represent widely divergent approaches to the collections program.

Advantages

Sales personnel know the customer. They tend to have a personal relationship with the customer[21] and understand what is required to motivate the customer to take specific actions.

Disadvantages

One frequently mentioned disadvantage centers around the potential confusion that this dual role may cause the salesperson. It is commonly thought that the salesperson who must also be "bill collector" cannot possibly be as effective.

Tricks

There seems to be an irresistible urge by managers to devise a new and novel approach that will be extremely effective in getting the customer's money sooner. The authors have encountered many such tactics and will relate three of the more interesting actual cases.

One owner-manager with particularly large and difficult collections informed several of the major late paying customers that he was being audited by the Internal Revenue Service. He further explained it was his understanding that one of the ways the IRS decided whom to audit next was to identify individuals and companies who had large outstanding bills. Clearly, those people must be having financial problems and might be hiding something from the Internal Revenue Service. This particular individual reported payments by return mail.

Another owner-manager hired a retired banker to pursue particularly difficult collections. The banker's method of operation was to go through the banking system to locate the

EXHIBIT 2-11
CHART ILLUSTRATING TWO COMMON ORGANIZATIONS AND
DIFFERENT AREAS WHERE PRINCIPAL COLLECTIONS EFFORTS RESIDE

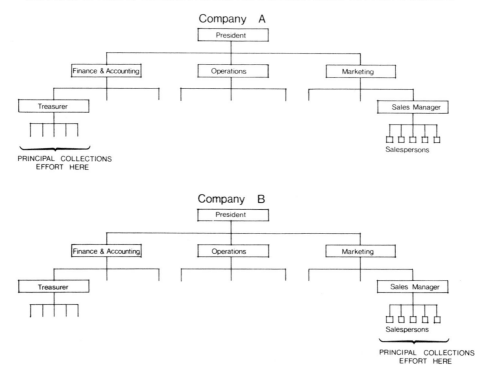

customer's banker. The retired banker then persuaded the customer's banker to exert pressure on the customer. The customers did not like the idea of their banker thinking that they engaged in poor management practices. This owner-manager's collections problems all but disappeared.

Still another owner-manager was experiencing flagrant abuse of the sales terms by the single largest customer. Net 30 invoices were approaching 90 days in age before payment was received. Monthly billing to this customer totaled $10,000. The owner-manager learned that invoices of less than $250 in amount were immediately processed by this large customer as not worth delaying. Needless to say, the customer began receiving more than 40 invoices per month; each was less than $250 in amount. The customer's computer automatically processed payment and the average age of the receivables moved from about 90 days to approximately 15 days.

Advantages

If a successful novelty approach can be devised, an exceptionally high collections rate may result. If this collection method utilizes form letters, then it may also be very cost effective.

Disadvantages

A disadvantage of using gimmick or novel approaches is the possibility of reducing the dignity of the business organization in the eyes of its customers. In addition, if repeat business is carried on with the same customers, it is not only difficult to continue to produce top flight stunts but the effect on an account tends to lessen with repeated use.[22]

MOST EFFECTIVE TECHNIQUES

Success in using the preceding techniques for getting your customer's money sooner is dependent upon the specific conditions between customer and supplier. In the wide range of techniques that may be applied to encourage timely payment, the authors classify these commonly used ones as only moderately effective. There are, however, four practices or techniques which the authors have observed produce better than average results.

Invoicing Procedures

One important thing that can be done to get your customer's money sooner is to institute good invoicing procedures. Many hours and many dollars could be saved in collections efforts if proper practices were followed at the time the invoice is sent. The following steps should be followed:

First, make sure that the invoice is accurate. Correct catalogue numbers, proper pricing, accurate additions and other computations, and correct addresses are simple tasks that can expedite the processing of an invoice. Inaccuracies can create endless delays of payment.

A second good practice is to be crystal clear when specifying the terms of payment. Misunderstandings regarding terms contribute to excessive and unnecessary delays. Some of the standard terms of sale are as follows:

- Cash with Order (C.W.O.)
- Cash in Advance (C.I.A.)
- Cash before Delivery (C.B.D.)
- Cash on Delivery (C.O.D.)
- Sight Draft—Bill of Lading (S.D.—B.L.)
- End-of-Month (E.O.M.)
- Middle-of-Month (M.O.M.)
- Proximo (Prox.)[23]

Sight Draft—Bill of Lading is a term of sale under which a negotiable bill of lading, accompanied by the invoice and a sight draft drawn on the buyer, is forwarded by the seller to the customer's bank or a banking connection in the same city for collection.[24] (For a sample sight draft, refer to *Warren's Forms of Agreement* or consult your attorney.) Proximo is Latin for "next" or "next following" and signifies payment in the month following shipment. For example, terms of net 10th prox. means payment by the 10th of the following month.[25]

A third recommended practice is to make sure that the method of payment is clearly agreed upon at the time of invoicing. Common methods of payment include a check, an approved credit card, a post-dated check, a promissory note, a sight draft or a bartered item.[26]

A fourth recommended practice is to follow the customer's instructions to the letter with regard to invoicing. For example, send exactly the right number of copies and be sure that they are sent to the correct person in the customer's organization. For companies with several locations, be certain that the invoice is sent to the right address.

A fifth recommended practice is to process and send the invoice rapidly. An invoice that is a week late being sent is one that encourages the customer to pay a week later than normal. By processing invoices quickly, mistakes and problems are discovered early and perhaps soon enough so that no delay in payment results.

Factoring

Factoring is selling the accounts receivable to organizations that specialize in buying and collecting them. Factors represent one of our oldest financial institutions. Their origin can be traced to ancient Rome. In fact, the term "factor" stems from the Latin verb "fasio" and literally means "he who does things."[27] The commercial factor developed as an institution in connection with the growth of the wool industry in England in the beginning of the late 14th century.[28] The development of American mills led to the development of factors for those mills. A factor, located in New York, for example, might represent several New England mills. From their early origins, where they assisted in the merchandising function, factors have evolved into the modern financial function of a non-bank lender.[29]

There are two types of fees charged by factoring organizations. First, there is a fee for receivables bookkeeping, collection and assumption of credit risks.[30] This fee is typically three-fourths of 1% to 2% of the invoice amount. If one also desires to be paid the invoice amount at the time the invoice is turned over to the factor, then there is an interest charge from the time the factor pays the vendor for an invoice to the time the factor collects from the customer.[31] The interest rate is generally slightly higher than bank rates.[32] Because disputes may arise between customer and vendor, it is common practice for the factor to hold back some percentage of the invoice amount, perhaps 25%, and pay this to the vendor upon satisfactory completion of the transaction.

There are several variations of the basic factoring proposition. A vendor's invoice may be factored with or without recourse back to the vendor. With notification factoring, the customer is instructed to pay the factor, whereas with non-notification factoring, the vendor does all of the collections bookkeeping and the customers are not notified.[33]

There are two major types of factoring: maturity factoring and advance factoring. With maturity factoring, the factor pays the vendor on the maturity date of the receivables whether the customers do or do not pay promptly.[34] With advance factoring, the vendor is advanced money against the receivables at the time the receivables are forwarded to the factor. This advance payment will frequently solve most of the client's financing problems. It is comparable to the client's selling for cash on delivery less the factor's fee.

Legitimate factoring organizations do not really deserve the "shady operators" reputation that some individuals feel they have. Certain smaller factoring organizations charge a flat 5-6% of the invoice amount and advance money immediately. If the invoice is collected in 30 days, then the factor can repeat this transaction 12 times in a year. Many are inclined to multiply 5% times 12 months and arrive at a 60% annual interest rate. This is not really a fair calculation. In addition to charging a fee for the use of money over time, the factor is engaging in the assumption of credit risk, collections bookkeeping and wide-ranging time and money-consuming collection activities.

Any metropolitan area should provide a selection of both large and small factoring organizations. In a metropolitan area, the largest one or two banks in town will probably have factoring departments. The yellow pages of one city having a population of 1.3 million listed 13 different factoring organizations.

Advantages

Factoring organizations offer expertise in collections work. These organizations also provide timely collections bookkeeping, typically on a weekly basis. Another advantage of dealing with factors is that the customer's credit worthiness is in question and not that of the vendor. Still another advantage is that factoring does not result in a liability appearing on the balance sheet as would be the case if a loan had been secured with accounts receivable pledged as collateral.

Disadvantages

One obvious disadvantage of factoring is the cost associated with it. Also the interest rate charged for advanced money is probably greater than that normally charged by a bank. Another potential disadvantage is the presence of feelings in some industries that a company is in severe financial difficulty if it factors its accounts receivable.

Using Intimate Information About Your Customer

Accumulating and utilizing intimate information about your customer's organization is one of the most consistently effective techniques for getting your money sooner. Acquiring knowledge about a customer's accounts payable policies and procedures as well as learning a great deal about those individuals who implement these policies and procedures can be invaluable. When dealing with a large number of customers, it may be impractical to accumulate this kind of intimate information about all of them. It is common, however, that something like 80% of one's business comes from 20% of the customers. Consequently, one should gain a lot of knowledge about the internal workings of the largest and most important customers. Owner-managers skilled in managing accounts receivable frequently report that in their largest customer's organization they get to know every individual on a first name basis who has anything to do with the processing and payment of an invoice. They make a special note of birthdays, information about these individuals' families and personal likes and dislikes, including whether an individual prefers paper clips or staples with invoice correspondence.

One owner-manager reported using this technique very successfully on large U.S Government receivables. The age of his "Uncle Sam" receivables was approaching the 90 days mark. Financial pressures on this person's company necessitated some sort of decisive action. This individual selected the nicest personality in his business and sent this employee to Washington with instructions to get to know a lot about everyone who influenced processing of the company's invoices. Subsequently, this employee hand-delivered exactly the right number of copies of all paperwork to each of the required persons in that department. The employee also took the opportunity to engage in friendly dialogue regarding the family, the weather, etc. This intimate interaction with key individuals in the customer's organization eventually resulted in a reduction of the age of the typical receivable from 90 days to approximately 15 days. The size of the monthly invoices was sufficiently large that the cost of the employee's time and travel was small by comparison. Getting paid an average of 75 days sooner relieved this particular closely held business of its major financing worries.

Top Management Intervention

Perhaps the most powerful weapon in the owner-manager's arsenal is personal involvement and communication with the customer regarding payment. In larger corporations, top management involvement in the collection process may not occur until very advanced stages have been reached. In closely held companies, it is beneficial and often necessary that the owner-manager be involved in the process from early negotiation of terms of sale to advanced collections activities.

When collection is the problem, the authors have found that results are produced when top management of the vendor's organization personally communicates with top management of the customer's organization. The flavor of the communication should be that receipt of payment for the outstanding balance due is essential if we are to continue doing business. What can we work out to resolve this matter?

Personally communicating does not mean write a letter. A telephone call or a personal visit produces results. In smaller companies, we mean presidents talking to presidents. In larger companies, the owner-manager must get beyond the clerical level and communicate with someone in a decision-making capacity. This should be someone who has the authority to make an agreement on behalf of the customer's company.

If top management's personal involvement in collections is one of the most effective techniques available, why do so many owner-managers utilize this technique last? Even worse, many owner-managers will allow an account to go uncollected rather than become personally involved. There appear to be at least three major reasons why these managers do not choose to become involved. First, many owner-managers do not seem to understand the incredible impact that a slight variation in the timing of collections can have on the company's bank account. As pointed out in Exhibit 2-7, the timing of collections can make or break a company.

Second, many owner-managers believe the collections process is strictly clerical. "An inexpensive clerical person can handle the 'bill collections.'" The cash flow statements presented earlier in this chapter, however, portray receipts from sales as typically the largest numbers on that statement. If concern for this is not a presidential responsibility, what is?

A third reason that owner-managers are reluctant to become involved in the collections process is that many feel this will cost the company substantial sales. Discussions with several thousand owner-managers have convinced the authors that the opposite is true. The vast majority of customers will react with respect for the good management practices of their supplier.

LAST RESORT TECHNIQUES

After reasonable efforts have been expended and standard techniques have been exhausted, final stage techniques must be employed. Most companies wait two or, possibly, three months before concluding that the final stage has been reached. The owner-manager should not wait too long in instituting specific actions because surveys have indicated that the percentage of recovery diminishes quite rapidly as account ages go beyond the 90-day mark.

Final stage techniques may be grouped into three categories: Special agreements, referral to collection agencies and institution of legal action.

Special Agreements

The most desirable way to resolve a collections problem is to enter into a special agreement with the customer. Converting the standard sales terms to C.O.D. on all future shipments is an example of one such agreement. Stopping all present shipments until the account is "cleaned up" represents another. In certain instances, it is desirable to convert an unsecured receivable into a promissory note. This note might be personally guaranteed by the customer and it might name some special collateral as security.

Special pay out arrangements also fall in this group. For example, the customer might agree that all future shipments will be on a C.O.D. basis. In addition, for each dollar paid on new shipments, an equal amount will be paid to reduce past due accounts.

The usual security devices of mortgage, pledge, conditional sale, trust receipt, or their variances, permit today's creditor to obtain a lien on property of the debtor to secure the liability.[35] A lien may be described as the right of someone to retain possession of personal property until some duty owing from the owner of the property is satisfied.[36] In a lien, one who makes no claim to the ownership of chattels (personal property) nevertheless claims the right to detain them until payment is received for materials or services expended. At common law, a mechanic was given a lien and so were an innkeeper, a warehouseman and a common carrier. Also, a landlord had a lien for unpaid rent and an unpaid seller had a vendor's lien where title to the goods had passed but the goods themselves remained in the possession of the seller.[37]

For the creditor who has not secured a lien by agreement and is not given one by statute, the law provides other means of reaching the debtor's property. The unsecured creditor has available such remedies as attachment, garnishment and execution to subject the debtor's property to his claim.[38]

Collection Agencies

When other efforts have failed to produce results, it is sometimes desirable to call upon outside agencies to assist in the collection of past due accounts. There is no shortage of such outside agencies. The yellow pages of a city having a population of 1.3 million indicated 73 separate collection agencies. Such agencies can be extremely helpful but should be selected with care. Some collection agencies tend to resort to thinly disguised threats. Because of a few ill chosen phrases, their letters can reflect unfavorably upon the creditor whom they represent. One should also consider whether the collection medium is bonded. Many firms, having placed accounts for collection with an outside agency, have then spent more time trying to get the money from the collection medium than they ever spent trying to get it from the customer.[39] Considering the service provided, the fee charged by reputable firms is reasonable. A fairly typical commission schedule might be 25% for the first $2,000 recovered and 20% on the excess up to $25,000. Rates would probably be negotiated beyond $25,000.[40] Collection of retail accounts may cost as much as 50%.

Legal Action

Instead of using a collection agency, the creditor can submit a delinquent account to an attorney for appropriate action. If a suit is initiated, the creditor can assist the attorney by furnishing the records that will be needed: (1) A sworn affidavit of account which sets out the state in which the company is incorporated, if it is a corporation, or the names of the partners if it is a partnership, (2) the original note if the account is on a note and (3) copies of each outstanding invoice and an itemized statement of account.[41]

If court action becomes necessary, the company's books of original entry—the first place that a charge appears on a company's records—will also be needed. These may take the form of the order, shipping list or invoice upon which the pricing is done. Either the individual who made the entries or the individual in charge of the department should be ready to testify that the charges were made at the time indicated and that the entries are correct. It is sometimes necessary to prove that the charges are reasonable by establishing that the charge for any particular item was reasonable as compared with charges made for similar items by other concerns. In some instances, it may be necessary to prove delivery. In general, the lawyer's case can be no stronger than the facts presented. The client must provide all the essential data.[42]

Even when the case goes to trial and a judgment is obtained, voluntary payment does not necessarily follow. The lawyer may have to order an execution so that property can be sold, if necessary, to satisfy the judgment. To assure prompt action and maximum salvage, the creditor's attorney should be provided with all available information regarding the debtor's assets.[43]

For a financially distressed debtor, bankruptcy may result. If a voluntary bankruptcy is involved (the debtor initiates the proceedings), the creditors should proceed with the advice of their attorneys. In some cases, it may be necessary for the creditors to initiate involuntary bankruptcy proceedings against the debtor.

A debtor who is subjected to bankruptcy on the petition of his creditors is known as an "involuntary bankrupt." Under the revised Bankruptcy Act (effective October 1979) the court, after the trial, shall order relief against the debtor only if:

1. the debtor is generally not paying such debtor's debts as such debts become due; or

2. within 120 days before the date of the filing of the petition, a custodian, other than a trustee, receiver, or agent appointed or authorized to take charge of less than substantially all of the property of the debtor for the purpose of enforcing a lien against such property, was appointed or took possession.

This is in contrast to the prior Bankruptcy Act in which the petitioning creditors were required to allege in their petition that the debtor, within the immediate four months prior to filing of the petition, committed one or more of the following six acts of bankruptcy:[44]

1. The debtor concealed, removed, or permitted to be concealed or removed any part of his property, with intent to hinder, delay or defraud his creditors.

2. The debtor, while insolvent, made a preferential transfer of a portion of his property to a creditor, the effect of which was to enable such creditor to obtain a greater percentage of his debt than some other creditor of the same class.

3. The debtor suffered or permitted, while insolvent, any creditor to obtain a lien upon any of his property.

4. The debtor made a general assignment to a trustee for the benefit of his creditors.

5. The debtor procured, permitted or suffered the appointment of a receiver or trustee to take charge of his property.

6. The debtor admitted in writing his inability to pay his debts and his willingness to be adjudged a bankrupt.[45]

The privilege of filing an involuntary proceeding is regulated as follows: The liabilities of the debtor must amount to $5,000 or more; there must be at least three petitioning creditors if the debtor has 12 or more creditors; one petitioning creditor is sufficient if the debtor has fewer than 12 creditors; the petitioning creditor or creditors must hold claims that are provable, fixed as to liability and amount and that aggregate $5,000 over and above the value of any security held by the creditor.[46]

Since bankruptcy laws are periodically revised, you may want to refer to a resource such as *Collier Bankruptcy Act and Rules* (New York: Matthew Bender) for the latest regulations.

NOTES FOR CHAPTER 2

[1]*Profit Forecasting*, THAT'S BUSINESS™ Educational Films, Produced by John A. Welsh and Jerry F. White, The Owner-Managed Business Center, Inc., Dallas, 1978.

[2]*Cash Flow Forecasting*, THAT'S BUSINESS™ Educational Films, Produced by John A. Welsh and Jerry F. White, The Owner-Manager Business Center, Inc., Dallas, 1978.

[3]John A. Welsh and Jerry F. White, *Profit and Cash Flow Management for Non-Financial Managers*, 1974.

[4]*Accounts Receivable*, THAT'S BUSINESS™ Educational Films, Produced by John A. Welsh and Jerry F. White, The Owner-Managed Business Center, Inc., Dallas, 1978.

[5]Ibid.

[6]Ibid.

[7]Ibid.

[8]Ibid.

[9]Ibid.

[10]*Credit Management Handbook*, National Association of Credit Management, edited by Credit Research Foundation, (Homewood, Illinois: Richard D. Irwin, Inc., 1965) p. 313.

[11]Bernie J. Grablowsky, "Mismanagement of Accounts Receivable by Small Business," *Journal of Small Business Management*, Vol. 14, (October, 1976), p. 25.

[12]*Credit Management Handbook*, p. 145.

[13]Ibid., p. 143. Reprinted with permission.

[14]Grablowsky, p. 23.

[15]*Credit Management Handbook*, p. 133. Reprinted with permission.

[16]Ibid., p. 134. Reprinted with permission.

[17]Ibid., p. 505.

[18]Ibid., p. 322.

[19]Ibid., p. 312.

[20]Ibid., p. 311.

[21]Ibid., p. 301.

[22]Ibid., p. 310. Reprinted with permission.

[23]H.N. Broom and Justin G. Longenecker, *Small Business Management*, 3rd Edition (Cincinnati: South-Western Publishing Co., 1971), p. 436.

[24]*Credit Management Handbook*, p. 528. Reprinted with permission.

[25]Ibid., p. 530.

[26]Ibid., pp. 317-319.

[27]Monroe R. Lazere, *Commercial Financing*, (New York: The Ronald Press Company, 1967), p. 10.

[28]Ibid., p. 10.

[29]Ibid., p. 11.

[30]*Credit Management Handbook*, p. 639.

[31]Ibid., p. 639.

[32]William R. Gruttemeyer, "Factoring: Is It a Dirty Word," *Journal of Small Business Management*, Vol. 13, No. 1, (January, 1975), p. 39.

[33]Ibid., p. 40.

[34]Ibid., p. 39.

[35]James William Moore, Walter Ray Phillips, *Debtors' and Creditors' Rights*, Fourth Edition, (New York: Matthew Bender, 1975), p. 1.3.

[36]*Credit Management Handbook*, p. 571. Reprinted with permission.

[37]Ibid., p. 571.

[38]James William Moore, p. 13. Reprinted with permission.

[39]*Credit Management Handbook*, p. 330. Reprinted with permission.

[40]Lawrence Rout and David P. Garino, "As Many Firms Delay Remitting Their Bills, Suppliers Try Dunning," *Wall Street Journal*, Southwest Edition, (August, 1978), p. 1.

[41]*Credit Management Handbook*, p. 331.

[42]Ibid., p. 331. Reprinted with permission.

[43]Ibid., p. 332. Reprinted with permission.

[44]Asa S. Herzog, Lawrence P. King and William T. Laube, *1976 Collier Pamphlet Edition Bankruptcy Act and Rules*,(New York: Matthew Bender, 1976) p. 23.

[45]John W. Wyatt and Madie B. Wyatt, *Business Law Principles and Cases*, Fifth Edition, (New York: McGraw-Hill Book Company, 1975), p. 820.

[46]Ibid., p. 821.

3

Inventory Management – Key to Financial Prosperity in the Closely Held Firm

---

Having access to enough of the right kind of inventory is crucial to the survival and prosperity of many businesses. Consequently, industrial as well as academic literature has documented many concepts directed at proper management of inventory.

STANDARD CONCEPTS

Among the more frequently mentioned concepts are inventory turnover, economic order quantity (EOQ) and economic lot size (ELS).

Inventory Turnover

Inventory turnover is an indication of the velocity with which merchandise moves through the business. It is expressed as a relationship between the annual cost of goods sold and the average inventory level. As an equation, the relationship is:[1]

$$\text{Inventory Turnover} = \frac{\text{Cost of Goods Sold}}{\text{Average Inventory}}$$

If the average inventory should begin to increase while a fixed amount of goods is being sold in a given period of time, the inventory turnover will be reduced. This could alert management to a potential danger signal.

Another aspect of the inventory turnover calculation relates to the efficiency of investment in inventory. To illustrate, consider the simplified annual income statement which follows:

SALES	$1,000,000
EXPENSES	
Cost of Goods Sold	500,000
General & Administrative	200,000
Marketing	200,000
Total Expenses	$900,000
Pre-Tax Profit	$100,000

If the average inventory level for this business is $125,000, then the inventory turnover would be calculated as follows:

$$\text{Inventory Turnover} = \frac{\text{Cost of Goods Sold}}{\text{Average Inventory}}$$

$$= \frac{\$500,000}{\$125,000}$$

$$= 4$$

As may be seen, the inventory turns four times per year for this business. From the preceding income statement, $100,000 in pre-tax profits resulted during this year of operation.

Suppose that, by clever management, the inventory turnover rate could be increased from four times per year to five times per year. The inventory turnover equation may be rearranged algebraically as follows with five turns per year being utilized:

$$\text{Average Inventory} = \frac{\text{Cost of Goods Sold}}{\text{Inventory Turnover}}$$

$$= \frac{\$500,000}{5}$$

$$= \$100,000$$

Thus, if the inventory turnover rate increases from four times per year to five times per year, the level of the average inventory would decrease from $125,000 to $100,000 assuming a constant cost of goods sold figure.

If the $100,000 in pre-tax profit indicated on the preceding income statement can be earned with a $100,000 investment in inventory, clearly, that is more efficient utilization of the company's capital than if the same amount of money is earned on a $125,000 inventory investment.

Many managers conclude that the higher the inventory turnover figure, the more efficient the utilization of the money invested in inventory.

Economic Order Quantity

The concept of economic order quantity (E.O.Q.) suggests that for a given item of inventory, there is an optimum order quantity that will tend to minimize total inventory costs. The economic order quantity formula is written as follows:[2]

$$\text{E.O.Q.} = \sqrt{\frac{2FS}{C}}$$

where: E.O.Q.   is the economic ordering quantity in units, or the optimum quantity to order each time an order is placed.

F   is the fixed cost of placing and receiving an order (i.e. the ordering costs in $ per order that includes the cost of placing orders, shipping, handling, etc.).

S   is the annual sales in units.

C   is the carrying cost per unit of inventory (i.e., the holding costs in dollars per unit for one year and includes storage costs, insurance, taxes, depreciation, spoilage, cost of funds tied up in inventory, etc.).

This formula is used as an aid in deciding how much to buy. It attempts to trade off the cost of ordering inventory against the cost of carrying inventory. It attempts to determine at what order quantity the sum of these two costs will be at a minimum.

Economic Lot Size

Economic lot size is a concept that helps a manufacturer decide how many units to make. A variety of expressions may be derived for calculation purposes depending upon how the business actually operates. One such expression attempting to determine economic lot size is described by Broom and Longenecker.[3]

The economic lot size is the number of units per lot that minimizes the cost of a month's supply of the given product. A manufacturer is subject to two conflicting forces in determining economic lot size. On the one hand, a larger number of units per lot will lower the unit cost of production. This is because the fixed preparation costs—such as machine setup, labor and ticket writing—are spread over a larger number of units per lot. On the other hand, expenses involved in carrying finished goods inventory would be decreased by having a smaller lot. The E.L.S. technique attempts to determine a point of balance. It attempts to determine the number of units per lot that will minimize the total of these two types of costs over a period of time.

SPECIAL CONSIDERATIONS OF THE OWNER-MANAGER

Many owner-managers do not utilize these industry concepts and practices. The person who has ultimate responsibility for management of the total enterprise, in addition to inventory management, is continually bombarded by options, opportunities and special situations from suppliers and from the marketplace that seem to make standard practices less than useful. Possible materials shortages, quantity purchasing discounts, variable lead times for ordering, new policies regarding minimum order quantities and company liquidity (the ability to meet the payroll) are typical of the myriad of considerations faced daily by the owner-manager who must make inventory decisions. Unlike large, well-staffed, well-equipped and well-financed companies, most closely held businesses have to be especially careful not to make inventory decisions that could inadvertently create financial crises.

How Stockpiling Creates A Pitfall

Periodically, managers feel a need to stockpile higher than normal inventory levels. A strike at the supplier's plant, disruptions in transportation, natural disasters, substantial price increases and raw materials shortages can contribute to the manager's feeling a need to stockpile. While the attempt to guarantee adequate supplies of inventory on hand might appear to be a conservative management posture, stockpiling can, in certain operating situations, create a hazardous pitfall.

To illustrate, consider Intercity Assembly Company, Inc. whose future performance was portrayed in detail in Exhibits 1-5 and 1-6. The specific assumptions involved in these forecasts are also presented in Chapter 1. A summary of management's income statement forecast is presented in Exhibit 3-1 and a summary of the cash flow statement forecast is presented in Exhibit 3-2.

This company is making a solid, respectable profit but will need some additional outside financing over the next seven months as indicated by the projected bank overdrafts of Exhibit 3-2. If things go according to projections, approximately $12,000 will be needed to resolve the maximum anticipated bank deficit that occurs in Month 2.

EXHIBIT 3-1

SUMMARY OF ORIGINAL
PRO FORMA INCOME STATEMENT
FOR
INTERCITY ASSEMBLY COMPANY, INC.

Month	1	2	3	4	5	6	7
REVENUES	$ 80,000	84,000	88,000	94,000	100,000	106,000	110,000
EXPENSES	70,770	74,670	77,770	83,670	88,670	93,970	97,470
Pre-Tax Profit	9,230	9,330	10,230	10,330	11,330	12,030	12,530
Income Taxes	2,769	2,799	3,069	3,099	3,399	3,609	3,759
Net Profit	$ 6,461	6,531	7,161	7,231	7,931	8,421	8,771

EXHIBIT 3-2

SUMMARY OF ORIGINAL
PRO FORMA CASH FLOW STATEMENT
FOR
INTERCITY ASSEMBLY COMPANY, INC.

Month	1	2	3	4	5	6	7
RECEIPTS	$ 74,000	252,000	80,000	84,000	88,000	94,000	100,000
DISBURSEMENTS	83,000	256,100	74,100	84,737	83,150	90,800	102,457
Cash Flow	(9,000)	(4,100)	5,900	(737)	4,850	3,200	(2,457)
Beginning Balance	1,100	(7,900)	(12,000)	(6,100)	(6,837)	(1,987)	1,213
Ending Balance	$ (7,900)	(12,000)	(6,100)	(6,837)	(1,987)	1,213	(1,244)

EXHIBIT 3-3

INVENTORY SCHEDULE (IN UNITS) & PURCHASES OVERVIEW
FOR STOCKPILING EXAMPLE

Month	1	2	3	4	5	6	7
Beginning Inventory	43,500	43,500	46,500	147,500	150,500	155,500	157,500
–Shipments (Out)	40,000	42,000	44,000	47,000	50,000	53,000	55,000
+Purchases (Received)	40,000	45,000	145,000	50,000	55,000	55,000	55,000**
Ending Inventory	43,500	46,500	147,500	150,500	155,500	157,500	157,500
Purchases Overview							
Value of Purchases (Received)	$ 40,000	45,000	145,000	50,000	55,000	55,000	55,000
Cash Disbursements (Net 30)	$ 40,000*	40,000	45,000	145,000	50,000	55,000	55,000

*Due to a transaction of a prior period.

**The assumption has been made that sales for Month 8 will be the same as for Month 7.

EXAMPLE OF HOW A COMPANY CAN GO BROKE PLAYING IT SAFE

Suppose that Intercity's management becomes concerned over the possibility of a raw materials shortage. In Month 3, the decision is made to bring in an extra 100,000 units to have on hand (this represents about two months extra supply). The revised inventory forecast shown in Exhibit 3-3 would result.

During the period in which the materials shortage is impending but has not yet occurred, the company is engaged in stockpiling. This is reflected in the higher inventory levels for Months 3, 4, 5, 6 and 7.

When the units costing $1.00 each are received, the obligations for payment are reflected in the purchases overview. Separate from the stockpiling consideration, inventory is purchased such that the ending inventory for a given month will be sufficient to cover the following month's anticipated sales. Orders must be in multiples of 5,000 units with 5,000 units representing the minimum amount that may be ordered. Payment is due 30 days after receipt of goods.

The mere decision to stockpile does not change the number of units projected to be sold, nor does it change the cost of the units to be sold over the next seven months. Consequently, there will be no change in the projected income statement that was summarized in Exhibit 3-1. The projected cash flow statement is a different matter. The extra large shipment received in Month 3 must be paid for in Month 4. The impact on Intercity's projected cash flow is detailed in Exhibit 3-4.

EXHIBIT 3-4

INTERCITY ASSEMBLY COMPANY, INC.
PRO FORMA CASH FLOW STATEMENT
FOR STOCKPILING EXAMPLE

Month	1	2	3	4	5	6	7
RECEIPTS							
Sales Receipts	$ 74,000*	77,000*	80,000	84,000	88,000	94,000	100,000
Common Stock	—	175,000	—	—	—	—	—
Total Received	74,000	252,000	80,000	84,000	88,000	94,000	100,000
DISBURSEMENTS							
Direct Materials	40,000*	40,000	45,000	**145,000**	50,000	55,000	55,000
Direct Labor	4,000	4,200	4,400	4,700	5,000	5,300	5,500
Overhead	1,300	1,300	1,300	1,300	1,300	1,300	1,300
Manufacturing Equip.	—	180,000	—	—	—	—	—
Salaries	6,900	7,450	7,500	8,350	8,350	9,000	9,000
Rent	2,000	2,000	2,000	2,000	2,000	2,000	2,000
Insurance	6,000	—	—	—	—	—	—
Office Equipment	—	3,000	—	—	—	—	—
Other G&A	2,800*	3,000	4,100	4,550	5,500	6,600	7,050
Advertising	9,000*	9,750	9,800	10,200	11,000	11,600	12,500
Brochures	—	5,400	—	—	—	—	—
Taxes	11,000*	—	—	8,637	—	—	10,107
Total Disbursed	83,000	256,100	74,100	**184,737**	83,150	90,800	102,457
Total Cash Flow	$ (9,000)	(4,100)	5,900	**(100,737)**	4,850	3,200	(2,457)
Beginning Balance	$ 1,100	(7,900)	(12,000)	**(6,100)**	**(106,837)**	**(101,987)**	**(98,787)**
Ending Balance	$ (7,900)	(12,000)	(6,100)	**(106,837)**	**(101,987)**	**(98,787)**	**(101,244)**

*From operations during prior periods.

EXHIBIT 3-5
COMPARISON OF STOCKPILING EXAMPLE WITH OPERATING RESULTS
FOR THE ORIGINAL FORECAST

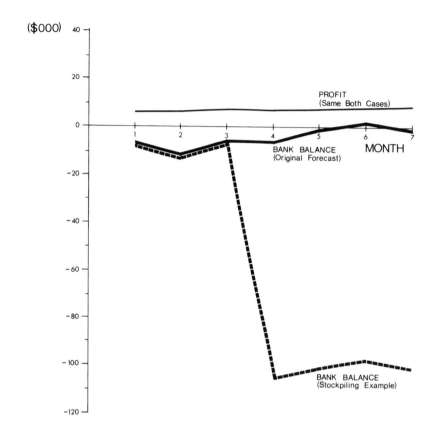

From the standpoint of inventory, the company is in a very comfortable position. From the standpoint of liquidity, the company is in a disastrous position. Instead of an anticipated need for approximately $12,000 in additional cash over the next seven months, the company's decision to stockpile in Month 3 creates a need for more than $100,000 in additional, external cash by Month 4. Operating results are graphically portrayed in Exhibit 3-5.

Regardless of whether or not the company stockpiles, the profit remains unchanged. Bank balances, however, are dramatically altered. This phenomenon is created by the decision to hold more inventory than is absolutely needed.

The situation would have been even worse if holding costs (carrying costs) were considered. Some slight decline in profit, as well as a detrimental change in bank balance, would result if additional costs related to such items as storage, insurance and taxes were added to the forecast due to increased inventory levels.

Imagine the predicament of the manager who only receives an income statement.

As an additional point, consider the relationship between month-ending inventory levels and the company's month-ending bank balance that is portrayed in Exhibit 3-6.

In this example, as well as in many operating companies, an increase in the level of inventory, for whatever reason, creates a corresponding increase in the need for external cash.

EXHIBIT 3-6
COMPARISON OF INVENTORY LEVELS WITH COMPANY BANK BALANCE
WHEN A COMPANY STOCKPILES

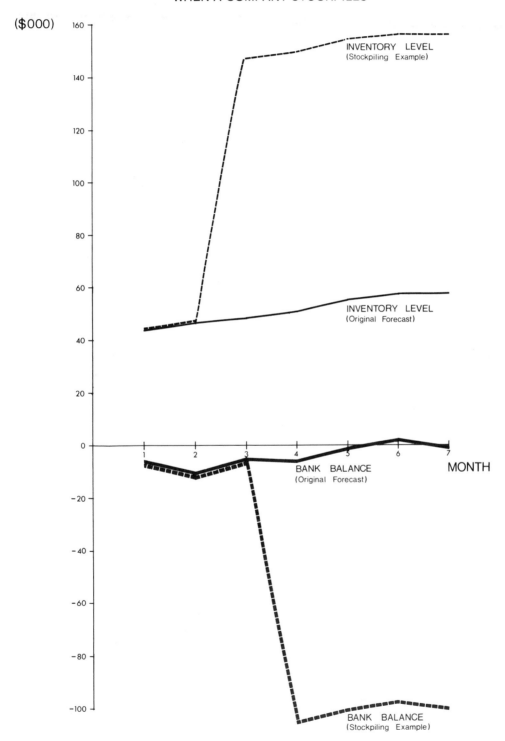

It is interesting that the dramatic change in inventory levels is displaced in time from the dramatic change in company bank balances. The difference in timing between these two major events depends on what kind of deal management has made with the supplier. If stockpiling becomes inevitable, one way to cope with the decreasing liquidity of the company is to negotiate different payment terms with the supplier.

HIGH VERSUS LOW INVENTORY LEVELS: PROS AND CONS

High inventory levels tend to insure an ability to ship to the customer and reduce the risk of stockouts. The opposite is true of very low inventory levels. On the other hand, high inventory levels are more expensive to hold. Increased storage costs, insurance costs and taxes tend to erode net margins. Since the inventory is not turned as rapidly with a high level of inventory, the increase in age of some of the units could result in an increased spoilage rate. As a general rule, high inventory levels consume more cash than low inventory levels and in the worst case, high inventory levels could jeopardize the company's liquidity.

How Quantity Discounts Can Create a Financial Dilemma

Suppliers who offer quantity discounts present the owner-manager with a common option. Buy a specific quantity at a specific price or buy a larger quantity at a reduced price per unit. Under certain conditions, the decision to buy larger quantities at a cheaper price can create a financial dilemma.

EXAMPLE OF WHAT CAN HAPPEN TO A COMPANY TAKING QUANTITY DISCOUNTS

To illustrate what can happen to a company taking quantity discounts on purchases of materials, consider once again Intercity Assembly Company, Inc. In the original forecasts of Exhibit 1-5 and Exhibit 1-6 that are summarized in Exhibits 3-1 and 3-2, management purchased raw material units at a cost of $1.00 per unit in quantities of 5,000. If a 5% discount is available on purchases of 35,000 units and multiples of 35,000 units and if management decides to take advantage of these discounts beginning in Month 3, the revised inventory forecast presented in Exhibit 3-7 would result.

Inventory is purchased such that the ending inventory will be sufficient to cover the following month's anticipated sales. Payment for raw material units received is 30 days after receipt of the goods. As seen from the purchases overview, the per unit cost of the materials received decreases. There will likewise be a decrease in the amount of cash disbursed on a per-unit basis beginning 30 days later.

EXHIBIT 3-7
INVENTORY SCHEDULE (IN UNITS) & PURCHASES OVERVIEW
FOR QUANTITY DISCOUNT EXAMPLE

Month	1	2	3	4	5	6	7
Beginning Inventory	43,500	43,500	46,500	72,500	60,500	80,500	62,500
–Shipments (Out)	40,000	42,000	44,000	47,000	50,000	53,000	55,000
+Purchases (Received)	40,000	45,000	70,000	35,000	70,000	35,000	70,000
Ending Inventory	43,500	46,500	72,500	60,500	80,500	62,500	77,500
Purchases Overview							
Value of Purchases (Received)	$ 40,000	45,000	66,500	33,250	66,500	33,250	66,500
Cash Disbursements (Net 30)	$ 40,000*	40,000	45,000	66,500	33,250	66,500	33,250

*Due to a transaction of a prior period.

When the expense of these cheaper units is reflected in a forecasted income statement on a first in-first out basis, the results presented in Exhibit 3-8 occur. Net profit in Months 4, 5, 6 and 7 is perceptibly higher than in the original forecast of Exhibit 3-1.

If the cash flow counterpart to Exhibit 3-8 is prepared, the events described by Exhibit 3-9 result.

EXHIBIT 3-8
INTERCITY ASSEMBLY COMPANY, INC.
PRO FORMA INCOME STATEMENT
FOR QUANTITY DISCOUNT EXAMPLE

Month	1	2	3	4	5	6	7
REVENUES							
Units Sold	40,000	42,000	44,000	47,000	50,000	53,000	55,000
Sales	$ 80,000	84,000	88,000	94,000	100,000	106,000	110,000
EXPENSES							
Direct Materials	40,000	42,000	44,000	**44,775**	**47,500**	**50,350**	**52,250**
Direct Labor	4,000	4,200	4,400	4,700	5,000	5,300	5,500
Overhead	4,000	4,000	4,000	4,000	4,000	4,000	4,000
Cost of Goods Sold	48,000	50,200	52,400	**53,475**	**56,500**	**59,650**	**61,750**
Gross Profit	32,000	33,800	35,600	**40,525**	**43,500**	**46,350**	**48,250**
General & Administrative							
Salaries	6,900	7,450	7,500	8,350	8,350	9,000	9,000
Rent	2,000	2,000	2,000	2,000	2,000	2,000	2,000
Insurance	500	500	500	500	500	500	500
Depreciation	170	170	170	170	170	170	170
Other G&A	3,000	4,100	4,550	5,500	6,600	7.050	7,850
Marketing							
Advertising	9,750	9,800	10,200	11,000	11,600	12,500	13,000
Brochures	450	450	450	450	450	450	450
Total Expense	70,770	74,670	77,770	**81,445**	**86,170**	**91,320**	**94,720**
Taxable Income	9,230	9,330	10,230	**12,555**	**13,830**	**14,680**	**15,280**
Income Taxes	2,769	2,799	3,069	**3,767**	**4,149**	**4,404**	**4,584**
Net Profit	$ 6,461	6,531	7,161	**8,788**	**9,681**	**10,276**	**10,696**

While the company is improving its profits in Months 4 to 7, it consumes more cash as indicated by the increased magnitude of the overdrafts of Months 4, 5 and 6.

Exhibit 3-10 graphically illustrates what can happen to a company that elects to take quantity purchasing discounts.

In this example, profits beginning in Month 4 increase somewhat. The effect on the company's bank balance, however, is alarming. The need for additional external cash in Month 4 alone increases by more than $20,000. In this situation, the decision to take quantity discounts could create severe liquidity problems.

It is normal to believe that an increase in profits over a long period of time will create improved bank balances. That may be possible. The problem caused by most quantity discounts, however, does not occur in the "long run" but in the "short run." One cannot make extra profits for the coming year if one cannot figure out how to get through the next 90 days.

This "cheaper by the dozen" option presents the owner-manager with a financial dilemma, more profit or more liquidity. The warning is "Don't make that extra profit unless you can finance it."

EXHIBIT 3-9
INTERCITY ASSEMBLY COMPANY, INC.
PRO FORMA CASH FLOW STATEMENT
FOR QUANTITY DISCOUNT EXAMPLE

Month	1	2	3	4	5	6	7
RECEIPTS							
Sales Receipts	$74,000*	77,000*	80,000	84,000	88,000	94,000	100,000
Common Stock	—	175,000	—	—	—	—	—
Total Received	74,000	252,000	80,000	84,000	88,000	94,000	100,000
DISBURSEMENTS							
Direct Materials	40,000*	40,000	45,000	**66,500**	**33,250**	**66,500**	**33,250**
Direct Labor	4,000	4,200	4,400	4,700	5,000	5,300	5,500
Overhead	1,300	1,300	1,300	1,300	1,300	1,300	1,300
Manufacturing Equip.	—	180,000	—	—	—	—	—
Salaries	6,900	7,450	7,500	8,350	8,350	9,000	9,000
Rent	2,000	2,000	2,000	2,000	2,000	2,000	2,000
Insurance	6,000	—	—	—	—	—	—
Office Equipment	—	3,000	—	—	—	—	—
Other G&A	2,800*	3,000	4,100	4,550	5,500	6,600	7,050
Advertising	9,000*	9,750	9,800	10,200	11,000	11,600	12,500
Brochures	—	5,400	—	—	—	—	—
Taxes	11,000*	—	—	8,637	—	—	**12,320**
Total Disbursed	83,000	256,100	74,100	**106,237**	**66,400**	**102,300**	**82,920**
Total Cash Flow	$ (9,000)	(4,100)	5,900	**(22,237)**	**21,600**	**(8,300)**	**17,080**
Beginning Balance	$ 1,100	(7,900)	(12,000)	(6,100)	**(28,337)**	**(6,737)**	**(15,037)**
Ending Balance	$ (7,900)	(12,000)	(6,100)	**(28,337)**	**(6,737)**	**(15,037)**	**2,043**

*From operations during prior periods.

QUANTITY DISCOUNTS: PROS AND CONS

Perhaps the most obvious thing in favor of quantity purchasing discounts is that there is a possibility for higher profit margins. One of the major disadvantages is that quantity purchasing usually consumes greater quantities of cash in the short range. Another negative aspect is that holding costs or carrying costs of inventory are very likely increased. Also, if the quantity purchased is significantly more than one currently needs, then a higher rate of deterioration and spoilage may occur, since the inventory sits for longer periods of time prior to usage.

Some enlightened owner-managers feel that taking quantity discounts is a form of stockpiling with an incentive attached.

Inventory Procurement: Two Red Flags

Owner-managers are frequently presented with a variety of purchasing terms and conditions. Some procurement conditions can be a setup for subsequent financial problems. Two red flags are long lead times when ordering materials or other merchandise and large minimum order quantities.

EXHIBIT 3-10
COMPARISON OF QUANTITY OF DISCOUNT EXAMPLE WITH OPERATING
RESULTS FOR THE ORIGINAL FORECAST

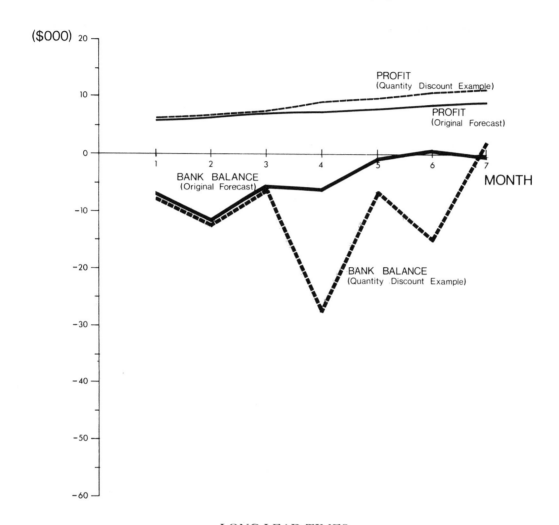

LONG LEAD TIMES

The length of time between the ordering of inventory items and their actual receipt can vary based on economic conditions, geographical distances between supplier and customer, different delivery practices among various suppliers and supply and demand factors. Industry practices, seasonal dating, transportation vagaries and raw material shortages may also influence the length of time between placing of the order and receipt of the goods. Long lead times alone can be planned for and dealt with. When the unexpected occurs, however, major financial problems can result.

Consider once again Intercity Assembly Company, Inc. whose performance is projected for the next seven months in the summarized income forecast of Exhibit 3-1 and the summarized cash flow forecast of Exhibit 3-2. Suppose that Intercity has one unexpected "bad" month, Month 3. Instead of the anticipated shipments to the customers totaling 44,000 units, only 20,000 units are actually sold in Month 3. The projected income statement would be altered as indicated in Exhibit 3-11.

The gross profit of $14,000 in Month 3 is not adequate to cover the fixed general and administrative as well as marketing expenses. This results in a net loss for the month of $7,959. (This substantial loss in Month 3 creates an income tax credit in the form of a loss carryforward based on the effective tax rate of 30%.)

If the company does not have a long lead time for materials that it purchases, the projected inventory schedule may be adjusted to compensate for the reduced requirements caused by Month 3, the "bad" month. The revised inventory schedule is presented in Exhibit 3-12.

Raw materials are purchased such that the ending inventory will be adequate to cover the following month's projected sales. Orders are in multiples of 5,000 units with 5,000 units being the minimum order. Payment is 30 days after receipt of goods.

When the cash disbursements (see Purchases Overview of Exhibit 3-12) for the materials purchased are reflected in a revised cash flow forecast, the impact on the company's liquidity may be observed. This change is reflected in the forecasted cash flow statement of Exhibit 3-13.

The bank balances that will occur are very different from those portrayed in the original forecast summarized in Exhibit 3-2. In the original forecast, the largest cash deficit occurred in Month 2 and totaled $12,000. If Month 3 turns out to be a "bad" month as described, the maximum cash deficit would be more than $21,000 and would occur in Month 5.

When the operating results of the original forecast are compared graphically with those

EXHIBIT 3-11
INTERCITY ASSEMBLY COMPANY, INC.
PRO FORMA INCOME STATEMENT
FOR BAD MONTH EXAMPLE

Month	1	2	3	4	5	6	7
REVENUES							
Units Sold	40,000	42,000	**20,000**	47,000	50,000	53,000	55,000
Sales	$ 80,000	84,000	**40,000**	94,000	100,000	106,000	110,000
EXPENSES							
Direct Materials	40,000	42,000	**20,000**	47,000	50,000	53,000	55,000
Direct Labor	4,000	4,200	**2,000**	4,700	5,000	5,300	5,500
Overhead	4,000	4,000	4,000	4,000	4,000	4,000	4,000
Cost of Goods Sold	48,000	50,200	**26,000**	55,700	59,000	62,300	64,500
Gross Profit	32,000	33,800	**14,000**	38,300	41,000	43,700	45,500
General & Administrative							
Salaries	6,900	7,450	7,500	8,350	8,350	9,000	9,000
Rent	2,000	2,000	2,000	2,000	2,000	2,000	2,000
Insurance	500	500	500	500	500	500	500
Depreciation	170	170	170	170	170	170	170
Other G&A	3,000	4,100	4,550	5,500	6,600	7,050	7,850
Marketing							
Advertising	9,750	9,800	10,200	11,000	11,600	12,500	13,000
Brochures	450	450	450	450	450	450	450
Total Expense	70,770	74,670	**51,370**	83,670	88,670	93,970	97,470
Taxable Income	9,230	9,330	**(11,370)**	10,330	11,330	12,030	12,530
Income Taxes	2,769	2,799	**(3,411)**	3,099	3,399	3,609	3,759
Net Profit	$ 6,461	6,531	**(7,959)**	7,231	7,931	8,421	8,771

for the "bad" month example, an interesting picture emerges as depicted in Exhibit 3-14. A traumatic but common phenomenon is portrayed. Since customers in this example pay the company on a net 60-day basis, there is no change in the ending bank balance in Month 3, the "bad" month. One month after the "bad" month, bank balances increase dramatically. But two months after the "bad" month, bank balances plunge to a level far below the worst deficit originally forecast. A "bad" month for this company having no long lead times on receipt of raw materials results in surplus cash for a short period of time and then a disastrous liquidity bind. The frustrating part of this phenomenon is that the cash bind occurs long after the sales problems have been rectified and the monthly units shipped are back on forecast.

Suppose that the same "bad" month condition develops in Month 3. Consider now what happens if the company is locked into a long lead time for receipt of materials. If the company is committed to firm, irrevocable orders 90 days in advance of when the materials are actually received, a new set of events would ensue. Normally, there would not be an effect on the sale price or the expenses incurred by a mere difference in when materials are ordered. Exhibit 3-15 is a revised forecast for the same "bad" month when a long materials lead time is involved.

It is not surprising that this revised income statement is identical to that of Exhibit 3-11. It may be surprising that a very different picture emerges if the revised inventory schedule is prepared incorporating a long lead time for materials. The difference in receipt of materials and in inventory levels is portrayed in Exhibit 3-16.

EXHIBIT 3-12
INVENTORY SCHEDULE (IN UNITS) & PURCHASES OVERVIEW
FOR BAD MONTH EXAMPLE

Month	1	2	3	4	5	6	7
Beginning Inventory	43,500	43,500	46,500	**51,500**	**54,500**	**54,500**	**56,500**
–Shipments (Out)	40,000	42,000	**20,000**	47,000	50,000	53,000	55,000
+Purchases (Received)	40,000	45,000	**25,000**	50,000	**50,000**	55,000	55,000
Ending Inventory	43,500	46,500	**51,500**	**54,500**	54,500	**56,500**	**56,500**
Purchases Overview							
Value of Purchases (Received)	$ 40,000	45,000	**25,000**	50,000	**50,000**	55,000	55,000
Cash Disbursements (Net 30)	$ 40,000*	40,000	45,000	**25,000**	50,000	**50,000**	55,000

*Due to a transaction of a prior period.

The rescheduling of a given month's purchases requires 90 days. The discovery that fewer units would be needed in Month 3 cannot be reflected in adjusted receipts from the supplier until Month 6. The orders placed for the materials of Months 4 and 5 became firm and irrevocable in Months 1 and 2. By the end of Month 6, the ending inventory amount can be

EXHIBIT 3-13
INTERCITY ASSEMBLY COMPANY, INC.
PRO FORMA CASH FLOW STATEMENT
FOR BAD MONTH EXAMPLE

Month	1	2	3	4	5	6	7
RECEIPTS							
Sales Receipts	$ 74,000*	77,000*	80,000	84,000	**40,000**	94,000	100,000
Common Stock	—	175,000	—	—	—	—	—
Total Received	74,000	252,000	80,000	84,000	**40,000**	94,000	100,000
DISBURSEMENTS							
Direct Materials	40,000*	40,000	45,000	**25,000**	50,000	**50,000**	55,000
Direct Labor	4,000	4,200	**2,000**	4,700	5,000	5,300	5,500
Overhead	1,300	1,300	1,300	1,300	1,300	1,300	1,300
Manufacturing Equip.	—	180,000	—	—	—	—	—
Salaries	6,900	7,450	7,500	8,350	8,350	9,000	9,000
Rent	2,000	2,000	2,000	2,000	2,000	2,000	2,000
Insurance	6,000	—	—	—	—	—	—
Office Equipment	—	3,000	—	—	—	—	—
Other G&A	2,800*	3,000	4,100	4,550	5,500	6,600	7,050
Advertising	9,000*	9,750	9,800	10,200	11,000	11,600	12,500
Brochures	—	5,400	—	—	—	—	—
Taxes	11,000*	—	—	2,157	—	—	10,107
Total Disbursed	83,000	256,100	**71,700**	58,257	83,150	**85,800**	102,457
Total Cash Flow	$ (9,000)	(4,100)	**8,300**	25,743	**(43,150)**	8,200	(2,457)
Beginning Balance	$ 1,100	(7,900)	(12,000)	**(3,700)**	22,043	**(21,107)**	**(12,907)**
Ending Balance	$ (7,900)	(12,000)	**(3,700)**	22,043	**(21,107)**	**(12,907)**	**(15,364)**

*From operations during prior periods.

corrected such that the desired levels exist from that point forward.

Again the basic inventory philosophy is to have enough units on hand at the end of the month to cover the following month's anticipated sales volume. Orders are still in multiples of 5,000 units with 5,000 units the minimum order. Payment to the materials supplier is 30 days after receipt of goods.

When the disbursements brought about by this new inventory schedule are reflected in the forecasted cash flow statement for Intercity Assembly Company, the operating results portrayed in Exhibit 3-17 occur.

When this company has a "bad" month and is simultaneously locked into a long lead time (90 days) for receipt of materials, the maximum deficit that would arise in the company's bank account is more than $40,000 and occurs in Month 5. This is in contrast to the same company with the same bad month but no long lead time on receipt of materials having a maximum cash deficit of approximately one half of that. The company having a 90-day lead time on materials would consume approximately $20,000 in additional cash by the end of Month 5. This difference is dramatized graphically in Exhibit 3-18.

The "bad" month both with and without a long lead time for materials results in a substantial drop in profit. Both "bad" month examples, however, resulted in improved bank balances for the month following the "bad" month. In Month 5, the company's bank account in both examples plummets. When a 90-day lead time on receipt of materials is imposed, the liquidity is seriously injured.

Again, for a moment, think about the predicament of the manager who only receives an income statement. The income statement in this situation did not change while the cash flow statement changed dramatically.

EXHIBIT 3-14
COMPARISON OF OPERATING RESULTS FOR ORIGINAL FORECAST AND
BAD MONTH EXAMPLE

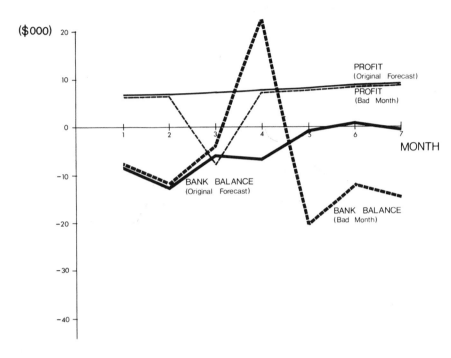

EXHIBIT 3-15
INTERCITY ASSEMBLY COMPANY, INC.
PRO FORMA INCOME STATEMENT
FOR BAD MONTH PLUS LONG MATERIALS
LEAD TIME EXAMPLE

Month	1	2	3	4	5	6	7
REVENUES							
Units Sold	40,000	42,000	**20,000**	47,000	50,000	53,000	55,000
Sales	$ 80,000	84,000	**40,000**	94,000	100,000	106,000	110,000
EXPENSES							
Direct Materials	40,000	42,000	**20,000**	47,000	50,000	53,000	55,000
Direct Labor	4,000	4,200	**2,000**	4,700	5,000	5,300	5,500
Overhead	4,000	4,000	4,000	4,000	4,000	4,000	4,000
Cost of Goods Sold	48,000	50,200	**26,000**	55,700	59,000	62,300	64,500
Gross Profit	32,000	33,800	**14,000**	38,300	41,000	43,700	45,500
General & Administrative							
Salaries	6,900	7,450	7,500	8,350	8,350	9,000	9,000
Rent	2,000	2,000	2,000	2,000	2,000	2,000	2,000
Insurance	500	500	500	500	500	500	500
Depreciation	170	170	170	170	170	170	170
Other G&A	3,000	4,100	4,550	5,500	6,600	7,050	7,850
Marketing							
Advertising	9,750	9,800	10,200	11,000	11,600	12,500	13,000
Brochures	450	450	450	450	450	450	450
Total Expense	70,770	74,670	**51,370**	83,670	88,670	93,970	97,470
Taxable Income	9,230	9,330	**(11,370)**	10,330	11,330	12,030	12,530
Income Taxes	2,769	2,799	**(3,411)**	3,099	3,399	3,609	3,759
Net Profit	$ 6,461	6,531	**(7,959)**	7,231	7,931	8,421	8,771

EXHIBIT 3-16

INVENTORY SCHEDULE (IN UNITS) AND PURCHASES OVERVIEW
FOR BAD MONTH PLUS LONG MATERIALS LEAD TIME EXAMPLE

Month	1	2	3	4	5	6	7
Beginning Inventory	43,500	43,500	46,500	**71,500**	**74,500**	**79,500**	56,500
–Shipments (Out)	40,000	42,000	**20,000**	47,000	50,000	53,000	55,000
+Purchases (Received)	40,000	45,000	45,000	50,000	55,000	**30,000**	55,000
Ending Inventory	43,500	46,500	**71,500**	**74,500**	**79,500**	**56,500**	**56,500**
Purchases Overview							
Value of Purchases (Received) $	40,000	45,000	45,000	50,000	55,000	**30,000**	55,000
Cash Disbursements (Net 30) $	40,000*	40,000	45,000	45,000	50,000	55,000	**30,000**

*Due to a transaction of a prior period.

LARGE MINIMUM ORDER QUANTITIES

It is reasonable and common that many suppliers require a minimum order quantity for the goods that they sell. It is not feasible for example to sell one paper clip. There is a certain minimum order quantity that makes a shipment economically justifiable. For Intercity

EXHIBIT 3-17

INTERCITY ASSEMBLY COMPANY, INC.
PRO FORMA CASH FLOW STATEMENT
FOR BAD MONTH PLUS LONG MATERIALS
LEAD TIME EXAMPLE

Month	1	2	3	4	5	6	7
RECEIPTS							
Sales Receipts	$ 74,000*	77,000*	80,000	84,000	**40,000**	94,000	100,000
Common Stock	—	175,000	—	—	—	—	—
Total Received	74,000	252,000	80,000	84,000	**40,000**	94,000	100,000
DISBURSEMENTS							
Direct Materials	40,000*	40,000	45,000	45,000	50,000	55,000	**30,000**
Direct Labor	4,000	4,200	**2,000**	4,700	5,000	5,300	5,500
Overhead	1,300	1,300	1,300	1,300	1,300	1,300	1,300
Manufacturing Equip.	—	180,000	—	—	—	—	—
Salaries	6,900	7,450	7,500	8,350	8,350	9,000	9,000
Rent	2,000	2,000	2,000	2,000	2,000	2,000	2,000
Insurance	6,000	—	—	—	—	—	—
Office Equipment	—	3,000	—	—	—	—	—
Other G&A	2,800*	3,000	4,100	4,550	5,500	6,600	7,050
Advertising	9,000*	9,750	9,800	10,200	11,000	11,600	12,500
Brochures	—	5,400	—	—	—	—	—
Taxes	11,000*	—	—	2,157	—	—	10,107
Total Disbursed	83,000	256,100	**71,700**	78,257	83,150	90,800	**77,457**
Total Cash Flow	$ (9,000)	(4,100)	**8,300**	5,743	**(43,150)**	3,200	**22,543**
Beginning Balance	$ 1,100	(7,900)	(12,000)	**(3,700)**	2,043	**(41,107)**	**(37,907)**
Ending Balance	$ (7,900)	(12,000)	**(3,700)**	2,043	**(41,107)**	**(37,907)**	**(15,364)**

*From operations during prior periods.

Assembly Company, Inc., it is reasonable to expect the supplier of the raw materials to have a minimum quantity that can be shipped.

It is not minimum order quantities per se that create a red flag for owner-managers. The red flag situation is created by minimum order quantities that are sufficiently large that they cause management to consistently purchase and regularly have on hand more units than would normally be desired. To get some quantitative feeling for how large minimum quantities impact the operations of a business, refer to Exhibits 3-8 and 3-9. Large minimum order

EXHIBIT 3-18
COMPARISON OF OPERATING RESULTS FOR ORIGINAL FORECAST, BAD
MONTH EXAMPLE AND BAD MONTH PLUS LONG MATERIALS LEAD TIME
EXAMPLE

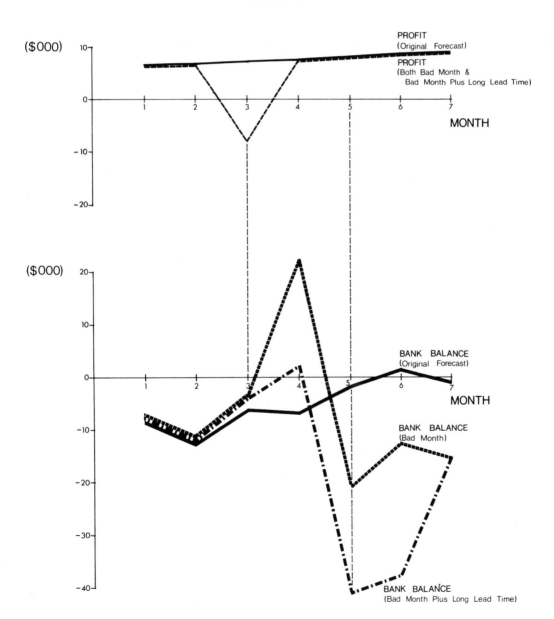

quantities create the same kind of phenomenon caused by taking quantity discounts when the quantity purchased is larger than the amount management would normally procure. As a matter of fact, large minimum order quantities would produce results slightly worse than those depicted in Exhibit 3-10 for large quantity discounts. The reason is large minimum order quantities alone do not have the associated reduction in unit cost created by the discount.

When minimum order quantities are specified and are much larger than management really desires, it may be worthwhile to consider an alternate source of supply even though that alternate source may charge more on a per unit basis. These smaller order quantities, though more expensive from an income statement point of view, may prevent a liquidity crisis. One technique for evaluating the various alternatives is to prepare an income and a cash flow forecast of the type utilized in this chapter and see what profit and cash flow conditions result from the various possible purchase options.

INVENTORY AS TYPE II MONEY

Money comes in different forms. The highest order, the most liquid and perhaps the most desirable form is "cash money." The authors refer to this as Type I money. It is measured in dollars.

Accounts receivable, inventory, equipment and other assets are things of value and may be thought of as forms of money. However, they are not Type I money, even though they may be valuable to certain individuals and they may have an established market value. The authors refer to these forms of money as Type II money also measured in dollars.

Four significant points emerge from the consideration of Type I and Type II money:

1. There are transactions, crucial to the survival of a business, that may be completed only with Type I money. For example:

    a. You cannot meet the payroll with Type II money.

    b. You cannot repay bank debt with Type II money.

    c. You cannot pay most creditors with Type II money.

    d. You cannot pay taxes with Type II money.

    e. You cannot pay rent with Type II money.

    f. You cannot pay insurance with Type II money.

    g. You cannot pay the utilities bill with Type II money.

    h. You cannot pay the phone bill with Type II money.

2. The timing of many of these transactions is critical and precise. For example, payday is a fixed date with no flexibility.

3. Type II money is not necessarily convertible into Type I money. It is almost never immediately convertible.

4. If you are forced to convert Type II money into Type I money under pressure of time, the conversion ratio is frequently less than one to one. Borrowing against inventory may yield only 50¢ on the dollar depending on the type of inventory. Factoring accounts receivable may result in only 70¢ on the dollar in the short run and 95¢ on the dollar in the long run. An inventory clearance sale may occur at 10% to 50% off regular price.

While many companies must have inventory to conduct their business, it is important to recognize that this is Type II money. The common occurrence in closely held companies of too much Type II money and too little Type I money on specific dates, such as payday, can create a potentially fatal lack of liquidity.

NOTES FOR CHAPTER 3

[1]Robert N. Anthony, *Management Accounting,* 4th Edition (Homewood, Illinois: Richard D. Irwin, Inc., 1970), p. 301.

[2]J. Fred Weston, *Financial Management,* (Homewood, Illinois: Richard D. Irwin, Inc., 1975), p. 49.

[3]H. N. Broom and Justin G. Longenecker. *Small Business Management,* 3rd Edition (Cincinnati: South-Western Publishing Co., 1971), p. 629.

4

Administering Accounts Payable –
Making Money in the Way You Pay Your Bills

In the eyes of many enlightened managers, individuals are naive who view accounts payable management as merely the timely paying of bills. Some skillful managers even view what is paid and when it is paid as crucial elements to achieving a competitive edge in the marketplace.

FINANCIAL CONSIDERATIONS

Accounts payable management is largely financial management and a significant portion of the considerations are financial. Basic to the financial considerations is the decision to write a check. Since the owner-manager controls when checks are written (one can refuse to write a check even in the face of a law suit), a variety of choices usually exist regarding (1) how much is actually paid and (2) when payment is made. To illustrate this, consider Exhibit 4-1. This "decision tree" diagrams the various management choices available. Starting from the left, the first two branches relate to whether the company does or does not have the money to pay the account in question. If a business simply cannot pay the supplier, about the only alternative is to negotiate some arrangement. If, however, a business has the funds available to pay a given account, then a variety of options present themselves.

The next level of branching in this "decision tree" considers paying before the due date, paying on the due date or paying after the due date of the payable in question. A third level of branching occurs with two of these options. If a decision is made to pay before the due date, there may or may not be a tangible monetary incentive involved. Following another branch, if the decision is made to pay after the due date, there may or may not be a specific monetary penalty.

There are three lines of choice that are of particular interest to the astute accounts payable manager. These three are as follows:

1. Can Pay & Pay Before Due & With Incentive
2. Can Pay & Pay After Due   & No Penalty
3. Can Pay & Pay After Due   & With Penalty

EXHIBIT 4-1
THE ACCOUNTS PAYABLE MANAGEMENT DECISION TREE

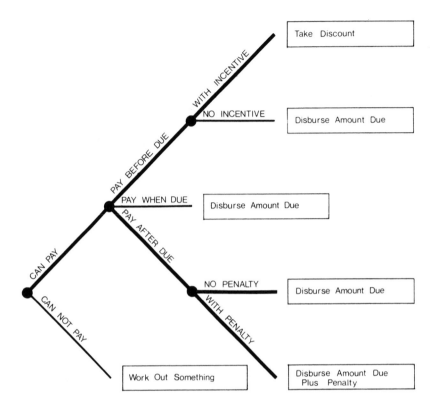

The first line of choices results in the decision to take a supplier's discount for quick payment. A typical discount might be 1% within 10 days; net due in 30 days or, perhaps 2% within 10 days; net due in 30 days. The second line of choices has to do with paying late but not incurring a penalty for doing so. The third line of choices results in paying late and incurring a penalty for late payment.

The first line of choices presents the owner-manager with the question, "Should one take the discount or not?"

Conventional Approach To Evaluating A Discount

A cash discount is a benefit to the customer that the seller is willing to offer for certain benefits that accompany prompt turnover of his funds. The practice of offering cash discounts arose during the Civil War period because of fear that unstable economic conditions would impair the seller's ability to collect. Cash discounts were commonly 8% or higher, but as competitive selling forced declining profit margins, discount rates were gradually reduced in most lines.[1]

Failure to take a discount amounts to the customer's paying a fee for use of supplier financing for an extra period of time. Consequently, one method of evaluating different discounts is to compare the effective annualized interest rates associated with each discount proposition. The expression for calculating an annualized interest rate is as follows:

$$\text{Annualized Rate} = \frac{\begin{array}{c}\text{Number of Days}\\\text{in a Year}\end{array}}{\begin{array}{c}\text{Number of Days}\\\text{Financing Is Used}\end{array}} \times \begin{array}{c}\text{Percent of Principal}\\\text{Amount Charged}\end{array}$$

How to Determine the Cost of
Supplier Financing

To calculate the annualized interest rate associated with supplier financing when the supplier offers a cash discount, the annualized rate expression would be written

$$\text{Annualized Rate} = \frac{\text{Number of Days in A Year}}{\left[\begin{array}{c}\text{Net Credit}\\\text{Period in Days}\end{array}\right] - \left[\begin{array}{c}\text{Cash Discount}\\\text{Period in Days}\end{array}\right]} \times \text{Discount}$$

Utilizing this relationship, the annualized interest rate associated with three common cash discounts,

½% 10 days; Net 30 days,
1% 10 days; Net 30 days, and
2% 10 days; Net 30 days

would be as follows;

½% 10; Net 30 $\text{Annualized Rate} = \dfrac{365 \text{ days}}{(30\text{-}10) \text{ days}} \times \text{½\%}$

$= \dfrac{365}{20} \times \text{½\%}$

$= 9.125\%$

1% 10; Net 30 $\text{Annualized Rate} = \dfrac{365 \text{ days}}{(30\text{-}10) \text{ days}} \times 1\%$

$= \dfrac{365}{20} \times 1\%$

$= 18.25\%$

2% 10; Net 30 $\text{Annualized Rate} = \dfrac{365 \text{ days}}{(30\text{-}10) \text{ days}} \times 2\%$

$= \dfrac{365}{20} \times 2\%$

$= 36.5\%$

If one takes the discount within the discount period, then that individual is electing not to utilize supplier financing. If one elects to ignore the discount and to use supplier financing for the net credit period, the annualized rate associated with supplier financing would be as calculated. The implication is that if supplier financing as calculated is more costly than alternative sources of financing, then one should take the discount.

This represents a common conventional approach utilized by owner-managers and certain members of the financial community to evaluate cash discounts.

Fallacies of the Conventional Approach

There are several problems associated with this conventional approach to determining whether a cash discount should be taken. One troublesome area involves the liquidity status of a business after it takes a cash discount. A second shortcoming has to do with the inflexibility of the assumptions used when calculating the cost of supplier financing. Both of these fallacies will be examined.

The Liquidity Pitfall

The evaluation of a cash discount by analyzing equivalent annualized interest rates does not consider the liquidity ramifications in a particular company's bank account. Entirely too many owner-managers have the feeling that reducing the cost of purchases by taking a cash discount improves profits and simultaneously improves the status of their bank balance. "After all, I write a smaller check. The difference remains in the bank. Doesn't it?"

EXAMPLE OF A COMPANY THAT TOOK THE DISCOUNT AND ALMOST WENT BROKE

To explore what can happen to a company that decides to take the discount, consider once again Intercity Assembly Company, Inc. The next seven months' performance of this company was originally forecast in Exhibit 1-5 (a pro forma income statement) and in Exhibit 1-6 (a pro forma cash flow statement). The forecasted performance of these two exhibits is summarized in Exhibits 4-2 and 4-3.

EXHIBIT 4-2
SUMMARY OF ORIGINAL
PRO FORMA INCOME STATEMENT
FOR
INTERCITY ASSEMBLY COMPANY, INC.

Month	1	2	3	4	5	6	7
REVENUES	$ 80,000	84,000	88,000	94,000	100,000	106,000	110,000
EXPENSES	70,770	74,670	77,770	83,670	88,670	93,970	97,470
Pre-Tax Profit	9,230	9,330	10,230	10,330	11,330	12,030	12,530
Income Taxes	2,769	2,799	3,069	3,099	3,399	3,609	3,759
Net Profit	$ 6,461	6,531	7,161	7,231	7,931	8,421	8,771

The projected income statement of Exhibit 4-2 indicates that the Intercity Assembly Company's management expects conservative growth and very respectable net profits. The projected cash flow statement summarized in Exhibit 4-3 indicates that without additional external financing, the company will be somewhat short of cash most of the time during the coming seven months. The worst anticipated cash deficit of $12,000 in Month 2 is not overly bothersome at this point, in light of the company's profit performance. The company should be able to borrow moderate sums on a short-term basis if it so desires.

Intercity Assembly Company has one major supplier. Suppose that in Month 3, the materials supplier informs Intercity that a 3% 10 days; net 30 days cash discount will go into effect. The conventional approach to evaluating this cash discount would calculate the equivalent annualized interest rate associated with the supplier's financing if one elects to pay in 30 days and not take the discount. This computation would yield the following:

$$3\% \ 10; \ \text{Net } 30 \qquad \text{Annualized Rate} \ = \frac{365 \text{ days}}{(30\text{-}10) \text{ days}} \times 3\%$$

$$= \frac{365}{20} \times 3\%$$

$$= \ 54.8\%$$

Conventional calculations indicate that if management does not take the discount, and thereby elects to utilize supplier financing, the cost of supplier financing on an annualized rate basis is 54.8%. When one thinks in terms of bank interest rates, it is difficult to justify this apparent financing cost. Based on the preceding calculation, Intercity would probably take the discount as soon as it becomes available (i.e., Month 3).

EXHIBIT 4-3
SUMMARY OF ORIGINAL
PRO FORMA CASH FLOW STATEMENT
FOR
INTERCITY ASSEMBLY COMPANY, INC.

Month	1	2	3	4	5	6	7
RECEIPTS	$ 74,000	252,000	80,000	84,000	88,000	94,000	100,000
DISBURSEMENTS	83,000	256,100	74,100	84,737	83,150	90,800	102,457
Cash Flow	(9,000)	(4,100)	5,900	(737)	4,850	3,200	(2,457)
Beginning Balance	1,100	(7,900)	(12,000)	(6,100)	(6,837)	(1,987)	1,213
Ending Balance	$ (7,900)	(12,000)	(6,100)	(6,837)	(1,987)	1,213	(1,244)

To examine the impact of taking the 3% 10 days; net 30 days cash discount on Intercity's operations, first examine the exact procedure for recognizing when the discount is earned. Exhibit 4-4 is helpful in this regard.

EXHIBIT 4-4
DIAGRAM ILLUSTRATING WHEN DISCOUNTS MAY BE TAKEN RELATIVE
TO WHEN SHIPMENTS ARE RECEIVED

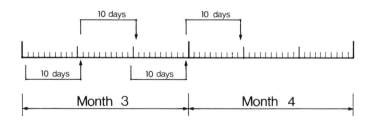

Since the discount must be taken within 10 days of the date the shipment is received (or perhaps the invoice date), a shipment received during the first 10 days of Month 3 must have its discount taken during the second 10 days of Month 3. Likewise, a shipment received in the second 10 days of Month 3 must have its discount taken within the third 10-day period of Month 3. A shipment received during the third 10-day period of Month 3 must have its discount taken during the first 10-day period of Month 4. As an average, two-thirds of those shipments received in Month 3 will have their associated discount taken in Month 3 and one-third of the shipments received in Month 3 will have their associated discount taken the following month. This general logic also holds true for those months following Month 3.

The total shipments received (purchases) are projected in the inventory schedule of Exhibit 4-5. This inventory schedule is based upon minimum orders of 5,000 units and orders in multiples of 5,000 units. It is Intercity's policy to have enough units on hand at the end of a given month to be certain next month's anticipated volume can be shipped.

If Exhibit 4-5 is viewed in relationship to Exhibit 4-4, a scheme may be evolved for recognizing when the discounts are earned. A schedule that calculates the discounts earned is presented in Exhibit 4-6.

EXHIBIT 4-5
INVENTORY SCHEDULE (IN UNITS)
FOR MATERIALS

Month	1	2	3	4	5	6	7
Beginning Inventory	43,500	43,500	46,500	47,500	50,500	55,500	57,500
–Shipments (Out)	40,000	42,000	44,000	47,000	50,000	53,000	55,000
+Purchases (Received)	40,000	45,000	45,000	50,000	55,000	55,000	55,000
Ending Inventory	43,500	46,500	47,500	50,500	55,500	57,500	57,500

EXHIBIT 4-6
SCHEDULE OF RECOGNITION OF DISCOUNTS EARNED
3% 10; Net 30 Example

Month	1	2	3	4	5	6	7
Value of Discount Earned (3% of shipments Received)			$1,350	1,500	1,650	1,650	1,650
Recognition of Discount (⅔ Same Month, ⅓ Next Month)			$ 900	1,000 450	1,100 500	1,100 550	1,100 550
Total Discount Recognized			$ 900	1,450	1,600	1,650	1,650

In these calculations, two-thirds of the discount related to a given month's purchases received is recognized in that month and one-third in the following month. If these monthly discounts are thought of as a reduction in the materials cost, the revised pro forma income statement of Exhibit 4-7 results. The exhibit demonstrates a reduction in the cost of goods sold and, consequently, an increase in the gross profit of the business beginning in Month 3. Net profit is increased in Months 3 through 7 by an attractive amount. A comparison of the total net profits for the next seven months indicates the expected improvement.

EXHIBIT 4-7
INTERCITY ASSEMBLY COMPANY, INC.
PRO FORMA INCOME STATEMENT
with 3% 10; Net 30 Cash Discount

Month		1	2	3	4	5	6	7
REVENUES								
Units Sold		40,000	42,000	44,000	47,000	50,000	53,000	55,000
Sales	$	80,000	84,000	88,000	94,000	100,000	106,000	110,000
EXPENSES								
Direct Materials		40,000	42,000	44,000	47,000	50,000	53,000	55,000
less Discount Earned		—	—	(900)	(1,450)	(1,600)	(1,650)	(1,650)
Direct Labor		4,000	4,200	4,400	4,700	5,000	5,300	5,500
Overhead		4,000	4,000	4,000	4,000	4,000	4,000	4,000
Cost of Goods Sold		48,000	50,200	51,500	54,250	57,400	60,650	62,850
Gross Profit		32,000	33,800	36,500	39,750	42,600	45,350	47,150
General & Administrative								
Salaries		6,900	7,450	7,500	8,350	8,350	9,000	9,000
Rent		2,000	2,000	2,000	2,000	2,000	2,000	2,000
Insurance		500	500	500	500	500	500	500
Depreciation		170	170	170	170	170	170	170
Other G&A		3,000	4,100	4,550	5,500	6,600	7,050	7,850
Marketing								
Advertising		9,750	9.800	10,200	11,000	11,600	12,500	13,000
Brochures		450	450	450	450	450	450	450
Total Expense		70,770	74,670	76,870	82,220	87,070	92,320	95,820
Taxable Income		9,230	9,330	11,130	11,780	12,930	13,680	14,180
Income Taxes		2,769	2,799	3,339	3,534	3,879	4,104	4,254
Net Profit	$	6,461	6,531	7,791	8,246	9,051	9,576	9,926

TOTAL PROFIT FOR
NEXT SEVEN MONTHS

Original Forecast (No Discount)	$52,507
Revised Forecast (With Discount)	$57,582

Since profits were so handsomely improved by taking the discount, one might be inclined to think that down at the bank cash flow and bank balances would likewise be improved.

To determine the impact on company cash flow, it is helpful to refer again to Exhibits 4-4 and 4-5. If payment is made 10 days after units are received, then, as an average, two-thirds of the units received in a given month are paid for in that month and one-third of the units received in a given month are paid for in the following month. This series of disbursements for materials received is reflected in the schedule of Exhibit 4-8. If this new series of disbursements is incorporated into the company's forecasts, the revised pro forma cash flow statement shown in Exhibit 4-9 results.

Instead of increasing significantly as profit did, the cash flow is much worse for the seven-month period and the bank balances suggest a small disaster. Instead of being overdraft a maximum of $12,000 as originally forecast, by taking the discount, Intercity must cover overdrafts in excess of $38,000 during the next seven months. The requirement to pay for materials in 10 days instead of the customary 30 days caused a subtle but common pitfall. The liquidity bind created for Intercity by the 3% 10 days; net 30 days discount is graphically

EXHIBIT 4-8
SCHEDULE OF DISBURSEMENTS FOR MATERIALS
3% 10; Net 30 Example

Month	1	2	3	4	5	6	7
Value of Units Received (@ 1.00/Unit)	$40,000	45,000					
Value of Units Received (with 3% Discount)			$43,650	48,500	53,350	53,350	53,350
Cash Disbursements (Net 30 Days)	$40,000*	40,000	45,000				
Cash Disbursements ⅔ Same Month			$29,100	32,333	35,567	35,567	35,567
⅓ Following Month				14,550	16,167	17,783	17,783
Total Disbursed	$40,000	40,000	74,100	46,883	51,734	53,350	53,350

*From transactions of a prior period.

EXHIBIT 4-9
INTERCITY ASSEMBLY COMPANY, INC.
PRO FORMA CASH FLOW STATEMENT
with 3% 10; Net 30 Cash Discount

	Month	1	2	3	4	5	6	7
RECEIPTS								
Sales Receipts	$	74,000*	77,000*	80,000	84,000	88,000	94,000	100,000
Common Stock		—	175,000	—	—	—	—	—
Total Received		74,000	252,000	80,000	84,000	88,000	94,000	100,000
DISBURSEMENTS								
Direct Materials		40,000*	40,000	74,100	46,883	51,734	53,350	53,350
Direct Labor		4,000	4,200	4,400	4,700	5,000	5,300	5,500
Overhead		1,300	1,300	1,300	1,300	1,300	1,300	1,300
Manufacturing Equip.		—	180,000	—	—	—	—	—
Salaries		6,900	7,450	7,500	8,350	8,350	9,000	9,000
Rent		2,000	2,000	2,000	2,000	2,000	2,000	2,000
Insurance		6,000	—	—	—	—	—	—
Office Equipment		—	3,000	—	—	—	—	—
Other G&A		2,800*	3,000	4,100	4,550	5,500	6,600	7,050
Advertising		9,000*	9,750	9,800	10,200	11,000	11,600	12,500
Brochures		—	5,400	—	—	—	—	—
Taxes		11,000*	—	—	8,907	—	—	11,517
Total Disbursed		83,000	256,100	103,200	86,890	84,884	89,150	102,217
Total Cash Flow	$	(9,000)	(4,100)	(23,200)	(2,890)	3,116	4,850	(2,217)
Beginning Balance	$	1,100	(7,900)	(12,000)	(35,200)	(38,090)	(34,974)	(30,124)
Ending Balance	$	(7,900)	(12,000)	(35,200)	(38,090)	(34,974)	(30,124)	(32,341)

*From transactions of a prior period.

portrayed in Exhibit 4-10. As indicated, profit did increase, but the negative impact on the company's bank account is so significant that it cannot be ignored.

Those desiring to take supplier discounts must be prepared to make substantial cash investments.

EXHIBIT 4-10
COMPARISON OF OPERATING RESULTS FOR A COMPANY THAT DOES
AND DOES NOT TAKE A 3% 10; NET 30 CASH DISCOUNT

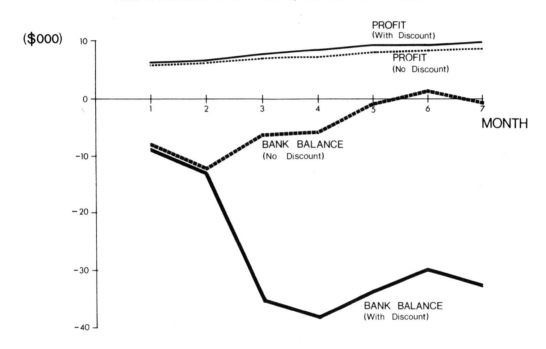

HOW BORROWING FROM A BANK TO TAKE THE DISCOUNT
CAN CREATE ANOTHER PITFALL

According to the conventional approach, the cost of supplier financing for a 3% 10 days; net 30 days discount is 54.8% on an annualized basis. It seems irresistible to want to borrow from a bank and take the discount. After all, the logic frequently goes, if one can borrow from the bank at 10%, take the discount and not utilize supplier financing at 54.8%, one should be able to make the "spread" between the two annualized interest rates, i.e., 44.8%.

Suppose that Intercity Assembly Company, Inc. did just that. The revised cash flow forecast of Exhibit 4-9 indicates a deficit in the company's bank account of more than $35,000 in Months 3 and 4. If Intercity arranged a $40,000 loan to be received at the beginning of Month 3, it would seem that one could make a substantial amount of money using the bank's funds.

If a $40,000 installment loan at 10% annual interest rate is received at the beginning of Month 3, logically it might be repaid monthly. Suppose further that this is a one-year note with

12 equal monthly payments. Payments are to be made on the last day of each month beginning with Month 3. An amortization table for this loan is presented in Exhibit 4-11.

If the interest for the loan payments made in Months 3, 4, 5, 6 and 7 are reflected in the pro forma income statement that also contains the reduction in materials cost due to taking the discount, the revised income statement of Exhibit 4-12 results.

EXHIBIT 4-11
Loan Amortization Table for
Installment Loan of $40,000
at 10% Interest Rate for
1 Year with 12 Equal
Monthly Payments

Loan Payment Number	Size of Payment	Interest Due	Reduction of Principal Amount
1	$3,516.64	$ 333.32	$3,183.32
2	3,516.64	306.80	3,209.84
3	3,516.64	280.04	3,236.60
4	3,516.64	253.08	3,263.56
5	3,516.64	225.88	3,290.76
6	3,516.64	198.48	3,318.16
7	3,516.64	170.80	3,345.84
8	3,516.64	142.92	3,373.72
9	3,516.64	114.80	3,401.84
10	3,516.64	86.48	3,430.16
11	3,516.64	57.88	3,458.76
12	3,516.52	29.08	3,487.44

If the receipt of the loan principal and the loan payments (interest plus principal) are reflected in the pro forma cash flow statement, the revised forecast of Exhibit 4-13 emerges.

A comparison of the three different examples, that is, taking the discount, not taking the discount and borrowing the money to take the discount, is made graphically in Exhibit 4-14.

While there appears to be only a moderate difference in the net profit for each of the three examples, there seems to be a profound difference in what is happening down at the bank. At the end of Month 7, the company's bank account is significantly worse off when it takes the cash discount. The same is true when the company borrows the money to take the discount. Many owner-managers walk into this common trap and can frequently be heard to remark, "You know that extra profit I'm making, where is it? It's not down at the bank."

There are several factors at work when one decides to borrow money to take a discount. On the positive side, taking the discount results in a lower per unit cost for materials. On the negative side, there are (1) increased income tax deposits due to more profit, (2) added new costs in the form of interest and (3) repayments (or amortization) of loan principal.

Is it possible that this particular company would be better off to forget the discount and just pay its bills?

You Can Change the Cost of
Supplier Financing

A second major fallacy of the conventional approach to evaluating a discount has to do with the assumption that if one does not take the discount, then one will pay exactly at the end

EXHIBIT 4-12
INTERCITY ASSEMBLY COMPANY, INC.
PRO FORMA INCOME STATEMENT
Illustrating Use of
Borrowed Money to Take Cash Discount

Month	1	2	3	4	5	6	7
REVENUES							
Units Sold	40,000	42,000	44,000	47,000	50,000	53,000	55,000
Sales	$ 80,000	84,000	88,000	94,000	100,000	106,000	110,000
EXPENSES							
Direct Materials	40,000	42,000	44,000	47,000	50,000	53,000	55,000
less Discount Earned	—	—	(900)	(1,450)	(1,600)	(1,650)	(1,650)
Direct Labor	4,000	4,200	4,400	4,700	5,000	5,300	5,500
Overhead	4,000	4,000	4,000	4,000	4,000	4,000	4,000
Cost of Goods Sold	48,000	50,200	51,500	54,250	57,400	60,650	62,850
Gross Profit	32,000	33,800	36,500	39,750	42,600	45,350	47,150
General & Administrative							
Salaries	6,900	7,450	7,500	8,350	8,350	9,000	9,000
Rent	2,000	2,000	2,000	2,000	2,000	2,000	2,000
Insurance	500	500	500	500	500	500	500
Depreciation	170	170	170	170	170	170	170
Interest	—	—	333	307	280	253	226
Other G&A	3,000	4,100	4,550	5,500	6,600	7,050	7,850
Marketing							
Advertising	9,750	9,800	10,200	11,000	11,600	12,500	13,000
Brochures	450	450	450	450	450	450	450
Total Expense	70,770	74,670	77,203	82,527	87,350	92,573	96,046
Taxable Income	9,230	9,330	10,797	11,473	12,650	13,427	13,954
Income Taxes	2,769	2,799	3,239	3,442	3,795	4,028	4,186
Net Profit	$ 6,461	6,531	7,558	8,031	8,855	9,399	9,768

of the net credit period. This is, of course, not necessarily true. If one does not elect to take a cash discount and then pays on the due date, the effective annualized interest rate as calculated in the conventional manner would be accurate. Suppose that a company decides to pay after the due date knowing that a late penalty will not be imposed. The company that elects to play this game is making the series of decisions pointed out as being one of the paths of the accounts payable management decision tree presented in Exhibit 4-1. The lines of decision would be "Can Pay and Pay After Due and No Penalty."

To analyze what it means to pay after the due date with no penalty, consider again the expression for calculating the annualized rate associated with supplier financing.

$$\text{Annualized Rate} = \frac{\text{Number of Days in a Year}}{\text{Number of Days Financing Is Used}} \times \text{Discount}$$

For the cash discount 2% 10 days; net 30 days, the conventional approach would take the attitude that the cost (2% of invoice) is associated with the difference between the discount period and the net credit period or 20 days. Therefore, the annualized interest rate for supplier financing would be

$$\text{Annualized Rate} = \frac{365 \text{ days}}{20 \text{ days}} \times 2\%$$

$$= 36.5\%$$

EXHIBIT 4-13
INTERCITY ASSEMBLY COMPANY, INC.
PRO FORMA CASH FLOW STATEMENT
Illustrating Use of Borrowed Money to Take Cash Discount

Month	1	2	3	4	5	6	7
RECEIPTS							
Sales Receipts	$ 74,000*	77,000*	80,000	84,000	88,000	94,000	100,000
Common Stock	—	175,000	—	—	—	—	—
Loans Received	—	—	**40,000**	—	—	—	—
Total Received	74,000	252,000	**120,000**	84,000	88,000	94,000	100,000
DISBURSEMENTS							
Direct Materials	40,000*	40,000	**74,100**	46,883	51,734	53,350	53,350
Direct Labor	4,000	4,200	4,400	4,700	5,000	5,300	5,500
Overhead	1,300	1,300	1,300	1,300	1,300	1,300	1,300
Manufacturing Equip.	—	180,000	—	—	—	—	—
Salaries	6,900	7,450	7,500	8,350	8,350	9,000	9,000
Rent	2,000	2,000	2,000	2,000	2,000	2,000	2,000
Insurance	6,000	—	—	—	—	—	—
Office Equipment	—	3,000	—	—	—	—	—
Other G&A	2,800*	3,000	4,100	4,550	5,500	6,600	7,050
Advertising	9,000*	9,750	9,800	10,200	11,000	11,600	12,500
Brochures	—	5,400	—	—	—	—	—
Loan Repayment	—	—	3,517	3,517	3,517	3,517	3,517
Taxes	11,000*	—	—	8,807	—	—	11,265
Total Disbursed	83,000	256,100	**106,717**	90,307	88,401	92,667	105,482
Total Cash Flow	$ (9,000)	(4,100)	**13,283**	**(6,307)**	**(401)**	**1,333**	**(5,482)**
Beginning Balance	$ 1,100	(7,900)	**(12,000)**	**1,283**	**(5,024)**	**(5,425)**	**(4,092)**
Ending Balance	$ (7,900)	(12,000)	**1,283**	**(5,024)**	**(5,425)**	**(4,092)**	**(9,574)**

*From operations during prior periods.

If the invoice is paid 25 days late and no penalty is incurred, however, the same discount lost becomes associated with a much longer period of time and reduces the effective annualized rate associated with vendor provided financing as follows:

$$\text{Annualized Rate} = \frac{365 \text{ days}}{(20 + 25) \text{ days}} \times 2\%$$

$$= \frac{365}{45} \times 2\%$$

$$= 16.2\%$$

If one can delay paying 55 days past the due date without penalty, the rate becomes

$$\text{Annualized Rate} = \frac{365 \text{ days}}{(20 + 55) \text{ days}} \times 2\%$$

$$= \frac{365}{75} \times 2\%$$

$$= 9.7\%$$

EXHIBIT 4-14
COMPARISON OF OPERATING RESULTS FOR A COMPANY THAT
(1) TAKES A 3% 10; NET 30 CASH DISCOUNT, (2) DOES NOT TAKE THE
DISCOUNT AND (3) BORROWS MONEY TO TAKE THE DISCOUNT

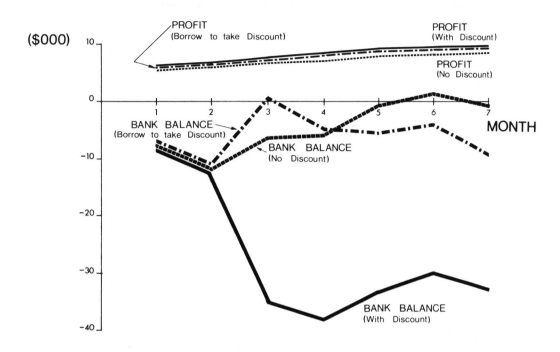

which may be less expensive than alternative sources of financing.

If this annualized rate calculation is performed for a variety of cash discounts, an interesting family of curves emerges as shown in Exhibit 4-15.

The annualized interest rate associated with supplier financing can be read immediately from this chart for various times of payment beyond the original invoice date. For example, if a 1% 10 days; net 30 days cash discount is ignored and the invoice is paid in 90 days, the annualized interest rate associated with supplier financing is only 4.6%.

It is clearly possible to change the cost of supplier financing. Certain circumstances may make it attractive not to take the discount.

The Reverse Discount Strategy

The reverse discount is a strategy used by the authors for dealing with certain suppliers who offer cash discounts. The concept works as follows: Suppose that ABC Company offers you a cash discount, perhaps 2% 10 days; net 30 days. Instead of taking the 2% for paying in 10 days, you offer the supplier a reverse discount. You offer to pay regular invoice price plus an extra 2% for the right to pay a certain number of days later (i.e., days beyond the cash discount period of 10 days from date of invoice).

The obvious question arises as to how many days beyond the cash discount period should one attempt to negotiate. Should a longer time period be requested for a 2% reverse discount compared to a 1% reverse discount?

EXHIBIT 4-15
ANNUALIZED INTEREST RATE ASSOCIATED WITH SUPPLIER FINANCING
VS. AGE OF INVOICE

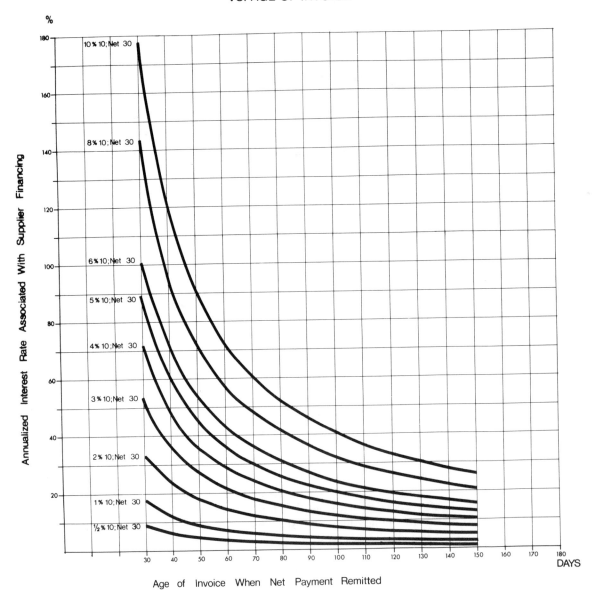

Age of Invoice When Net Payment Remitted

One way to think of this question is in terms of the cost of financing provided by the supplier. A fee for the use of someone else's money for a period of time bears a marked resemblance to the interest associated with loans.

The basic equation for interest is

$$i = p\,r\,t$$

where,

> i is the interest (in dollars)
> p is the principal amount (in dollars)
> r is the annualized interest rate (in decimal equivalent of percent)
> t is the time the principal is used (in years)

To derive an expression relating the number of days beyond the cash discount period (reverse discount period) to the equivalent annualized interest rate associated with supplier financing, it is necessary to first interpret the four preceding variables. The interest, i, is the cost associated with delayed payment. This cost is the discount lost plus the reverse discount or

$$i = (2 \times discount) \times p$$

where p is the invoice amount or principal.

Rewriting the original equation to solve for the reverse discount period

$$t_{rev} = \frac{i}{p \times r}$$

The variable t represents the reverse discount period and r is the equivalent annualized interest rate associated with vendor provided financing for the period beyond the cash discount period.

Now, substituting the reverse discount expression for i, we get

$$t_{rev} = \frac{(2 \times discount) \times p}{p \times r}$$

By canceling out p from the equation and expressing t in terms of days and not years, we have

$$t_{rev} \text{ in days} = \frac{365 \, (2 \times discount)}{r}$$

To apply this expression, assume that 2% 10 days; net 30 days is offered by a vendor. You instead negotiate a reverse discount. Suppose that you are not willing to pay more than 18% annualized interest rate for supplier financing. The reverse discount period (number of days beyond the cash discount period) to be negotiated would be

$$t_{rev} = \frac{365 \, (2 \times discount)}{r}$$

$$= \frac{365 \, (2 \times 2\%)}{18\%}$$

$$= \frac{365 \, (4)}{18}$$

$$= 81 \text{ days}$$

If this exercise is conducted for a variety of common discount situations, a useful working aid emerges as shown in Exhibit 4-16.

For a number of common discounts and reasonable annual interest rates, the reverse discount period to be negotiated can be read directly from the graph of Exhibit 4-16.

Two additional points should be made. First, if one adds the regular discount period to the reverse discount period and associates the same interest, 2 times discount rate times p, then a slightly different and *lower* equivalent annualized interest rate results. Second, the reverse discount strategy is not for every owner-manager to use with every supplier who offers a cash discount. The supplier must be able and willing to negotiate. The owner-manager must

EXHIBIT 4-16
REVERSE DISCOUNT STRATEGY CHART INDICATING DAYS BEYOND
THE DISCOUNT PERIOD THAT MUST BE EFFECTED FOR A GIVEN COST
OF FINANCING

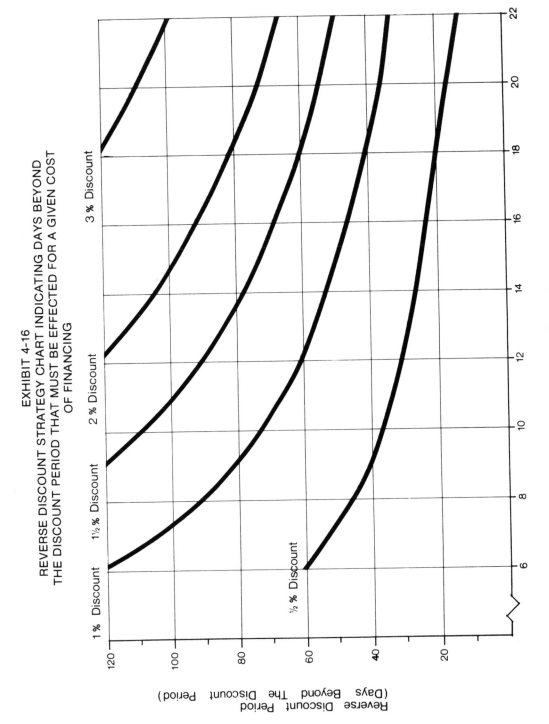

precisely understand this negotiation process and should have a desire for non-bank financing. In addition, as Exhibit 4-16 illustrates, there are practical limitations for discounts greater than 3%.

Is the Late Payment Penalty a Bargain?

One of the interesting options pointed out in the accounts payable management decision tree of Exhibit 4-1 was the series of judgments whereby one has the ability to pay the supplier but elects to pay after the due date and incur a late payment penalty.

When no discount is involved but a late payment penalty, such as 1% per month on past due balances, is imposed, the annual interest rate associated with supplier financing is straightforwardly calculated. Since there are 12 months in a year, x% per month equals 12x% per year (that is 1% per month equals 12% per year, 1½% per month equals 18% per year, etc.).

For payment terms of net 30 days, 1% per month on past due balances, this approach implies that there is zero cost for 30 days' financing and 12% annualized interest rate thereafter. This is accurate; however, there is another way to look at the proposition. If one considers the total length of time that the supplier's financing is utilized (net credit period plus late period) and relates the interest paid (late payment fee) to that total period, an annualized cost for the use of supplier money can be determined as follows:

$$\text{Average Annualized Interest Rate} = \frac{\text{Monthly penalty percent} \times 12 \times \text{Months late in paying}}{(\text{Months in normal credit period}) + (\text{Months late in paying})}$$

For example, suppose that one supplier offered the following financing terms:

Net 30 days;
1% per month on all past due balances

Also, assume that payment is one month late. The conventional calculation would hold that the 1% charged for the extra one month taken amounts to an annual interest rate of:

$$\text{Annualized Rate} = 1\%/\text{month} \times \frac{12 \text{ months}}{\text{year}}$$

$$= 12\% \text{ per year}$$

On the other hand, for the 60 days (two months) that the supplier's money was actually used in this example, 1% of the invoice amount was charged. As an average this works out to be

$$\text{Average Annualized Interest Rate} = \frac{1(\%/\text{month}) \times 12(\text{months/year}) \times 1(\text{month})}{1(\text{month}) + 1(\text{month})}$$

$$= \frac{12(\%/\text{year})}{2}$$

$$= 6\%/\text{year}$$

While the annualized rate is 12%, the average annualized rate is only 6% per year.

Consider another example. Suppose supplier financing terms are

Net 60 days
1½ per month on all past due balances

The annualized rate calculation would be

$$\text{Annualized Rate} = 1\frac{1}{2}\%/\text{month} \times \frac{12 \text{ months}}{\text{year}}$$

$$= 18\% \text{ per year}$$

If the customer is two months late in paying the invoice, the average annualized interest rate would be

$$\text{Average Annualized Interest Rate} = \frac{1\frac{1}{2}(\%/\text{month}) \times 12(\text{months/year}) \times 2(\text{months})}{2(\text{months}) \times 2(\text{months})}$$

$$= \frac{36(\%/\text{year})}{4}$$

$$= 9\%/\text{year}$$

As in the case of the reverse discount, the authors are not recommending that everyone should consider the average annualized interest rate approach. For the particular situations available to you, we are posing a provocative question, "Is the late payment penalty a bargain?"

We have found that a large percentage of those suppliers who impose a late penalty are unwilling to enforce it rigorously. When the risk of customer good will is at stake, they frequently ignore their own late penalty. If an owner-manager is inclined to protest late penalties and does so successfully, then the management game reverts back to the one already described under the heading "You Can Change the Cost of Supplier Financing." In this event, one would in effect be following the branch of the decision tree indicating the ability to pay but choosing to pay after the due date with no penalty.

Compensating Balances and
the Real Cost of Bank Financing

Much of the discussion thus far has involved evaluation of the cost of supplier financing under various arrangements and conditions. Analogies to loans were implied in much of the annualized interest rate discussions. If the cost of supplier financing was 13% and that of a bank loan was 12%, one might quickly conclude that bank financing was less expensive. This may not be the case.

Most owner-managers have at one time or another been confronted by the banker requiring a compensating balance, especially when tight monetary conditions prevail in the economy. If a $100,000 loan at 10% is made and a 15% compensating balance is required, then the borrower may never use more than $85,000 of the amount loaned. An annual interest of 10% for the $100,000 amount is paid but only $85,000 may be used since the $15,000 compensating balance never leaves the borrower's checking account.

How does one determine the *effective* annualized interest rate of bank financing when a compensating balance is required? The basic interest equation referred to in a previous section

$$i = prt$$

may be adapted to calculate this rate. If a variety of bank loans and compensating balance criteria are considered, a helpful working aid may be derived. The family of curves portrayed in Exhibit 4-17 demonstrates the relationship between quoted interest rates and effective interest rates.

Illustrating the usage of this chart, suppose that a 10% loan is negotiated and a 15% compensating balance is required. The chart of Exhibit 4-17 indicates that the effective cost of bank financing to the borrower is approximately 11.8% and not 10%. Of course, if no compensating balance is required, then the quoted annualized rate and the effective annualized rate are identical.

EXHIBIT 4-17
EFFECTIVE COST OF BANK FINANCING WHEN A COMPENSATING
BALANCE IS REQUIRED

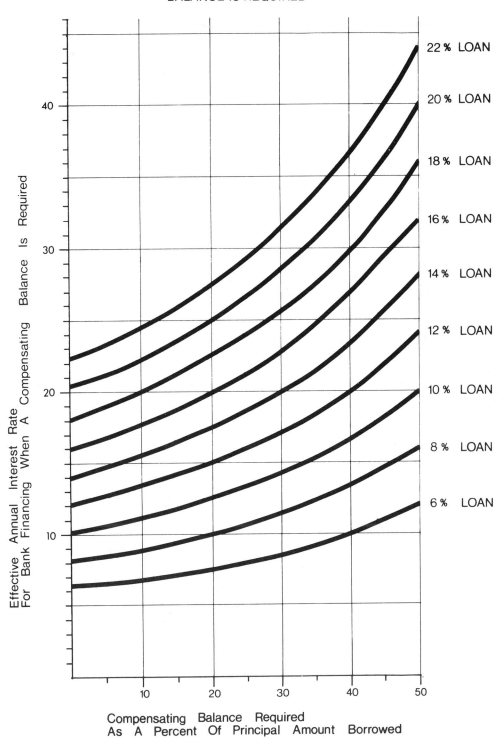

Compensating Balance Required
As A Percent Of Principal Amount Borrowed

NON-FINANCIAL CONSIDERATIONS

Many owner-managers who conduct one of the analyses mentioned in this chapter select an accounts payable strategy not supported by the financial considerations alone. Other non-financial considerations enter the picture and influence their final decisions. For example, in an industry environment characterized by raw materials shortages, a supplier's representative may subtly disclose that if you do not take their discount, then you may have difficulty in receiving materials ordered. The necessity to receive these materials may dominate over other financial considerations.

Credit reporting agencies are fond of saying wonderful things about companies that pay their bills exactly on time and those that take cash discounts. A closely held business interested in building its reputation among present and future creditors may manage its accounts payable according to a scheme designed to enhance its credit rating.

In a very competitive, fast growing, flexible and dynamic market, there may be a desire to see "what you can get away with regarding late payment." A controlled series of experiments designed to discover how much "slack" is in various suppliers' accounts receivable management systems might be conducted. The owner-manager's mind is usually very creative when it comes to designing such experiments.

One might decide to pay cash in advance or cash on delivery to a small but very important supplier. Certain vendors such as this may lack a financial track record and have difficulty in securing adequate working capital. Advance payments and prompt payments from customers can enhance the chances of survival and success of a small and fledgling supplier.

Internal management policies may dominate other financial considerations. For example, a company may decide that it is simpler to have a basic policy which states "Take the discount on all invoices of less than $50 and for all invoices over $50, pay 10 days late." A policy such as this tends to eliminate hassle and top management involvement in relatively minor day-to-day procedures.

The authors are not recommending that financial considerations alone determine the ultimate decision with regard to accounts payable management. They are recommending that monetary considerations be examined first to determine which course of action is financially prudent. The financial considerations are then to be reviewed in light of the non-financial considerations. The ultimate series of judgments will depend upon the specifics of each individual case.

OLD TECHNIQUES FOR DELAYING PAYMENT

There are a number of very old and very worn-out techniques for delaying payment to the supplier. These techniques include:

Forget to sign the check you sent.

Send payment to a slightly incorrect address.

Send payment to the wrong person.

Forget to place adequate postage on envelope.

Or when called by the supplier regarding a past due payment, you reply:

"You mean they didn't send that check last week? I will investigate this immediately."

or

"The computer fouled up."

or

"There has been an organizational change and your invoice must have been misplaced."

or

"We've been growing so fast our bookkeeping just hasn't kept up."

or

"I guess your invoice must have fallen through a crack. Could you send us another copy?"

or

"One of the items you sent us is defective. We can't pay you until we have this straightened out."

About all that can be said for these old techniques is that suppliers are sick and tired of them. The same handful of ploys are so frequently utilized that not only are they ineffective, but they destroy credibility and rapport with the vendor. If special terms cannot be negotiated with the supplier in advance, at least try to come up with a creative, innovative excuse for late payment.

HOW TO IMPROVE CASH FLOW THROUGH ACCOUNTS PAYABLE MANAGEMENT

As pointed out in the discussion surrounding Exhibits 4-12, 4-13 and 4-14, there can be a number of items that influence the impact of accounts payable management strategies on the company's cash flow. The dominant variable usually is timing of the payment of the bulk of the invoice. Most of the previously discussed techniques for evaluating and strategies for taking cash discounts caused substantially worse cash flow and, consequently, worse cash balances in the bank account. This was associated with paying the bulk of the invoice sooner.

The observation is that cash flow (at least in the short run) is improved by delaying payments. The longer the delay, the greater the improvement. There are, of course, practical limitations and important non-financial considerations. Nevertheless, the principle is clear.

The authors suggest that major delays in payment be negotiated with suppliers in advance rather than relying afterwards on old techniques which destroy credibility and jeopardize your sources of supply.

NOTES FOR CHAPTER 4

[1]*Credit Management Handbook*, Credit Research Foundation, Second Edition, (Homewood, Illinois: Richard D. Irwin, Inc., 1965), p. 533. Reprinted with permission.

5

Powerful Profit and Cash Flow Techniques
Using Depreciation and the Investment Tax Credit

Depreciation and the investment tax credit are separate and distinct concepts. Regulatory authorities, however, have written the rules in such a way that it is difficult to consider one without examining the other.

DEPRECIATION: A CRUCIAL CONCEPT

Depreciation represents the using up of an asset having a useful life greater than one year. It is a very real phenomenon that nibbles away at most assets until one day they no longer have any usefulness to the business. The assets are then typically disposed of for whatever amount may be obtained.

Depreciation is the orderly expensing of an asset over its useful life. Confusion often arises when the owner-manager hears statements such as: "Depreciation is a source of funds"; "Depreciation is a means of recovering your investment in property . . . "; "Your depreciation reserve is adequate"; "Depreciation is a non-cash expense."

These statements are reasonable in a specialized context and when used by accountants, stockbrokers, and financial professionals. For owner-managers, these utilizations of the word cloud the issue and detract from the fact that depreciation is the expensing of something already owned.

Depreciation as an Operating Reality

When an office desk is purchased it remains "as good as new" for several years. Eventually, it will become so shabby and dilapidated that one must dispose of it. This process of deterioration that decreases the usefulness of an asset over time is depreciation. As an operating phenomenon, depreciation is an eroding process that eventually causes furniture, typewriters, trucks, buildings and other assets to become useless.

Depreciation as an Accounting Technique

Once depreciation is accepted as a real phenomenon, the problem arises as to how to account for it in the company's books. Some assets do not last as long as others. Some assets are more heavily used when they are new (and hence more reliable). There are a number of key concepts and generally accepted techniques for recording depreciation. It is important to recognize that the specific accounting technique selected may or may not be descriptive of how the asset is actually used up from an operating point of view. It is only important that the recording procedure be reasonable and according to generally accepted accounting principles.

Depreciation: The Effect on Profit

Profit equals revenues less expenses. Depreciation is an expense of doing busines and, hence, affects the company's profit. The more depreciation recognized during a given operating period, the less profit and visa versa. Management interested in demonstrating as much profit as possible will naturally lean toward using an acceptable depreciation technique that recognizes less expense and, hence, more profit. Depreciation is, therefore, a profit management technique.

Depreciation: The Effect on Cash Flow

An asset is paid for, based upon when it was purchased and the purchase terms. Depreciation, on the other hand, is recognized as the asset is used up. Consequently, depreciation is not directly connected with the disbursement of cash.

There is, however, an indirect linkage. A profitable business will pay income taxes. More profit means more tax. Since depreciation is a deductible expense, it affects the computation of profit and income tax. The resulting tax must be paid in cash. Since cash flow equals receipts of cash less disbursements of cash, the cash flow is indirectly affected by depreciation through the income tax mechanism. This important mechanism is fully discussed in Chapter 8.

Keys To Skillful Application

There are numerous rules and practices that affect the different applications of depreciation. Knowledge of a few key principles is paramount to skillful depreciation usage.

GENERALLY ACCEPTED PRINCIPLES

Among the generally accepted principles related to depreciation are the following ones mentioned in Internal Revenue Service publication 534, Tax Information on Depreciation:

- The kind of property on which one may ordinarily claim the depreciation deduction is property with a useful life of more than one year. Examples are buildings, machinery, equipment, trucks, etc. [1]
- The depreciation deduction is allowed only for property which is used in a trade or business or held for the production of income. You may not deduct depreciation on property you and your family use as a residence or your automobile used solely for pleasure purposes or for commuting.[2]
- If property is used for both business and personal use, depreciation is deductible only to the extent that the property is used in your business.[3]
- Property held primarily for sale to customers or property that is properly includible in inventory is not depreciable property used in the business.[4]
- The basis for determining depreciation is the same as the basis one would use to determine gain if the property were sold. Usually, the cost of property is its basis. If the

property is materially improved, the additional costs are added to the basis; casualty losses reduce the basis.[5]

- One may deduct depreciation on tangible property only to the extent that it is subject to wear and tear, to decay or decline from natural causes, to exhaustion, and to obsolescence.[6]

- If an intangible asset such as a patent or copyright is used in your business and has a limited period of usefulness, it may be depreciated.[7]

- Land is never subject to an allowance for depreciation.[8]

- Goodwill is an intangible capital asset that is not subject to depreciation.[9]

- Trademarks and trade names usually have an indefinite life and the purchase price of such intangible property is not deductible or depreciable.[10]

- Professional libraries are depreciable if their value will diminsh. The cost of technical books, journals, and services that have a usefulness of one year or less is deducted as a business expense.[11]

- If a portion of the purchase price for a business is for a covenant not to compete, and the covenant is for a fixed number of years, the amount paid for the covenant is deductible as a business expense proportionally over the life of the covenant. A covenant not to compete is an agreement whereby the seller of a business agrees not to compete with the buyer for a limited time or within an agreed area, or a combination of both.[12]

These principles represent many of the ground rules for utilization of depreciation.

THREE IMPORTANT VARIABLES

There are three important variables to be considered when making management decisions regarding depreciation: basis, salvage value and useful life.

Basis

There is only so much depreciation in a given asset depending on its basis. Basis is determined by the way a business acquires the property. The cost of the property is generally the original basis. If, however, the property was acquired by gift, by inheritance or in some other manner, the original basis other than cost must be used. [13]

The cost of property is the amount one pays for it either in cash, debt obligations or other property. Under certain circumstances property acquired on any time payment arrangement under which either no interest or only a low amount of interest is charged, may have a basis that is the purchase price less an amount considered to represent interest,[14] (i.e., a portion of the purchase price is imputed interest and not included in the property's basis).

If one acquires property that includes both depreciable and non-depreciable property, the total basis must be allocated between the depreciable and non-depreciable property. As an example of this, consider the following illustration presented in Internal Revenue Service publication 534:

> You purchased a building and the land on which it stands for $30,000. If the value of the building is two-thirds of the total value of the land and building, your basis for depreciating the building, before considering salvage, is $20,000 (i.e. 2/3 × $30,000).[15]

For a detailed discussion of allocation of cost, obtain a copy of publication 551, Tax Information on Cost or Other Basis of Assets, which is available at any Internal Revenue Service office.

Salvage Value

Salvage value is the amount (determined at the time of acquisition) estimated to be realized on the sale or other disposition of an asset when it is no longer useful in your business or in the production of your income, and is to be retired from service. Salvage value is not subsequently adjusted merely because of price-level changes. If a business customarily uses an asset for its full inherent useful life, salvage value may be no more than junk value. But, if it is the company's policy to retire assets that are still in good operating condition, salvage value may represent a relatively large portion of the original cost or basis of the asset.[16]

Useful Life

Useful life is not necessarily the useful life inherent in the asset, but is the period over which the asset may reasonably be expected to be useful in the trade or business or for the production of income. The useul life of property may be determined from your particular operating conditions and experience.

No average useful life for an item is applicable in all businesses. The useful life of any item depends upon such things as the frequency with which it is used, its age when acquired, the policy as to repairs, renewals and replacements, the climate in which it is used, the normal progress of the arts, economic changes, inventions and other developments within the industry or trade.[17]

The useful life of the depreciable property should be determined on the basis of your particular operating conditions and experience. If one's experience is inadequate, the general experience in the industry may be utilized until one's own experience forms an adequate guide for making the determination.

One convenient method for determining the useful life of an asset is the Class Life Asset Depreciation Range System outlined by the Internal Revenue Service and elected by filing Form 4832 annually. Special tables formulated by the IRS are at the heart of this system. A copy of the Class Life Asset Depreciation Range Tables is presented in Appendix A.

When using the Class Life Asset Depreciation Range System, one is restricted to using only the straight-line depreciation method, the sum-of-the-years-digits method, or the declining-balance method.[18] Each of these methods will be discussed later in this chapter. Under this system salvage value can be disregarded, but in no event may an asset be depreciated below its reasonable salvage value. Additional information regarding utilization of the Class Life Asset Depreciation Range System may be obtained by contacting the nearest office of the Internal Revenue Service and requesting publication 534, Tax Information on Depreciation.

Depreciation Techniques

Depreciation, like any other management tactic, should be utilized in a way to help achieve organizational objectives. Crucial to the selection of the best method is a precise understanding of the various depreciation techniques and how they affect company operations.

THE STRAIGHT-LINE TECHNIQUE

The straight-line technique, a very common one, recognizes an equal amount of depreciation each period of the asset's useful life. For an asset costing $180,000, having a useful life of five years and an estimated salvage value of 10% of the purchase price ($18,000), the depreciation would be:

$$\text{Straight-Line Depreciation} = \frac{\text{Cost-Salvage}}{\text{Useful Life}}$$

$$= \frac{\$180,000 - \$18,000}{5 \text{ years}}$$

$$= \frac{\$162,000}{5 \text{ years}}$$

$$= \$32,400/\text{year}$$

The depreciation for each of the next five years is 20% of the cost minus salvage value as follows:

Year	Annual Depreciation
1	$ 32,400
2	32,400
3	32,400
4	32,400
5	32,400
	$162,000

At the end of five years, one might sell the asset at salvage or $18,000 since it (hypothetically) has reached the end of its useful life.

The depreciation per month in year one would be:

$$\frac{\$32,400}{12 \text{ mos.}} = \$2,700/\text{month}$$

Internal Revenue Service literature states that "this method must be used for any depreciable property for which you have not adopted a different acceptable method."[19]

THE DECLINING-BALANCE TECHNIQUE

There are several variations of this technique. One frequently used version applies twice the straight-line depreciation rate (*without* regard to salvage value) to the declining book value (cost less accumulated depreciation to date) of the asset. This is called the double-declining-balance method.

To illustrate the mechanics of this method, consider the $180,000 asset previously discussed having a five-year useful life. Calculation of the double-declining-balance rate of depreciation as twice the straight-line rate would yield:

$$\text{Straight-Line (S.L.) Rate} = \frac{100\%}{5 \text{ years}}$$

$$= 20\% \text{ per year}$$

$$\text{Double-Declining-Balance Rate} = 2 \times \text{S.L. Rate}$$

$$= 2 \times 20\% \text{ per year}$$

$$= 40\% \text{ per year}$$

The following table illustrates a method for computing the annual depreciation amount under this version of the method:

EXHIBIT 5-1
ANNUAL DEPRECIATION FOR DOUBLE-DECLINING-BALANCE
Depreciation Per $1,000 in Asset Cost

Useful Life Selected (in Years)	1	2	3	4	5	6	7	8	9
3	$666.67	222.21	74.06						
4	500.00	250.00	125.00	62.50					
5	400.00	240.00	144.00	86.40	51.84				
6	333.33	222.20	148.14	98.77	65.85	43.90			
7	285.71	204.08	145.77	104.12	74.38	53.13	37.95		
8	250.00	187.50	140.63	105.47	79.10	59.33	44.49	33.37	
9	222.22	172.83	134.42	104.56	81.32	63.25	49.20	38.27	29.76
10	200.00	160.00	128.00	102.40	81.92	65.54	52.43	41.94	33.56
11	181.82	148.76	121.71	99.59	81.48	66.66	54.54	44.63	36.51
12	166.67	138.92	115.76	96.46	80.38	66.98	55.82	46.51	38.76
13	153.85	130.18	110.15	93.21	78.87	66.73	56.47	47.78	40.43
14	142.86	122.48	104.98	89.98	77.12	66.10	56.65	48.56	41.62
15	133.33	115.55	100.13	86.78	75.22	65.19	56.50	48.97	42.44
16	125.00	109.38	95.70	83.74	73.27	64.11	56.10	49.09	42.95
17	117.65	103.77	91.57	80.80	71.30	62.91	55.51	48.99	43.22
18	111.11	98.76	87.79	78.03	69.36	61.67	54.81	48.72	43.30
19	105.26	94.21	84.29	75.42	67.47	60.37	54.01	48.33	43.24
20	100.00	90.00	81.00	72.90	65.61	59.05	53.14	47.83	43.05

Year	Cost	Accumulated Depreciation at Beginning of Year	Book Value at Beginning of Year	Rate	Depreciation for Year
1	$180,000	-0-	$180,000	40%	$ 72,000
2	"	$ 72,000	108,000	"	43,200
3	"	115,200	64,800	"	25,920
4	"	141,120	38,880	"	15,552
5	"	156,672	23,328	"	9,331
			Total Depreciation		$166,003

In this example, the first year's depreciation is $72,000. Distributing this equally over 12 months gives:

$$\frac{\$72,000}{12 \text{ mos.}} = \$6,000/\text{month}$$

One obvious question results from depreciation calculated in this manner, "How do you account for salvage value?" In response, it is interesting to note that the mechanics of this method automatically leave an effective salvage value on the books. In this case, the cost ($180,000) less the total amount depreciated ($166,003) leaves $13,997 on the books. Under the straight-line method used previously, a salvage value of $18,000 was selected. Normally, the difference in salvage value between that resulting from a choice based on reasonableness and

EXHIBIT 5-1 *(cont.)*

10	11	12	13	14	15	16	17	18	19	20
24.44										
29.87	24.44									
32.30	26.91	22.43								
34.21	28.94	24.49	20.72							
35.67	30.57	26.20	22.46	19.25						
36.78	31.88	27.63	23.95	20.76	17.99					
37.58	32.89	28.77	25.18	22.03	19.28	16.87				
38.14	33.66	29.70	26.20	23.12	20.40	18.01	15.89			
38.49	34.22	30.42	27.04	24.03	21.36	18.99	16.88	15.00		
38.68	34.61	30.97	27.70	24.79	22.18	19.84	17.75	15.88	14.21	
38.74	34.87	31.38	28.24	25.42	22.88	20.59	18.65	16.68	15.01	13.51

that determined by the mechanics of the double-declining-balance method is not excessive. If, for some reason, it is crucial that a particular salvage value be utilized then, during the last year of useful life, depreciate the asset down to the point that the desired salvage value is left on the books. At that point, stop the depreciating process.

Since the declining-balance method will never completely depreciate the asset, it is common to switch to straight-line depreciation during the last year or two of the asset's useful life. Of course, if a switch is made to the straight-line method, a reasonable salvage value must be subtracted from the remaining book value. The new depreciation method is then applied to the difference between salvage and book values.

The table presented in Exhibit 5-1 describes the annual depreciation that would occur under the double-declining-balance method for a variety of different useful lives. This table may be considered a working tool to aid in the decision of which useful life to select and whether or not double-declining-balance is the desired depreciation method.

There are two additional versions of the declining-balance method, 150% declining balance and 125% declining balance. The maximum rate one can use under the declining-balance method on used tangible personal property having a useful life of three years or more, is 1½ times the straight-line rate. The maximum rate that one can use under the declining-balance method on used residential rental property and having a useful life of 20 years or more is 1¼ times the straight-line rate.[20] The table shown in Exhibit 5-2 depicts the first year depreciation under each of these three declining-balance methods for a variety of useful lives.

EXHIBIT 5-2
FIRST YEAR DEPRECIATION FOR
THREE DECLINING BALANCE METHODS

Useful Life Selected (in Years)	First Year Depreciation Per $1,000 in Asset Cost		
	Double (2.0) Declining Balance Method*	1.5 Declining Balance Method*	1.25 Declining Balance Method**
3	$ 666.67	$ 500.00	$ —
4	500.00	375.00	—
5	400.00	300.00	—
6	333.33	250.00	—
7	285.71	214.29	—
8	250.00	187.50	—
9	222.22	166.67	—
10	200.00	150.00	—
11	181.82	136.36	—
12	166.67	125.00	—
13	153.85	115.39	—
14	142.86	107.14	—
15	133.33	100.00	—
16	125.00	93.75	—
17	117.65	88.24	—
18	111.11	83.33	—
19	105.26	78.95	—
20	100.00	75.00	62.50
21	95.24	71.43	59.52
22	90.91	68.18	56.82
23	86.95	65.21	54.34
24	83.33	62.50	52.08
25	80.00	60.00	50.00
26	76.92	57.69	48.08
27	74.07	55.55	46.30
28	71.43	53.57	44.64
29	68.97	51.72	43.10
30	66.67	50.00	41.67

*Applies to assets with useful life of three years or greater.
**Applies to certain assets with useful life of 20 yrs. or greater.

THE SUM OF THE YEARS-DIGITS TECHNIQUE

The sum of the years-digits (S.O.Y.D.) method also provides a steadily declining periodic depreciation charge over the estimated life of the asset. This is accomplished by applying a successively smaller fraction each year to the cost less the residual (salvage) value. The numerator of the changing fraction is the number of remaining years of life and the denominator is the sum of the digits representing the years of life. In the case of an asset with a useful life of five years, the denominator would be:

$$1 + 2 + 3 + 4 + 5 = 15$$

The numerator would be the number of remaining years of life such that the fraction for each year would be:

Year of Asset Life	Fraction to be Applied to Cost Less Salvage
1	5/15
2	4/15
3	3/15
4	2/15
5	1/15

If the cost of the fixed asset is $180,000 and the salvage value is 10%, ($18,000), the sum of the years-digits depreciation would be:

Year	Cost Less Residual Value	Rate	S.O.Y.D. Depreciation for Year	Accum. Depreciation at End of Yr.	Book Value at End of Yr.
1	$162,000	5/15	$ 54,000	$ 54,000	$ 126,000
2	"	4/15	43,200	97,200	82,800
3	"	3/15	32,400	129,600	50,400
4	"	2/15	21,600	151,200	28,800
5	"	1/15	10,800	162,000	18,000*

---

*The book value at the end of the last year is, of course, the estimated salvage value.

The depreciation for the first year is $54,000. The monthly depreciation for the first year would be:

$$\frac{\$54,000}{12 \text{ mos.}} = \$4,500/\text{month}$$

The sum of the years-digits method may be used only on tangible property having a useful life of three years or more.[21]

A graph of the first-year depreciation per $1,000 of asset cost versus asset useful life selected is presented in Exhibit 5-3 for both the sum of the years-digits and the straight-line methods. The contrast between the two methods for several common salvage values is demonstrated.

THE UNITS-OF-PRODUCTION TECHNIQUE

The units-of-production method relates depreciation to the estimated productive capacity of the asset irrespective of the lapse of time. Depreciation is first computed for an appropriate unit of production such as hours, miles, number of operations, number of units produced, etc.

The depreciation per unit is then calculated as follows:

$$\text{Depreciation per Unit} = \frac{\text{Cost} - \text{Salvage}}{\text{Total Units (in useful life)}}$$

To illustrate, assume the estimated useful life of the previously mentioned $180,000 asset is 2.5 million units instead of five years. With a salvage value of 10%, or $18,000, the depreciation expense per unit would be:

$$\text{Depreciation per Unit} = \frac{\$180,000 - \$18,000}{2,500,000 \text{ units}}$$

$$= \$ .0648/\text{unit}$$

EXHIBIT 5-3
FIRST YEAR DEPRECIATION VS. ASSET USEFUL LIFE FOR STRAIGHT
LINE AND SUM OF THE YEARS-DIGITS

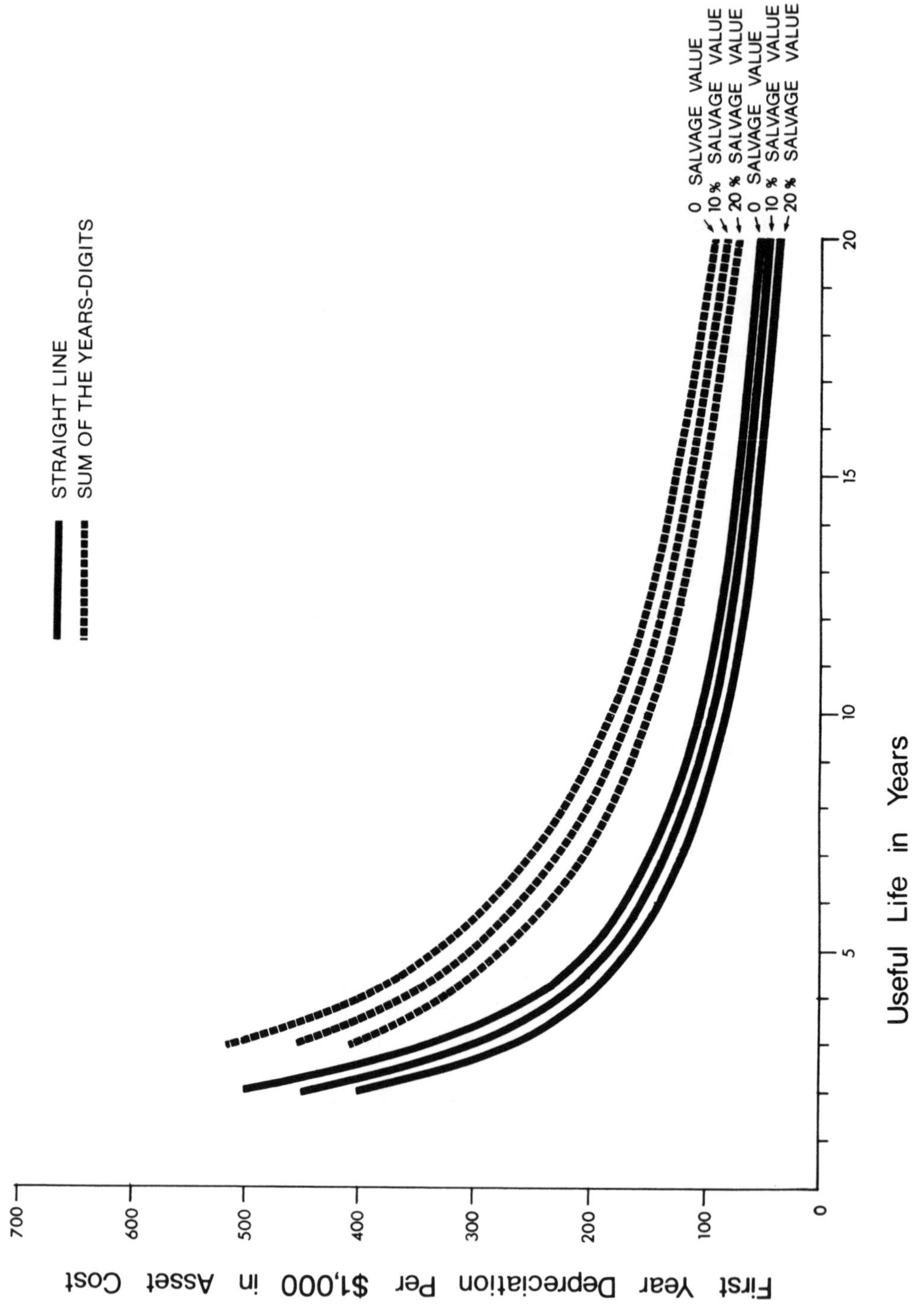

Utilizing the sales projections of Intercity Assembly Co. (see Exhibit 1-5 for monthly forecast) in which sales increase over the next seven months, the units-of-production depreciation would be as follows:

Month	Units Shipped	Units-of-Production Depreciation per Unit	Units-of-Production Depreciation
1	40,000	$.0648	$2,592
2	42,000	"	2,722
3	44,000	"	2,851
4	47,000	"	3,046
5	50,000	"	3,240
6	53,000	"	3,434
7	55,000	"	3,564

In constrast to the methods previously discussed that yielded the same or a decreasing depreciation rate over time, this method in this company setting yields a monthly depreciation that increases over time.

As a further illustration of the usefulenss of this depreciation technique, consider a machine that produces Christmas tree holders. This piece of equipment could very likely be running two shifts a day, seven days a week during the months of October and November. During the months that this machine is contributing to a high level of sales it would be nice to have a non-cash expense to write off against those sales in an effort to reduce taxes accrued during those two months. For the remaining 10 months of the year this piece of equipment might be stored with a canvas over it. During those 10 months, management might prefer not to be saddled with a large fixed expense resulting from a piece of equipment that was not contributing to the sales and earnings of the enterprise.

OTHER DEPRECIATION TECHNIQUES

Any other consistent method may be used for computing depreciation. Three additional methods are: Remaining-Life Plan, Operating-Day Method, and Income-Forecast Method.

Remaining Life Plan: This technique is a variation of the sum of the years-digits method. Under this technique, depreciation is computed by applying changing fractions to the *unrecovered* cost less any salvage value taken. The numerator changes each year to correspond with remaining useful life of the asset (including the year for which the allowance is computed), and the denominator changes each year to correspond with the sum of the numbers representing the remaining useful life.

Operating-Day Method: This method may be used when the major depreciation factor on equipment (such as rotary oil drilling rigs) is wear and tear from use rather than obsolescence. Useful life is the estimated number of days the equipment can be operated; depreciable basis is prorated on number of days used.

Income-Forecast Method: This method may be used to depreciate the cost of rented television film, taped shows and motion picture films. A fraction is applied, using the film's income for the year as the numerator, and the estimated income to be received over the film's useful life as the denominator. This fraction is multiplied by the adjusted cost of films that produced income during the year.[22]

During the first two-thirds of the useful life of the property, depreciation deductions under any such method must not result, at the end of any tax year, in accumulated allowances that are greater than the total that could have been deducted if the declining-balance method had been used. The limitations on the use of the declining-balance and sum of the years-digits methods apply equally to any consistent method used other than the straight-line method.

EXHIBIT 5-4
GRAPHICAL COMPARISON OF FOUR DEPRECIATION METHODS FOR A
FIVE-YEAR USEFUL LIFE ASSET

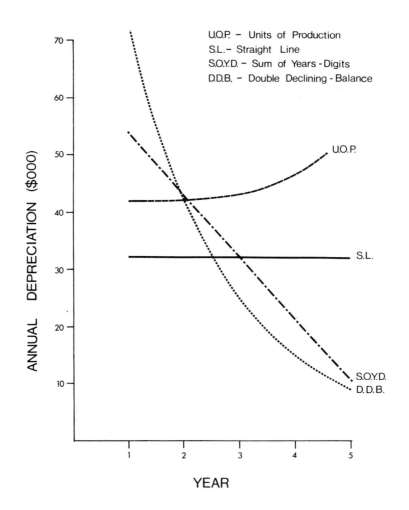

COMPARISON OF THE MORE COMMON
DEPRECIATION TECHNIQUES

In attempting to select a specific depreciation method, it is helpful to consider how some of the more common techniques compare in a business situation. If one considers the depreciation during the next seven months for the previously discussed $180,000 asset utilizing four common depreciation methods, a comparison may be made as follows:

Month	Straight-Line	Double-Declining-Balance	Sum of the Years-Digits	Units-of-Production
1	$2,700	$6,000	$4,500	$2,592
2	"	"	"	2,722
3	"	"	"	2,851
4	"	"	"	3,046
5	"	"	"	3,240
6	"	"	"	3,434
7	"	"	"	3,564

As may be seen, there is considerable flexibility in the management of depreciation. High, intermediate and low levels of depreciation may be chosen as well as depreciation that varies with utilization of the asset and, hence, the activity of the business.

EXHIBIT 5-5

GRAPHICAL COMPARISON OF FOUR DEPRECIATION METHODS FOR AN
EIGHT-YEAR USEFUL LIFE ASSET

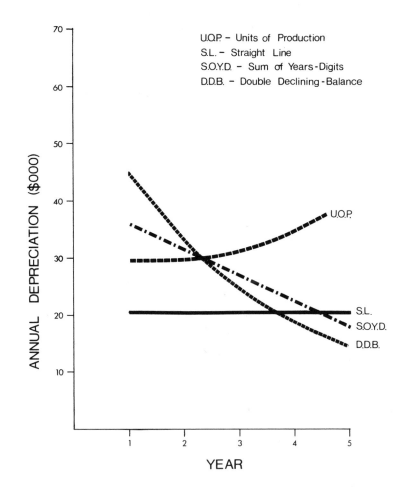

U.O.P. – Units of Production
S.L. – Straight Line
S.O.Y.D. – Sum of Years-Digits
D.D.B. – Double Declining-Balance

EXHIBIT 5-6
GRAPHICAL INDICATION OF POSSIBLE FIRST YEAR DEPRECIATION
RANGE FOR FOUR DEPRECIATION METHODS AND TWO DIFFERENT
USEFUL LIVES

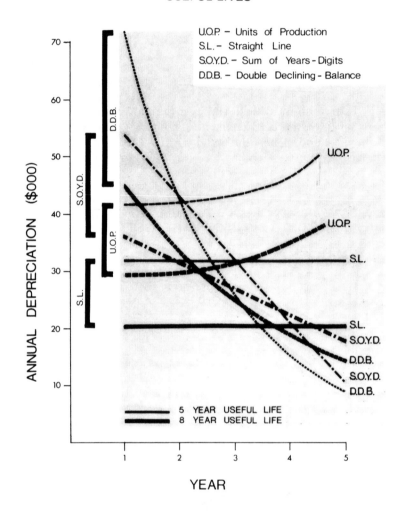

A comparison of the characteristics of these methods may be made graphically for the $180,000 asset owned by Intercity Assembly Co. If the annual depreciation for the five years useful life is plotted for the straight-line, double-declining-balance, sum of the years-digits and units-of-production (assuming 648,000 units produced this year) methods, the graph as shown in Exhibit 5-4 would result.

This graph demonstrates why declining-balance and sum of the years-digits methods are referred to as accelerated depreciation. In the early years of life of an asset, depreciation is recognized at a faster rate than that resulting from straight-line.

If the asset depreciation range for this equipment is five to eight years, then management could just as easily select eight years as five years for the useful life. If eight years useful life is selected and if the units of production useful life is varied from 2.5 million units to 3.5 million units, the preceding graphical comparison would appear as shown in Exhibit 5-5.

If these two comparative graphs are superimposed, the very interesting picture seen in Exhibit 5-6 emerges. By skillful selection of useful life and depreciation method (not to mention salvage value) any first-year depreciation amount from $20,250 to $72,000 may be selected for the asset under consideration. Since depreciation is an expense that appears on the income statement, the dramatic impact on profit of various decisions regarding depreciation is obvious. Innovative managers are creative with depreciation.

Switching Depreciation Methods

One may change from the declining-balance method to the straight-line method at any time during the useful life of a given piece of property without the consent of the Internal Revenue Service. When this change is made, the unrecovered cost or other basis less the estimated salvage value must be spread over the estimated remaining useful life determined at the time of the change of depreciation method. After changing to the straight-line method for any specific piece of property, you generally may not change to the declining-balance or to another method of depreciating that property for a period of 10 years, without written permission from the IRS.[23]

Except as previously noted any change in method of computing depreciation generally requires the consent of the Internal Revenue Service. A request for change in depreciation method should be filed on Internal Revenue Service form 3115.

Additional First Year's Depreciation

One may elect to deduct 20% of the cost of qualifying property as additional first-year depreciation in addition to the regular depreciation. Do not use salvage value in computing this deduction. Qualifying property consists of new or used tangible personal property having a useful life of at least six years (determined at date of acquisition). The cost of property on which one may take this additional depreciation allowance is limited to $10,000 on a separate return and $20,000 on a joint return. If a corporation purchases the property, its deduction would be 20% of only $10,000.[24]

The following example presented in Internal Revenue Service publication 534, is helpful in understanding how to calculate additional first-year depreciation:[25]

> You use the calendar year. On July 1 you bought a used pile driver for $14,500. It had an estimated useful life of 10 years and a salvage value of $500. Your depreciation deduction is computed as follows:

SEPARATE RETURN

Additional First-Year Depreciation: 20% of $10,000 ($14,500 limited to $10,000)	$2,000
Regular Depreciation: 10% of $12,000 ($14,500 less the $2,000 and less $500 salvage) × ½ year	600
Total Depreciation for the Year	$2,600

Other rules and latest updates related to the use of additional first-year depreciation are outlined in IRS publications 334 and 534.

Identical Assets/Different Depreciation Methods

The cost or other basis of every asset subject to depreciation is recorded in an asset account. One may establish as many accounts for depreciable property as desired. To utilize different depreciation methods for identical assets, all that must be done is to classify them and record them in different accounts in the company's books.

EXAMPLE OF A COMPANY THAT
ELECTED ACCELERATED DEPRECIATION

To illustrate the impact of different depreciation methods on a company's performance, consider Intercity Assembly Company, Inc., whose forecasted performance over the next seven months was detailed in Exhibits 1-5 and 1-6. That performance is summarized as follows:

EXHIBIT 5-7
Summary of Original
Pro Forma Income Statement
for
Intercity Assembly Co., Inc.[26]

Month	1	2	3	4	5	6	7
REVENUES	$80,000	84,000	88,000	94,000	100,000	106,000	110,000
EXPENSES	70,770	74,670	77,770	83,670	88,670	93,970	97,470
Pre-Tax Profit	9,230	9,330	10,230	10,330	11,330	12,030	12,530
Income Taxes	2,769	2,799	3,069	3,099	3,399	3,609	3,759
Net Profit	$ 6,461	6,531	7,161	7,231	7,931	8,421	8,771

EXHIBIT 5-8
Summary of Original
Pro Forma Cash Statement
for
Intercity Assembly Co., Inc.[27]

Month	1	2	3	4	5	6	7
RECEIPTS	$74,000	252,000	80,000	84,000	88,000	94,000	100,000
DISBURSEMENTS	83,000	256,100	74,100	84,737	83,150	90,800	102,457
Cash Flow	(9,000)	(4,100)	5,900	(737)	4,850	3,200	(2,457)
Beginning Balance	1,100	(7,900)	(12,000)	(6,100)	(6,837)	(1,987)	1,213
Ending Balance	$(7,900)	(12,000)	(6,100)	(6,837)	(1,987)	1,213	(1,244)

These forecasts are based on the straight-line depreciation of a $180,000 piece of equipment acquired in Month 1. A five-year useful life and a salvage value equal to 10% of the purchase price are utilized.

If, instead, management elects double-declining-balance depreciation, an accelerated method, and keeps the same useful life, the operating performance shown in Exhibit 5-9 results. The revised Manufacturing Overhead category is composed of $1,300 per month in

EXHIBIT 5-9
INTERCITY ASSEMBLY COMPANY, INC.
PRO FORMA INCOME STATEMENT
WITH DOUBLE-DECLINING BALANCE DEPRECIATION

Month	1	2	3	4	5	6	7
REVENUES							
Units Sold	40,000	42,000	44,000	47,000	50,000	53,000	55,000
Sales $	80,000	84,000	88,000	94,000	100,000	106,000	110,000
EXPENSES							
Direct Materials	40,000	42,000	44,000	47,000	50,000	53,000	55,000
Direct Labor	4,000	4,200	4,400	4,700	5,000	5,300	5,500
Overhead	7,300	7,300	7,300	7,300	7,300	7,300	7,300
Cost of Goods Sold	51,300	53,500	55,700	59,000	62,300	65,600	67,800
Gross Profit	28,700	30,500	32,300	35,000	37,700	40,400	42,200
General & Administrative							
Salaries	6,900	7,450	7,500	8,350	8,350	9,000	9,000
Rent	2,000	2,000	2,000	2,000	2,000	2,000	2,000
Insurance	500	500	500	500	500	500	500
Depreciation	170	170	170	170	170	170	170
Other G&A	3,000	4,100	4,550	5,500	6,600	7,050	7,850
Marketing							
Advertising	9,750	9,800	10,200	11,000	11,600	12,500	13,000
Brochures	450	450	450	450	450	450	450
Total Expense	74,070	77,970	81,070	86,970	91,970	97,270	100,770
Taxable Income	5,930	6,030	6,930	7,030	8,030	8,730	9,230
Income Taxes	1,779	1,809	2,079	2,109	2.409	2,619	2,769
Net Profit	4,151	4,221	4,851	4,921	5,621	6,111	6,461

EXHIBIT 5-10
INTERCITY ASSEMBLY COMPANY, INC.
PRO FORMA CASH FLOW STATEMENT
WITH DOUBLE-DECLINING BALANCE DEPRECIATION

Month	1	2	3	4	5	6	7
RECEIPTS							
Sales Receipts $	74,000*	77,000*	80,000	84,000	88,000	94,000	100,000
Common Stock	—	175,000	—	—	—	—	—
Total Received	74,000	252,000	80,000	84,000	88,000	94,000	100,000
DISBURSEMENTS							
Direct Materials	40,000*	40,000	45,000	45,000	50,000	55,000	55,000
Direct Labor	4,000	4,200	4,400	4,700	5,000	5,300	5,500
Overhead	1,300	1,300	1,300	1,300	1,300	1,300	1,300
Manufacturing Equip.	—	180,000	—	—	—	—	—
Salaries	6,900	7,450	7,500	8,350	8,350	9,000	9,000
Rent	2,000	2,000	2,000	2,000	2,000	2,000	2,000
Insurance	6,000	—	—	—	—	—	—
Office Equipment	—	3,000	—	—	—	—	—
Other G&A	2,800*	3,000	4,100	4,550	5,500	6,600	7,050
Advertising	9,000*	9,750	9,800	10,200	11,000	11,600	12,500
Brochures	—	5,400	—	—	—	—	—
Taxes	11,000*	—	—	5,667	—	—	7,137
Total Disbursed	83,000	256,100	74,100	81,767	83,150	90,800	99,487
Total Cash Flow $	(9,000)	(4,100)	5,900	2,233	4,850	3,200	513
Beginning Balance $	1,100	(7,900)	(12,000)	(6,100)	(3,867)	983	4,183
Ending Balance $	(7,900)	(12,000)	(6,100)	(3,867)	983	4,183	4,696

*From operations during prior periods.

cash expenses and $6,000 per month in double-declining-balance depreciation on the $180,000 asset. Profits are still respectable.

Down at the bank a different story is emerging, as indicated in Exhibit 5-10.

The monthly profit dropped somewhat as a result of accelerated depreciation. On the other hand, the ending balance improved dramatically and shifted from an overdraft position in Month 7 to a positive bank balance for that same month. The end result of selecting the accelerated-depreciation method is dramatized in the following summary table:

EXHIBIT 5-11
Table Summarizing Operations
Under Two Different Depreciation Methods

	Net Profit for 7 Months	Ending Bank Balance Month 7
Straight-Line	$52,507	$(1,244)
Double-Declining-Balance	36,337	4,696

This table demonstrates a common dilemma facing many managers. The decision that improved cash flow and ending cash balances was one that decreased the total profit earned. The dilemma is that it is frequently difficult to make a decision that improves both profit and cash at the same time. For the most part the manager must be content with trading profit for cash or cash for profit.

Strong Points of Depreciation as
a Profit and Cash Flow Strategy

There are two major reasons why depreciation is such an important profit and cash flow management technique: flexibility and ease of implementation. The flexibility of depreciation in attempting to make the company's profit and cash flow work out as desired is dramatically demonstrated by the graphs shown in Exhibit 5-4, 5-5 and 5-6. As an extreme case for the asset shown in these graphs, management had the ability to select a first-year depreciation of anything from $20,250 to $72,000 as pointed out in Exhibit 5-6.

With respect to ease of implementation, all that is necessary to institute a particular depreciation tactic is to make an entry each month in the company's books. This ease of implementation is in dramatic contrast to other approaches such as bringing the accounts receivable in sooner. One may spend a great deal of time and energy in attempting to reduce the average age of outstanding receivables. The effort could meet with little success. Entering a particular depreciation number in the business's financial recordkeeping system is something that is immediate and complete.

How to Select the Best Depreciation
Method for Your Business

A managerial focus on profit and cash flow provides one approach to selecting the most appropriate depreciation method for a given business. The first step is to determine which depreciation methods are applicable for the particular asset under consideration. The range of useful lives that would be appropriate, as well as the various possibilities for salvage value, should then be identified. Several depreciation possibilities should be formulated. Next, portray these possible choices in the company's income forecast and cash flow forecast. That depreciation method is best that generates the most profit while simultaneously maintaining the desired liquidity (cash balance).

INVESTMENT TAX CREDIT: A POSSIBLE BONUS FOR THE QUALIFIED

Investment tax credit is linked to depreciation through the useful life of the asset in question. The useful life selected for depreciation purposes is the one that must also be used for investment tax credit purposes.

The investment tax credit is also discussed in Chapter 8. The focus there is on the credit as a specific technique for minimizing taxes.

The investment tax credit is a credit directly applicable to one's income tax liability. The amount of the investment tax credit is periodically modified by Acts of Congress. An investment tax credit of 10% of the purchase price applies to investment credit property acquired and placed in service during the tax year.[28]

The investment tax credit is available for the year the property is placed in service. Property is considered to be placed in service when one begins to depreciate that property or when the property is placed in a condition or state of readiness and availability for service.

Since the investment tax credit is, in fact, a credit to one's tax liability, its favorable use makes the fundamental assumption that one's company is making enough profit to pay taxes. A business that is not paying income tax and has no future anticipation of income tax liabilities does not benefit from this regulatory provision.

Qualifying Property

For property to qualify for the investment tax credit it must: (1) be depreciable, (2) have a useful life of at least three years, (3) be tangible personal property or other tangible property (except buildings or their structural components) used as an integral part of manufacturing, production, extraction, etc., and (4) be placed in service in a trade or business or for production of income during the year.[29]

Tangible personal property includes depreciable tangible property except land and land improvements (such as buildings and other permanent structures and their components). Property in the nature of machinery is the principal type of property that qualifies as tangible personal property. Buildings, swimming pools, paved parking areas, wharves and docks, for example, are not tangible personal property. Assets such as grocery store counters, printing presses and individual air conditioning units normally qualify as tangible personal property. Assets of a mechanical nature, such as gasoline pumps, even though located outside a building, also qualify. Generally, central heating and air conditioning systems, plumbing and wiring are structural components of a building and do not qualify as tangible personal property.[30]

If individuals lease property rather than purchase it outright, they are allowed the investment tax credit provided the owner elects to pass the credit to them. The property in question must be considered qualifying new property, both to the lessee, and to the lessor (owner).[31] For specific problems, talk with your tax professional.

Intangible property, horses or real property other than that already referred to does not qualify for the investment credit.[32]

For additional information regarding qualifying property refer to Internal Revenue Service publication 572, Tax Information on Investment Credit. This publication is available free at your nearest Internal Revenue Service office.

Limitations

Property with a useful life of less than three years does not qualify for the credit. Only one-third of the investment in qualifying property with a useful life of at least three years but less than five years is subject to the credit. Two-thirds of the amount invested is subject to the credit if the property has a useful life of at least five years but less than seven years. The full investment is subject to the credit, if the property has a useful life of at least seven years.[33]

The investment credit allowable is 10% of the eligible investment.

Qualifying used property is treated differently from qualifying new property. One may count no more than $100,000 of the cost of qualifying used property in any one year for purposes of the investment credit.[34] A lessor cannot pass the credit for used property to the lessee.[35] (See IRS publication 572 for the latest update.)

An unused credit exists if the sum of the investment credit carryovers to the current tax year, plus the credit allowable for the current tax year, exceed the limitation based on your tax liability. Unused credit may be carried back to the three preceding tax years, and the balance still unused in those years may be carried over to succeeding tax years.[36]

Recapture: A Potential Pitfall

Recapture is a concept that is related to "settling accounts" with the Internal Revenue Service when an asset is disposed of for which investment credit was claimed in a prior year. One must compare the actual useful life (determined by the date of disposition) with the estimated useful life originally used in computing the credit. If one disposes of an asset before the end of the estimated useful life used in computing the credit, the credit must be recomputed substituting actual useful life for the estimated useful life used originally. If the recomputed credit is less than the credit that actually reduced the tax liability, one must add to the tax liability for the year the asset is disposed of any excess of the credit allowed for all affected years over the recomputed credit.[37]

This recomputation of the investment credit is intended to place one in the position that would have existed if the actual useful life had been used in computing the credit originally. One must determine if all or part of the credit must be recaptured. No recapture determination need be made if one holds the property for seven years or more.[38]

Since recapture considerations arise upon disposition of an asset for which investment credit has been claimed, the topic of disposition itself becomes a crucial consideration. A disposition occurs in any transaction in which one ceases to own property.[39] For example, property has been disposed of if it is abandoned or otherwise retired from use. Disposition for recapture purposes includes sales, exchanges, gifts, trade-ins and involuntary conversions. It also includes a sale in sale-leaseback transactions and a transfer on the foreclosure of a security interest. It does not include: a transfer of title to a creditor on the creation of a security interest; transfer at death; corporate tax-free transfers; and changes in the form of doing business. Property may be treated as disposed of, if the taxpayer fails to keep adequate records showing: (1) cost or other basis; (2) estimated useful life; (3) the date property was placed in service; and (4) the date of disposition.[40]

Example of a Company Benefiting
From Investment Tax Credit

Consider the example of Intercity Assembly Company, Inc., discussed earlier in this chapter. The performance of the company is described in Exhibit 5-7 and Exhibit 5-8 with a proforma income statement and a proforma cash flow statement. If the $180,000 asset purchased by Intercity Assembly Company, Inc. in Month 1 is a non-qualifying asset for investment credit purposes, the summarized performance for the seven months in question would be that portrayed in Exhibit 5-12 as follows.

EXHIBIT 5-12
Intercity Assembly Company, Inc.
Seven-Month Performance, No
Investment Credit

Income Statement for Seven Months		Cash Flow Statement for Seven-Month Period	
Revenues	$662,000	Receipts	$772,000
Expenses	586,990	Disbursements	774,344
Pre-Tax Profit	75,010	Cash Flow	(2,344)
Income Taxes	22,503	Beginning Balance	1,100
Net Profit	52,507	Ending Balance	(1,244)

If, on the other hand, the $180,000 asset is qualifying property and the investment credit applied, a substantially different picture emerges. With investment credit, the performance of Exhibit 5-13 results.

EXHIBIT 5-13
Intercity Assembly Company, Inc.
Seven-Month Performance,
With Investment Credit

Income Statement for Seven Months		Cash Flow Statement for Seven Month Period	
Revenue	$662,000	Receipts	$772,000
Expenses	586,990	Disbursements	762,344
Pre-Tax Profit	75,010	Cash Flow	9,656
Income Tax	22,503		
Before Credit		Beginning Balance	1,100
Investment Credit	12,000*	Ending Balance	10,756
Net Profit	64,507		

*For a five-year useful life two-thirds of the purchase price qualifies for the tax credit.

A summary of the company's performance both with and without the benefit of the investment credit is presented in the following table:

	Profit for 7 Months	Cash Balance Month 7
Original Forecast	$52,507	$(1,244)
(Straight-Line Depreciation and No Investment Tax Credit)		
Revised Performance	$64,507	$10,756
(Straight-Line Depreciation plus Investment Tax Credit)		

NOTES FOR CHAPTER 5

[1]*Tax Information on Depreciation* Publication 534, (Washington D.C.: Internal Revenue Service, 1978), p. 1.
[2]Ibid.
[3]Ibid.
[4]Ibid.
[5]*Tax Information* Publication 534, p. 2.
[6]Ibid.
[7]Ibid.
[8]Ibid.
[9]Ibid.
[10]Ibid.
[11]Ibid.
[12]Ibid.
[13]*Tax Guide for Small Business* Publication 334, (Washington D.C.: Internal Revenue Service, 1978), p. 17.
[14]*Tax Guide* Publication 334, p. 17.
[15]*Tax Information* Publication 534, p. 3
[16]*Tax Information* Publication 534, p. 4.
[17]*Tax Information* Publication 534, p. 3.
[18]*Federal Tax Handbook*, (Englewood Cliffs: Prentice-Hall, Inc., 1978), p. 285.
[19]*Tax Information* Publication 534, p. 6.
[20]Ibid.
[21]*Tax Information* Publication 534, p. 7.
[22]*Federal Tax Handbook*, p. 279.
[23]*Tax Information* Publication 534, p. 7.
[24]*Tax Information* Publication 534, p. 5.
[25]Ibid.
[26]John A. Welsh and Jerry F. White, *Profit & Cash Flow Management for Non-Financial Managers*, 1974, p. 17-18B.
[27]Ibid.
[28]*Tax Information on Investment Credit* Publication 572, (Washington, D.C.: Internal Revenue Service, 1978), p. 1.
[29]Ibid.
[30]Ibid.
[31]*Tax Information* Publication 572, p. 3.
[32]Ibid.
[33]*Tax Information* Publication 572, p. 5.
[34]*Tax Information* Publication 572, p. 6.
[35]*Tax Information* Publication 572, p. 3.
[36]*Tax Information* Publication 572, p. 6.
[37]*Tax Information* Publication 572, p. 9.
[38]*Tax Information* Publication 572, p. 7.
[39]Ibid.
[40]*Federal Tax Handbook*, p. 298.

6

Smart Administration with LIFO and FIFO Inventory Costing Techniques

THE BASIC CONCEPT

When calculating the cost of goods sold for the income statement, one commonly arrives at the cost of the inventory consumed in the process of producing the goods by solving the algebraic equation:

Cost of inventory consumed during a given period

        EQUALS   The cost of the inventory on hand at the beginning of the period

        PLUS   The cost of the purchases for inventory during the period

        MINUS   The cost of the goods remaining in inventory at the end of the period.

This simple algebraic equation is precise and exact. However, practical application of this formula creates a formidable task even in some small and relatively uncomplicated businesses. The inventory consists of many items, small and large, new and not so new, some in boxes, some in bags and some not packaged at all. The individual items are purchased at various times at various prices. They are consumed as needed, usually without regard to when and at what price they were purchased.

To apply the equation accurately, it is necessary for each item in the inventory to be identified by its cost and for the sum total cost of the items in the inventory to be counted at the beginning *and* at the end of the period under consideration. Since even a small owner-managed business may have thousands of items in its inventory, the time and manpower required to count and record each item with its cost would consume more time and manpower than the business could afford.

Accountants have overcome this dilemma by accepting a count of the number of items in the inventory independent of the price at which they were purchased. They then deduct the number of items consumed from the total number of such items recorded in the accounting books, attaching to them a cost easily identified in the books. As purchase prices fluctuate up and down over an extended period of time, this method of removing cost from the recorded value of the inventory will tend to average out the fluctuating costs. The method is an excellent approximation as long as the purchase prices tend to fluctuate around some average price.

The cost easiest to identify in the books is either the most recent purchase price or the most distant price. If the cost of items added to the inventory is tabulated chronologically, it is easy to remove this cost chronologically. This is the method most widely used[1] and is referred to as the FIFO method or first-in-first-out method. The most common alternative method is to remove cost from the tabulation of purchases in the reverse order, or LIFO, last-in-first-out.

One way to think about this process is to imagine that as various supplies are received they are recorded together with their unit cost on a series of cards. For each shipment received a card is created and the cards are filed chronologically as shown in Exhibit 6-1.

EXHIBIT 6-1
ILLUSTRATION OF CHRONOLOGICAL RECORDING OF SHIPMENTS
RECEIVED

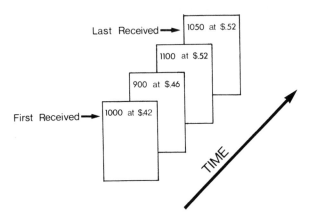

When using the FIFO method of costing inventory consumed, the bookkeeping department subtracts the unit cost from the oldest unit record card first. Under the LIFO method, unit costs are taken from the most recent unit record card first as illustrated in Exhibit 6-2.

EXHIBIT 6-2
ILLUSTRATION OF FIFO ORDER OF USAGE AND LIFO ORDER OF USAGE

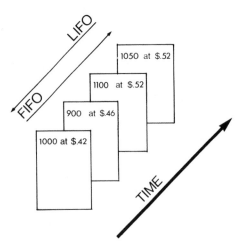

PROS AND CONS: THE PROFESSIONALS CONTINUE TO ARGUE

Over the years, various arguments have developed concerning the pros and cons of the LIFO versus the FIFO inventory costing methods, and their respective effects on the operating statement (income statement) and the statement of financial position (balance sheet). Owner-managers and the lay public are often baffled by these arguments and misled by the terminology used. Before discussing the pros and cons it might be helpful to try to understand who is making the arguments and what their objectives are.

Keeping a count of each and every item, identified with its actual cost, entering and leaving the inventory, can become a costly and time-consuming task even for a relatively small business. Consider the problem of preparing such information monthly for the companies listed on the New York Stock Exchange. The accounting profession was long ago forced to create methods for estimating such data at a reasonable cost to the companies. The FIFO and LIFO methods described above are examples of such methods of estimating.

Costing the inventory consumed in making the product and generating the sales is only one of many areas in the practical application of accounting where similar problems arise. The profession is faced with producing a numerical representation of what has occurred in the business without overburdening the business with the cost of producing that representation.

In order to resolve this practical problem the accounting profession has established a policy-making body which determines acceptable methods. These acceptable methods are then provided as rules for certified accountants to follow. In this way the users of financial reports can rely on consistency from one report to another and from one accountant to another. One rule-making group in the United States is the Financial Accounting Standards Board.

The perspective of the FASB is that they serve the best interests of the *users* of the financial reports. These users include investors, stock brokers, analysts, bankers, government statisticians, government regulatory agencies and, of course, the managers of the companies described by the reports. The FASB produces accounting standards which will make it possible for an outsider to understand the inside workings of the business.

One of the most fundamental principles of the accounting profession is called "matching." It refers to relating Revenue from sales to the Expense incurred in producing that Revenue. Therein lies a basic problem when determining the cost of inventory consumed in making a sale. The FIFO method may be attributing the cost of inventory to something purchased many months ago. The LIFO method attributes the cost to something purchased more recently. During periods of rapid inflation, however, even the cost of the most recent purchase may not be representative of what the inventory would have cost when the sale was made.

The perspective of the professionals who offer the arguments, pro or con, for FIFO or LIFO is from the position of "exact current matching between Revenue and Expense at the time the Revenue was realized." The most exact current matching would occur if all of the expenses associated with a revenue were incurred at exactly the same time the revenue was obtained.

Income Statement Considerations

One of the advantages of LIFO most often suggested is that during periods of rising costs, reported profits are lower (than for the same company using FIFO) and, thus, the tax liability is lower for the business. As long as costs continue to rise, LIFO will provide a tax advantage.[2] Once a business elects the LIFO method, however, it cannot readily switch* to another method and must use LIFO for both tax and financial reporting purposes.[3] Consequently, if prices fall, the business will lose the tax advantage while FIFO users may gain the advantage.

---

*For additional information regarding switching refer to LIFO discussion of Chapter 8.

Proponents of LIFO argue that the income realized under the last-in-first-out pricing system more closely matches revenue and expense. They say that the increases in unit costs of inventory items are unrealized gains (when prices are rising) and that these inventory holding gains and losses (discussed later in this chapter) are excluded from the income accounts. Because the cost of goods sold, under LIFO, fluctuates with the general purchase price fluctuations, reported profits are "smoothed." LIFO thus ignores gains or losses from cost-level changes.[4]

Adversaries of LIFO argue that LIFO does not completely adjust to cost-level changes. Costs may increase or decrease subsequent to the last purchase price of inventory. The latest purchases or costs may or may not be close to the current replacement costs.[5]

FIFO advocates argue that their method allows the firm's real reported income to "keep up" with specific inventory cost-level changes and reality is reflected on the income statement. The "reality" argument of FIFO is based upon the assumption that the investment in the inventory of a business is similar to any other investment by a firm. The inventory holding gains or losses due to cost-level changes are similar to any other non-operating investment income and should be reflected as income upon realization. FIFO, it is said, recognizes income from the firm's most important income-producing asset, inventory.

Balance Sheet Considerations

By using FIFO the ending inventory value on the asset side of the balance sheet reflects a closer approximation to reality than under LIFO because the most recent inventory purchase cost is closer to the current replacement cost. The LIFO ending inventory figure may even be a fixed cost that is unrealistic during cost increases or declines. When the LIFO ending inventory value is fixed (because the number of units sold approximates the number of units purchased), values may be drastically understated when costs rise, and drastically overstated when costs decline.

FIFO, then, accounts for cost-level changes to a much greater extent than does LIFO. But the same argument used against LIFO on the income statement can now be used against FIFO on the balance sheet. FIFO does not technically reflect cost-level adjustments for ending inventory values because the cost level can change subsequent to the last purchase of inventories. FIFO inventory values are simply an approximation to replacement costs, just as the LIFO cost of goods sold is simply an approximation to current inventory costs.

Further Considerations

While either method is a generally accepted accounting principle, the presentation of both financial position (balance sheet) and results of operations (income statement) may be significantly different depending upon whether LIFO or FIFO is used.

For example, the current ratio (current assets divided by current liabilities) under FIFO, when compared to that of a similar firm using LIFO, will appear much stronger because inventory values are higher when costs are rising. When costs are falling, the opposite is true. Under LIFO, the inventory turnover figure is higher because the cost of goods sold during inflation is higher while the inventory figure is lower.

The same problem of comparability is seen when operating ratios are compared among LIFO and FIFO users. For example, during inflation, FIFO invariably reports a higher return on assets and equity than does LIFO.

If is difficult to compare a FIFO user with a LIFO user, or a recently converted LIFO user to its previous statements under FIFO. Comparability and consistency are basic accounting objectives. They may appear to be violated by the divergence of accounting principles allowable for inventory valuation.

Perhaps the only real solution to the problem of which inventory valuation method you should implement is to define management objectives first and then realize all the implications, real or imagined, of LIFO and FIFO.

How to Determine Holding Gains and Losses Under FIFO

Inventory gains and losses are equal to the difference between the reported cost of inventory consumed in making a sale and what the inventory would have cost had it been purchased at the time of the sale.

During periods of rapidly changing costs, holding gains and losses can be significant and, in inflationary periods, FIFO recognizes more of these gains. Consider the case of a company which has the following inventory transactions during the course of a year:[6]

Beginning Inventory	10,000 @ $.25
Sales Price	$.50 per unit

Period	Purchases			Units Shipped
1	12,000	@	$.30	8,000
2	13,000		.40	12,000
3	11,000		.35	14,000
4	10,000		.40	11,000

The cost of inventory consumed in making these shipments using the FIFO costing method may be calculated as follows:

Beginning Inventory	Purchases Received	Shipments (FIFO)	Cost of Units Shipped	Ending Inventory
10,000 @ $.25	12,000 @ $.30	8,000 @ $.25	$ 2,000	2,000 @ $.25 12,000 @ .30
2,000 @ .25 12,000 @ .30	13,000 @ .40	2,000 @ .25 10,000 @ .30	3,500	2,000 @ .30 13,000 @ .40
2,000 @ .30 13,000 @ .40	11,000 @ .35	2,000 @ .30 12,000 @ .40	5,400	1,000 @ .40 11,000 @ .35
1,000 @ .40 11,000 @ .35	10,000 @ .40	1,000 @ .40 10,000 @ .35	3,900	1,000 @ .35 10,000 @ .40
Total cost of units shipped (using FIFO)			$14,800	

The cost of inventory consumed in making these shipments using the most current cost of purchases may be calculated as below:[7]

Purchases Received	Shipments in Units	Current Cost of Shipments
12,000 @ $.30	8,000	$ 2,400
13,000 @ .40	12,000	4,800
11,000 @ .35	14,000	4,900
10,000 @ .40	11,000	4,400
Total current cost of units shipped		$16,500

The inventory holding gain, the difference in calculated cost of units shipped is $1,700 and is included in the profit when using the FIFO method.

The LIFO method also recognizes inventory holding gains and losses. The cost of inventory consumed in making these shipments using the LIFO costing method may be calculated as follows:

Beginning Inventory	Purchases Received	Shipments (LIFO)	Cost of Units Shipped	Ending Inventory
10,000 @ $.25	12,000 @ $.30	8,000 @ $.30	$ 2,400	10,000 @ $.25 4,000 @ .30
10,000 @ .25 4,000 @ .30	13,000 @ .40	12,000 @ .40	4,800	10,000 @ .25 4,000 @ .30 1,000 @ .40
10,000 @ .25 4,000 @ .30 1,000 @ .40	11,000 @ .35	11,000 @ .35 1,000 @ .40 2,000 @ .30	4,850	10,000 @ .25 2,000 @ .30
10,000 @ .25 2,000 @ .30	10,000 @ .40	10,000 @ .40 1,000 @ .30	4,300	10,000 @ .25 1,000 @ .30
Total cost of units shipped (using LIFO)			$16,350	

The inventory holding gain, the difference between the LIFO cost and the current cost, is $150 and is included in the profit when using the LIFO method. The LIFO method recognizes holding gains and losses, but not nearly to the extent that FIFO does.

How FIFO Can Pay Off on the Balance Sheet

The ending inventory amount in the previous illustration is 11,000 units regardless of which method of inventory valuation is utilized. However, different unit costs can be associated with the unsold units on hand at the end of the last period.[8]

FIFO Valuation			LIFO Valuation		
Ending Inventory	=	11,000 Units	Ending Inventory	=	11,000 Units
10,000 @ $.40	=	$4,000	10,000 @ $.25	=	$2,500
1,000 .35	=	350	1,000 .30	=	300
Tot. End. Inventory		$4,350	Tot. End. Inventory		$2,800

FIFO tends to paint a picture portraying more assets and specifically more current assets during times of rising prices. This makes many (including your banker!) who review your balance sheet feel more comfortable. As illustrated later in this chapter, FIFO can substantially improve various measures of financial performance during inflationary periods.

Cash Flow Impact of Purchases and Sales

To illustrate the impact of purchases and sales on company cash receipts and disbursements, consider the business we have been examining.[9]

Date	Purchases (Units)	Cost	Sales (Units)	Price
Beginning Inventory Jan 1	10,000	$.25	-0-	-0-
Apr 1	12,000	.30	8,000	$.50
Jul 1	13,000	.40	12,000	.50
Oct 1	11,000	.35	14,000	.50
Dec 1	10,000	.40	11,000	.50

Regardless of whether it uses FIFO or LIFO on its financial statements, it must pay out, in either case, $3,600 for the 12,000 units that cost $.30/unit, and it will still receive $4,000 for the 8,000 units it sold for $.50/unit. What is paid out and what comes in is the same under both methods of inventory valuation.

Impact On Profits

The impact on company profits is one of the major considerations when choosing between LIFO and FIFO. For the business previously discussed, net profit after taxes under the FIFO method is more than three times greater than net profit under LIFO, as demonstrated in the following illustration:[10]

	FIFO			LIFO		
Sales	45,000 × $.50	=	$22,500	45,000 × $.50	=	$22,500
Cost of Goods Sold	10,000 × .25	=	2,500	10,000 × .40	=	4,000
	12,000 × .30	=	3,600	11,000 × .35	=	3,850
	13,000 × .40	=	5,200	13,000 × .40	=	5,200
	10,000 × .35	=	3,500	11,000 × .30	=	3,300
Total Cost of Goods Sold			14,800			16,350
Gross Profit			7,700			6,150
G&A and Marketing Expenses			5,450			5,450
Total Expenses			20,250			21,800
Pre-Tax Profit			2,250			700
Income Taxes (17%)*			383			119
Net Profit			1,867			581

---

*Assumes the business estimates an effective tax rate of 17% for the year.

From the above income statements it may be seen that sales in either case are the same in units and dollar amounts, since the selling price is constant. However, under FIFO, the cost of goods sold figure is significantly less than under the LIFO method. This is because prices are, for the most part, rising and the lower costs of inventories were associated with the cost of goods sold first. Under LIFO, the higher prices incurred for inventory purchases throughout the year were first associated with the cost of goods sold (most recent costs), thus reducing net income. Because net income is lower under LIFO, taxable income is lower and taxes are thereby reduced. Lower taxes represent a cash saving at the time a tax deposit is made.

Financial Performance Ratios

Because of different reported incomes, cash flows and ending inventory figures, various liquidity and profitability ratios will be affected differently, depending upon which inventory costing method is employed. For the example under consideration, a balance sheet would include the following items:[11]

BALANCE SHEET*

	FIFO	LIFO
Current Assets		
Cash	$ 2,000	$ 2,000
Inventory	4,350	2,800
Fixed Assets		
Property & Equipment	20,000	20,000
Current Liabilities		
Accounts Payable	4,000	4,000
Taxes Payable	383	119
Owner's Equity		
Capital Stock	15,000	15,000

When common liquidity, profitability and return ratios are calculated, the difference in financial performance becomes evident as shown in the following table:[12]

RATIOS	FIFO	LIFO
Current Ratio (Current Assets/Current Liab.)	1.45	1.17
"Quick Ratio" (Cash/Current Liabilities)	.46	.49
Inventory Turnover (Cost of Goods Sold/Inventory)	3.40	5.84
Gross Profit Margin (Gross Profit**/Sales)	.34	.27
Net Profit Margin (Net Profit/Sales)	.08	.27
Return on Assets (Net Profit/Total Assets)	.07	.02
Return on Invested Capital (Net Profit/Capital Stock)	.12	.04

Astute managers can be creative when portraying their financial performance. LIFO and FIFO represent valuable techniques for making financial statements come out the way you would like them.

EXAMPLE OF A COMPANY THAT ELECTED LIFO VERSUS FIFO

To compare the difference in operating results produced by LIFO versus FIFO, consider what might happen to Intercity Assembly Company, Inc. during a period of inflation. A detailed forecast of the income statement for Intercity was originally presented in Exhibit 1-5. The forecasted cash flow statement was presented in Exhibit 1-6. These two statements are summarized in Exhibits 6-3 and 6-4 respectively.

---

*Selected Balance Sheet items as of December 31. Total Assets do not equal Total Liabilities plus Owner's Equity because certain Balance Sheet items have not been listed.

**Gross Profit = Sales – Cost of Goods Sold

EXHIBIT 6-3
SUMMARY OF ORIGINAL
PRO FORMA INCOME STATEMENT
FOR
INTERCITY ASSEMBLY COMPANY, INC.

Month	1	2	3	4	5	6	7
REVENUES	$ 80,000	84,000	88,000	94,000	100,000	106,000	110,000
EXPENSES	70,770	74,670	77,770	83,670	88,670	93,970	97,470
Pre-Tax Profit	9,230	9,330	10,230	10,330	11,330	12,030	12,530
Income Taxes	2,769	2,799	3,069	3,099	3,399	3,609	3,759
Net Profit	$ 6,461	6,531	7,161	7,231	7,931	8,421	8,771

EXHIBIT 6-4
SUMMARY OF ORIGINAL
PRO FORMA CASH FLOW STATEMENT
FOR
INTERCITY ASSEMBLY COMPANY, INC.

Month	1	2	3	4	5	6	7
RECEIPTS	$ 74,000	252,000	80,000	84,000	88,000	94,000	100,000
DISBURSEMENTS	83,000	256,100	74,100	84,737	83,150	90,800	102,457
Cash Flow	(9,000)	(4,100)	5,900	(737)	4,850	3,200	(2,457)
Beginning Balance	1,100	(7,900)	(12,000)	(6,100)	(6,837)	(1,987)	1,213
Ending Balance	$ (7,900)	(12,000)	(6,100)	(6,837)	(1,987)	1,213	(1,244)

Suppose that management of Intercity expects a 15% increase in the cost of materials received beginning in Month 2 and an additional 15% increase in the cost of materials received beginning in Month 4. If the selling price to the customer is raised 15% in Month 2 and an additional 15% in Month 4, the resulting impact on forecasted profit would be reflected in the revised pro forma income statement shown in Exhibit 6-5.

With the cost of materials rising to $1.15 and $1.32 and an increase in the sales price to $2.30 and $2.65 in Months 2 and 4, the net profit levels are generally higher as one might expect in a situation where prices are increased but general and administrative as well as marketing costs remain the same (in the near future). The direct materials flow schedule portrayed in Exhibit 6-6 illustrates how the calculation for the cost of direct materials expense was made for the units shipped. (The FIFO method was used.)

Exhibit 6-6 also illustrates how the disbursements for direct materials were calculated The column designated "Purchases Received" indicates the value of the units received for each month of the forecast. Payment for these units occurs 30 days after their receipt. The pro forma cash flow statement for Intercity Assembly Company, assuming FIFO inventory costing in an inflationary environment, is portrayed in Exhibit 6-7.

The balances shown in Exhibit 6-7 were sufficiently discouraging that management decided to investigate what impact electing the LIFO method of inventory costing would have. If, under the same inflation conditions, the last-in-first-out method is utilized, then the profit indicated in Exhibit 6-8 would result.

The cost of the direct materials shipped is calculated using the LIFO method as shown in Exhibit 6-9.

EXHIBIT 6-5
INTERCITY ASSEMBLY COMPANY, INC.
REVISED PRO FORMA INCOME STATEMENT
FIFO WITH INFLATION

Month	1	2	3	4	5	6	7
REVENUES							
Units Sold	40,000	42,000	44,000	47,000	50,000	53,000	55,000
Sales $	80,000	96,600	101,200	124,550	132,500	140,450	145,750
EXPENSES							
Direct Materials	40,000	42,000	50,375	54,050	65,915	69,960	72,600
Direct Labor	4,000	4,200	4,400	4,700	5,000	5,300	5,500
Overhead	4,000	4,000	4,000	4,000	4,000	4,000	4,000
Cost of Goods Sold	48,000	50,200	58,775	62,750	74,915	79,260	82,100
Gross Profit	32,000	46,400	42,425	61,800	57,585	61,190	63,650
General & Administrative							
Salaries	6,900	7,450	7,500	8,350	8,350	9,000	9,000
Rent	2,000	2,000	2,000	2,000	2,000	2,000	2,000
Insurance	500	500	500	500	500	500	500
Depreciation	170	170	170	170	170	170	170
Other G & A	3,000	4,100	4,550	5,500	6,600	7,050	7,850
Marketing							
Advertising	9,750	9,800	10,200	11,000	11,600	12,500	13,000
Brochures	450	450	450	450	450	450	450
Total Expense	70,770	74,670	84,145	90,720	104,585	110,930	115,070
Taxable Income	9,230	21,930	17,055	33,830	27,915	29,520	30,680
Income Taxes	2,769	6,579	5,117	10,149	8,375	8,856	9,204
Net Profit	6,461	15,351	11,938	23,681	19,540	20,664	21,476

EXHIBIT 6-6
INTERCITY ASSEMBLY COMPANY, INC.
DIRECT MATERIALS FLOW SCHEDULE

Month	Beginning Inventory	Purchases Received	Inventory Avail. for Shipment (FIFO)	Shipments (FIFO)	Ending Inventory (FIFO)
1	43,500 @ $1.00	40,000 @ $1.00	43,500 @ $1.00 40,000 @ $1.00	40,000 @ $1.00	3,500 @ $1.00 40,000 @ $1.00
2 (15% Increase)	3,500 @ $1.00 40,000 @ $1.00	45,000 @ $1.15	3,500 @ $1.00 40,000 @ $1.00 45,000 @ $1.15	3,500 @ $1.00 38,500 @ $1.00	1,500 @ $1.00 45,000 @ $1.15
3	1,500 @ $1.00 45,000 @ $1.15	45,000 @ $1.15	1,500 @ $1.00 45,000 @ $1.15 45,000 @ $1.15	1,500 @ $1.00 42,500 @ $1.15	2,500 @ $1.15 45,000 @ $1.15
4 (15% Increase)	2,500 @ $1.15 45,000 @ $1.15	50,000 @ $1.32	2,500 @ $1.15 45,000 @ $1.15 50,000 @ $1.32	2,500 @ $1.15 44,500 @ $1.15	500 @ $1.15 50,000 @ $1.32
5	500 @ $1.15 50,000 @ $1.32	55,000 @ $1.32	500 @ $1.15 50,000 @ $1.32 55,000 @ $1.32	500 @ $1.15 49,500 @ $1.32	500 @ $1.32 55,000 @ $1.32
6	500 @ $1.32 55,000 @ $1.32	55,000 @ $1.32	500 @ $1.32 55,000 @ $1.32 55,000 @ $1.32	500 @ $1.32 52,500 @ $1.32	2,500 @ $1.32 55,000 @ $1.32
7	2,500 @ $1.32 55,000 @ $1.32	55,000 @ $1.32	2,500 @ $1.32 55,000 @ $1.32 55,000 @ $1.32	2,500 @ $1.32 52,500 @ $1.32	2,500 @ $1.32 55,000 @ $1.32

EXHIBIT 6-7
INTERCITY ASSEMBLY COMPANY, INC.
PRO FORMA CASH FLOW STATEMENT
FIFO WITH INFLATION

Month	1	2	3	4	5	6	7
RECEIPTS							
Sales Receipts	$ 74,000*	77,000*	80,000	**96,600**	**101,200**	**124,550**	**132,500**
Common Stock	—	175,000	—	—	—	—	—
Total Received	74,000	252,000	80,000	**96,600**	**101,200**	**124,550**	**132,500**
DISBURSEMENTS							
Direct Materials	40,000*	40,000	**51,750**	**51,750**	**66,000**	**72,600**	**72,600**
Direct Labor	4,000	4,200	4,400	4,700	5,000	5,300	5,500
Overhead	1,300	1,300	1,300	1,300	1,300	1,300	1,300
Manufacturing Equip.	—	180,000	—	—	—	—	—
Salaries	6,900	7,450	7,500	8,350	8,350	9,000	9,000
Rent	2,000	2,000	2,000	2,000	2,000	2,000	2,000
Insurance	6,000	—	—	—	—	—	—
Office Equipment	—	3,000	—	—	—	—	—
Other G&A	2,800*	3,000	4,100	4,550	5,500	6,600	7,050
Advertising	9,000*	9,750	9,800	10,200	11,000	11,600	12,500
Brochures	—	5,400	—	—	—	—	—
Taxes	11,000*	—	—	**14,465**	—	—	27,380
Total Disbursed	83,000	256,100	**80,850**	97,315	99,150	108,400	137,330
Total Cash Flow	$ (9,000)	(4,100)	**(850)**	**(715)**	2,050	16,150	**(4,830)**
Beginning Balance	$ 1,100	(7,900)	(12,000)	**(12,850)**	**(13,565)**	**(11,515)**	4,635
Ending Balance	$ (7,900)	(12,000)	**(12,850)**	**(13,565)**	**(11,515)**	4,635	**(195)**

*From operations during prior periods.

EXHIBIT 6-8
INTERCITY ASSEMBLY COMPANY, INC.
REVISED PRO FORMA INCOME STATEMENT
LIFO WITH INFLATION

Month	1	2	3	4	5	6	7
REVENUE							
Units Sold	40,000	42,000	44,000	47,000	50,000	53,000	55,000
Sales	$ 80,000	**96,600**	**101,200**	**124,550**	**132,500**	**140,450**	**145,750**
EXPENSE							
Direct Materials	40,000	**48,300**	**50,600**	**62,040**	**66,000**	**69,960**	**72,600**
Direct Labor	4,000	4,200	4,400	4,700	5,000	5,300	5,500
Overhead	4,000	4,000	4,000	4,000	4,000	4,000	4,000
Cost of Goods Sold	48,000	**56,500**	**59,000**	**70,740**	**75,000**	**79,260**	**82,100**
Gross Profit	32,000	**40,100**	**42,200**	**53,810**	**57,500**	**61,190**	**63,650**
General & Administrative							
Salaries	6,900	7,450	7,500	8,350	8,350	9,000	9,000
Rent	2,000	2,000	2,000	2,000	2,000	2,000	2,000
Insurance	500	500	500	500	500	500	500
Depreciation	170	170	170	170	170	170	170
Other G&A	3,000	4,100	4,550	5,500	6,600	7,050	7,850
Marketing							
Advertising	9,750	9,800	10,200	11,000	11,600	12,500	13,000
Brochures	450	450	450	450	450	450	450
Total Expense	70,770	**80,970**	**84,370**	**98,710**	**104,670**	**110,930**	**115,070**
Taxable Income	9,230	**15,630**	**16,830**	**25,840**	**27,830**	**29,520**	**30,680**
Income Taxes	2,769	**4,689**	**5,049**	**7,752**	**8,349**	**8,856**	**9,204**
Net Profit	6,461	**10,941**	**11,781**	**18,088**	**19,481**	**20,664**	**21,476**

EXHIBIT 6-9
INTERCITY ASSEMBLY COMPANY, INC.
DIRECT MATERIALS FLOW SCHEDULE

Month	Beginning Inventory	Purchases Received	Inventory Avail. for Shipment (LIFO)	Shipments (LIFO)	Ending Inventory (LIFO)
1	43,500 @ $1.00	40,000 @ $1.00	43,500 @ $1.00	40,000 @ $1.00	43,500 @ $1.00
			40,000 @ $1.00		
2 (15% Increase)	43,500 @ $1.00	45,000 @ $1.15	43,500 @ $1.00	42,000 @ $1.15	43,500 @ $1.00
			45,000 @ $1.15		3,000 @ $1.15
3	43,500 @ $1.00	45,000 @ $1.15	43,500 @ $1.00	44,000 @ $1.15	43,500 @ $1.00
	3,000 @ $1.15		3,000 @ $1.15		3,000 @ $1.15
			45,000 @ $1.15		1,000 @ $1.15
4 (15% Increase)	43,500 @ $1.00	50,000 @ $1.32	43,500 @ $1.00	47,000 @ $1.32	43,500 @ $1.00
	3,000 @ $1.15		3,000 @ $1.15		3,000 @ $1.15
	1,000 @ $1.15		1,000 @ $1.15		1,000 @ $1.15
			50,000 @ $1.32		3,000 @ $1.32
5	43,500 @ $1.00	55,000 @ $1.32	43,500 @ $1.00	50,000 @ $1.32	43,500 @ $1.00
	3,000 @ $1.15		3,000 @ $1.15		3,000 @ $1.15
	1,000 @ $1.15		1,000 @ $1.15		1,000 @ $1.15
	3,000 @ $1.32		3,000 @ $1.32		3,000 @ $1.32
			55,000 @ $1.32		5,000 @ $1.32
6	43,500 @ $1.00	55,000 @ $1.32	43,500 @ $1.00	53,000 @ $1.32	43,500 @ $1.00
	3,000 @ $1.15		3,000 @ $1.15		3,000 @ $1.15
	1,000 @ $1.15		1,000 @ $1.15		1,000 @ $1.15
	3,000 @ $1.32		3,000 @ $1.32		3,000 @ $1.32
	5,000 @ $1.32		5,000 @ $1.32		5,000 @ $1.32
			55,000 @ $1.32		2,000 @ $1.32
7	43,500 @ $1.00	55,000 @ $1.32	43,500 @ $1.00	55,000 @ $1.32	43,500 @ $1.00
	3,000 @ $1.15		3,000 @ $1.15		3,000 @ $1.15
	1,000 @ $1.15		1,000 @ $1.15		1,000 @ $1.15
	3,000 @ $1.32		3,000 @ $1.32		3,000 @ $1.32
	5,000 @ $1.32		5,000 @ $1.32		5,000 @ $1.32
	2,000 @ $1.32		2,000 @ $1.32		2,000 @ $1.32
			55,000 @ $1.32		

Exhibit 6-9 also provides the information to calculate what disbursements must be made for materials purchased and received. This allows recalculation of the pro forma cash flow forecast. The revised cash flow forecast for Intercity Assembly Company, utilizing the last-in-first-out method, is represented in Exhibit 6-10.

A comparison of the operating results for Intercity with the given inflation scenario is shown in Exhibit 6-11.

This exhibit graphically illustrates the classic trade-off presented by the LIFO/FIFO option. Profits under FIFO are significantly better. The bank balance under LIFO, however, is the more attractive. From a liquidity point of view, the company is approximately $4,381 better off down at the bank in Month 7 if it elects the LIFO method. Reported net profit after tax, however, will not be as attractive using the LIFO method.

It is interesting to consider the fact that approximately $4,381 in additional, real, spendable cash exists in the bank account at the end of Month 7, and the only thing done differently is that the bookkeeper for Intercity recognizes the expense of materials in a slightly different fashion, merely the modification of a paper transaction. Some owner-managers refer to this phenomenon as manufacturing money without a printing press.

EXHIBIT 6-10
INTERCITY ASSEMBLY COMPANY, INC.
PRO FORMA CASH FLOW STATEMENT
LIFO WITH INFLATION

Month	1	2	3	4	5	6	7
RECEIPTS							
Sales Receipts	$ 74,000*	77,000*	80,000	**96,600**	101,200	124,550	132,500
Common Stock	—	175,000	—	—	—	—	—
Total Received	74,000	252,000	80,000	**96,600**	101,200	124,550	132,500
DISBURSEMENTS							
Direct Materials	40,000*	40,000	**51,750**	51,750	66,000	72,600	72,600
Direct Labor	4,000	4,200	4,400	4,700	5,000	5,300	5,500
Overhead	1,300	1,300	1,300	1,300	1,300	1,300	1,300
Manufacturing Equip.	—	180,000	—	—	—	—	—
Salaries	6,900	7,450	7,500	8,350	8,350	9,000	9,000
Rent	2,000	2,000	2,000	2,000	2,000	2,000	2,000
Insurance	6,000	—	—	—	—	—	—
Office Equipment	—	3,000	—	—	—	—	—
Other G&A	2,800*	3,000	4,100	4,550	5,500	6,600	7,050
Advertising	9,000*	9,750	9,800	10,200	11,000	11,600	12,500
Brochures	—	5,400	—	—	—	—	—
Taxes	11,000*	—	—	12,507	—	—	24,957
Total Disbursed	83,000	256,100	**80,850**	95,357	99,150	108,400	134,907
Total Cash Flow	$ (9,000)	(4,100)	**(850)**	1,243	2,050	16,150	(2,407)
Beginning Balance	$ 1,100	(7,900)	(12,000)	**(12,850)**	**(11,607)**	**(9,557)**	6,593
Ending Balance	$ (7,900)	(12,000)	**(12,850)**	**(11,607)**	**(9,557)**	6,593	4,186

*From operations during prior periods.

EXHIBIT 6-11
GRAPH COMPARING OPERATING RESULTS IN A COMPANY ELECTING
LIFO VS. FIFO

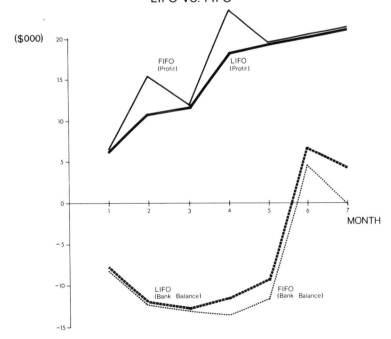

NOTES FOR CHAPTER 6

[1]C. R. Niswonger and P. E. Fess, *Accounting Principles* (Cincinnati: South-Western Publishing Company, 1965), p. 236.

[2]James D. Edwards and Homer A. Black, *The Modern Accountant's Handbook* (Homewood, Illinois: Dow Jones-Irwin, 1976), p. 113.

[3]*Federal Tax Handbook*, (Englewood Cliffs: Prentice-Hall, Inc., 1978), p. 359.

[4]Niswonger, p. 238.

[5]Robert N. Anthony, *Management Accounting* (Homewood, Illinois: Richard D. Irwin, Inc., 1970), p. 231.

[6]John A. Welsh and Jerry F. White, *Profit and Cash Flow for Non-Financial Managers*, 1974, p. 24.

[7]Ibid.

[8]Ibid.

[9]Welsh, p. 23.

[10]Ibid.

[11]Welsh, p. 25.

[12]Ibid.

A Special Approach for Boosting
Cash Flow and Bank Balances for
Closely Held Enterprises

"The profit and cash flow game" implies that there is an overall game involving both of these vital quantities. That is true; there is. It may not seem evident that there is a "big picture" business strategy that links two such dissimilar quantities.

PROFIT AND CASH FLOW ARE DIFFERENT

The forecasted income statement and forecasted cash flow statement in Exhibits 1-5 and 1-6, respectively, as well as those that were utilized extensively in Chapters 2 through 6, are consistent with regard to one very obvious point.

PROFIT IS NOT CASH FLOW

As Chapter 1 also pointed out, neither one of these quantities can be reliably deduced from the other by any simple rule of thumb such as cash flow equals net profit plus depreciation.

If these two quantities are so dramatically different, then it stands to reason that the way you manage to bring about improvement in profit will be different from the way you manage to enhance cash flow.

PLAYING THE PROFIT GAME

Most people instinctively understand how to play the "profit game." Since profit is defined as the difference between revenues and expenses for a particular period of time, the obvious approach is to increase revenues whenever possible and simultaneously decrease expenses when feasible. The spread between revenues and expenses will be reflected in the quantity referred to as profit. This general principle is illustrated symbolically in the diagram in Exhibit 7-1.

The "profit game" is a game of magnitudes of numbers. The strategy is to generate larger numbers in the category referred to as revenues and smaller numbers in the category referred to as expenses. This increases profit and, hence, contributes to winning the game. Focusing on magnitudes of numbers, however, is not the fundamental approach for playing the "cash flow game."

EXHIBIT 7-1
DIAGRAM DEMONSTRATING THE BASIC PRINCIPLE
FOR PLAYING THE PROFIT GAME

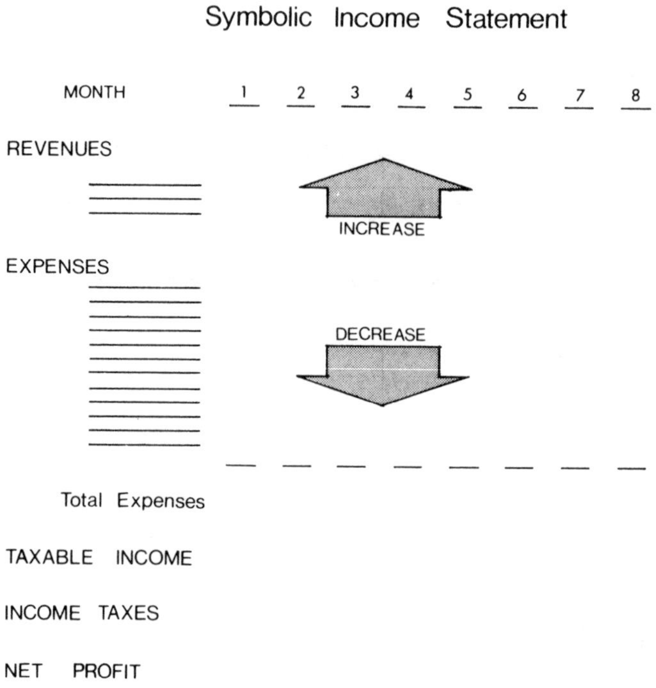

Symbolic   Income   Statement

MONTH	1	2	3	4	5	6	7	8

REVENUES

INCREASE

EXPENSES

DECREASE

Total Expenses

TAXABLE   INCOME

INCOME   TAXES

NET   PROFIT

PLAYING THE CASH FLOW GAME

The "cash flow game" is primarily one of timing. The basic strategy is to identify those transactions called receipts and make them happen faster. In addition, identify those transactions referred to as disbursements and make them happen slower. Faster receipts and slower disbursements represent the fundamental approach to winning the "cash flow game." This approach is symbolically illustrated in the diagram in Exhibit 7-2.

There are practical limits as to how long various disbursements can be delayed. Playing that part of the game too well is called "out of business." Nevertheless, the opportunities to negotiate faster receipts and slower disbursements are virtually limitless.

Case in Point

A closely held chemicals manufacturing company with $600,000 in annual sales was reported to be 60 days away from bankruptcy. Quality control and product rejection problems had created such operating losses that company financial resources were exhausted. Private investors, banks and financing companies no longer represented realistic sources of funds. Management believed it had about solved the technical problems associated with the product. The president had no idea, however, where to turn to procure the operating capital needed to survive an additional 60 to 90 days while resolving the technical problems.

EXHIBIT 7-2
DIAGRAM DEMONSTRATING THE BASIC PRINCIPLE
FOR PLAYING THE CASH FLOW GAME

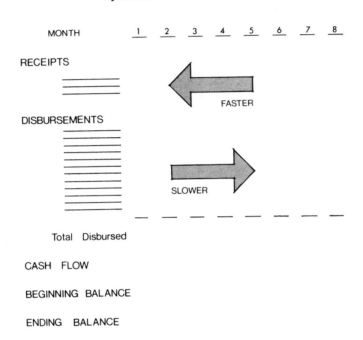

Symbolic Cash Flow Statement

Upon investigation, it was learned that the owner-manager took all the 10-day cash discounts offered by suppliers. In addition, the average age of the accounts receivable was 74 days. He wanted to keep the cost of materials low by taking discounts and he wanted to insure customer good will by not bothering them with collection activities.

By getting the owner-manager to discontinue taking cash discounts for several months (as well as riding the suppliers to 60 days) and by instituting a vigorous accounts receivable collection program that reduced the average age to 46 days, enough cash was generated to buy the time needed to resolve the technical problems. Today that company is growing rapidly and is very profitable. Faster receivables and slower payables were the keys to survival for this closely held business.

To demonstrate the application of this fundamental cash flow management tactic, it is helpful to focus on the most critical receipt and disbursement transactions. In any given business, the most critical receipts and the most critical disbursements are, when considered simultaneously, referred to by the authors as the critical receipts and disbursements module (CRDM).

The CRDM Approach

There is an old saying among owner-managers that business is governed by the "eighty/twenty" rule. For example, 80% of the sales comes from 20% of the customers, 80% of the expense dollars comes from 20% of the expense items or 80% of the total shipments comes from 20% of the product line. Among the many receipt and disbursement transactions influencing cash flow, it would seem reasonable that a small number of critical ones tends to dominate, perhaps in agreement with the eighty/twenty rule. Consequently, a focus on the critical receipts and disbursements group or module (CRDM) of transactions should prove beneficial, especially from the "big picture" point of view.

To illustrate the CRDM approach, consider the critical receipts and disbursements (usually the largest or most dominant ones) for a retail business, a service business and a contracting business.

How a Retail Business Can Play the Cash Flow Game

Consider a retail business that sells $1,000 of merchandise. The owner-manager might decide that the critical receipt is from sales to the customer and the critical disbursement is to the merchandise supplier. Suppose that as an average, one-half of the sales are for cash and one-half of the sales are on credit, paid for in 30 days. If merchandise is received an average of two months prior to the month of the sale, and paid for 30 days after receipt of the merchandise, the CRDM cash flow shown in Exhibit 7-3 would result.

EXHIBIT 7-3

Profit and Cash Flow Charts for Examining
the Critical Receipts & Disbursements Module (CRDM)
for a Retail Business

	CRDM Income Statement					CRDM Cash Flow Statement				
Month	1	2	3		Month	1	2	3	4
REVENUES	$			1,000	RECEIPTS					
EXPENSES					Sales	$			500	500
Merchandise				600	DISBURSEMENTS					
					Merchandise		x ------- 600			
CRDM Contribution	$			400	CRDM Cash Flow			(600)	500	500
					Cumulative CRDM Cash Flow*	$		(600)	(100)	400

*As of the end of each month.

As may be seen, $1,000 in sales occurring in Month 3 would yield a $400 CRDM contribution on the CRDM Income Statement. But the resulting combination of receipts and disbursements portrayed on the CRDM Cash Flow Statement creates a severe negative cash flow the month prior to the month of sale, and creates cumulative CRDM cash flow deficits for two months, Month 2 and Month 3. A nice gain of $400 (before other expenses) is realized from an income point of view but cumulative cash flow problems are created by this series of events. In an effort to improve the CRDM cash flow, suppose the retailer pays a 1% late payment penalty to the merchandise supplier for the right to pay 30 days late. The resulting improvement in cash flow is demonstrated in Exhibit 7-4.

EXHIBIT 7-4

Cash Flow Chart for Examining
the Critical Receipts & Disbursements Module (CRDM)
for a Retail Business
Paying a 1% Late Penalty
To Merchandise Supplier

	Month	1	2	3	4
RECEIPTS					
Sales	$			500	500
DISBURSEMENTS					
Merchandise		x---------•→		606	
CRDM Cash Flow				(106)	500
Cumulative CRDM Cash Flow*	$			(106)	394

*As of the end of each month.

By slowing down the critical disbursements for one additional month, even with a 1% penalty, the maximum cumulative cash flow deficit is reduced by almost $500. Suppose that the retailer then attempts to accelerate collection of the critical receipts from sales. By switching to the utilization of credit cards rather than charge accounts, the customer's money can be received in the month of sale, Month 3. There would be a nominal charge, perhaps 4%, by the bank for sales using charge cards, such as Mastercharge and Visa. While some profit may have to be relinquished, this particular retailer will succeed in eliminating cumulative CRDM cash flow deficits as shown in Exhibit 7-5. For this retailer, who is desiring to improve cash flow, the CRDM approach suggests a very meaningful strategy.

How a Service Business Can Play the Cash Flow Game

The owner-manager of a professional service business, such as a consulting company, might logically conclude that the critical receipt comes from sales to the company's clients and the critical disbursement results from salaries to a group of well-paid professionals. If payment is received from the customers in an average of 60 days after they are invoiced, and if the employees must be paid within the same month the work was invoiced, the critical receipts and disbursements module portrayed in Exhibit 7-6 results.

EXHIBIT 7-5
Cash Flow Chart for Examining
the Critical Receipts & Disbursements Module (CRDM)
for a Retail Business
Using Credit Cards instead of Charge Accounts and
Paying a 1% Penalty to Merchandise Supplier

Month	1	2	3	4
RECEIPTS				
Sales	$		500	
DISBURSEMENTS			480	
Merchandise		x --------- • ——►	606	
CRDM Cash Flow			374	
Cumulative CRDM Cash Flow*	$		374	

*As of the end of each month.

EXHIBIT 7-6
Profit and Cash Flow Charts for Examining
the Critical Receipts & Disbursements Module (CRDM)
for a Professional Service Business

CRDM Income Statement				CRDM Cash Flow Statement				
Month	1	2	3	Month	1	2	3	4
REVENUES	$	1,000		RECEIPTS				
EXPENSES				Sales	$	x----------- 1,000		
Salaries		700		DISBURSEMENTS				
				Salaries		700		
CRDM Contribution	$	300		CRDM Cash Flow		(700)	—	1,000
				Cumulative CRDM Cash Flow*	$	(700)	(700)	300

*As of the end of each month.

This scheme of receipts and disbursements creates severe cumulative CRDM cash flow problems. While a $300 gain does eventually result, a cash flow deficit of $700 occurs during the month of the sale and in the following month. That is, $700 for 60 days for every $1,000 of professional services invoiced.

If the manager factors one-half of the accounts receivable (i.e., sells one-half of the invoices to a factoring organization) at a cost of 5% of the invoice amount, the severity of the cumulative CRDM cash flow deficit can be reduced from $700 for 60 days to $225 for 60 days as shown in Exhibit 7-7. If, in addition to factoring one-half of the accounts receivable, the

EXHIBIT 7-7
Cash Flow Chart for Examining
the Critical Receipts & Disbursements Module (CRDM)
for a Professional Service Business
That Factors ½ of Its Accounts Receivable
at a Cost of 5% of Invoice Amount

Month	1	2	3	4
RECEIPTS				
Sales	$	475	⟵	500
DISBURSEMENTS				
Salaries		700		
CRDM Cash Flow		(225)	—	500
Cumulative CRDM Cash Flow*	$	(225)	(225)	275

*As of the end of each month.

owner-manager of this professional service business elects to utilize contract labor for one-half of the work performed, then payment to the contract professionals might be delayed or negotiated on a 30-day basis. This possibility is reflected in the chart in Exhibit 7-8.

EXHIBIT 7-8
Cash Flow Chart for Examining
the Critical Receipts & Disbursements Module (CRDM)
for a Professional Service Business
That Uses Contract Professionals for ½ Its Work
and Also Factors ½ of Its Accounts Receivable

Month	1	2	3	4
RECEIPTS				
Sales	$	475	⟵	500
DISBURSEMENTS				
Salaries		350 ⟶	350	
CRDM Cash Flow		125	(350)	500
Cumulative CRDM Cash Flow*	$	125	(225)	275

*As of the end of each month.

The combination of factoring one-half of the accounts receivable together with the utilization of subcontract professionals could reduce the cumulative CRDM cash flow deficit to $225 for only 30 days per $1,000 in services invoiced. It is easy to imagine that by factoring a larger percent of the accounts receivable or by subcontracting a larger percent of the company's business, the cumulative CRDM cash flow deficit could be reduced still further. It is not uncommon, for example, to pay independent professionals 60 days after they perform their services.

How a Contracting Business Can Play the Cash Flow Game

Consider a contracting business whose owner-manager determines that the critical receipts come from sales and the critical disbursements are related to materials and labor. The CRDM Income Statement and Cash Flow Statement of Exhibit 7-9 reflect sales receipts that are collected an average of 60 days after the invoice is sent to the customer, materials that are received the month the invoice is sent and paid for on a net 30-day basis, and labor that is paid in the month the work is invoiced to the customer.

As indicated in Exhibit 7-9, this scheme of CRDM receipts and disbursements results in severe negative, cumulative CRDM cash flow. Each $1,000 in sales creates a maximum cash deficit of $600 in the month following the month of the sale. To improve this situation, suppose

EXHIBIT 7-9
Profit and Cash Flow Charts for Examining
the Critical Receipts & Disbursements Module (CRDM)
for a Contracting Business

	CRDM Income Statement				CRDM Cash Flow Statement				
Month	1	2	3		Month	1	2	3	4
REVENUES	$	1,000		RECEIPTS					
EXPENSES				Sales	$	x ----------- 1,000			
Materials		300		DISBURSEMENTS					
Labor		300		Materials			x ----- 300		
				Labor		300			
CRDM Profit	$	400		CRDM Cash Flow			(300)	(300)	1,000
				Cumulative CRDM Cash Flow*	$		(300)	(600)	400

*As of the end of each month.

the manager reviews the impact of much stricter collections practices. If one-half of the accounts receivable are collected in 30 days and the other half in 60 days, the CRDM cash flow picture improves substantially as seen in Exhibit 7-10. The maximum cumulative CRDM cash flow deficit is reduced from $600 to $300.

If the owner-manager also negotiates 60-day payment terms with one-half of the materials suppliers by agreeing to pay a 1% late payment penalty and utilizes one-third contract labor that can be paid 30 days after the work is performed, then even with a 10% higher cost for that portion of the labor contracted, the CRDM cash flow picture is improved. This additional delay in paying the materials supplier combined with utilizing some contract labor yields the improved performance indicated in Exhibit 7-11.

EXHIBIT 7-10
Cash Flow Chart for Examining
the Critical Receipts & Disbursements Module (CRDM)
for a Contracting Business
That Improves its Collections

Month	1	2	3	4
RECEIPTS				
Sales	$		500 ◄── 500	
DISBURSEMENTS				
Materials		x ──────── 300		
Labor		300		
CRDM Cash Flow		(300)	200	500
Cumulative CRDM Cash Flow*	$	(300)	(100)	400

*As of the end of each month.

EXHIBIT 7-11
Cash Flow Chart for Examining
the Critical Receipts & Disbursements Module (CRDM)
for a Contracting Business
That Utilizes ⅓ Contract Labor,
Delays Paying Materials Supplier for 30 Days
with a 1% Penalty
and Also Improves Collections

Month	1	2	3	4
RECEIPTS				
Sales	$		500 ◄── 500	
DISBURSEMENTS				
Materials		x ───── 150 ──► 152		
Labor		200 ──► 110		
CRDM Cash Flow		(200)	240	348
Cumulative CRDM Cash Flow*	$	(200)	40	388

*As of the end of each month.

Through this series of ploys, the maximum cumulative CRDM cash flow deficit is further reduced by a third from $300 per $1,000 of sales to only $200 per $1,000 of sales. If, in addition to these techniques, the owner-manager institutes a 5% discount for all deposits in advance of the starting of work, the picture can be improved still further. Suppose an average of 20% of a contract job can be collected prior to the starting of work. A greatly improved cash flow picture emerges as demonstrated in Exhibit 7-12.

What was initially a $600 maximum cumulative CRDM cash flow deficit for each $1,000 in sales now becomes only a $10 maximum cumulative CRDM cash flow deficit. Obviously, the impact on this contracting business' liquidity is profound. While some real scheming and hard negotiation may be involved in implementing these CRDM techniques, the payoff could be well worth the effort.

EXHIBIT 7-12
Cash Flow Chart for Examining
the Critical Receipts & Disbursements Module (CRDM)
for a Contracting Business
That Negotiates 20% Advance Deposits,
Utilizes ⅓ Contract Labor,
Delays Paying Materials Supplier
and Also Improves Collection

	Month	1	2	3	4
RECEIPTS					
Sales		$190	◄———	400 ◄—	400
DISBURSEMENTS					
Materials			x -----	150 ——►	152
Labor			200 ——►	110	
CRDM Cash Flow		190	(200)	140	248
Cumulative CRDM Cash Flow*		$190	(10)	130	378

*As of the end of each month.

Caveat: A Limitation of the CRDM Approach

The CRDM approach is not a final decision technique since it does not consider all the detailed ramifications of major management decisions. The result of CRDM "scheming" should be subjected to additional examination. The CRDM's value lies in its being a simple and practical working and planning tool to formulate initial profit and cash flow management strategies. The CRDM yields concepts and approximations that may be later refined with detailed calculations.

Once a desired critical receipts and disbursements policy has been evolved using the CRDM approach, it may be further evaluated using the Welsh-White Profit and Cash Flow Technique.

THE WELSH-WHITE PROFIT AND CASH FLOW TECHNIQUE

The profit and cash flow game implies a consideration beyond merely maximizing profit or maximizing cash flow. Since a management decision that improves profit usually affects cash flow adversely, and one that improves cash flow frequently is detrimental to profit, the effective owner-manager will simultaneously consider the impact of a given decision on both profit and cash flow. Skillful maneuvering to favorably influence both profit and cash flow is "playing the profit and cash flow game."

After working with numerous owner-managers, the authors have evolved a simple approach that has been found to be very effective.

The Technique

The Welsh-White technique is to first prepare a month-by-month accrual-basis income forecast and a counterpart receipts and disbursements cash flow forecast for the business in question, similar to that illustrated in Exhibits 1-5 and 1-6. A time period of 6 to 24 months into the future (depending on the nature of the business) is usually adequate.

Next, reflect in that forecast a proposed management decision that is under consideration. Re-calculate the net profit and the forecasted bank balances and record for future reference. Repeat the process for each major management decision being contemplated.

For those who like to use the old tired refrain, "But you can't forecast in my business," we contend that you can. While no one has a perfect crystal ball, a workable forecast suitable for evaluating management alternatives is feasible for every business we have ever examined.

The Decision Criteria

The recommended series of management decisions, from a profit and cash flow point of view, will be the combination that generates the most profit while *simultaneously* maintaining a comfortable liquidity (bank balance).

Profit and cash flow are, of course, not the only criteria in financial decision making. Conscientious application of this technique before decisions are made, however, will eliminate many of the common problems which threaten the survival and prosperity of closely held businesses.

$$8$$

Approaches to Cutting the Company's Taxes Versus the Owner - Manager's Taxes

Successful owner-managers commonly share the same feeling, "I work night and day in the face of enormous adversity to create something, and then I end up paying it out in taxes." Regardless of how one feels, taxes are a fact and they cannot be avoided. Within the rules, however, there are numerous ways to lighten the burden.

Before discussing tax minimization, several major considerations should be kept in mind. First, tax laws are constantly changing. An apparently endless shopping list of social and economic goals are continually in front of lawmakers, and they often respond to these through the tax laws. Evidence of this constant change was reflected by the prominent notice on the cover of the 1977 and 1978 Federal Income Tax Form for individuals (See Exhibit 8-1).

Another consideration is that the Internal Revenue Service is interested in substance rather than form. If, for example, one establishes a corporation with a view to being taxed at the corporate rate but, in fact, behaves as a sole proprietor, the Internal Revenue Service will look beyond the form of the corporation and will levy a tax rate based on the proprietorship, that is the substance organization.

Still another consideration is that the owner-manager, generally speaking, is not a tax specialist. The amount of time devoted to making sales, delivering the product or the service, and responding to the myriad of daily interruptions makes it virtually impossible for the owner-manager to devote the time necessary to understand the fine nuances and the esoteric elements of the vast and ever-changing set of tax laws.

The final major consideration is that there is no "*the* method" for minimizing taxes. In any given business, the method, or combination of tactics selected, will reflect one's personal goals and the goals for the business.

This chapter is primarily concerned with minimizing income taxes but it will also address other tax areas when appropriate. The objective is to point out some of the more significant, time-proven techniques and to suggest a systematized approach to thinking about the problem. An explanation of the techniques will be followed by comments regarding advantages, disadvantages and pay-offs when relevant. One should then be able to make a few major decisions regarding the tactics to be used in a personally tailored game plan.

EXHIBIT 8-1
EXAMPLE OF CHANGING TAX LAWS

1977 Federal Income
Tax Forms

Watch for Tax Law Changes

At the time Form 1040 and instructions were printed, Congress was considering legislation that would allow credits for energy saving expenses for your personal residence. We have set aside lines 45 and 61a on Form 1040 for these credits. If this legislation is passed, we will do our best to tell you about it in radio, television and newspaper announcements. Please watch for this information which will also tell you about the energy credit form and instructions.

1978
Federal Income
Tax
Forms

Tax Law Changes

Congress recently enacted legislation that allows credits for energy saving expenses for your personal residence. Line 45 of Form 1040 should be used to claim these credits. Congress also enacted legislation that, among other things, raises the capital gains exclusion starting November 1, 1978, and changes the treatment of the sale of a personal residence for individuals 55 and over. These changes are reflected in the 1978 forms and instructions. See the Highlights on page 3 for more information.

THE BASIC TAX PRINCIPLE

In its simplest form, the calculation of taxes to be paid is:

$$\text{TAXABLE AMOUNT} \times \text{TAX RATE} = \text{TAX DUE}.$$

If one wishes to minimize the TAX DUE, there are two prominent variables to focus on, the TAXABLE AMOUNT and the TAX RATE. A reduction of either one or both of these will reduce the TAX DUE. Also, there are opportunities to reduce the TAX DUE directly by taking advantage of certain credits and avoiding specific penalties. The approach will be to consider strategies and techniques to reduce TAXABLE INCOME, TAX RATE and TAX DUE, respectively.

REDUCING THE TAXABLE AMOUNT (INCOME TAX)

Five major strategies will be discussed. They will be generally referred to as Postponement, Creative Spending, Consumption, Benevolence and Philanthrophy.

Postponement

Postponement refers to delaying taxes directly, or indirectly, to a subsequent fiscal year. The motive of the owner-manager is the anticipation that perhaps the business or the individual will be in a more favorable tax posture at some future period. For many managers this simply means not paying the taxes this year. They frequently feel, "This gives me another year to figure out something else." This strategy is fine with the Internal Revenue Service, because taxes that aren't paid this year must be paid in a subsequent year.

The following discussion explains several techniques that may be used to effect postponement of taxes.

ACCELERATED DEPRECIATION

Accelerated depreciation is discussed in detail in Chapter 5 as a profit and cash flow management device. Here, accelerated depreciation is examined as a technique for reducing the taxable income in a particular year by postponement to a subsequent year.

The total amount of depreciation that can be taken on an asset depends upon the cost of the asset. Within limits, it is immaterial to the Internal Revenue Service whether one uses up most of the depreciation in the early years, as with accelerated depreciation, or spreads this expense out in equal amounts over the useful life of the asset. Obviously, the large portion of depreciation that is expensed (deducted) in the early years of a given asset using accelerated depreciation is not available for deduction in subsequent years.

Depreciation is an expense of doing business and it reduces profit. It is, also, a deductible expense and reduces taxable income. To illustrate, consider the following business engaged in tax planning for next year. With no purchases of new equipment, next year's forecast would be:

Projection for Next Year

Revenues	$200,000
Expenses	180,000
Pre-Tax Profit	20,000
Federal Income Tax (17%)°	3,400
Net Profit After Tax	$16,600

Suppose that the owner-manager of this business buys a truck (over-the-road tractor) next year for $18,000. For financial purposes, straight-line depreciation over four years with a 10% salvage value seems reasonable. For tax purposes, double-declining-balance depreciation is selected and a three-year useful life is chosen. The two different pictures of next year's operations are portrayed in the following projected income statements (operating and financing expenses related to ownership of the truck are not considered here):

°Assuming that this owner-manager forecasts the effective average tax rate for the year to be 17%.

Projected Income Statement Financial Purposes (for Banker, Stockholders, etc.)		Projected Income Statement Tax Purposes (for Internal Revenue Service)	
Revenues	$200,000	Revenues	$200,000
Expenses		Expenses	
Depreciation (S.L.)	4,050	Depreciation (D.D.B.)	12,000
All Other	180,000	All Other	180,000
Total Expenses	184,050	Total Expenses	192,000
Pre-Tax Profit	15,950	Taxable Income	8,000
Federal Income Tax (17%)	2,712	Federal Income Tax (17%)	1,360
Net Profit After Tax	$13,238	Net Income	$ 6,640

With no new depreciation the Federal income tax paid would be $3,400 (preceding example). The new straight-line depreciation associated with the truck in the above example reduces the projected income tax to be paid to $2,712. The double-declining-balance depreciation with a larger deduction lowers the projected income tax to $1,360. The difference between $1,360 and $2,712, amounting to $1,352, represents income tax postponed to subsequent years by the difference in the two depreciation methods.

Pursuing this further, the amount of tax saved next year by the straight-line depreciation associated with the proposed new asset is $3,400 minus $2,712, or $688. Dividing $688 by 18, the Federal income tax saved per $1,000 of asset cost is determined to be $38 (using a four-year useful life and a 10% salvage value). Likewise, the double-declining-balance depreciation associated with the truck saves $3,400 minus $1,360, or $2,040. Dividing $2,040 by 18, gives $113 in Federal income tax saved per $1,000 of asset cost when a three-year useful life is selected and this accelerated depreciation method is employed.

If a variety of useful lives are examined and alternative depreciation methods are considered, a family of curves emerges for the first-year tax saved versus the asset useful life selected. Three families of curves for each of the common depreciation methods: straight-line, double-declining-balance, and sum of the years-digits are presented in Figure 8-2.

This chart can be very useful to the owner-manager for tax-planning purposes. Think about the depreciable assets that your business might effectively utilize, estimate the tax bracket you are likely to be in, then refer to Figure 8-2 to see which useful-life and depreciation method will give the desired first-year tax saving. Use the curves for both financial planning and tax planning purposes.

There is one additional aspect to this chart. The straight-line and sum of the years-digits families of curves assume a salvage value of zero. If a salvage value of 15% is desired, for example, just read from the graph the first-year tax saved for the elected depreciation method and useful life. Now, reduce the amount of tax saved (from the chart) by the same percentage as that selected for the salvage value, in this case, 15%. In a like manner, the amount of tax saved by the straight-line or sum of the years-digits method for any desired salvage value can be determined. Salvage value is not a consideration at this point with the double-declining-balance method.

INVESTMENT TAX CREDIT

While tax credits in general are discussed later in this chapter under the section entitled, "Reducing Taxes Due (Directly)," the investment tax credit is reviewed here because it is integrally linked to the preceding topic of depreciation. The asset useful life selected for tax purposes is the one that must be used for determining the amount of investment tax credit for which one qualifies.

A description of the investment tax credit and its ramifications as a profit and cash flow management tool was presented in Chapter 5. It will be examined here from a tax reduction point of view.

While this credit has been occasionally changed, it is generally in the range of 10% of the purchase price of the asset. For a selected useful life of at least three, but less than five years, one is eligible for one-third of the investment tax credit on qualifying property. For a useful life of at least five years, but less than seven years, two-thirds of the investment tax credit is available. Finally, for a useful life of seven years or greater, the full investment tax credit is available.

EXHIBIT 8-2
FIRST YEAR TAX SAVED VS. ASSET USEFUL LIFE SELECTED FOR THREE
DEPRECIATION METHODS AND FOR 15%, 45% AND 70% EFFECTIVE TAX
BRACKETS

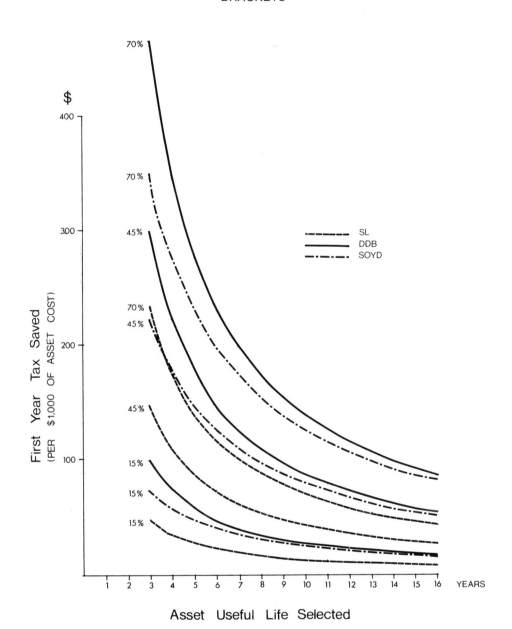

Asset Useful Life Selected

As was mentioned in Chapter 5, the investment tax credit is not a deductible expense. It is a credit directly applied to one's tax bill. Consequently, it is not a function of one's tax bracket.

The graph in Figure 8-3 illustrates the tax saved during the year of purchase (per $1,000 of asset cost) for various asset useful lives. The greatest incentive is obviously for long life assets such as major manufacturing equipment, locomotives and petroleum exploration equipment.

Consider what is implied when Exhibit 8-2 is viewed in relation to Exhibit 8-3. Depreciation yields the greatest first year tax savings when a shorter useful life is selected;

EXHIBIT 8-3
TAX SAVED VS. ASSET USEFUL LIFE SELECTED FOR
INVESTMENT TAX CREDIT

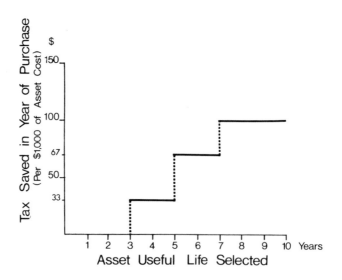

investment tax credit yields the greatest tax savings when a longer useful life is selected. The owner-manager is, therefore, in a trade-off situation regarding useful life selected. The matter is further complicated because tax benefits of depreciation depend not only on useful life, but also on the taxpayer's tax bracket.

To avoid the numerous calculations necessary for analyzing the trade-offs, you may refer to Exhibit 8-4. This exhibit portrays three families of curves for three common depreciation methods. Each family is calculated for three tax brackets. The curves are per $1,000 of asset cost and assume a salvage value of zero. Under these conditions the investment tax credit is the more dominant variable in low tax brackets, while accelerated depreciation is the more dominant variable in higher tax brackets.

LIFO INVENTORY COSTING

LIFO and FIFO principles were discussed in Chapter 6. The emphasis was on pros and cons and use as a profit and cash flow management device. Here the emphasis is on tax ramifications and dealings with the Internal Revenue Service.

LIFO application is made on Internal Revenue Service Form 970. Once adopted, this method must be continued unless the Revenue Service requires a change to another method, or, on application, authorizes such a change.[1]

LIFO represents a strategy for reducing the taxable income by postponement during inflationary periods when inventory costs are rising. Since the cost of the most recent unit (and,

EXHIBIT 8-4
FIRST YEAR TAX SAVED VS. ASSET USEFUL LIFE SELECTED FOR
DEPRECIATION AND INVESTMENT TAX CREDIT AND FOR 15%, 45% AND
70% EFFECTIVE TAX BRACKETS

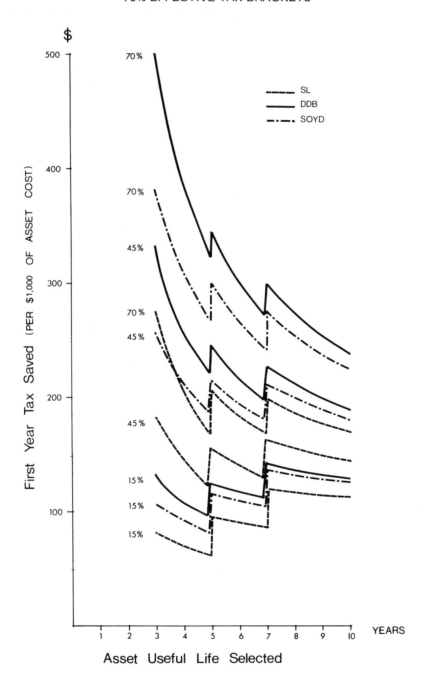

hence, the most expensive) is the one deducted, a bookkeeping increase in cost of goods sold occurs. This increase in a deductible expense reduces taxable income and, hence, Federal income tax. As pointed out in Chapter 6, LIFO works in reverse to increase tax paid during periods of deflation. Since the United States historically has had an inflationary trend, many managers believe that LIFO postpones a portion of the income tax indefinitely.[2]

LIFO was first used during the 1930s by some of the oil companies. The Revenue Act of 1938 authorized the use of LIFO for income tax purposes but only in specified and narrow cases. The Revenue Act of 1939 permitted any taxpayer to use LIFO but made it impractical for most companies. Finally, in 1948, a tax court case made the use of LIFO available to a wide variety of companies.[3]

To illustrate the tax reduction benefit of LIFO over FIFO, consider the example in Exhibit 8-5, adapted from Internal Revenue Service publication 334.

EXHIBIT 8-5.

Example of the Difference in Costing Inventory Under FIFO and LIFO.

"In tax year 1979 you have an opening inventory of 1,000 units of a commodity. This is comprised of:
500 units purchased in 1977 at $1.00 per unit
500 units purchased in 1978 at $1.50 per unit
In 1979, you purchased an additional 500 units as follows:
In February—200 units at $2.00 per unit
In July—300 units at $3.00 per unit
By the close of the tax year 1979, 1,250 units were sold leaving a closing inventory of 250 units."

COST OF GOODS SOLD UNDER
FIRST-IN-FIRST-OUT METHOD

Opening Inventory		
500 units @ $1.00	$500	
500 units @ $1.50	750	$1,250
Plus:		
Goods purchased during the year		
200 units @ $2.00	$400	
300 units @ $3.00	900	1,300
Cost of goods available for sale		$2,550
Less:		
Closing inventory (1,500 − 1,250 = 250)		
250 @ $3.00 (i.e., the last 250 units		
purchased remain in inventory)		750
Cost of goods sold		$1,800

COST OF GOODS SOLD UNDER
LAST-IN-FIRST-OUT METHOD

Opening Inventory (adjusted to average cost)		
1,000 units @ $1.25		$1,250.00
Plus:		
Goods purchased during the year		
200 @ $2.00	$400.00	
300 @ $3.00	900.00	1,300.00
Cost of goods available for sale		$2,550.00
Less:		
Closing inventory 250 units @ average cost		
of $1.25 per unit (i.e., units in opening		
inventory to the extent thereof, remain in		
inventory)		312.50
Cost of goods sold		$2,237.50

In this example the difference in deductible expenses (due to the difference of cost of goods sold) is $2,237.50 minus $1,800.00, or, $437.50. An indication of the amount of Federal income tax saved by the LIFO method in this example is indicated in the following table.

Increase in Deduction due to LIFO Method	Tax Bracket of Taxpayer	Tax Saved
$437.50	15%	$ 65.63
437.50	25%	109.38
437.50	40%	175.00
437.50	70%	306.25

The actual amount of tax saved, of course, depends on the tax bracket of the taxpayer.

Who Should Use LIFO

The importance of the method of inventory costing varies among companies. LIFO is an important consideration for companies where the following is true:[4]

1. Material costs constitute a relatively large part of total cost.
2. The inventory is comparatively large.
3. The manufacturing process is relatively long, which means there is a large "work in process" inventory.
4. Selling price is closely linked in a definite relationship to current cost.

Advantages and Disadvantages

There are many items that the owner-manager must consider before making the decision to implement the LIFO inventory costing method. Some advantages and disadvantages of LIFO are as follows:

Advantages: 1. Decreases income taxes through bookkeeping methodology in time of inflation.

2. Not only applicable to the entire inventory, but may also be used for a specific or selected part of the inventory.

Disadvantages: 1. Decreases reported profits from the stockholder's and creditor's point of view.[5]

2. Decreases value of inventory on the balance sheet which might be an important point when borrowing money against inventory.[6]

3. Increases TAX PAID in periods of deflation.

4. More accounting work frequently results when LIFO is used.

5. LIFO is based on cost and the marking down of inventory to the lower of cost or market is not allowed. Furthermore, the opening inventory for the first year that LIFO is used must be valued at actual cost regardless of market value. In this case the unit cost for an item is the average of the cost of all items, as if they were all bought at the same time at the same price.[7]

6. LIFO is not recognized by most other countries for income tax purposes. There is, therefore, a disadvantage when valuing foreign inventories.[8]

7. Distribution of LIFO inventory by a corporation to its shareholders may result in a taxable event.

8. When a taxpayer elects the LIFO method the Internal Revenue Service may also require that LIFO be used for similar goods of any other trade or business of the taxpayer.

Even though the number of disadvantages may appear to be greater than the number of advantages of LIFO, the decrease in taxes, due to the use of this method during periods of inflation, may outweigh all of the apparent disadvantages.

TAX SHELTERS

The pressure of Federal income taxes on the successful owner-manager is frequently perceived to be onerous. Consequently, finding a haven for hard-earned dollars has been an endless problem. The customary term used for investments that provide such a shield from income taxes for earned money is tax shelter.

EXHIBIT 8-6
TYPICAL TAX SHELTER PERFORMANCE

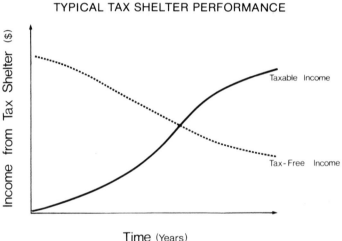

Tax shelters are commonly employed as a tax postponement strategy. The general concept is to create an investment situation where little or no taxable income is produced in the early years. Significant tax-free income (ideally in the form of spendable cash) should result, however. In addition, there should be the definite prospect of long-term appreciation of the investment itself. Hopefully, some or all of the long-term gains would be taxed at a more favorable rate (capital gains).

The income performance of a typical tax shelter is illustrated in Exhibit 8-6. Taxable income is low during the early years. Tax-free income on the other hand is high in the early years but tapers off as the mechanisms of the tax shelter are consumed.

It is important to point out that the quality tax shelter does not lose money. It should, in fact, result in a very favorable return on investment over time.

Tax Shelter Example

An example of a tax shelter is presented in Exhibit 8-7.[9]

An asset is purchased for $80,000 that has a useful life of seven years. This asset is projected to produce revenues over its useful life of $100,000 in Year 1 and increasing to $300,000 in Year 7.

EXHIBIT 8-7.
Example of a Tax Shelter
(in $000)

Year	1	2	3	4	5	6	7
Revenues	$100.0	150.0	200.0	225.0	250.0	275.0	300.0
Operating Expenses	68.0	102.0	136.0	153.0	170.0	187.0	204.0
Operating Income	32.0	48.0	64.0	72.0	80.0	88.0	96.0
Interest Paid	8.0	7.2	6.2	5.2	4.1	2.9	1.5
Income before Depreciation	24.0	40.8	57.8	66.8	75.9	85.1	94.5
Depreciation	22.9	16.3	11.7	8.3	6.0	4.3	3.0
Taxable Income	1.1	24.5	46.1	58.5	69.9	80.8	91.5
Tax Sheltered Income	$22.9	16.3	11.7	8.3	6.0	4.3	3.0

EXHIBIT 8-8
TABLE DEMONSTRATING INTEREST ON LOAN

LOAN $ **80,000.00**   RATE **10.000%**   PAYMENT $ **16,432.44**

TERMS: YEARS **7**   MONTHS   PERIODS **7**

PAYMENT NUMBER	PAYMENT		UNPAID BALANCE
	INTEREST	PRINCIPAL	
1	8,000.00	8,432.44	71,567.56
2	7,156.76	9,275.68	62,291.88
3	6,229.19	10,203.25	52,088.63
4	5,208.86	11,223.58	40,865.05
5	4,086.51	12,345.93	28,519.12
6	2,851.91	13,580.53	14,938.59
7	1,493.86	14,938.59	16,432.45**

The asset is purchased with debt utilizing a loan of $80,000 at 10% interest rate and payable in annual installments over seven years. The deductible interest payments are illustrated in Exhibit 8-8.

Double-declining-balance depreciation is elected using a seven-year useful life. A table demonstrating computation of the double-declining-balance depreciation is shown in Exhibit 8-9 (note that the rate of 28.57% is double the straight-line rate for seven years of 14.286%).

Hopefully, the revenues and the operating income increase over the life of the investment. The characteristics of interest and of double-declining-balance depreciation over the useful life of the asset are such that they decrease with time. Taxable income increases dramatically over time until in Year 7 it approaches operating income. The tax sheltered income, sometimes

EXHIBIT 8-9.

Table Computing Double-Declining-Balance Depreciation

Year	Cost	Accumulated Depreciation Beginning of Year	Book Value Beginning of Year	% Rate	Double-Declining-Balance Depreciation for the Year
1	$80,000	$ -0-	$80,000	28.57	$22,856
2	80,000	22,856	57,144	28.57	16,326
3	80,000	39,182	40,818	28.57	11,662
4	80,000	50,844	29,156	28.57	8,330
5	80,000	59,174	20,826	28.57	5,950
6	80,000	65,124	14,876	28.57	4,250
7	80,000	69,374	10,626	28.57	3,036

referred to as the tax free income, begins as a substantial amount in the early years and tapers off to a relatively low amount toward the end of the useful life of the asset involved in this investment. The common terminology, "tax sheltered income," results primarily from the depreciation utilized in the structuring of this particular investment. The depreciation in turn is merely a function of accounting practices and is determined by the desires of the investor. Depreciation, like amortization, is, in fact, a real expense of doing business but it is a non-cash expense. Depreciation and amortization are in that regard commonly considered a shelter for a portion of the taxable income. Some individuals also view the interest expense along with the depreciation as a part of the sheltering mechanism.

Tax Shelter Opportunities

Successful businesses and individuals have historically been very creative in designing and implementing tax shelters. A few of the popular investment situations that have been successfully utilized in the past are listed below:

1. Farming
2. Leasing personal property
3. Commercial feedlots
4. Orchards and vineyards
5. Income property
6. Exploring for or exploiting oil and gas resources
7. Real Estate
8. Holding, producing or distributing motion picture films and video tapes.
9. Certain Public stocks issuing dividends that represent non-taxable capital distributions.

Caution When Using Tax Shelters

Federal income tax laws are constantly changing and the goal of much recent legislation has been to reduce or eliminate many of the advantages of tax shelters. After designing or selecting a desirable tax shelter, run the proposed scheme by your tax professional, C.P.A., or attorney specializing in Federal income tax to make sure that it does not violate current tax rules.

ACCOUNTING MANEUVERS

There are several statements in Internal Revenue Service publication 334 that set the stage for accounting techniques with regard to income taxation:

1. "Taxable income must be computed on the basis of a fixed accounting period and in accordance with a set of rules to determine the time and manner of reporting income and deductions."
2. "A method of accounting is that set of rules under which one ascertains when and how to record income and expenses in the books and how to prepare the profit and loss statement for an accounting period."
3. "No particular method of accounting is prescribed for all taxpayers. Each must adopt a system that is best suited to the individual's purpose and one that will clearly reflect income."
4. "One must be consistent from year to year and compute taxable income in accordance with the method of accounting regularly used in keeping the books."

Within this framework there are frequent opportunities for a particular business to postpone income tax by skillful use of the different methods of accounting.

Principal Accounting Techniques

There are two principal accounting techniques: (1) the accrual method and (2) the cash receipts and disbursements method.

A hybrid combination of these two may also be used. Furthermore, a taxpayer engaged in two or more separate and distinct businesses may use a different method of accounting for each trade or business. Complete and separate books and records must be maintained, however.

The accrual method recognizes revenues when they are earned (typically when the customer is invoiced) and recognizes expenses when they are incurred (typically when the supplier's invoice is received). The process of recognizing revenues and expenses is uncoupled from the actual receiving and sending of payments and the actual receiving of materials. This method is, in essence, the one demonstrated in Chapter 1 as an income forecast. It is the method that resulted in what was humorously referred to as a "use 'em up chart."

The cash receipts and disbursements method recognizes revenues when cash or its equivalent is actually received (irrespective of when the liability for payment by a customer originated), and recognizes expenses when cash or its equivalent is actually disbursed (irrespective of when the liability for payment to a supplier originated). This method is similar (but not identical) to that demonstrated in Chapter 1 as a cash flow forecast (a picture of the company's checkbook).

*Example of How to Use an Accounting
Maneuver*

To illustrate a business situation where one method is clearly preferable to the other, consider a business that has had the following sales performance based on when the customer was invoiced.

Month	Sales Last Year	Sales This Year
1	$ 34,000	$ 66,000
2	37,000	68,000
3	40,000	69,000
4	44,000	70,000
5	47,000	72,000
6	50,000	74,000
7	51,000	76,000
8	54,000	77,000
9	56,000	79,000
10	60,000	81,000
11	62,000	83,000
12	65,000	85,000
	$600,000	$900,000

If the business incurred total deductible expenses this year of $756,000 against $900,000 in revenues, the accrual basis income statement would be as follows:

INCOME STATEMENT
FOR THIS YEAR
ACCRUAL METHOD

Revenues	$900,000
Expenses	756,000
Taxable Income	144,000
Federal Income Tax°	44,640
Net Income	$99,360

Using the accrual method, an estimated income tax liability of $44,640 arises for This Year.

Now, suppose that in this business the accounts receivable are collected in an average of 45 days (i.e., one-half of a given month's sales is collected the following month, that is in 30 days; and the other one-half is collected in the month after that, that is in 60 days). If all monthly expenses are paid in the month they are recognized (as items such as rent and payroll typically are), the operations shown in Exhibit 8-10 would emerge as an income statement using the cash receipts and disbursements method. Using the cash receipts and disbursements method, an income tax liability of $35,185 arises for This Year.

The difference between $44,640 and $35,185, or $9,455, represents Federal income tax postponed to subsequent tax periods. In both cases, the amount of goods or services actually sold by the business and the expenses deducted were identical.

°Assume that this owner-manager forecasts the effective average tax for the year to be 31%.

EXHIBIT 8-10.
INCOME STATEMENT FOR THIS YEAR
CASH RECEIPTS & DISBURSEMENTS METHOD

RECEIPTS
    From Sales of Last Year
        ½ of Month 11 $31,000
        All of Month 12   65,000

    From Sales of This Year
        All of Months 1 thru 10   732,000
        ½ of Month 11   41,500
        None of Month 12   -0-
        Total Receipts $869,500

DISBURSEMENTS
    For Operating Expenses This Year   756,000

Taxable Income   113,500
Federal Income Tax*   35,185
Net Income $78,315

*Estimated at an effective annual rate of 31%.

In this example, growth of the business is a factor contributing to the advantage of the cash receipts and disbursements method over the accrual method. This phenomenon is coupled with the fact that the receipts from sales are slower, on the average, than disbursements for expenses.

If, on the other hand, payment for sales is immediate and payment for expenses is substantially delayed (in a growing company situation), the accrual basis would tend to provide tax advantages.

*Five Cautions When Using Accounting
Maneuvers*

A number of basic rules promulgated by the Internal Revenue Service represent cautions for the owner-manager desiring to reduce taxes through use of accounting maneuvers. Among these rules are the following:

1. The accrual method must be used for purchases and sales by every business in which the production, purchase or sale of goods is an income-producing factor (i.e., every business that sells out of its inventory).[10]

2. A cash receipts and disbursements basis taxpayer may be required to include in revenue the amount of revenue "constructively" received. This is revenue that the taxpayer has not actually received but that is so much within his control and disposition as to amount to actual receipt.[11]

3. Changing accounting methods normally requires consent of the Internal Revenue Service. Application is made on form 3115 and must be filed with the Commissioner of Internal Revenue, Washington, D. C. 20224. Application must be filed within 180 days after the start of the year for which the change is desired.[12]

4. Taxable income is figured on the basis of the taxpayer's annual accounting period (fiscal year). A sole proprietor may not use one tax year for his business income and a different tax year basis for income from other sources.[13]

5. Changes in accounting periods may be made. Generally, application is made on form 1128. Changes should be justified on the basis of a substantial business reason. A requested change ordinarily will not be approved if it substantially reduces a taxpayer's tax liability by shifting a taxpayer's income or deductions to another year or to another taxpayer.[14]

CURRENT DEDUCTIONS AND CAPITALIZATION

The cost of certain assets with a useful life greater than one year must be capitalized and then expensed over their useful life as previously discussed. Other costs, as in the example of this month's rent, must be expensed in the current period. In certain instances, the Federal income tax laws permit one to choose either to claim a current deduction or to capitalize specific types of expenditures. Deducting in the current period increases expenses and reduces taxes, thereby postponing the tax to subsequent taxable years. The opportunity to decide between deducting now and deducting later allows latitude for manipulating the timing of income tax in certain situations.

Specific Opportunities

Some of the more common opportunities for electing to deduct currently rather than to capitalize include:

Research and Experimental Expenditures—You may deduct currently or capitalize costs incident to the development of an experimental pilot model, a plant process, product, formula, invention or similar property, and the improvement of already existing property of this type. Also included is the cost of any research or experimental work carried on for you by another person or organization such as an engineering company.

Exploration Expenditures—May be deducted currently or capitalized and expensed over time. These expenditures must be paid or incurred during the tax year for ascertaining the existence, location, extent or quality of any deposit of ore or other mineral (other than oil or gas) before the development stage begins.

Circulation Expenditures—Circulation expenditures (such as hiring extra employees for a limited time to get new subscribers through telephone calls) made by a publisher to establish, maintain or increase the circulation of a newspaper, magazine or other periodical are deductible in the year of the expense or may be capitalized.

Repairs, Moving and Rearranging Expenditures—May present opportunities for choosing between current deductions and capitalization.

A Caution When Using Current Deductions Tactics

Many expenses that are incurred currently but benefit future periods may not be allowed as current deductions and must be capitalized for expensing over subsequent periods. Internal Revenue Service publication 334 cites one such example:

"A manufacturer and marketer of locks and locking devices issues a merchandise catalog. The products are not subject to rapid changes in style, etc. and the catalog is expected to remain unchanged for several years. The production costs of the catalog are capital expenditures" and must be expensed over time through the mechanism of depreciaton.[15]

When in doubt as to whether a proposed expense may or may not qualify as a current deduction, consult your tax professional.

RETIREMENT PLAN TACTICS

Under certain circumstances, the government allows individuals to create their own retirement program. Payments by those eligible are fully deductible in the current tax period. Federal income tax is postponed until retirement when the taxpayer is likely to be in a lower tax bracket. There are two major programs of interest to the owner-manager: individual retirement savings programs and self-employed retirement plans.

Individual Retirement Savings Program (IRA)

To be eligible to establish your own individual retirement savings program you must not have been covered at any time during the tax year by a qualified employer's plan, a government retirement plan or a tax sheltered annuity. A principal difference between the individual retirement savings program as opposed to the self-employed retirement plan discussed in the following section is that individuals, whether employer or employee, may independently establish their own plan. If eligible, one may contribute to the individual retirement savings program an amount equal to 15% of annual earnings (up to a maximum contribution of $1,500) and deduct the entire amount from the current year's income.[16]

Additional information regarding individual retirement savings programs may be obtained through IRS publication 590.[17]

Self-Employed Retirement Plans (Keogh)

If one is a sole proprietor or a partner of a partnership and owns more than 10% of the trade or business, that person may be entitled to a limited deduction for contributions that provide retirement benefits. If the plan qualifies, one may contribute and, consequently, deduct the lesser of $7,500 or 15% of the net earnings from self-employment. To initiate a self-employed retirement plan, one may design a personalized written plan or utilize a written plan prepared by certain sponsoring organizations that generally have received prior Internal Revenue Service approval of the form of their plan.[18]

There are several reporting forms associated with self-employed retirement plans. To determine exactly which form to file, consult Internal Revenue Service publication 560.[19]

Creative Spending

Creative spending is one strategy for reducing the *taxable amount*. It is available primarily to successful businesses that have the opportunity to make more money than is necessary to meet their bottom-line goals. This strategy involves taking the difference between the company's goal for the bottom line and what is otherwise produced and spending it "creatively" to benefit the company in future periods.

Consider the following example. Suppose a company is under the management obligation to produce 16% of its sales as pre-tax profit or taxable income. If the company has the following performance, it will have exceeded its bottom-line goal by 2%:

	Percent
Sales	100
Operating Expenses	−82
Taxable Income	18

The company might decide to spend "creatively" the difference between the 16% taxable income goal and the 18% actually produced. The distribution of the sales dollar would then appear as follows:

	Percent
Sales	100
Operating Expenses	−82
Operating Income	18
Creative Spending Expense	−2
Taxable Income	16

The purpose here is to focus on those expenses (ones the company would not necessarily make if it were struggling to meet minimum performance standards) that are currently deductible as far as the Internal Revenue Service is concerned but ones that management knows will produce future (as well as current) benefits even though these benefits may be intangible. "Creative spending," as it is used here, does not imply lavish, extravagant or wasteful expenditures.

Some examples of "creative spending" follow:

Image Advertising	This tactic involves engaging in advertising to enhance the company's image in the marketplace. This type of advertising is not absolutely essential to the present or immediate future sales of the business. This kind of advertising increases marketplace recognition of the company, its products and its trademarks. Items such as a handsomely illustrated annual report might even fall in this category, since it tends to paint an image of a more substantial and high-quality company.
Additional Fringe Benefits	This tactic focuses on retaining key and quality employees. This might include some of the traditional fringe benefits such as hospital protection, or it may include unusual benefits related to "working for our company." Special employee training and educational programs might be one such benefit. An annual company picnic might even qualify.
New Product Development	The central thought of this tactic is to be more competitive in future periods. Quality market surveys, market research, new product design and development all might be possibilities for "creative spending."
Increased Compensation	This tactic is designed to attract and keep quality personnel. Paying employees wages that are competitively higher and giving bonuses selectively come under "creative spending." Financially rewarding employees in innovative ways at higher rates than the rest of the industry should tend to cause a long-term migration from the competitor's company to your company.

Once a business becomes very successful, "creative spending" represents an interesting strategy for reducing the taxable amount.

Consumption

After the postponement and creative spending options have been explored, one might consider the strategy referred to here as consumption.

Frequently, the successful owner-manager has "carved his business out of the forest," after long years of hard work. With little support and scarce resources a substantial and profitable entity has finally been created. When success has reached the point that income tax seems burdensome, one valid alternative is the decision to live better.

DEDUCTIBLE WAYS TO LIVE BETTER

A very successful business that is paying considerable income tax offers numerous opportunities for the owner-manager to live better. Among the categories of deductible expenses conducive to this improved quality of living are:

TRAVEL—Many owner-managers are required to travel as part of their day-to-day business activity. If driving is practical, a more comfortable and better quality of vehicle might be considered. For example, one might select a full-size Ford instead of a compact. If you wish to spend less time commuting, you might decide to fly rather than drive. You might elect to fly first class instead of flying coach.

The Internal Revenue Service has basic rules regarding what travel is actually deductible. With regard to travel, one must prove the following:

1. The amount of each separate expenditure for traveling away from home, such as the cost of transportation or lodging (the daily cost of your breakfast, lunch and dinner, and other incidental elements of such travel may be aggregated, if they are set forth in reasonable categories, such as meals, gasoline and oil, and taxi fares);

2. The dates of your departure and return home for each trip, and the number of days spent on business away from home;

3. The destination or locality of your travel; and

4. The business reason for your travel or the nature of the business benefit derived or expected to be derived as a result of your travel.[20]

ENTERTAINMENT—Certain types of entertainment are considered normal business expenses and are deductible. A successful business paying a large amount of income tax may provide the owner-manager with the opportunity to entertain more and to engage in more expensive entertainment. Since entertainment might represent an opportunity for abuse of the deduction privilege, the Internal Revenue Service insists that the following be proved in order that entertainment be deductible.

1. The amount of each separate expenditure for entertaining, except that incidental items like cab fares and telephone calls may be aggregated on a daily basis;

2. The date the entertainment took place;

3. The name (if any), address or location, and the type of entertainment, such as dinner or theater, if it is not apparent from the name or designation of the place;

4. The reason you entertained or the nature of the business benefit derived or expected to be derived as a result of entertaining and, except for certain business meals, the nature of any business discussion or activity that took place; and

5. The occupation or other information relative to the person or persons entertained, including name, title or other designation, sufficient to establish such person's business relationship to you.[21]

For additional information regarding the nature of deductible entertainment and travel expenditures, refer to Internal Revenue Service publication 463, available from your local IRS Office.

ENERGY—Energy costs to a business have for the last few years been substantial. Consequently, many companies have instituted procedures that make the working environment less comfortable. Thermostat settings in the '60s during the winter and in the upper '70s during the summer represent efforts to curtail and minimize energy costs. The owner-manager who is paying a large amount of income tax might decide to set thermostat controls to temperature levels that create a more comfortable working environment (within regulatory limits).

EQUIPMENT—Many owner-managed businesses prosper while using what might be referred to as fully-depreciated assets. Obsolete copying machines that produce copies at a low quality and low cost, mechanical typewriters and hard, unattractive furniture are common in fast-growing and entrepreneurial businesses. The taxable income can be decreased by utilizing more modern copying machines and memory typewriters, acquiring attractive and comfortable furniture, modernizing the decor, selecting carpet for the offices and, perhaps, even moving to a more convenient and attractive location. Additional tax benefits can result from then giving the old equipment to a charity.

EDUCATION—The very successful business affords its owner-manager the opportunity to attend seminars and other educational experiences to improve already existing skills. As long as there is clearly an educational activity being conducted, there is no restriction on where the seminar is held: Palm Springs, Palm Beach or Vail, might be the scene of a very meaningful, educational experience.

STAFF—Another common characteristic of fast-growing entrepreneurial companies is a critical shortage of staff. Everyone wears several hats. The president may very well be the president from eight a.m. until five p.m., the "janitor" from five p.m. until seven p.m. and a part of the accounting staff from seven p.m. until nine p.m. A business paying a large amount of income tax may decide to reduce its taxable income by hiring more qualified and competent employees who, hopefully, will reduce the workload of the owner-manager. Such additions to the payroll may never before have been viewed as economically feasible. The central thought here is using an increased staff to make the owner-manager's job easier.

CAUTIONS WHEN USING THE CONSUMPTION STRATEGY

A few words of caution are in order when seeking deductible ways to live better. The Internal Revenue Service is particularly sensitive with regard to expenditures for travel, entertainment and gifts. In general, they will require that one prove five critical elements for the expense to be deductible. These elements are: (1) time, (2) cost, (3) place, (4) business relationship of the expenditure and (5) business purpose of the expenditure.[22]

Business expenses are deductible only if they are ordinary and necessary to carry on the trade or business and are adequately substantiated. Furthermore, the deduction will be allowed only if the expenditures are directly related to or associated with the active conduct of the trade or business.

Lavish or extravagant expenses are not allowed.[23] This applies especially to travel and business entertainment expenses. In general, records must be accurate, thorough and timely in order to substantiate any deductible expenditure. No deductions are allowed for approximations or estimates.

Benevolence

Another strategy for reducing the taxable amount is benevolence. Benevolence is used here to refer to the concept of giving a portion of the created resources to those who built the business, namely the employees (that may include owner-managers). This can be done directly as in the example of a reasonable bonus. While payments such as bonuses are deductible by the company, they are taxable to the employee. The more interesting types of benevolence seek to provide a deduction for the company that is not currently taxable to the employee. There are several tactics for accomplishing this.

PENSION AND PROFIT-SHARING PLANS

Qualified pension and profit-sharing plans have some attractive tax benefits. First, the amount contributed by the employer represents an immediate deduction just as though ordinary salary raises were given. Second, even though this contribution is made on behalf of an employee, it is not considered part of the employee's current taxable income. Third, the amount set apart and accumulated in the qualified plan may be used to produce additional income. This additional income is not taxed until distribution upon retirement. Fourth, favorable tax treatment is available on distributions made after retirement. Fifth, the distribution made from a qualified plan may under certain circumstances be excluded from an employee's taxable estate for Federal estate tax purposes.[24]

Although the phrase "pension and profit-sharing plans" is commonly used as though they were just one concept, pension and profit-sharing plans are distinctively different. Understanding the differences is essential to intelligent use of these tactics.

Pension Plans

Traditionally, pension plans are those that are designed primarily to provide for the payment of precisely determinable benefits for the covered employees over a period of years. This period is usually for life after retirement. At the heart of the pension concept is the characteristic of definitely determinable future benefits.[25]

Profit Sharing Plans

In contrast to the pension plan, a profit-sharing plan is one that is designed to allow the employees participation in the profits of the business. While contributions by the employer may be a predetermined percentage of annual profits, there is no general requirement that the employer must adhere to a percentage allowance. Since the employer's contributions will typically fluctuate from year to year, the benefits ultimately paid to covered employees will necessarily be indeterminate. The most obvious difference existing between pension plans and profit-sharing plans is the concept of definitely determinable future benefits versus indeterminate future benfits.[26]

Money Purchase Pension Plans

There is a gray area between pension plans and profit-sharing plans. This hybrid type of plan is known as the money purchase pension plan. Under a money purchase pension plan the employer is obligated to contribute a certain percentage of the covered employee's compensation. Since any given employee's compensation is subject to variation over time, the ultimate benefits are not definitely determinable at any point prior to the employee's retirement. This variation is unlike the traditional pension plan because future benefits are not definitely determinable. Furthermore, it is not like profit-sharing plans because the contribution formula of the employer is not linked to profits of the company.[27]

General Requirements

Qualifying pension and profit-sharing plans are typically created by the execution of a written trust agreement (generally prepared by an attorney) describing the particular plan.[28] Prior to implementation all proposed plans should be submitted to the Office of District Director of Internal Revenue for the district in which the corporation's principal place of business is located.[29] Penalties for errors may be drastic.

The plan should be amendable and capable of being terminated by the company. It should be authorized by the board of directors and the stockholders.

There are numerous requirements that must be met to have a plan qualify for the tax benefits. One of the most significant requirements is that the plan must not discriminate in favor of employees who are officers, shareholders or highly compensated employees.[30]

Payments to the qualifying plan plus regular salaries paid to the covered employees must not exceed reasonable compensation for past and present services rendered. Any contribution to an employee pension over the amount necessary to provide a reasonable pension is not deductible by the employer.[31] Certain limitations govern annual additions to an employee's account under a qualified plan.[32]

Pros and Cons of Pension vs. Profit-Sharing Plans

Pension plans, unlike profit-sharing plans, provide fixed and predetermined benefits upon retirement. This fosters a sense of financial security. Consequently, the pension plan is frequently more attractive to relatively low-paid personnel and to labor unions and is not as attractive to officers and highly paid personnel.[33]

Pension plans, on the other hand, do not provide a great deal of incentive for above-average performance. Therefore, profit-sharing plans are preferable when considering this factor. Management-oriented employees are typically more interested in the profit-sharing plan than the pension plan.[34]

Trustees of both pension and profit-sharing plans have a great deal of flexibility in their investment of the funds. Trustees of a profit-sharing plan, however, usually feel at greater liberty to invest in equities and other items having some degree of risk than do the trustees of a pension plan.[35]

Establishment of a qualified pension plan involves undertaking a relatively fixed commitment for an indeterminate number of years. On the other hand, a profit-sharing plan involves no commitment in the absence of profits. This flexibility makes a profit-sharing plan in many cases more attractive to the small or expanding company.[36]

MEDICAL AND DENTAL PAYMENT PLANS

One important fringe benefit that is simultaneously deductible to the company but not taxable to the employee is a medical and dental payment plan. A company may arrange with its employees to pay in part or in total their hospital, medical and dental expenses. It is also permissible for the employee to be directly reimbursed by the company for these same expenditures. Plans of this type may be either limited or broad in scope. Since a very liberal plan might result in a heavy burden on the company, it is not uncommon to limit benefits to a fixed percentage of the employee's direct compensation.[37]

No particular formality is necessary in establishing a medical and dental payment plan. It is unnecessary to submit such a plan to the Internal Revenue Service for advance approval as is the case with pension and profit-sharing plans. Adoption of a resolution by the board of directors is usually sufficient to institute the plan.

GROUP TERM-LIFE INSURANCE PLANS

Another popular fringe benefit that is deductible by the company is group term-life insurance for the employees. If insurance protection is generally less than $50,000, then the deductible contribution by the employer is not includable in the employee's income.[38]

Group term-life insurance may be provided to employees subject to certain standards. For example, employees under a stated age might be excluded. Unmarried employees might be excluded.[39]

Philanthropy

After one achieves a certain plateau of success, mere accumulation of wealth may no longer have the motivating appeal it once did. The way created wealth will be used often becomes as important as the actual creation itself. Last on most owner-managers' lists of preferences is spending hard-earned resources on taxes. The successful owner-manager may (rather than letting government dictate the use of his property) decide on philanthropy in an effort to control the use to which society puts a portion of his created resources. While the humanitarian and moral aspects of private philanthropy have always been important, the tax benefits from charitable giving are becoming increasingly important.

THE COST OF GIVING

The actual cost to a donor for making a charitable contribution depends on that individual's income tax bracket. The higher the tax bracket the lower the relative cost of the charitable contribution. The government, in effect, participates in the cost of making a donation.

To illustrate, consider the following table.[40]

	Taxpayer A 25% Bracket	Taxpayer B 50% Bracket
Amount of Contribution	$ 5,000	$ 5,000
Reduction in Tax Due to Contribution	1,250	2,500
Net Cost of Contribution to Donor	$ 3,750	$ 2,500

As seen, the net cost of the contribution to the donor varies dramatically with the tax bracket.

YOU CAN CONTRIBUTE PROPERTY

The simplest method of charitable giving is a payment of cash. There is no question concerning the value of the contribution and proof of payment can be easily established. Property, however, may also be contributed. Consider the contribution of appreciated property:[41]

Mr. Smith, an owner-manager, bought a small boat five years ago for use by his business in transporting special cargo down the river to the next city. The vessel cost $18,000 and has been subject to $4,500 of depreciation. Today Mr. Smith gave the boat to State University School of Oceanography. The boat was recently appraised and found to have a fair market value of $20,000. Mr. Smith's charitable deduction is $15,500 (fair market value of $20,000, less $4,500, the amount of depreciation recaptured that would have been realized if the boat had been sold).

There are numerous rules associated with the giving of property. The example above illustrates one such rule with regard to depreciation on donated appreciated property. The importance of how a transaction is handled is further illustrated by considering the situation where: 1) a gift of property is made and 2) property is sold and a gift of the proceeds is made. Under both situations a contribution deduction would arise in the amount of the value of the property contributed. If, however, sale of property is made first and the proceeds are then given as a gift, a long-term capital gain representing the difference between the cost of the property and the sale price of the property results. While a contribution deduction does arise, a new tax liability in the form of a capital gain tax would occur. Significantly different tax consequences result from the contribution of essentially the same property, depending upon how the transaction is handled mechanically.

LIMITATIONS ON DEDUCTIONS

For an individual the deductions for a given tax year for contributions to qualified organizations is limited to various percentages of the taxpayer's adjusted gross income.[42]

A corporation is allowed to deduct contributions not in excess of a fixed percentage of its taxable income. Subject to certain limitations, excess contributions may be carried over to following years.[43]

CAUTIONS WHEN MAKING CONTRIBUTIONS

Since a number of unexpected pitfalls may be encountered when making charitable contributions, a few cautions are in order. One of the more obvious is to make absolutely certain that the contribution is, in fact, deductible. For a list of organizations to which a contribution is deductible see publication 78, available from the Superintendent of Documents, U.S. Government Printing Office, Washington, D.C. 20402.

A deduction will not be allowed if any of the net earnings of an organization that receives the contribution are used for the benefit of any private shareholder or individual.

Dues paid to a qualified organization are deductible to the extent they exceed the value of the benefits and privileges received. For example, suppose $20 is paid for a box lunch that has a fair market value of $5. The charitable contribution that may be deducted is only $15.[44]

No deduction is allowed for the donation of services or for the use of property.[45]

A deduction is allowable only for the tax year in which the contribution is actually paid, whether the taxpayer is on the cash or the accrual accounting basis.[46]

The law permitting individuals to claim a limited deduction or credit for certain political contributions does not entitle corporations to claim this deduction for credit.

One should keep records, receipts, canceled checks and all other evidence to substantiate deductions. For contributions in property other than money, one must state the kind of property contributed, the cost, the fair market value, the method used to determine its fair market value at the time of the contribution and whether the amount of the contribution was affected by an appreciation in value.

REDUCING TAX RATE (INCOME TAX)

In trying to minimize taxes, one of the major objectives relates to reducing the TAX RATE. Obviously, a given taxable amount taxed at a lower rate results in fewer tax dollars.

Selecting the Most Favorable Rate

Fundamentally, there are two tax rates that may be used: the individual rate and the corporate rate. Key elements of the rules governing individual taxes are discussed in Internal Revenue Service publication 17, available at no cost from the IRS.

Key elements of the rules governing corporate taxes are discussed in Internal Revenue Service Publication 334, also available at no cost from the IRS.

HOW THE GAME IS PLAYED

The individual rate and the corporate rate are basically quite *different.* Taking this into consideration, create (or gain access to) a proprietorship (taxed at the individual rate) and a corporation (taxed at the corporate rate). The game then becomes:

... skillfully control the amount of taxable income that is taxed at the individual rate and the amount that is taxed at the corporate rate so that the total income tax paid is minimized.

THE TAX-ESTIMATING AND PLANNING CHART

For most owner-managers, when thoughts turn to tax planning, the appropriate tax table is frequently not handy or the tax references at hand may be out of date (rules change frequently). If this isn't an impediment, then the arithmetic necessitates a calculator (that may not be presently available). This frustrating process can be avoided if the owner-manager will adopt the following three-step procedure:

1. Call or write the nearest Internal Revenue Service Office and request publication 17 with regard to individual taxes and publication 334 with regard to corporate taxes.

2. After determining the current and applicable individual and corporate tax rates, set up a table to calculate data that allows portrayal of the relevant tax rules in a simple graphical chart.

3. Use this chart (instead of tables, references and calculators) for simple and fast tax estimating and planning.

How to Create the Tax Chart

As an illustration of how to prepare a tax-estimating and planning chart suppose that an owner-manager files individually on a married, joint return basis. The applicable tax table would be IRS Schedule Y. The corporate rate, on the other hand, would be obtained from IRS publication 334. For varying taxable income amounts from $5,000 to $1 million, calculate the tax to be paid filing the joint return and alternatively filing the corporate return.

A tax-estimating and planning chart then may be plotted, preferably in two sections, to enhance the detail at low taxable income levels as well as at high taxable income levels. For a prior period, the chart presented in Exhibit 8-11 would result.

How to Use the Tax Chart

To use a tax-estimating and planning chart, first consider the taxable income you might expect during the coming year (the profit forecast technique demonstrated in Chapter 1 is useful for this purpose). Next, find this amount on the relevant horizontal axis of your chart. Then examine the graph to determine whether the corporate rate or your individual rate produces the least tax to be paid. You may want to experiment with taking the total taxable

EXHIBIT 8-11
INCOME TAX ESTIMATING AND PLANNING CHART

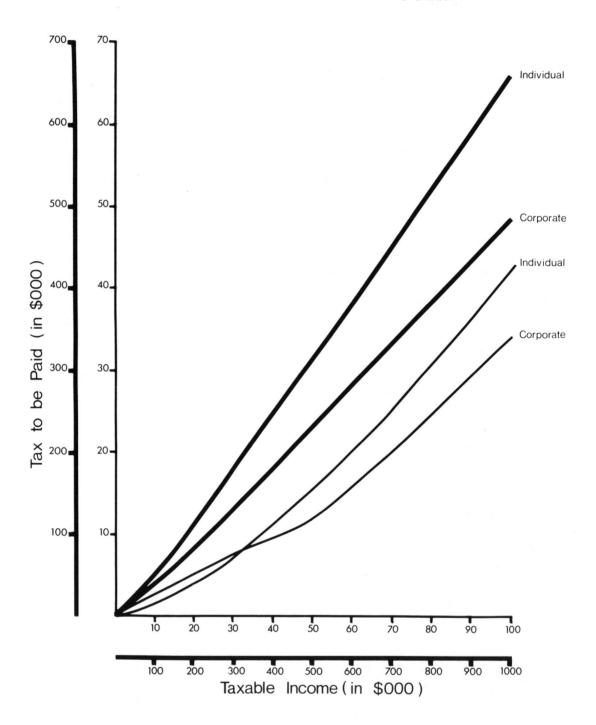

income and breaking it into two parts to see if one portion taxed at your individual rate plus the other portion taxed at the corporate rate produces less total tax.

A working table is already set up in Exhibit 8-12 for calculating data necessary for preparation of your own tax-estimating and planning chart. After a customized table is completed, plot the data on the prepared chart form in Exhibit 8-13.

You now have a tailored, tax-estimating and planning chart that can be used expeditiously without additional references or a calculator.

EXHIBIT 8-12.
WORKING FORM FOR YOUR TAX ESTIMATING AND
PLANNING CHART DATA TABLE

Taxable Income	Tax to be Paid @ Your Individual Rate	Tax to be Paid @ Your Corporate Rate
$ 5,000	$_____	$_____
10,000	_____	_____
20,000	_____	_____
25,000	_____	_____
30,000	_____	_____
50,000	_____	_____
70,000	_____	_____
100,000	_____	_____
200,000	_____	_____
400,000	_____	_____
600,000	_____	_____
800,000	_____	_____
1,000,000	_____	_____

MECHANISMS FOR MANIPULATING THE TAX RATE

There are a number of mechanisms useful in controlling which tax rate should be applied to a given taxable income. The more common business entities and the tax rate associated with each are summarized below:

Entities Resulting in Taxation at the Corporate Tax Rate	Entities Resulting in Taxation at the Individual Tax Rate
Corporation	Proprietorship
Limited Partnership	Partnership
	Subchapter S Corporation
	Limited Partnership

EXHIBIT 8-13
WORKING FORM FOR YOUR TAX ESTIMATING AND PLANNING CHART

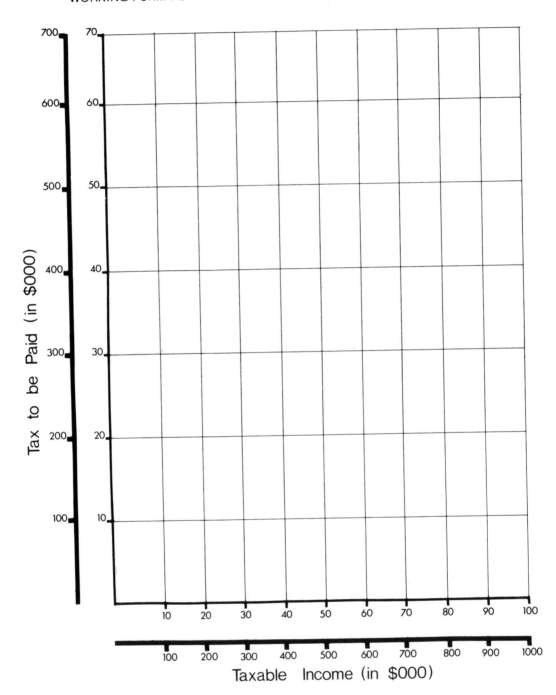

Corporation

The corporation developed as the legal response to the economic need for a means to amass large sums of capital to conduct modern business activities. Roman lawyers are given credit for inventing the corporate idea. The original concept of a corporation was what we would call a municipal or a public corporation and not a private corporation.[47] During the 12th and 13th centuries teachers and students formed corporations (as universities) for the promotion of higher education.[48] The practice of incorporating craft guilds dates back to at least 1407 with the incorporation of the haberdashers.[49]

The corporation as a form of doing business has numerous advantages. The more prominent ones include: limited liability of the shareholders for the debts of the business, ready transferability of ownership and perpetual existence of the entity.

With regard to taxation, the rules applying to corporations are specified in IRS publication 334. Taxable income of the ordinary corporation does not pass on to its individual owners. Rather, it resides in the corporate entity and is taxed according to the previously mentioned rules. For example, the following corporation would have taxable income of $16 subject to the corporate rate:

EXHIBIT 8-14.
CORPORATION

Revenues	$100
Expenses	−84
Taxable Income	$ 16

A corporation must annually file Internal Revenue Service form 1120.

Sole Proprietorship

The sole proprietorship is a natural form for the one-person business in which the same individual is the owner and worker. Advantages of the sole proprietorship entity revolve around the absence of formalities. Not subjected to as many regulatory and reporting requirements as other forms of business enterprise, the owner is his own boss and delays and ceremonious duties in dealing with a board of directors can be avoided.

Disadvantages do exist, however, with the sole proprietorship form of business. The owner is subject to unlimited personal liability, the business is subject to disintegration upon the death or incapacity of the owner and the equity captial in the business is limited by the resources of the sole owner.

Taxable income passes directly from the business entity to the individual. This is demonstrated in Exhibit 8-15. The taxable income produced by the proprietorship is added to all other individual income created by the taxpayer, and the sum of the two are then taxed at the individual tax rate. The individual tax rate is available in publication 17 from the Internal

Revenue Service. Internal Revenue Service Schedule C must be completed and accompany form 1040 when business has been conducted in the proprietorship entity.

EXHIBIT 8-15
PROPRIETORSHIP

Revenues	$ 100
Expenses	84
Taxable Income	$ 16

Adds to the individual 's other taxable income;
the sum is taxed at the individual rate.

Partnership

The Uniform Partnership Act defines a partnership as "an association of two or more persons to carry on as co-owners a business for profit." Distinctive characteristics of the partnership form of doing business include the ability of every partner to act on behalf of the business, the preclusion of any person from becoming a partner without the consent of all the partners and the dissolution of the partnership by the death of any one partner.

EXHIBIT 8-16
PARTNERSHIP

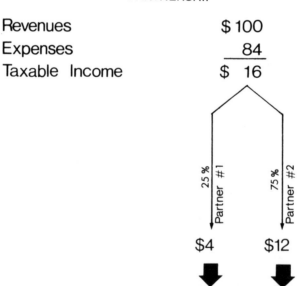

Revenues	$ 100
Expenses	84
Taxable Income	$ 16

25 % Partner #1   75 % Partner #2

$4 $12

Adds to the individual 's other taxable income;
the sum is taxed at the individual rate.

A partnership as such does not pay tax on its income. Each partner includes his distributive share of partnership income in his own return whether or not any distribution is actually received. This is illustrated by the diagram in Exhibit 8-16. In this figure there is assumed to be one 25% ownership partner and one 75% ownership partner.

The partnership must file a return that is Internal Revenue form 1065. This form must be filed whether or not the partnership has a book profit.

Subchapter S Corporation

Subchapter S corporations are very popular because once established, they are exempt from Federal income taxes and will continue to be exempt so long as the Subchapter S election is in effect. Confusion, though, surrounds the Subchapter S entity itself. There is no such thing as a Subchapter S corporation per se that is a different kind of legal entity from the ordinary corporation. For qualifying ordinary corporations, some may elect (by completing an Internal Revenue Service form) to be taxed under a section of the law referred to as Subchapter S. Subchapter S corporations are no more than ordinary corporations that fill out a particular Internal Revenue Service form and meet certain criteria.

To qualify for the Subchapter S election, a corporation must meet the following requirements of a small business corporation:

- It must be a domestic corporation.
- It must not be a member of an affiliated group.
- It must have only one class of stock.
- It must not have more than 15 shareholders (except under special rules).
- It must have only individuals or estates as shareholders.
- It must not have a non-resident alien as a shareholder.

The election may be made by a qualified corporation at any time during the year preceding the tax year or during the first 75 days of the first tax year. The election should be made on form 2553, entitled Election by Small Business Corporations and filed with the Internal Revenue Service according to the instructions on the reverse side of form 2553.

Since there are potentially serious consequences of termination or revocation of election, one should be aware of the events causing termination. Termination may be caused if:

1. A new shareholder affirmatively refuses to consent to the election.
2. All shareholders in the corporation consent to revoke the election.
3. The corporation ceases to be a small business corporation (see list of preceding requirements for a small business corporation).
4. More than 80% of the corporation's gross receipts for the tax year are from sources outside the United States.
5. More than 20% of the corporation's gross receipts for a tax year are from passive investment income.

The rules for taxing taxable income of Subchapter S corporations are similar (but not exactly) to the rules for partnerships. As demonstrated in Exhibit 8-17, the taxable income or loss passes to the shareholders in proportion to the number of shares that they hold in the Subchapter S corporation. This taxable income or loss passes to the individuals whether there is an actual distribution to these individuals or not.

A Subchapter S corporation, like any corporation, continues to have the advantage of limited liability for the stockholders.

A Subchapter S corporation must file a return on form 1120S for each tax year in which the election is effective.[50] In addition, the corporation must complete a separate schedule K-1 (entitled Shareholders Share of Undistributed Taxable Income) for each shareholder. Additional information regarding Subchapter S corporations is available in Internal Revenue Service publication 589 (entitled Tax Information on Subchapter S Corporations).

EXHIBIT 8-17
CORPORATION SUBCHAPTER S ELECTION

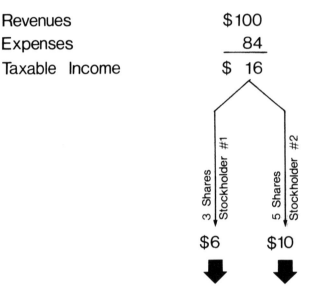

Revenues	$100
Expenses	84
Taxable Income	$ 16

Adds to the individual 's other taxable income; the sum is taxed at the individual rate.

Limited Partnership

The limited partnership is a statutory form of doing business and is defined as a "partnership formed by two or more persons ... having as members one or more general partners and one or more limited partners."[51] The general partner or partners have personal liability as in the case of an ordinary partnership. The limited partners on the other hand have limited liability similar to that of shareholders in a corporation. Characteristics of a limited partnership include: the limited partners are excluded from control of the business and from participation in its management; there can be no continuity of a limited partnership's existence in the event of death of a limited partner; a limited partner may assign his interest in the business without the consent of the other partners; and the general partner may be either an individual or a corporation subject to certain rules.[52]

The treatment of taxable income in a limited partnership is demonstrated in Exhibit 8-18. The taxable income or loss passes to the partners in proportion to their ownership. An added feature that is not available for Subchapter S corporations is the fact that one of the partners, the general partner, may be a corporation.

In the final analysis, the taxable status of limited partnerships depends on the characteristics they have under the state law where they are created. A limited partnership may be classified as an ordinary partnership or as an association taxable as a corporation, depending upon its characteristics. Limited partnerships in states whose laws are patterned after the Uniform Limited Partnership Act usually are taxed as partnerships.

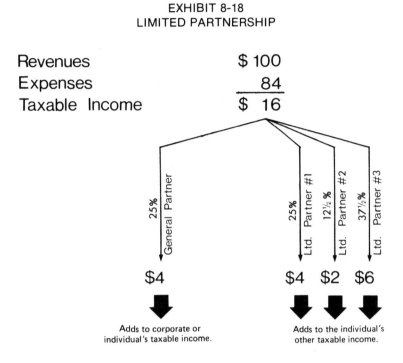

EXHIBIT 8-18
LIMITED PARTNERSHIP

Selecting a Different Tax Law

Taxes are imposed by governmental units that may be local, state or national. These various governmental units impose taxes in different manners and amounts. If you find the tax laws in one particular location unfavorable, you might decide to select the tax laws imposed by a different location. Some cities and, indeed, some states are favorably disposed toward business and some are unfavorably inclined toward business. Some states have an income tax on business, others do not. Some states have an individual income tax, others do not. Some regions are trying to encourage commerce and employment, while other regions are more interested in preserving the natural environment.

Even more dramatic differences become apparent between different nations. Some countries are interested in attracting investment, developing technology and providing employment for their citizens. As a result, certain foreign governments offer attractive tax holidays and interesting tax incentives. It is not uncommon, however, to have restrictions imposed by the host government on repatriation of profits.

Moving to a new area or establishing subsidiaries or branches in a different location may have very attractive tax ramifications.

Taking Advantage of Special Rules

To encourage specific national and economic goals, lawmakers frequently provide specialized incentives. A few of the more common ones are reviewed here.

CAPITAL GAINS AND LOSSES

Gains and losses from transactions involving capital assets are subject to well-defined rules and limitations. For example, a difference is drawn between short-term capital gains and losses and long-term capital gains and losses. Since 1977 one must have owned the capital asset for more than 12 months if the gain or loss is to receive long-term treatment.[53] Generally speaking, net long-term capital gains receive a more favorable tax treatment than the ordinary income tax rate.

The rules for individuals differ from those for corporations.[54]

An individual may claim a capital loss deduction if capital losses exceed capital gains.[55] For additional detailed information regarding capital gains and losses for individuals, refer to publication 17 available from the Internal Revenue Service.

Corporations, on the other hand, may deduct capital losses only to the extent of capital gains. For additional information regarding capital gains and losses for corporations, refer to IRS Bulletin 334.

SECTION 1244 STOCK

Under normal rules of income taxation, a shareholder who suffers a loss on an investment in common stock may obtain only a capital loss deduction. If, on the other hand, an individual or a partnership realizes a loss on what is referred to as Section 1244 stock a portion or all of that loss can be taken as an ordinary deduction.[56]

In order to qualify as Section 1244 stock, the security must meet certain qualifications. First, it must be common stock of a domestic corporation. Second, the stock must be issued under a written plan to issue the stock within two years. Appropriate minutes of a corporation's board of directors meeting can qualify as a "plan" if necessary requirements are met.[57] Third, the corporation must be a small business corporation when the plan is adopted. To meet this criteria, paid-in-capital should not exceed $500,000 and total equity capital should not exceed $1,000,000. Fourth, the stock must be issued for money or property. In addition, no part of a prior offering of stock of any class may be outstanding at the time the Section 1244 plan is adopted. Finally, the corporation must, for the most part, be an operating company. Favorable tax advantages may be lost if for the five tax years of the corporation preceding the loss year of the stockholder, more than 50% of the gross receipts of the corporation were from investment sources such as interest, dividends or rents.[58]

MUNICIPAL BONDS

Interest on state and municipal bonds is tax exempt to both the corporate owner and individual investor. While these bonds may pay a lower interest rate than some other available investment instruments, the advantage of being tax free can substantially reduce the effective tax rate for a taxpayer in a relatively high income tax bracket.

REDUCING TAX DUE (DIRECTLY)

As mentioned previously, the TAX DUE is obtained by multiplying the TAXABLE AMOUNT by the TAX RATE. There are opportunities to reduce the TAX DUE directly by avoiding penalties and taking advantage of certain credits. Also, special taxes are imposed under certain operating circumstances.

Penalties

With regard to Federal taxes, penalties abound. First, a rule is passed and then one is penalized for not obeying it. For example, there is a rule stating when payroll taxes and employee-income-tax withholding is due. These taxes are reported on forms 941 and 941E.

The calendar quarters covered by forms 941 and 941E, due dates for these returns and the full payment of tax are as follows:

Quarter	Due Dates*
January—February—March	April 30
April—May—June	July 31
July—August—September	October 31
October—November—December	January 31

*If any due date falls on a Saturday, Sunday or legal holiday, the due date is extended to the next succeeding day that is not a Saturday, Sunday or legal holiday.

There are also rules as to when deposits must be made.

The estimated Federal income tax is to be deposited on or before the 15th day of each of the following months of the tax year (fiscal year):

Installments	4th mo. %	6 mo. %	9th mo. %	12th mo. %
4	25	25	25	25
3	—	33 1/3	33 1/3	33 1/3
2	—	—	50	50
1	—	—	—	100

Failure to respond to these and other tax rules results in penalties. There are penalties for failure to file a return, interest for delinquency in payment of tax, penalties for failure to make timely payment, penalties for underpayment of estimated tax by a corporation, penalties for failure to deposit taxes, penalties for failure to include proper identifying numbers on the returns and penalties for negligence.[59]

Penalties assessed for willful acts become more interesting. Willful filing of any known false or fraudulent document, including an income tax return, is a misdemeanor punishable by a fine of $10,000, imprisonment of not more than one year, or both. Willful attempt to evade or defeat the income tax is a felony punishable by a fine of $10,000 and imprisonment for not more than five years, or both.[60]

Timely and accurate filing of all required information can directly reduce the total TAX DUE.

Credits

The government "in all of its wisdom" provides tax incentives for certain socially worthwhile goals. These are expressed as tax credits and serve to reduce the amount of TAX DUE by the taxpayer. Some of the various credits are: Jobs Credit,[61] Work Incentive Credit,[62] Employee Stock Ownership Plan Credit,[63] and Investment Tax Credit (see Chapter 5).

Special Operating Circumstances

There are a number of special operating circumstances that give rise to undesirable taxable events. Two such circumstances involve: (1) reasonable salary limitations and (2) accumulated retained earnings tax.

REASONABLE SALARY LIMITATIONS

One disadvantage of corporations is the reasonable salary limitation criteria. Only a reasonable compensation for personal services is deductible by an employer. The amount is that which would be ordinarily paid for similar services under similar circumstances by similar enterprises.[64] The amount found to be excessive is treated as a non-deductible dividend distribution by the corporation and not as an ordinary and necessary expense of doing business. The disallowed portion of the compensation is taxed twice, once to the corporation and again to the shareholder/officer.[65] What is reasonable in any particular case depends upon the facts. Some of the factors considered are the character and amount of responsibility of the job, the ease or difficulty of the work itself, the time required, working conditions, future prospects, living conditions in the locality, technical training required and profitability to the employer of the services rendered.[66] Statistical data of an industry unrelated to the taxpayers is rarely helpful in proving a case with the Internal Revenue Service.

ACCUMULATED RETAINED EARNINGS TAX

Improper accumulation of earnings in a corporation can give rise to an extremely unpleasant taxable event known as the accumulated earnings tax. A very stiff penalty tax may be imposed on improper accumulations of taxable income.[67]

It is a common misconception that if the penalty tax is applicable, it is imposed on the corporation's entire accumulated retained earnings from the first day of its existence to the date of the imposition of the tax. Actually, the penalty tax is an annual tax. It is in addition to the regular corporate tax and is imposed on the corporation's accumulated taxable income for the particular year that is in question. In order to understand this penalty tax, one must realize that its applicability depends upon the presence of a bad purpose. Usually, this purpose is to avoid income tax to the shareholders. Where shareholders do not want to receive taxable dividends, the corporation will be subject to the tax.[68] The statute is directed at earnings accumulated beyond the reasonable needs of the business.[69]

Earnings accumulated for reasonable needs of the business are permitted. Reasonable needs include: bona fide expansion of the business or replacement of plant, acquisition of a business enterprise through purchasing stock or assets, retirement of bona fide indebtedness, providing necessary working capital for the business or providing investments or loans to suppliers or customers if necessary.[70]

Purposes that may indicate to the Internal Revenue Service that earnings are being accumulated beyond the reasonable needs of the business include: loans to shareholders, loans having no reasonable relation to the conduct of the business, investments in property or securities that are unrelated to the activities of the business of the taxpayer's corporation and retention of earnings and profits to provide against unrealistic hazards.[71]

Under certain conditions the directors may be personally liable to the corporation for allowing the corporation to become subject to the tax. If there is evidence of negligence in permitting the accumulation, an additional penalty tax can be imposed.[72]

MINIMIZING OTHER TAXES

There are numerous other taxes which the typical owner-manager is obligated to pay. Every employer must pay FICA (social security) taxes and Federal unemployment taxes. Other taxes for which one may be liable include: excise tax, occupational tax, wagering tax, highway use tax, civil aircraft use tax and self-employment tax. The individual seriously interested in minimizing taxes will not pass up the opportunity to analyze each and every one of these tax areas for possible minimizing opportunities.

To illustrate only one such opportunity, consider the social security tax paid by every employer. By consciously trying to decrease the percentage of the sales dollar that goes to employees, the social security tax may likewise be reduced. One of the things that this implies is that increased productivity will, in effect, reduce the labor cost as a percentage of the sales dollar and, consequently, the social security tax. Productivity is discussed further in Chapter 15. Since there is a wage base limitation, the use of relatively expensive personnel also represents an opportunity to reduce the effective percentage of social security taxes paid. If feasible, the use of contract labor where the employer does not pay the FICA tax may be attractive.

No stone should be left unturned in an effort to minimize other taxes.

CAVEAT: YOU CAN GO BROKE MINIMIZING TAXES

There is one common pitfall in which many managers of closely held companies find themselves. It results from a legitimate and conscientious attempt to minimize the tax liability produced by exceptional profit performance. To illustrate, consider the following corporation and the strategy utilized by its manager to reduce what was believed to be an excessive income tax liability.

How One Company Reduced its Taxes

Consider the company portrayed in Exhibit 8-19. As seen from the projected income statement for the year, a total taxable income of $100,000 is expected from sales totaling $703,000. Management feels that the projected Federal income tax liability of $25,000 is an amount that could be legitimately reduced to the benefit of the company and its employees. The projected cash flow statement indicates substantial bank balances throughout the next six months that represent the last half of the fiscal year. From a beginning bank balance of $2,000, a total of $29,000 will accumulate by the end of Month 12.

After reviewing the anticipated performance of the business, management decided on a four-part strategy for reducing the Federal income tax liability. As a postponement strategy, accelerated depreciation (double-declining-balance) would be used, as well as a contribution to the individual retirement account (IRA) of the owner-manager. Bonuses for the employees were selected as a benevolence strategy and charitable contributions were utilized as a philanthrophic strategy.

To take advantage of accelerated depreciation, a new tangible asset qualifying for the investment tax credit and costing $50,000 is proposed to be purchased in Month 7.
A five-year useful life is selected and the double-declining-balance depreciation method is utilized. The first year's depreciation under double-declining-balance method would be $20,000. This would amount to approximately $1.7 thousand per month in depreciation starting with Month 7 (the month of acquisition of the asset). It is anticipated that the manufacturer of the asset would expect payment upon delivery, that is in Month 7.

A contribution of $1,500 to the owner-manager's individual retirement account (IRA) plan would, of course, be a tax deduction. It is forecast that the contribution to the IRA plan would be made in Month 12 of the company's fiscal year.

Approximately 35% of the company's sales dollar goes to salaries. Management feels that giving part of the money made by the company back to the employees would provide an incentive for future performance. An amount roughly equal to 15% of the salaries is to be paid out in Month 12 for employee bonuses. The amount is $36,000.

The owner of the company also decides to make charitable contributions to five local organizations. A donation of $1,000 is scheduled to be made in each of the months beginning with Month 8 and ending with Month 12 of the fiscal year.

EXHIBIT 8-19
Example of a Company That Could Minimize Its Taxes
Projected Income Statement
(in $000)

	Total First 6 Mos.	7	8	9	10	11	12	Annual Total
REVENUES	$220	67	73	80	84	89	90	703
EXPENSES								
Operating (Cash)	80	26	28	31	33	35	35	268
Operating (30 Days)	100	33	36	39	41	43	43	335
Total Expenses	180	59	64	70	74	78	78	603
Taxable Income	40.0	8.0	9.0	10.0	10.0	11.0	12.0	100.0
Income Tax*	10.0	2.0	2.3	2.5	2.5	2.7	3.0	25.0
Net Income	$30.0	6.0	6.7	7.5	7.5	8.3	9.0	75.0

Projected Cash Flow Statement
(in $000)

	7	8	9	10	11	12
RECEIPTS (Net 30)	$60**	67	73	80	84	89
DISBURSEMENTS						
Operating (Cash)	26	28	31	33	35	35
Operating (30 Days)	31**	33	36	39	41	43
Income Tax Deposits	—	—	6.8	—	—	8.2
Total Disbursements	57	61	73.8	72	76	86.2
Cash Flow	3	6	(.8)	8	8	2.8
Beginning Bank Balance	2	5	11	10.2	18.2	26.2
Ending Bank Balance	$ 5	11	10.2	18.2	26.2	29.0

*Assume a forecasted effective average tax rate of 25%.

**From transactions of a prior period.

To examine the results of these combined tax-reduction strategies, refer to Exhibit 8-20. As may be seen, the taxable income is reduced from $100,000 to $47,300. Instead of having an accrued tax liability of $25,000, the new tax liability for the year would be only $6,800 (i.e., $11,800 less investment credit). A significant reduction in the amount of money to be paid in Federal income tax has been effected. Bottom-line performance for the company is still respectable and many benefits have been achieved through the strategies selected.

How to Go Broke Reducing Taxes

Management can take pride in the fact that first it created substantial bottom-line performance and then with additional strategies dramatically reduced the amount to be paid for Federal income tax. Let's hope that management takes this planning one step further and investigates what will be the ramification on the company's cash flow and bank balances of implementing these tax-reducing strategies. An overview of the cash flow is revealed in Exhibit 8-21. Fewer total dollars were paid for income tax but the combined strategies for minimizing taxes created a series of overdrafts at the bank that could force this company out of business. If the company had previously consumed all of its borrowing power, then a fatal series of decisions would have been made.

EXHIBIT 8-20.

Projected Income Statement
with Tax Saving Deductions
(in $000)

	Total First 6 Mos.	7	8	9	10	11	12	Annual Total
REVENUES	$220	67	73	80	84	89	90	703
EXPENSES								
Operating (Cash)	80	26	28	31	33	35	35	268
Operating (30 Days)	100	33	36	39	41	43	43	335
Subtotal Expense	180	59	64	70	74	78	78	603
Depreciation (5 yr. D.D.B)	—	1.7	1.7	1.7	1.7	1.7	1.7	10.2
IRA Contribution	—	—	—	—	—	—	1.5	1.5
Bonuses	—	—	—	—	—	—	36	36
Charitable Contributions	—	—	1	1	1	1	1	5
Total Expenses	180	60.7	66.7	72.7	76.7	80.7	118.2	655.7
Taxable Income	40	6.3	6.3	7.3	7.3	8.3	(28.2)	47.3
Federal Income Tax*	10.0	1.6	1.6	1.8	1.8	2.1	(7.1)**	11.8
Less Investment Tax Credit	—	5***	—	—	—	—	—	5
Net Income	$30.0	9.7***	4.7	5.5	5.5	6.2	(21.1)	40.5

*Assuming the same effective average tax rate of 25%.

**As a result of all the deductions taken, an income tax credit results.

***As a result of the investment tax credit.

EXHIBIT 8-21.

Projected Cash Flow Statement
with Tax Saving Deductions
(in $000)

Month	7	8	9	10	11	12
RECEIPTS	$60*	67	73	80	84	89
DISBURSEMENTS						
Operating (Cash)	26	28	31	33	35	35
Operating (30 Days)	31*	33	36	39	41	43
Equipment Purchase	50	—	—	—	—	—
IRA Contribution	—	—	—	—	—	1.5
Bonuses	—	—	—	—	—	36
Charitable Contributions	—	1	1	1	1	1
Income Tax Deposits	—	—	0**	—	—	(3.2)***
Total Disbursements	107	62	68	73	77	113.3
Cash Flow	(47)	5	5	7	7	(24.3)
Beginning Bank Balance	2	(45)	(40)	(35)	(28)	(21)
Ending Bank Balance	$(45)	(40)	(35)	(28)	(21)	(45.3)

*From transactions of a prior period.

**Net of Investment Credit (i.e., 5–5=0).

***Represents a net credit for the last quarter.

The problem did not result from income statement considerations, the problem resulted from the cash flow impact of those tax-minimizing decisions. Payments for equipment, lease-hold improvements and other tangible assets do not appear on the income statement. All of those deductions that produced tax benefits had to be paid in cash. It is unfortunate, although common, that closely held companies frequently experience near-fatal, liquidity crises as a result of avoiding current payment of taxes due.

Is it possible that this company would have been better off to go ahead and pay the taxes?

The Myth of Paying with "50¢" Dollars

A common expression has arisen with respect to minimizing taxes. A successful manager might say "I think I'll give the employees a bonus because, after all, I'll be paying for it with 50-cent dollars." This expression arises from the concept of a corporation being taxed at the maximum bracket that is approximately 50¢ for each dollar of taxable income. The thought is that, if one spends $1.00 on a legitimate, deductible expense, approximately 50¢ in taxes is saved. The fallacy with this whole concept is that one must write a check for $1.00. A tax benefit of 50¢ does result but a check for $1.00 is still written. There is a net outflow of 50¢ in company cash. If one really thinks about it, the concept of giving up a dollar to get 50¢ is like taking one step forward and two steps backward.

One is reminded of the entrepreneur who engaged in the business of walking into a hardware store, buying shovels for $1.00 and then walking out on the street and selling them for 75¢. When asked how he planned to win this game, he replied, "I'll make it up in volume."

Tax-minimizing strategies represent a wide variety of flexible techniques for planning out how the money in a business is utilized. They should, however, be used skillfully and with moderation. Failure to do so can, in extreme cases, result in a business that virtually goes broke minimizing taxes.

NOTES FOR CHAPTER 8

[1]James D. Edwards and Homer A. Black, *The Modern Accountant's Handbook* (Homewood, Illinois: Dow-Jones-Irwin, Inc., 1976), p. 113.

[2]*Financial Executives Handbook*, ed. Richard F. Vancil (Homewood, Illinois: Dow Jones-Irwin, Inc., 1970), p. 992.

[3]Edwards, p. 14.

[4]Robert N. Anthony, *Management Accounting* (Homewood, Illinois: Richard D. Irwin, Inc., 1970), p. 233.

[5]C. R. Niswonger and P. E. Fess, *Accounting Principles* (Cincinnati: South-Western Publishing Company, 1965), p. 237.

[6]Niswonger, p. 237.

[7]*Federal Tax Handbook*, (Englewood Cliffs: Prentice-Hall, Inc., 1979), p. 359.

[8]Edwards, p. 16.

[9]Alfred A. Ring, *Real Estate Principles and Practices* (Englewood Cliffs: Prentice-Hall, Inc., 1972), p. 237-240.

[10]*Federal Tax Handbook*, p. 356.

[11]*Federal Tax Handbook*, p. 364.

[12]*Federal Tax Handbook*, p. 365.

[13]*Federal Tax Handbook*, p. 369.

[14]*Federal Tax Handbook*, p. 370.

[15]*Tax Guide for Small Business* Publication 334, (Washington, D. C. : Internal Revenue Service, 1979), p. 15.

[16]*Tax Guide* Publication 334, p. 40.

[17]Ibid.

[18]Ibid.

[19]Ibid.

[20]*Tax Guide* Publication 334, p. 62.

[21]Ibid.

[22]Ibid.

[23]*Tax Guide* Publication 334, p. 59.

[24]Zolman Cavitch, *Tax Planning for Corporations and Shareholders* (New York: Matthew Bender, 1977), p. 510-522. Used by permission.

[25]Cavitch, p. 58.

[26]Cavitch, p. 59.

[27]Ibid.

[28]Cavitch, p. 524.

[29]Cavitch, p. 525.

[30]Cavitch, p. 535.

[31]*Federal Tax Handbook*, p. 221.

[32]*Federal Tax Handbook*, p. 223.

[33]Cavitch, p. 560.

[34]Ibid.

[35]Cavitch, p. 561.

[36]Ibid.

[37]Cavitch, p. 593.

[38]Cavitch, p. 595.

[39]Cavitch, p. 596.

[40]*Tax Economics of Charitable Giving* (Chicago: Arthur Andersen & Co., 1979), p. 19.

[41]*Tax Economics*, p. 10.

[42]*Federal Tax Handbook*, p. 263.

[43]*Tax Guide* Publication 334, p. 128.

[44]*Federal Tax Handbook*, p. 259.

[45]*Federal Tax Handbook*, p. 261.

[46]*Federal Tax Handbook*, p. 259.

[47]Frederick G. Kempin, Jr. and Jeremy L. Wiesen, *Legal Aspects of the Management Process* (St. Paul: West Publishing Co., 1976), p. 3.

[48]Kempin, p. 4.

[49]Kempin, p. 6.

[50]*Federal Tax Handbook*, p. 465.

[51]Chester Rohrlich, *Organizing Corporate and Other Business Enterprises* (New York: Matthew Bender, 1977), p. 238. Used by permission.

[52]Rohrlich, p. 239.

[53]*Tax Guide* Publication 334, p. 106.

[54]*Federal Tax Handbook*, p. 472.

[55]*Tax Guide* Publication 334, p. 107.

[56]Cavitch, p. 464.

[57]*Federal Tax Handbook*, p. 199.

[58]Cavitch, pp. 464, 467.

[59]*Federal Tax Handbook*, pp. 560, 561.

[60]*Federal Tax Handbook*, p. 564.

[61]*Federal Tax Handbook*, p. 302.

[62]*Federal Tax Handbook*, p. 300.

[63]*Federal Tax Handbook*, p. 299.

[64]*Federal Tax Handbook*, p. 221.

[65]Cavitch, p. 113.

[66]*Tax Guide* Publication 334, p. 33.

[67]Cavitch, p. 23.

[68]Cavitch, p. 25.

[69]*Federal Tax Handbook*, p. 461.

[70]Cavitch, p. 27.

[71]Cavitch, pp. 28, 210.

[72]*Federal Tax Handbook*, p. 461.

Eight Ratholes Where Profits Go
in the Closely Held Firm

Several messages have been stated and restated in this book. The first of these, that it is hoped will be heard and accepted at this point, is that profit is not cash flow.

A second message described in Chapter 1 is that growth consumes cash. Increasing sales are accompanied by increasing inventories, accounts receivable and investment in plant, equipment and training. There are some businesses that are exceptions to this rule but they are extremely rare. One obvious conclusion that a manager might draw from this is that growth should be constrained. Don't allow the business to grow, or at least, don't allow it to grow rapidly. This is a valid conclusion and a reasonable strategy. It is extremely difficult to accomplish, however, in the face of opportunities for growth.

Growth in sales is like motherhood and apple pie in our society. The American heritage is built on the concept of opportunity to accomplish new, better and bigger things. Growth provides realistic and valuable rewards other than just continuing the behavior of our forebears. Growth in sales provides opportunities for professional growth and career advancement for employees, managers and owners. Growth provides new jobs and opportunities for a greater number of people and has a beneficial ripple effect in the community in which the business is located.

Constraining growth in sales is often more difficult for managers to accomplish than firing a good and valuable employee who has given no cause for dismissal. Telling willing customers that you won't accept their orders gets right to your emotions. But the fact still remains that growth consumes cash. Managers find themselves on the "horns" of a dilemma.

Money In—Money Out

Since profit does not show up as cash in the bank, we have to conclude that all of the money that comes into a business also goes out of the business. Cash flow ebbs and flows. Examples in prior chapters demonstrate this. Plotting the profit and cash flow from examples in earlier chapters shows the profit generally trending upward with positive net profit all the time. Cash flow, on the other hand, fluctuates up and down, that is, positive and negative. Plotted bank balances at the end of the months reflect this same reaction. Profit and cash flow *seem* unrelated.

This conclusion permits us to look at the performance of a business in a slightly different fashion. In prior chapters, we have begun the description of operations with the units shipped and the sales. Having decided on what the sales are expected to be, the remainder of the forecasted income statement presentation records what expenses will be incurred in order to make those sales. The expenses must fit within the sales figure and are dependent upon how many units are shipped.

Since all the money that comes in goes out, we can look at this picture as the distribution of the sales dollar. As managers, we get to be the gatekeepers. We decide how much will be distributed here, how much there and how much somewhere else. All of the sales dollar gets distributed.

How to Distribute the Sales Dollar

An orderly listing might be made showing the distribution of the sales dollar. The first major distribution is for the materials that are needed to produce the product and for the wages of the labor to put the product together. There is also a distribution to pay for heat, light, rent, insurance, trash removal and all the things needed to provide the workers with a place to perform their work. This group of things taken together is called the overhead. The sum of the distributions to materials, labor and overhead is usually called the Cost of Goods Sold—an abbreviation for "the cost of the goods which were sold."

In a retail business, the manager buys the goods in a condition ready to be sold. The same would be true for a wholesale business or a distributorship. In these instances the cost going to materials, labor and overhead are not apparent but they still exist.

Cost of Goods Sold is the first major distribution from the sales dollar. The next one that managers usually think of includes themselves. In the owner-managed business, this is the president and those who work with the president. This includes the secretary, the bookkeepers, a fringe-benefits clerk and the purchasing person. These individuals are responsible for the whole business in general. They are the administration. They are the General & Administrative people. There is also a distribution needed to cover the heat, light, rent, trash removal and so on to provide these individuals with a place to do their work. This group of things taken together is the General & Administrative distribution from the sales dollar.

Making the product and watching over everything has been taken care of, but we are not finished distributing from the sales dollar. There is still the problem of actually making the sale. It takes people to talk people out of their hard-earned cash. There must be another major distribution from the sales dollar to cover the expense of people who bring about the sales. A common name for this distribution is Marketing.

It is normal in a financial presentation to add up the distributions at this point and get the total. If the sum is thought of as the total expense, then subtracting this from the sales will show the pre-tax profit. This number is needed to determine the next distribution, income tax.

Subtracting income tax from pre-tax profit, we arrive at the "bottom line," the net profit. If we stop here, we have the normal form of an income statement. Distribution from the sales dollar, however, is not yet finished.

Financial institutions and other lenders must have their claims satisfied. Interest on loans is included in the distributions already made. Now it is time to make the principal repayments. Many managers seem unaware of the size of their monthly principal repayments because these payments don't appear on the income statement presentation. When we think of a distribution of the sales dollar, however, the principal repayment is very prominently displayed.

It is not unusual to find that a business with a five-year loan for $150,000 has monthly principal repayments larger than the profits. The manager has distributed more of the sales dollar than is available, but didn't know it because this distribution doesn't appear on the income statement.

These major distributions of the sales dollar are indicated in Exhibit 9-1, "Distribution of the Sales Dollar."

EXHIBIT 9-1
Distribution of the Sales Dollar

Sales		000
Material	XX	
Labor	XX	
Overhead	XX	
Cost of Goods Sold		XXX
General & Administrative		XXX
Marketing		XXX
Income Tax		XX
Principal Repayment		XX

Example of a Detailed Distribution

Distributing the sales dollar to major categories provides a general overview of the operation of a business. Exhibit 9-2 provides an example of a detailed distribution of the sales dollar. This distribution emphasizes the people and the non-people expenditures.

EXHIBIT 9-2
Detailed Distribution of the Sales Dollar

Sales		000
Material	XX	
Labor	XX	
Overhead People	XX	
Overhead Other	XX	
Cost of Goods Sold		XXX
General & Administrative People	XX	
General & Administrative Other	XX	
General & Administrative		XXX
Marketing People	XX	
Marketing Other	XX	
Marketing		XXX
		XXX
Income Tax		XX
Principal Repayment		XX
Dividends		XX

One doesn't have to have many workers before there must be people to watch over the people. Since this kind of supervisory help is part of the overhead, the overhead category can be broken into Overhead People and Overhead Other. In the major category called General & Administrative, there are clearly people and non-people expenses. The same is true for Marketing.

Now the picture of the business seems more complete. But, you may ask, what about the profit? Some portion of it is probably used to make the principal repayments. Clearly, we are not yet finished distributing from the sales dollar. Just as there is more than one subcategory for Cost of Goods Sold, General & Administrative and Marketing, there is additional distribution from the major category called Profit.

It is unusual to find dividends being paid to owners by businesses which are not large and publicly held. An owner-managed business, a closely held business or a small business will seldom, if ever, formally declare dividends. On the other hand, they do sometimes provide the owners with cash. This would also be a distribution from the sales dollar.

Even now, after distributing to principal repayments and the owners, we are not yet finished with distributions from the sales dollar. Distribution of profit merits further consideration.

Distributing Profit

There are additional subcategories under profit where some portion of the sales dollar is distributed. Principal repayments and dividends or contributions to the owners are rather obvious ones. Other distributions are insidious in the way they creep into management decision making.

A major distribution goes into leasehold improvements. As a manager, you may recall walking into the shop one day and noticing how badly the place needed patching and painting. Perhaps, you remember the day your foreman made a very convincing argument for cutting a door into the back room. These are things that make the business a better and more efficient place to work.

On an income statement presentation, the result of these good works is a small increase in the amortization or depreciation portion of Overhead or General & Administrative. When viewed as a distribution from the sales dollars received, however, the sum involved is the total cost of the leasehold improvement.

While the expense is recognized over the remaining life of the lease on the property being improved, the painting contractor must be paid immediately.

Another distribution goes to small equipment. These small things are usually accounted for by choosing some arbitrary cutoff point. For example, a small piece of equipment like a desk calculator or a half-inch drill, costing less than $100 might be expensed as if used up immediately. Anything costing more than $100 is added to the equipment assets and depreciated over some reasonable lifetime. Hand tools, office equipment, small shop tools like portable compressors, chain saws and snow tires can find their way into the fixed assets of the business. As a result, a small monthly increase appears as depreciation under the Overhead or General & Administrative category on the income statement. The entire cost of these items, however, must be distributed from the sales dollars received.

Exhibit 9-3 shows a detail of where profits go. In addition to the items already discussed, there are distributions to Other Fixed Assets, Inventory Increases, Accounts Receivable Increases and Other. This is not a complete or comprehensive list. It mentions only major items.

A Business Has a Profile

Referring again to Exhibit 9-2, we may perceive something akin to a thumb print or profile. Businesses have profiles because of competition.

If two people are in the same business, making and selling the same item, they must first locate raw materials. Each will search the Yellow Pages, trade journals and trade conventions

EXHIBIT 9-3

Where Profits Go

Net Profit	000
Principal Repayments	XX
Dividends	XX
Leasehold Improvements	XX
Small Equipment	XX
Other Fixed Assets	XX
Inventory Increases	XX
Accounts Receivable Increases	XX
Other	XX

and, in time, contact the same supplier's salesperson.

Your cost for raw materials may be a little more or a little less than that of your competitor, but it will be very nearly the same price for the same thing from the same or a comparable supplier. And so it goes for all of the things needed to conduct the business: heat, light, rent, phone, paper, trash removal, etc. Even people have a market price. If you don't pay enough, they won't become your employees. If you pay too much, the business won't have any profit. The differences among competitors are relatively small. Major distributions from the sales dollar are very much the same when producing the same product or service in comparable quantities.

A Sample Business Profile

The profile of most businesses is well known. The examples given in prior chapters are primarily for a small manufacturing business that does its own selling. The profile for such a business, if it is doing well, looks like the one in Exhibit 9-4.

EXHIBIT 9-4

Typical Profile for a Small Manufacturing Business
Which Does Its Own Selling

Sales		100%
Materials	20	
Labor	20	
Overhead People	5	
Overhead Other	10	
Cost of Goods Sold		55
General & Administrative People	5	
General & Administrative Other	10	
General & Administrative		15
Marketing People	5	
Marketing Other	5	
Marketing		10
		80
Income Tax		10
Profit		10
		100%

Sales are shown as 100%. The other categories are shown as distributions from the sales dollar in percentages. Cost of Goods Sold is approximately 55%. If this is subtracted from the sales, the resulting Gross Profit Margin is 45% which is reasonable for this kind of business.

General & Administrative, in a closely held business, is hard to keep small. The president's salary alone makes up a significant portion. Add to that the president's secretary, some bookkeeping, the rent, heat, light, insurance and a few more things that the business has to have, and it is difficult to keep the General & Administrative down to 15% of the sales dollar.

In a smaller manufacturing business, the manager is frequently production oriented and is often reluctant to spend an adequate amount on promotion and advertising. To do well, however, the business must make a commitment to its promotion program. The figure usually found in this kind of business is 5-15% of the sales dollar. The 10% shown in the profile is reasonable.

In Exhibit 9-4, the taxes are shown as 50% of pre-tax profit for simplicity. For a small business, this number will be less, probably 20-30%. We would like to choose a figure more like that for a fully taxed business in order to emphasize the importance of this cost of doing business. The result is that 10% of the sales dollar is distributed to the taxing authorities.

This leaves 10% of the sales dollar for distribution to all of the sub-categories under profit. We might add that this is the profile of a business that is doing very well.

One interesting observation from Exhibit 9-4 is the importance of people. They are found under Labor, Overhead, General & Administrative and Marketing. Adding up the distributions of the sales dollar, 35% goes to people. A manager knows how important people are to the business. They consume most of the manager's time and 35% of the sales dollar, right off the top.

The "What Have You Done For Me Lately?" Syndrome

Seeing how important people are in the profile of a business and knowing that they consume most of the managment's time, it is interesting to consider the behavior of people. Most managers have noticed that employees seem always to be saying, "I'm looking for opportunities for growth and advancement." What the manager hears is "raise." Strangely, even after people have been given an evaluation and a raise, the manager hears that same old refrain. It sometimes sounds as if people are saying, "What have you done for me lately?"

Without people you can't build the business. When they are happy and working together, magic happens. When they become unhappy, it seems impossible to make the business work well.

As a manager, you sometimes wonder what makes people behave the way they do. Is there some basic explanation that will make it easier to understand why you keep hearing that old refrain? Perhaps there is. Certainly, people are too complex to have any simple explanation provide the entire story. There is one explanation, however, that goes a long way in helping to understand people's behavior.

A Reason for the Syndrome

Abraham Maslow[1] proposed a simple model of human behavior based upon a short list of human needs. There is a priority to the needs. Some must be satisfied, at least to some minimum level, before others become important.

Maslow illustrated the needs with a triangle. This is meant to suggest their priority and how they build upon each other. Physiological needs are the first which must be satisfied.

The physiological needs must be satisfied just to stay alive. A person must have food, water and shelter. An open wound cannot be left bleeding. One must find air to breathe regardless of the struggle required to obtain it. A person must be warm, but not too warm; dry, but not too dry. These needs must be satisfied sufficiently for the survival of the body.

When the physiological needs are satisfied just enough that life is not immediately threatened, another need emerges—safety. What safety refers to is the need to insure that life is not threatened by physical danger, even though the physiological needs have been satisfied sufficiently for the moment. Think of it this way. If you are starving and there is nothing but a bear in sight, well, you will go after the bear. If you have a choice between the bear or berries, the berries are safer.

When the safety needs are satisfied just enough that life is not immediately threatened, another need emerges. This one is called love. Exhibit 9-5 portrays Love Needs in Maslow's Hierarchy of Needs. Here the physiological and the safety needs are shown satisfied to some degree.

EXHIBIT 9-5
SHOWING LOVE NEEDS IN MASLOW'S HIERARCHY OF NEEDS

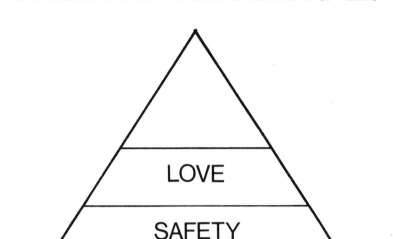

Love is a word with many meanings. What is meant here is that kind of love without which infants die. You may love roses. But, they don't love you back in a way that will satisfy these needs. Love is something that flows from individuals to individuals. Love comes from people.

It is interesting to observe that when the physiological needs are threatened, people care very little, if at all, about other people. It is as if they say to themselves, "If there are two of us, *he* might eat the bear." When the physiological needs are satisfied just enough that life is not immediately threatened and safety becomes important, people tend to agglomerate. People and animals learned a long time ago that there is safety in numbers. It is as if they are saying to themselves, "If there are a bunch of us, maybe the bear will eat *him*." People are still not interested in the other people. They tolerate them because the environment is safer with them around.

When the love needs become important, people need people. They need at least one person to satisfy an emptiness in their life. The family provides one opportunity to give and receive love.

When the love needs are satisfied enough that they are not a problem, another need arises. This one is called esteem. Esteem has to do with "how I feel about myself."

Once again, when this need is satisfied just enough that it is not an immediate problem, another need arises. This one is referred to as self-actualization. Exhibit 9-6 depicts Self-actualization Needs in Maslow's Hierarchy of Needs. Self-actualization is an unusual terminology that is frequently misused by those trying to discuss Maslow's Heirarchy of Needs.

Self-actualization means: What a person can become, a person will become. When all of the other needs have been satisfied enough that they are not of immediate concern, people will quite naturally do the things for which they have talent and aptitude. You get no satisfaction, no esteem, no love from doing things poorly. You get a warm and satisfying reaction and response to doing things well. Most human beings seek praise and compliments. They obtain these by doing what they do well, the things for which they have talent and aptitude.

EXHIBIT 9-6
SHOWING SELF-ACTUALIZATION NEEDS
IN MASLOW'S HIERARCHY OF NEEDS

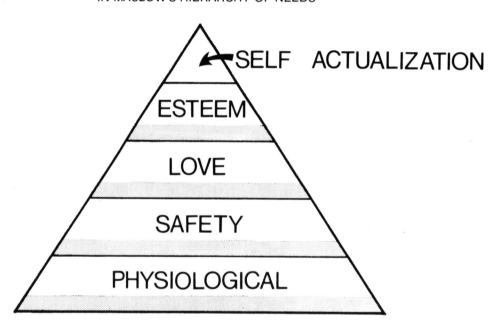

Maslow's Hierarchy of Needs

Exhibit 9-6 depicts the situation many of us find ourselves in if we live in the United States in the 20th century. We have satisfied all of the needs enough that we are working on satisfying all of them. Remember, the safety needs arise when the physiological needs are satisfied just enough that life is not immediately threatened. The physiological needs are not completely satisfied. They are still there demanding further satisfaction.

How are the physiological needs satisfied? When you are young and just starting out, you are content with a small apartment. Soon you want a small house and, in time a larger house. Later in life, you would like two houses, maybe one on the lake or in the mountains.

Remember the bear? You would like that bear finely ground. Eating ground meat every day creates a yearning for some unground meat, some chateaubriand. If you eat chateaubriand every day for a month, however, you get a craving for lobster. And so it goes.

The needs are growing and they appear to be insatiable. We are each working on all of the needs all the time and whenever we satisfy them, they grow and need greater satisfaction.

How are these needs typically satisfied? You can have chateaubriand instead of hamburger. It just costs a little more. It is safer to live in the suburbs than in the ghetto. It just costs a little more.

People spend a major portion of their time working to get just a little more money. Where do they get it? From the distribution of the sales dollar. Whether the employees realized it or not, whether they understood it or not, the manager was hearing them correctly. They were saying "What have you done for me lately?"

Re-Distributing the Sales Dollar

A manager who understands Maslow's Hierarchy of Needs and who has heard that old refrain from the employees may now see one way to solve the problem. The employees have real needs that are growing and are insatiable. What the employees need is a little more money from time to time. As the manager, you can handle that. After all, you control the distribution from the sales dollar.

Assume one is managing the business portrayed in Exhibit 9-4, and that its sales total $1,000,000 per year. The exhibit can be expressed in terms of dollars as shown in Exhibit 9-7, "Detailed Distribution of One Million Dollars in Sales."

EXHIBIT 9-7
Detailed Distribution of One Million Dollars
in Sales

Sales		$1,000,000
Material	$200,000	
Labor	200,000	
Overhead People	50,000	
Overhead Other	100,000	
Cost of Goods Sold		550,000
General & Administrative People	50,000	
General & Administrative Other	100,000	
General & Administrative		150,000
Marketing People	50,000	
Marketing Other	50,000	
Marketing		100,000
Income Tax		100,000
Profit		100,000
		$1,000,000

Suppose the manager of this business desires to be magnanimous by providing the employees with 10% annual raises to satisfy their growing needs. This would have to be a real increase, of course. A 10% raise in the face of 10% inflation is not very satisfying.

If the employees get 10% raises each year and the profile of the business remains the same, five years later this business would appear approximately as portrayed in Exhibit 9-8, "Same Business Five Years Later." If each category involving people grows by 10% each year, the

EXHIBIT 9-8
Same Business Five Years Later

Materials	$320,000	
Labor	320,000	
Overhead People	80,000	
Overhead Other	160,000	
Cost of Goods Sold		$ 880,000
General & Administrative People	80,000	
General & Administrative Other	160,000	
General & Administrative		240,000
Marketing People	80,000	
Marketing Other	80,000	
Marketing		160,000
Income Tax		160,000
Profit		160,000
Sales Needed		$1,600,000

other categories must grow by the same 10% because a business must retain its profile to stay competitive. That means that five years later the sales must have grown to $1,600,000.

To provide the employees with 10% real growth in compensation during these five years, the same employees need only provide the business with what it takes to increase sales to the new annual total of $1,600,000. To get the raises and keep the business competitive, the employees need to be more productive. The employee who picked up 10 boxes per hour must now, five years later, pick up 16 boxes. The clerk who prepared 10 invoices per hour must now prepare 16.

This doesn't imply that the people have to work harder. Profit has increased at the same rate. The business can make larger principal repayments. Management can invest in a hoist for one employee and a computer for the clerk. The company can make investments that increase productivity.

What this really says is if the managment and employees can create 10% annual increases in productivity, in constant dollars, then the people can have a 10% annual increase in compensation. This compensation provides the means with which they satisfy their growing needs. The matching increase in productivity allows the business profile to remain competitive.

The Inadequate Productivity Pitfall

Ten percent raises with 10% productivity increases allow management to be magnanimous. How realistic is 10% annual productivity increase? There have been times when this figure has been achieved and surpassed in this country and in others. A *Business Week* article [2] reported that the productivity of the American worker for the 15 years, 1960-75, ranged from +12% to –3% with an average for the 15 year period of 2.1%. Quarterly reports for the last half of the 1970s by the United States Department of Commerce indicate the average remains about 2%.

What would happen to our example if the manager gave 10% raises while the workers delivered productivity increases of only 2%? Of course, our employees are better than average. After all, they have had good raises and both management and employees have been working together to increase their productivity. Suppose our employees are able to deliver 5% productivity increases.

With a 5% annual productivity increase, the people could provide what it takes to increase sales by 5% per year for five years. Sales would be $1,276,000. Sales of $1,600,000 are needed, however, to provide the employees with their 10% raises. We are deficient $324,000 in sales.

This deficiency can be made up by hiring some additional help. The new help probably won't be as productive as our original employees but they should be as productive as our people were at the start of this five-year period. At that time, sales were $1,000,000 and people costs were $350,000. Dividing the latter into the former gives $2.86 sales per labor dollar, a kind of productivity figure.

Dividing this productivity into the sales needed, $324,000 yields the cost of the people needed to help our employees bring the sales up to $1,600,000. The requirement is $113,000 in payroll for the new people.

In the meantime, the original people have been getting their 10% raises so their cost is now up to $560,000 as seen in Exhibit 9-8. The total payroll after five years will be the cost of both the new people and the original people or $673,000.

Now, it all works out. Sales are increased to provide the raises for the people and help is brought in to make up for the deficiency in productivity increases.

Since we must maintain the profile of the business to keep it competitive, it would be wise to verify that it has been preserved. We know that people costs should be 35% of sales to maintain this profile. Dividing the new total people costs, $673,000 by 0.35 should yield the new total sales. Dividing those two numbers the new sales come out to be $1,923,000.

To provide the raises and add the help to make up for inadequate improvement in productivity, the sales have to grow even faster. Since this is not possible with the stated productivity of the original employees plus the new employees, the only remaining possibility is to change the distribution of the sales dollar to give a greater percentage to the employees. In a competitive market, however, this destroys the business' competitive profile. Granting raises at an annual rate greater than the rate of productivity increase produces a dilemma.

How Inadequate Productivity and Inflation Create a Dilemma

The example we used considered sales to be 100%. The actual sales could be $1,000,000, $100,000 or $100,000,000. The distributions are a percent of sales.

The increases chosen were so much per year as a percent of prior years. We selected raises of 10% per year and productivity increases of 5% per year. The resulting increase in sales was a percentage increase per year.

Whenever a quantity increases by a percentage with time its appearance when plotted on graph paper has a characteristic shape. That curve is known to mathematicians, engineers and scientists as an exponential curve. The characteristic of an exponential curve is that it always gets steeper. It begins to rise at some rate. While the rate of increase remains the same, the actual rise grows with time.

Exhibit 9-9, An Exponential Curve, is a plot of the relationship between sales and time (solid line) beginning with $1,000,000 and growing at 10% per year.

All of this analysis was done in constant dollars. If we now go back and add the effects of inflation, the curve gets even steeper (Exhibit 9-9, dotted line).

EXHIBIT 9-9
AN EXPONENTIAL CURVE

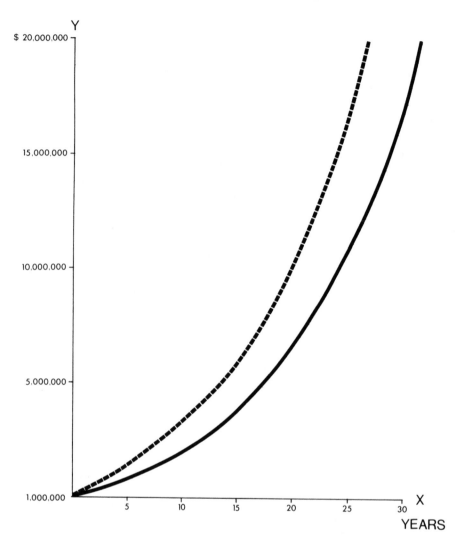

You may be saying to yourself that this can't go on. After all, some businesses have been around a long time and their sales have not gone through the sky. You have also heard of companies that fire or retire the high-priced employees and replace them with younger, less expensive employees. By doing this, they succeed in making the curve a little less steep. Their curve, however, is still an exponential curve as is the one for the companies listed on the New York and American Stock Exchanges. Think about it. Who is interested in a business with no growth? They all have some rate of growth, hence, an exponential curve.

One observation is suggested by this curve. All the competitors are going up an exponential curve. It is not hard to imagine that as they grow there is going to come a day when the marketplace just can't absorb all the products or services offered by all of the competitors.

When that day arrives, somebody has to get off the curve. Some competitor has to decline. That makes room for those who remain.

When productivity gains are less than the gains in the people's distribution from the sales dollar, the rate of growth in sales needs spiraling increases or the profile must be altered so that business is competitively weaker. Inflation increases the needed rate of growth even more. Each of these potentialities hastens the approach of the day when the weakest competitor will have to withdraw from the competition or be forced out.

Balancing the Needs of the People and the Needs of the Organization

A business is a group of people working together to satisfy their individual needs and goals and aspirations. The needs are real, innate and fundamental human needs that must be satisfied according to a priority. The needs, however, are never completely satisfied. They are growing and are insatiable.

Individuals obtain the means to satisfy their growing needs from a distribution of the sales dollar. They spend the biggest part of their time in this endeavor. They seek career growth and advancement in the organizational heirarchy to achieve greater means with which to satisfy their needs. Even without advancement, they seek increased compensation for longevity within the organization.

Meanwhile, the organization that provides them with their compensation must maintain a competitive profile in the distribution of its sales dollar or be forced to retreat from the marketplace. To provide the people with increases in their compensation the business must grow. But, growth consumes cash as explained in Chapter 1. The business needs an ever greater distribution from the sales dollar to support itself.

The rate of growth needed to maintain equilibrium is strongly affected by the productivity increases achieved by management and employees. The achievable increases in productivity are constrained by the ability of the business to make investments in new technology. The distribution of the sales dollar plowed back into the business must grow just to maintain the rate of growth and the rate of productivity increase.

The needs of the people and the needs of the business are competing for the distribution of the sales dollar. A business that does not grow will not satisfy the needs of its people. A business that grows while providing undue compensation to its people including the owners will not satisfy the needs of the business. To survive and endure, a business must grow and it must also balance the distribution of the sales dollar among the competing needs of the people and the needs of the business itself.

In the long run, owners, managers and employees who excessively indulge themselves in boats, planes, lake houses, motorhomes, luxury automobiles, country clubs and feather-bedding create an exponential curve too steep to climb and hasten the day when the weak competitor is driven from the marketplace. Non-productive distributions from the sales dollar weaken the business' ability to compete. In the end, the result is inevitable.

A Disturbing Afterthought

Exhibit 9-7 indicates an organization with revenues of one million dollars. Since the profile is a percentage distribution of the sales dollar, this initial sum could be any number. The total available could be several hundred billion dollars. Of course, only national economies and gross national products are nearly that big.

Distributions from the revenue dollar go for many purposes. A relatively small portion is distributed for the materials and labor which actually produce that which brings in the revenue. On the other hand, there are many services needed to get the finished product from the workers to the customers. There are also many services needed to watch over the operations, to police the people, to keep good records, to train people and to provide for their welfare. There are also needs for better facilities, tools, equipment, roads and parking lots.

Even in a one hundred billion dollar business, like a national economy, the people and the organization compete for the distribution of the revenue dollar. A business that grows while providing undue compensation to its people will not satisfy the needs of the organization. Managers, employees, consumers and decision-makers who indulge themselves in non-productive distributions weaken the organization's ability to compete. In time, the organization will become a weak competitor. In the end, the result is inevitable.

NOTES FOR CHAPTER 9

[1]Maslow, Abraham H., *Motivation and Personality*, 2nd Edition, (New York: Harper & Row, 1970)
[2]*Business Week*, November 15, 1976, p. 47.

10

Return on Investment or Liquidity:
Solving a Dilemma for the Closely Held Manager

Return on investment (ROI) usually encompasses the concept of economic productivity. "What do I get out for what I put in?" is as much a part of ROI as it is the productivity principles discussed in Chapter 15.

The authors have observed a curious phenomenon in our society regarding return on investment. The smallest economic entities, individuals, understand and apply the concept all the time. They place part of their savings in a passbook savings account and part in a certificate of deposit (CD). Individuals do this because CDs pay a higher interest rate and, thereby, provide a greater return on investment. There are, of course, trade offs. CDs require that money be committed for fixed periods of time and penalties usually result for early withdrawal.

At the other end of the spectrum, very large economic entities, such as members of the Fortune 500 corporations, routinely apply and use as a planning guideline the concept of return on investment. DuPont, one of the most ardent advocates of ROI, will get rid of departments, ventures or product lines that do not meet minimum ROI performance criteria.[1]

The curious phenomenon is that while very small entities, individuals, and very large entities, Fortune 500 corporations, understand and regularly apply ROI concepts, the in-between entities seldom do. The authors almost never encounter an owner-manager of a growing business who understands, utilizes or can even calculate return on investment. If ROI is ever considered, it is usually after the fact and then as a casual reference to what it was last year.

There are at least two reasons why most owner-managers do not focus on ROI as a major guideline for decision making. First, owner-managers have a unique ROI versus liquidity dilemma. Second, there is not a consensus as to how ROI should be calculated and applied.

THE ROI VS. LIQUIDITY DILEMMA

Owner-management is typically characterized by a hectic effort to make the sale and then produce and deliver the product. Punctuating this relentless struggle is an endless series of interruptions, phone calls, finanacial crises, people problems and operational "brush fires." The manager frequently feels that there is never enough time or money to do what is absolutely necessary for the health and sometimes even the survival of the business.[2]

For most owner-managers operating in this environment, return on investment and liquidity generally reduce to simple and earthy concepts. The question of return on investment really becomes a question of the return: typically, net profit. The question of profit often boils down to "How can I manage so that there will be some?" If a profit is already being earned, the pertinent question becomes, "Is there anything that can be done to increase it?" In a similar vein, the owner-manager's concern with liquidity is less often a concern with balance sheet ratios and more often a concern with how to meet the payroll due on Friday and the rent due on Tuesday.[3]

The owner-manager often thinks (and is seldom counseled to the contrary) that the answer to both return on investment and liquidity is to make more profit. This line of reasoning contributes to many financial management headaches. Consider the business portrayed in Exhibit 10-1 that sells its products for cash.

EXHIBIT 10-1
Forecasted Income Statement
(in 000's)

	Month	1	2	3	4	
Units Shipped		20	22	24	25	
REVENUES (Cash)		$ 40	44	48	50	
EXPENSES						
Materials		16	17	19	20	
Labor		8	9	10	10	
G&A & Marketing						
Paid Currently		7	8	8	9	
Paid in 30 Days		5	6	6	6	
Total Expense		36	40	43	45	
Profit		$ 4	4	5	5	

This business is making a respectable 10% profit on sales. The liquidity of the business is pragmatically described for the manager over the next four months by a counterpart statement of receipts and disbursements of cash. Units sell for $2 each. Materials cost 80¢ per unit, are paid for on a net 10-day basis (in the month of the expense) and must be purchased in lots of 15,000 units. It is desirable to carry a one-month supply in inventory. Labor is paid in the month of the expense, and the G & A and Marketing are paid as indicated.[4]

Before calculating the cash flow, it is necesssary to determine the schedule of receipts of materials (in lots of 15,000) and cash disbursements to pay for them (net 10 days). The inventory at the beginning of Month 1 is 30,000 units. Any number greater than the 20,000 to be shipped in Month 1 would have been adequate for the beginning inventory, but any number greater than 35,000 would be an excessive level. (The 20,000 needed plus one minimum order quantity, 15,000.) The materials disbursement was calculated using the schedule in Exhibit 10-2.

The statement of cash flows can then be portrayed as in Exhibit 10-3.

This owner-manager perceives an opportunity to improve profits. By extending 30 days credit to select customers, sales can be increased by 50% in four months while maintaining good margins. The new level of profits is indicated in the revised Income Statement shown in Exhibit 10-4.[5]

EXHIBIT 10-2
Materials Purchasing Schedule
(in 000's of units)

Month	1	2	3	4
Beginning Inventory	30	25	33	39
(−) Shipments	20	22	24	25
(+)Units Received	15	30	30	15
Ending Inventory	25	33	39	29
Value of Units Received @ 80¢/Unit	$ 12	24	24	12
Disbursement for Units Received	$ 12	24	24	12

EXHIBIT 10-3
Forecasted Cash Flow Statement
(in 000's)

Month	1	2	3	4
RECEIPTS				
Sales (Cash)	$ 40	44	48	50
DISBURSEMENTS				
Materials	12	24	24	12
Labor	8	9	10	10
G&A & Marketing				
Paid Currently	7	8	8	9
Paid in 30 Days	5*	5	6	6
Total Disbursed	32	46	48	37
Cash Flow	8	(2)	0	13
Beginning Cash Balance	5	13	11	11
Ending Cash Balance	$ 13	11	11	24

*The results of transactions of a prior period.

As may be seen, this decision would increase total profit over the next four months from $18,000 to $24,000. The company's liquidity, however, is another story. It is portrayed in Exhibit 10-5, the counterpart schedule of receipts and disbursements.

The manager who attempted to make more profit by introducing credit sales might be considered very successful. Down at the bank, however, overdrafts will occur three out of four

EXHIBIT 10-4
Forecasted Income Statement
Increased Sales Revision
(in 000's)

	Month	1	2	3	4
UNITS		20	27	33	38
REVENUES					
Sales (Cash)		$ 40	44	48	50
Sales (Credit)		—	10	18	26
Total Revenue		40	54	66	76
EXPENSES					
Materials		16	22	26	30
Labor		8	11	13	15
G&A & Marketing					
Paid Currently		7	9	11	13
Paid in 30 Days		5	7	9	10
Total Expense		36	49	59	68
Profit		$ 4	5	7	8

EXHIBIT 10-5
Forecasted Cash Flow Statement
Increased Sales Revision
(in 000's)

	Month	1	2	3	4
RECEIPTS					
Sales (Cash)		$ 40	44	48	50
Sales (Credit)		—	—	10	18
Total Receipts		40	44	58	68
DISBURSEMENTS					
Materials		24	24	24	36
Labor		8	11	13	15
G&A & Marketing					
Paid Currently		7	9	11	13
Paid in 30 Days		5*	5	7	9
Total Disbursed		44	49	55	73
Cash Flow		(4)	(5)	3	(5)
Beginning Cash Balance		5	1	(4)	(1)
Ending Cash Balance		$ 1	(4)	(1)	(6)

*The result of transactions of a prior period.

months. This increase in profit and decrease in liquidity dilemma is straightforwardly portrayed with the forecasted Income and Cash Flow Statements.[6]

Consider the same business that perceives that the way to solve the money shortage problem caused by credit sales is to make still more profit. If unfinished units are purchased in lots of 40,000 instead of 15,000, the supplier will offer a quantity discount of 10% of the purchase price. This appears to be a neat and simple way to get more money into the company by reducing the amount paid out. A revision of the preceding forecasted Income Statement, assuming both the extension of credit to the customers and the taking advantage of quantity discounts would yield an improved profit picture as shown in Exhibit 10-6.

EXHIBIT 10-6
Profit from Forecasted Income Statement
Increased Sales & Quantity Purchasing Revision
(in 000's)

Month	1	2	3	4
Profit	$ 6	7	10	11

Credit sales together with quantity purchasing yield a profit totaling $34,000, compared with an original profit of $18,000—practically doubled. Revision of the cash flow forecast (See Exhibit 10-7.) reveals the power of this tool in pointing out the liquidity ramifications. (A new schedule of receipts of materials and cash disbursements to pay for them was used to determine materials disbursements.)

Increasing sales through extension of credit to customers creates a maximum overdraft of

EXHIBIT 10-7
Forecasted Cash Flow Statement
Increased Sales & Quantity Purchasing Revision
(in 000's)

Month	1	2	3	4
RECEIPTS				
Sales (Cash)	$ 40	44	48	50
Sales (Credit)	—	—	10	18
Total Receipts	40	44	58	68
DISBURSEMENTS				
Materials	29	29	29	29
Labor	8	11	13	15
G&A & Marketing				
Paid Currently	7	9	11	13
Paid in 30 Days	5*	5	7	9
Total Disbursed	49	54	60	66
Cash Flow	(9)	(10)	(2)	2
Beginning Cash Balance	5	(4)	(14)	(16)
Ending Cash Balance	$ (4)	(14)	(16)	(14)

*The result of transactions of a prior period.

$6,000. If the business also takes advantage of supplier discounts for quantity purchasing, a maximum overdraft of $16,000 results.[7]

An overview of the three preceding management alternatives is given in Exhibit 10-8.

The financial dilemma which the owner-manager repeatedly experiences is pointed out in Exhibit 10-8. In the struggle to make or increase profits, returns, the manager aggravates the financial problems.

EXHIBIT 10-8

Overview of Three Management Alternatives

	PROFIT for 4 Months	CASH BALANCE at end of Month 4
Continue Present Operations	$ 18,000	$ 24,000
Extend Credit to Customers	24,000	(6,000)
Extend Credit to Customers and Take Quantity Discounts	34,000	(14,000)

In the second example, the desire to increase profits by extending credit to customers creates a financial problem which could jeopardize the company's ability to meet the payroll. To solve this liquidity problem, the manager decides to take advantage of quantity purchasing and thereby "make more money." More profit is created but a liquidity problem results that is more than twice as severe as before.

In some cases this difficulty can pick up momentum (credit unavailable, management incompetent, etc.) like a toboggan racing downhill. Each management decision trades liquidity for profit until all financial resources are exhausted and some major payment, like payroll, is missed. The company then fails to survive.[8]

Most attempts by an owner-manager to build the business result in painful liquidity problems. Increasing sales, increasing production, making a profit and maintaining a positive bank balance so consume the typical owner-manager that the question of maximizing the return on what is invested seldom gets considered.

RETURN ON INVESTMENT FORMULAS

It is interesting that in our free enterprise economy, there exists no universally accepted definition or measure of return on investment. The attempt to meaningfully quantify what you "get out" for what you "put in" is, with few exceptions, (such as interest on a savings account) a frustrating endeavor.

Common ROI Expressions

There are numerous expressions for arriving at the return on investment for a business. Some common ones include:

$$1.\ ROI = \frac{\text{Current-Year Profit (After Taxes)}}{\text{Shareholders Equity}}$$

and,

$$2.\ ROI = \frac{\text{Current-Year Cash Flow}}{\text{Shareholders Equity}}$$

where Shareholders Equity is typically the Paid in Captial (Common Stock) plus the Retained Earnings.[9]

Other measures of ROI include:

$$3. \ \text{ROI} = \frac{\text{Current-Year Profit (After Taxes)}}{\text{Gross Assets}}$$

$$4. \ \text{ROI} = \frac{\text{Current-Year Profit (After Taxes)}}{\text{Net Assets}}$$

$$5. \ \text{ROI} = \frac{\text{Current-Year Cash Flow}}{\text{Gross Assets}}$$

$$6. \ \text{ROI} = \frac{\text{Current-Year Cash Flow}}{\text{Net Assets}}$$

where Gross Assets are at cost and Net Assets are at cost less accumulated depreciation.[10]

$$7. \ \text{ROI} = \frac{\text{Current-Year Profit (After Taxes)}}{\text{Assets minus Current Liabilities}}$$

$$8. \ \text{ROI} = \frac{\text{Current-Year Cash Flow}}{\text{Assets minus Current Liabilities}}$$

$$9. \ \text{ROI} = \frac{\text{Current-Year Profit less Interest on Long Term Debt}}{\text{Assets}}$$

$$10. \ \text{ROI} = \frac{\text{Current-Year Cash Flow less Interest on Long Term Debt}}{\text{Assets}}$$

$$11. \ \text{ROI} = \frac{\text{Average Annual Profit}}{\text{Average Value of Assets Employed}}$$

$$12. \ \text{ROI} = \frac{\text{Average Annual Cash Flow}}{\text{Average Value of Assets Employed}}$$

where "Average Annual" is over a given number of years.[11]

Since combinations and rearrangements of the preceding expressions are also utilized, it is clear that one must decide which ROI definition to apply. Needless to say, the ROI for any specific company could be very low or very high depending on which definition is used.

The Owner-Manager's Special Perspective

While the expressions in the preceding section present an array of alternatives, they still do not reflect all of the input/output considerations that influence the owner-manager. Suppose that by working an additional four hours per day an owner-manager could improve the company's ROI by two percentage points annually. Many would not elect that increased output for the additional input required.

Suppose that by borrowing heavily, the business' ROI could be increased by three percentage points annually. Once again, a large number of owner-managers would elect to forego the better financial performance and preserve their borrowing power and managerial maneuverability.

Should an owner-manager invest in a risky enterprise that has the possibility of doubling the company's ROI? Many would refuse such an opportunity.

As a practical matter, what is invested and what is returned takes on a different implication for the owner-manager. The particular calculation method that happens to be in vogue may at some point in time answer the financial analyst's question as to how to compute ROI. The owner-manager, however, is engaged in an endless struggle of trying to relate personal and company objectives to the sacrifices necessary to achieve them.

The DuPont Formula

One common technique for calculating return on investment is the DuPont method. In fact, John Raskob, a financial manager with the DuPont Company in the early part of this century, is credited with originating the concept of relating the dollars produced by a business to the dollars invested in that business.[12]

Two versions of this approach are common. The first version computes a return on assets by considering two separate, basic ratios as follows:

$$\% \text{ return} = \frac{\text{Net Profit}}{\text{Sales}} \times \frac{\text{Sales}}{\text{Total Assets}}$$

In the jargon of the financial community, this might be expressed as:[13]

$$\% \text{ return} = \text{Return on Assets}$$
$$= \text{Net Profit Margin} \times \text{Asset Turnover}$$

A common graphical portrayal of this version of the formula is shown in Exhibit 10-9.

EXHIBIT 10-9
DIAGRAM OF RETURN ON ASSETS CALCULATION

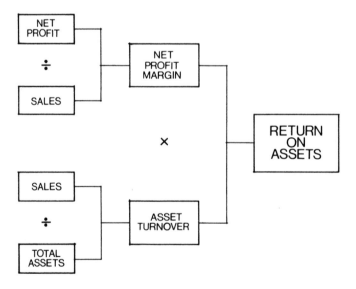

A second version of this approach attempts to determine return on net worth by including a third basic ratio as follows:

$$\% \text{ return} = \frac{\text{Net Profit}}{\text{Sales}} \times \frac{\text{Sales}}{\text{Total Assets}} \times \frac{\text{Total Assets}}{\text{Net Worth}}$$

A member of the financial community might concisely express this as

% return $\quad$ = Return on Investment

$$= \frac{\text{Net}}{\text{Profit}} \quad \times \quad \frac{\text{Asset}}{\text{Turnover}} \quad \times \quad \frac{\text{Financial}}{\text{Leverage}}$$
$$\quad\ \text{Margin}$$

This relationship is portrayed graphically in Exhibit 10-10.

In the diagrams of Exhibits 10-9 and 10-10, the basic terms have the following meanings:

1. Net Profit $\quad$ is $\quad$ Net Profit after Income Taxes
2. Sales $\quad$ are $\quad$ Net Sales
3. Total Assets $\quad$ are $\quad$ Current Assets plus Fixed Assets
4. Net Worth $\quad$ is $\quad$ Total Assets minus Total Liabilities

EXHIBIT 10-10
DIAGRAM OF RETURN ON INVESTMENT CALCULATION

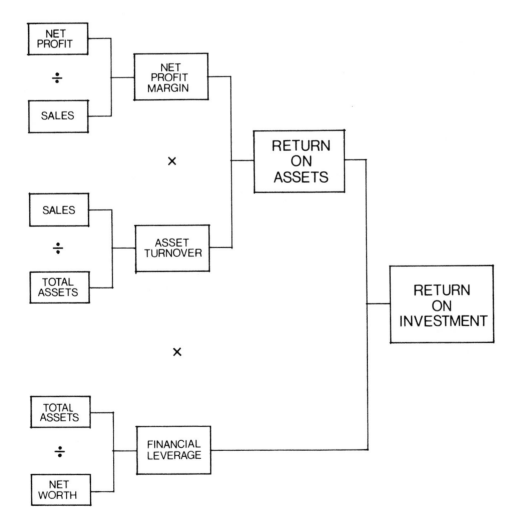

As pointed out earlier in this chapter, there are many versions of the ROI computation. There is no reason why the DuPont formula cannot be modified to respond to the various needs of different organizations. Gross profit could be used instead of net profit; net assets could be used instead of total assets; and equity plus long-term debt could be used instead of net worth. The final ROI calculation could be tailored to individual situations without altering the mechanics of the method.

One of the advantages of the DuPont method is that it allows a manager to observe the impact that changes in such items as sales, profits, assets, margins and leverage would have on the ultimate measure of return on investment. Activities under the responsibility of a middle-management person can be viewed by that individual in light of their contribution to total company ROI.

HOW TO USE ROI

ROI is one measure of performance. The obvious usefulness of the concept is that it can provide a benchmark against which the relative merits of an investment, a project or a company can be compared. Suppose management decides that no individual project will be undertaken unless it promises to deliver 20% return and no businesses will be considered for acquisition unless they can deliver 10% return on invested resources. A helpful screening policy is then established that can assist in the management decision process.

When thinking about ROI in the context of one's existing company, there are a couple of common utilizations. Owner-managers compare their performance to the rest of the industry and they compare themselves to their own historical trends.

Comparison with the Industry

There are numerous sources of industry performance ratios such as ROI. Trade associations usually collect and disseminate this data for the types of businesses they represent. Robert Morris Associates publishes their *Annual Statement Studies*. (Your banker has a copy of this publication.) Also, Dun & Bradstreet publishes annually a booklet listing more than a dozen key operating ratios, including ROI, for more than 100 types of businesses including retail, wholesale, manufacturing and construction. This publication is entitled *Key Business Ratios*.

In addition, business periodicals frequently publish profitability and ROI data. As an example, the data of Exhibit 10-11 was compiled from an issue of *Business Week*.[14] This data is based on comparable nine-month periods in 1977 and 1978.

When considering this type of data, a few cautions are in order. First, note carefully the definition of the two quantities making up this ROI expression.

After Tax Return	Net income before discontinued operations and extraordinary items (most recent nine months), adjusted for minority interest and interest expense.
Average Invested Capital	Average funds invested in the company. Funds invested are the sum of stockholders equity, minority interest and long-term debt at the beginning and the ending of the most recent nine months divided by two.[15]

Also, this data is compiled from the largest companies in the industry.

EXHIBIT 10-11
SELECTED INDUSTRY RETURNS

| | | After Tax Return on Average Invested Capital | | | | | |
| | Number of | 1977 | | | 1978 | | |
Industry	Companies	Highest	Lowest	Composite	Highest	Lowest	Composite
Autos	19	15.7%	1.6%	12.7%	15.1%	3.4%	11.3%
Chemicals	24	11.6	4.1	8.5	10.9	4.8	8.3
Computers	21	24.2	2.3	11.8	27.1	6.4	12.7
Food	30	19.9	4.9	10.8	19.0	5.6	12.2
Machinery	14	14.3	4.7	9.1	17.3	5.0	10.2
Oil	30	12.8	4.5	8.1	13.3	4.2	7.7
Paper	15	10.9	4.5	8.0	10.6	4.9	7.9
Steel	16	NM*	NM*	NM*	12.2	2.5	4.8

*Not Meaningful

It is interesting to note the change in composite returns from one year to the next. In addition, the spread between the highest and lowest individual company returns is dramatic.

In a different survey, one author reviewed 143 New York Stock Exchange companies in 1969 and found that the median ROI was 8.2%.[16] This ROI calculation estimated cash flow as a percent of total assets.

Dun & Bradstreet reports an ROI statistic in their *Key Business Ratios* booklet for each of their more than 100 categories of business. Their calculation is net profit divided by tangible net worth. "Tangible net worth is the equity of stockholders in the business, as obtained by subtracting total liabilities from total assets, and then deducting intangibles."[17] Net profit is net profit after taxes. This data is primarily from corporations with a tangible net worth of over $100,000.

When using industry data, one should make sure it is current. One should also be aware of the size of the companies from which the data is compiled. In addition, it is crucial that the method of calculation of ROI used by the industry be compatible with or identical to the method you select. Out-of-date information, data from dramatically different size companies and incompatible calculation methods can make comparison with industry statistics virtually meaningless.

Comparison with Historical Trends

For most owner-managers, comparison with industry data is more a matter of interest than an integral part of company planning and management decision making. Comparison with one's own historical performance, however, can be very meaningful. The philosophy recommended by the authors is to continually attempt to better the preceding year's performance. If you produced an ROI of 8% last year, try for 9 or 10% this year. If you achieve 10% this year, shoot for 11% next year. This process of always trying to better the preceding year's performance will result in your striving for the upper limit that can be achieved in your industry in light of the competition.

If you would like some absolute benchmark to try and exceed, think in terms of the returns you could achieve by investing money some place other than your business. Savings accounts, bank certificates of deposit and U.S. Government Securities can produce secure returns on investment of 5, 6, 7, 8, 9, 10% and sometimes more (depending on general economic and monetary conditions). Clearly, money invested in a business, with all its risks, should produce a somewhat greater return. Many owner-managers are disappointed if they can't produce a return on investment of greater than 10% annually.

WHEN IS ROI IMPORTANT TO THE BUSINESS?

Comments at the beginning of this chapter pointed out that small, growing, entrepreneurial companies typically do not use ROI as important decision-making criteria and large, stable, professionally managed companies do. At what point in the evolution of a business does ROI become important?

The authors believe that there is a hierarchy of financial needs for a business much like Maslow's Hierarchy of Needs for an individual. (See Chapter 9.) One possible portrayal of this hierarchy is that shown in Exhibit 10-12.

EXHIBIT 10-12
A BUSINESS' HIERARCHY OF NEEDS

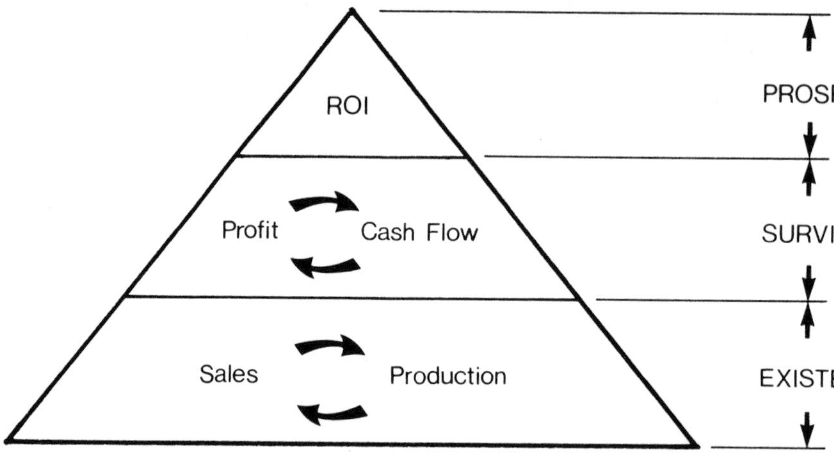

In the early years of a business, or when a business has its welfare threatened, management is frequently preoccupied with making sales and delivering the product or service. As one successful entrepreneur once put it, "If the sales don't occur, we can all go home. In fact, if the sales don't occur, we will be sent home." Making the sales and delivering the product or service must occur first merely for the business to exist.

Once the sales/production cycle begins to function adequately, another series of needs emerges that must be satisfied for the business to survive more than a few days. Revenues must exceed expenses such that the business makes a profit. Simultaneously, receipts of cash must exceed disbursements such that a positive bank balance exists. Making a profit and maintaining positive cash flow are not just neat corporate objectives. They are survival criteria. Failure to make a profit, like a chronic disease, will kill in the long run. Failure to maintain positive cash flow, like a slashed throat, will kill very quickly. Negative profit (losses) and negative cash flow will both kill a business—one just does it more quickly.

When a company grows and matures to the point that making the sales, delivering the product or service, making a profit and maintaining a positive cash flow do not totally consume management, another need becomes important. When not preoccupied with survival, managers and owners logically become concerned with whether the business is using its assets as efficiently as possible. Could the resources invested in the company be more productively utilized? Failure to produce an adequate ROI for several decades can weaken even the strongest companies to the point that management will become preoccupied with survival. Some individuals feel this thought is also valid for national economies.

It is the authors' observation that most owner-managed businesses are concerned with the survival and existence levels depicted in Exhibit 10-12. ROI is important to the long-range prosperity of a company. It is seldom considered, however, when survival and existence are an issue.

HOW TO COMPARE PRESENT DOLLARS AND FUTURE DOLLARS

Normally, investments are made and then returns occur sometime during the future. How does one relate a dollar invested today to a dollar returned five years from now?

There is a time value of money. Passbook saving accounts are one obvious manifestation of this. One dollar deposited today is worth more than one dollar 12 months later. To understand more about the time value of money, first, consider the concepts of compounding and discounting.

Compounding and Discounting

Suppose that $1,000 is invested at a compounded annual rate of 10%. In one year the investment would be worth

$$\text{Value in one year} = \$1,000 \times 1.10 = \$1,100$$

In two years the value of the investment would be

$$\text{Value in two years} = \$1,000 \times 1.10 \times 1.10 = \$1,100 \times 1.10 = \$1,210$$

A slightly different way of expressing this is

$$\text{Value in two years} = \$1,000 \times 1.10^2 = \$1,000 \times 1.21 = \$1,210$$

The number 1.21 is the factor for relating the present value of money to its value in two years at 10%.

The future value of $1,000 at 10% is portrayed in Exhibit 10-13 for each year during the next five years. Another way of stating this is that $1,000 is compounded at 10% for five years in the exhibit. One thousand dollars compounded at 10% has a value of $1,464 in four years.

EXHIBIT 10-13

Future Value of $1000 Today at 10% Rate.

Today	1 Year	2 Years	3 Years	4 Years	5 Years
$1000	1100	1210	1331	1464	1611

The concept of discounting takes a future cash benefit and calculates what must be invested now (at some selected annual rate) in order to generate that future benefit on a compounded basis. Exhibit 10-14 is helpful in relating present and future dollars through the compounding and discounting mechanism. Using this exhibit, one could conclude that $1,000 compounded for three years at 10% would yield $1,331. One could also conclude that $1,611 discounted at 10% for five years would yield $1,000. Exhibit 10-15 demonstrates how compounding and discounting factors are determined for a given annual percentage rate.

EXHIBIT 10-14

How Compounding and Discounting Relate
Present Dollars and Future Dollars

Present	1 Year	2 Years	3 Years	4 Years	5 Years
$1000	1100	1210	1331	1464	1611

Compounding at 10% →

← Discounting at 10%

EXHIBIT 10-15

EXAMPLE OF COMPOUNDING AND DISCOUNTING FACTORS

YEARS	1	2	3	4	5
10% Compounding Factor	1.10	$(1.10)^2$	$(1.10)^3$	$(1.10)^4$	$(1.10)^5$
10% Compounding Factor as a Decimal	1.100	1.210	1.331	1.464	1.611
10% Discounting Factor as a Fraction	$\frac{1}{(1.10)}$	$\frac{1}{(1.10)^2}$	$\frac{1}{(1.10)^3}$	$\frac{1}{(1.10)^4}$	$\frac{1}{(1.10)^5}$
10% Discounting Factor as a Decimal	.909	.826	.751	.683	.621

Examples of the Analysis of Potential Investments Using the Time Value of Money

To illustrate the dramatic effect of the time value of money and its impact on investment decisions, consider the following two streams of future benefits:

Year	1	2	3	4	5
Future Cash Benefits from Investment A	$600	100	100	100	100
Future Cash Benefits from Investment B	$100	100	100	100	600

The total cash benefits from the two investments are identical, $1,000. If we discount both streams to the present, using what we consider to be a reasonable rate of 10%, the following emerges:

INVESTMENT A

Year	Cash Benefit Stream	Discounting Factor @ 10%*	Present Value
1	$600	.909	$545
2	100	.826	83
3	100	.751	75
4	100	.683	68
5	100	.621	62
		Present Value	$833

INVESTMENT B

Year	Cash Benefit Stream	Discounting Factor @ 10%*	Present Value
1	$100	.909	$ 91
2	100	.826	83
3	100	.751	75
4	100	.683	68
5	600	.621	373
		Present Value	$690

Without commenting at this point as to what Investment A and Investment B are, we merely observe that although they both produce identical *total* future dollar benefits, the present values of these cash benefits (the value in today's dollars) are substantially different.

The process of discounting the stream of future cash benefits is often referred to as Discounted Cash Flow.

There are two common methods for using the discounting and present value concept in analyzing a potential investment. The first involves taking the present value of a stream of

----

*Present value tables are available which have already determined these values for various percentage rates. Many electronic calculators have these values built into their memory.

future benefits discounted at a rate *you* decide is reasonable for your business and comparing that present value with the initial investment. If the present value is greater than the intitial investment, then the investment is a good one for *you*, assuming the absence of non-monetary consideration such as having to purchase a new machine just to remain competitive.

As an example, consider the preceding investments, A and B. If the initial investment in both cases is $750, then at a 10% rate A is a good investment and B is not (from a financial point of view).

The second method involves computing the rate of return, using a trial and error procedure to find the discounting rate that will make the present value of the stream of future cash benefits equal to the initial investment. This technique is called the Internal Rate of Return Method and is illustrated in the following example:

EXAMPLE: Assume that an investment in a $1,000 asset is available. The asset has a useful life of five years at which time it will be sold for salvage at 10% of the purchase price. Annual receipts as a result of this asset's production total $890 (cash) and annual expenses (cash) associated with the asset total $130. The depreciation is computed on a straight-line basis considering the 10% salvage value. The effective income tax rate for this company is projected to be 35%.

STEP I: Portray the investment on an *annual* Income Statement basis for each of the five years of the investment's life.

Income Statement Impact of Proposed Investment°

Revenues	$ 890	(cash)
Expenses		
Operating Cost	130	(cash)
Depreciation	180	(non-cash)
Net Profit before Taxes	580	
Taxes (35%)	203	(cash)
Net Profit after Taxes	$ 377	

STEP II: Portray the annual *operating cash flow* statement (excluding the initial investment and salvage) as follows:

Operating Cash Flow Impact of Proposed Investment°

Receipts	$ 890
Disbursements	
Operating Cost	130
Taxes	203
Net Cash Flow	$ 557

°Identical for each of the five years in this example.

STEP III: Determine the annual cash benefit stream.

Total Cash Benefit Stream

Year	0	1	2	3	4	5
Inflows						
Net Cash Flow	—	$557	557	557	557	557
Salvage	—	—	—	—	—	100
Outflows						
Purchase	$1,000	—	—	—	—	—
Net Cash Benefits		$557	557	557	557	657

STEP IV: By trial and error, find the discounting rate that causes the present value of the cash benefit stream to equal the initial investment.

Trial #1—Use 20% Rate

Year	Cash Benefit	Discount Factor @ 20%	Present Value
1	$557	.833	$ 464
2	557	.694	387
3	557	.579	323
4	557	.482	268
5	657	.402	264
		Total Present Value	$1,706

The 20% rate was not high enough to bring the Present Value of the stream of future cash benefits down to the initial investment of $1,000.

Trial #2—Use 50% Rate

Year	Cash Benefit	Discount Factor @ 50%	Present Value
1	$557	.667	$372
2	557	.444	247
3	557	.296	165
4	557	.198	110
5	657	.132	87
		Total Present Value	$981

In this case, 50% was too high a discount rate.

Trial #2—Use 48% Rate

Year	Cash Benefit	Discount Factor @ 48%	Present Value
1	$557	.676	$ 377
2	557	.457	255
3	557	.308	172
4	557	.208	116
5	657	.141	93
		Total Present Value	$1,013

The 48% rate produces a present value greater than the original investment by about $13. The 50% rate produces a present value less than the original investment by approximately $19. The Internal Rate of Return is about halfway between 48% and 50%. It would be reasonable to conclude that the return on investment for this company is about 49% (a compounded rate of return). If greater accuracy is necessary, additional trials using 48.5%, 49% and 49.5% may be executed.

Since ROI is such an important concept for the long-range prosperity of a business, owner-managers should make time to at least give it an occasional consideration. Failure to do so can result in an eventual struggle for survival.

NOTES FOR CHAPTER 10

[1]"How DuPont Keeps Its Eye on Profit," *Business Week*, November 9, 1963, p. 144.

[2]John A. Welsh and Jerry F. White, "Return on Investment ... or Liquidity? A Manager's Dilemma," *Journal of Small Business Management*, April, 1978, Vol. 16, No. 2, p. 14.

[3]Ibid., p. 16.

[4]Ibid., p. 16.

[5]Ibid., p. 17.

[6]Ibid., p. 19.

[7]Ibid., p. 20.

[8]Ibid., p. 20.

[9]Robert A. Peters, *ROI Practical Theory and Innovative Applications*, (New York: AMACOM, 1974), p. 17.

[10]Ibid., p. 17.

[11]Ibid., p. 17.

[12]"ROI: ID Special Report,"*ID*, April, 1974, p. 21.

[13]Peters, p. 8.

[14]"Industrial Outlook 1979," *Business Week*, January 8, 1979, No. 2567, pp. 32-68.

[15]"Industrial Outlook 1979," p. 34.

[16]Peters, p. 45.

[17]*Key Business Ratios*, Dun & Bradstreet, Inc., New York, 1977.

11

Five Recurring Reasons Why Owner-Managed
Businesses Fail: Lining Up the Defenses

The authors cumulatively have more than 30 years experience founding companies, managing companies, counseling owner-managers and teaching entrepreneurs. During this time period, there have been many opportunities to visit owner-managed businesses. Sometimes the visit was made with the possibility of acquisition of the company in mind and, in other situations, the owner-manager was seeking counseling on some significant problem.

Many of these companies were failing at the time of the visit. If they were not failing, the current problems exceeded management's ability to deal with them. Five basic reasons why these businesses were in trouble were consistently identifiable.

FAILURE TO UNDERSTAND THE LANGUAGE

Imagine the typical visit to one of the businesses [previously mentioned]. Our party meets us at the local airport. Initial conversation includes, "Did you see the football game last night? How was the flight in?" a few niceties, small talk.

Very quickly, however, we begin inquiring about the business being visited. Questions might include, "Do you have a recent annual report? Have you prepared a cash flow forecast? What kind of margins does your business have?" When questions about the numbers of the business are asked, almost invariably the answer comes back, "Go talk to my accountant, he's expecting you. Go see my CPA and he'll tell you everything you want to know."

This presents a problem because the CPA is seldom a full-time employee located at the business. This professional is a valued counselor and advisor, but the CPA is not the manager. The part-time responsibility of providing advice is very different from the full-time responsibility of managing the company.

One can't help but wonder, "Doesn't this manager understand that if a manager can't describe the business with numbers, how is it possible to know what the business is like? How can one know what it's doing? How does one know how to make it better?" Numbers are the fundamental mechanism for describing the operations and condition of a business. One can use all kinds of words, with all kinds of embellishments, but when describing what the business is doing, it takes numbers. They're not calculus, just fourth grade arithmetic. These simple numbers are the very language of business. The managers of failing businesses typically do not speak (and apparently do not desire to understand) the basic language. Furthermore, they dismiss this crucial area of responsibility to other persons who typically are not full-time employees of the company.

FAILURE TO UNDERSTAND THE REGULATORY ENVIRONMENT

After some discussion about the numbers the conversation typically turns to a different kind of question. "Is this a corporation? Do you have pre-emptive rights? Do you have 1244 stock? Do you elect Subchapter S?" Almost invariably the answer comes back from the owner-manager in trouble, "I've talked with my lawyer who is expecting you. Go see my lawyer and he'll tell you everything you want to know."

Unfortunately, the lawyer isn't a full-time employee of the company either and often is not readily accessible. You wonder whether this manager comprehends the problem. There are all kinds of lawyers. To get a divorce requires one kind of lawyer. To reclaim a truck suggests another kind of lawyer. Public offerings, that's still another kind of lawyer. It's not adequate in today's business environment to get a "country lawyer" to take care of all of the company's affairs.

One owner-manager we know worked with a large law firm in New York City that had more than 150 partners. He had no idea how many junior associates were in the firm, but there were more than 150 partners. When he went to the law firm with a problem, the lawyer would get the in-house telephone book and he'd call his lawyer. That firm had specialists within the house for all the various fields of legal practice. Think about it, for every regulatory agency in the government, there's a specialty in the law. Quite often, there are many sub-specialties.

Apparently, many managers do not realize that this is is not exactly a free economic society. This is a free, *regulated* economic society. We live in an ocean of regulations, and we're responsible for all of them. They're for our protection and for our benefit. Managers of failing companies often abandon not only the numbers of their business but also the important legal responsibilities to other parties who aren't even employees of the company.

A PREOCCUPATION WITH FACADE

As a typical visit progresses, someone usually observes that it's about lunchtime. An offer is made to drive over to a "good" restaurant, typically in a Mercedes, Mark IV or Eldorado. The restaurant has tables covered with thick, heavy linen. Each place setting has three spoons and three forks (there seem to be so many that one doesn't know which to pick up first). The menus are two feet tall, covered with leather and written in French. It's lunchtime, but everything looks like dinner.

The lunch discussion hasn't continued for very long before you realize that the words being used are rather strange. One hears words like Acapulco and Honolulu. Reference is made to an exquisite menu in Boston and an annual meeting in Brussels.

There seems to be little reference to that truck out on the highway with a broken axle. Discussion does not center on the warehouse door that wouldn't open this morning or the shipping clerk who didn't appear for work. What one hears about is Jamaica and the Playboy Club. Many of the managers we visit act like they are very successful. They put on a facade of business success.

When talking with these managers who are in trouble we seldom hear anything about the substance of business.

The substance of business is customers parting with their hard-earned cash for whatever it is the business has to offer.

That's what it's all about. If that doesn't happen, we can all go home. In fact, if that doesn't happen, we will all be sent home.

It is very common that managers of failing enterprises preoccupy themselves with facade. In that process, they forget about the substance of business.

FAILURE TO UNDERSTAND THE PEOPLE NATURE OF BUSINESS

After lunch, the visit continues with the plant tour. At the plant, frequently, the first thing visible inside the front door is an area with living room furniture, carpet, drapes, colorful pictures on the wall and a cocktail table covered with colorful magazines.

Beyond this reception area is the remainder of the plant. Walking through the facility, one is greeted with, "Hello. How do you do?" and "It's nice to meet you." It's just wonderful. Everybody's smiling and everything is pleasant. As one passes by, however, something else is overheard. What is overheard is bickering and dissension. There's evidence of turmoil, turnover and trauma throughout the place. The manager is discussing the five-year corporate objective and making statements like, "We're going to move that wall back 40 feet and double the size of the warehouse. We're going to bring in a conveyor belt there and double the production on this line." What the employees in this kind of company display a real interest in is five o'clock and payday.

Remember the five-year objective? If management can ever get the employees' goals and the corporate goals together, magic happens. In these companies available for acquisition or otherwise in trouble, the manager has frequently forgotten what a business is in the first place. A business is a group of people. Those people are working together to satisfy their own individual needs and goals and aspirations. If their goals are in line with the corporate goals, the results are exciting. Satisfying the corporate goal, however, is not why the employees are there. These people are there to satisfy their needs and their goals and their aspirations.

A good manager knows that a business is people. An experienced manager also knows these people are very creative in the problems they present. When one has dealt with all the problems conceivable, they come up with another. One can handle the broken door or the damaged shipping crate or the truck stalled on the highway. What do you do, though, when an employee's third grandmother (this year) is having a funeral?

Managers of companies in trouble do not seem to really understand the people nature of business.

THE ABSENCE OF TIMELY FINANCIAL DATA

After the plant tour, one might as well go see the CPA who is almost never located next door. The trip is usually across town and very often to the next town. Upon arrival at the accountant's office, one typically discovers that the latest financial report is 90 days old. One is lucky if it's only 90 days. It is commonly five or six months old. In fact, it's not unusual to find that the latest report is an annual report dated nine months ago, and there hasn't been anything since. There is not a recent financial statement. There is an absence of timely financial data.

Consider what it means to have timely financial reports. Even if a business has in-house bookkeeping and the manager wants the financial reports out in a hurry and everyone is cooperative, it still takes time to collect all those little pieces of paper, put them together, make sure they're valid, add them up and produce some sort of report. It takes at least five to 10 working days. With luck, about the 10th of the following month, the manager will get a financial report.

Suppose the diagram in Exhibit 11-1 represents this month. Financial statements prepared in-house could be expected to arrive by the 10th. This statement reports about last month. The last report would have been about the 10th of last month as indicated in Exhibit 11-2.

Assume that the manager promptly reviews this month's statement. Usually, that individual would like to make the performance better or, at least, keep it from getting worse. Suppose specific actions are decided upon as a result of studying the report. After a day or two of reflection, the manager can start implementing a game plan. Nothing, however, happens in

EXHIBIT 11-1
DIAGRAM INDICATING WHEN THE FINANCIAL STATEMENT DESCRIBING
LAST MONTH'S PERFORMANCE MIGHT BE EXPECTED

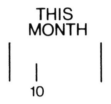

a day or two. It takes time to bring about change in business. For example, one could fire a couple of employees immediately. That's seldom done, however. They probably get until Friday of next week. After they have left, you discover they had accrued vacation and are still on the payroll.

On the other hand, you might decide to shrink the inventory; get rid of half of it. What are you going to do? Burn it? It won't go away.

EXHIBIT 11-2
DIAGRAM OF WHEN THE PRECEDING MONTH'S FINANCIAL STATEMENT
MIGHT BE EXPECTED

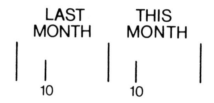

As another possibility, the manager might decide to acquire more warehouse space. One then has to locate space, negotiate for it and secure financing.

Nothing happens instantaneously in business. It takes time to bring about change.

The next financial report is prepared next month. It should arrive about the 10th. Next month's report tells about the business done this month. The first part of this month, however, looks like last month and the remaining portion of this month is in transition. One can't tell from next month's statement whether management succeeded by its actions this month in making last month's performance look better. This is illustrated in Exhibit 11-3.

EXHIBIT 11-3
DIAGRAM ILLUSTRATING HOW THE FINANCIAL STATEMENT PRODUCED
NEXT MONTH REFLECTS THE PERFORMANCE OF A MONTH IN
TRANSITION

To find out how successful management was, you have to wait still another month. It'll be the 10th of the month after next if you are right on top of everything and have in-house bookkeeping before it is possible to find out whether what management is doing right now made last month look better. That's a 100 days' blind spot as indicated in Exhibit 11-4. If a company's latest report is 90 days old, its manager has a 190 days' blind spot—that's 6 months.

EXHIBIT 11-4
DIAGRAM ILLUSTRATING MANAGEMENT'S 100 DAYS BLINDSPOT

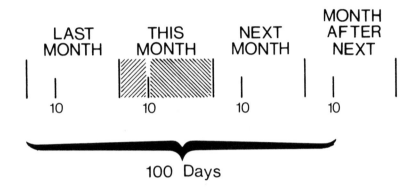

The business whose latest report is nine months old has a one-year blind spot. They could have been dead for six months and don't know it yet.

One can't manage the past and can barely influence the present. One can only manage the future. A manager has to decide what future events are desired and has to start taking action today to make those events come about.

There are severe limitations to timely financial statements. Managers of companies in trouble usually do not even have these.

12

How to Get a Fix on the Numbers of
Your Closely Held Business

One of the most consistently successful owner-managers the authors have ever met, an individual whose self-created net worth is in excess of 100 million dollars, made a profound statement during a meeting one day when he said, "An owner-manager *must* understand the numbers of his business." This particular owner-manager owns 18 companies and on any given day can reach into his shirt pocket and tell you the status of each company as of five p.m. the day before. He can read financial statements written in Spanish or Chinese as fluently as most individuals read the daily newspaper.

The importance of understanding the numbers in one's business supports the authors' observations of Chapter 11 that point out five reasons why owner-managed businesses fail. Two key reasons are: 1) failure of the owner-manager to understand the language of business and 2) failure of the owner-manager to receive timely financial reports.

This importance of the numbers and financial record systems which utilize the numbers was underscored more than 200 years ago by an inventor and struggling owner-manager who made this observation:

> My old competitor ... suffer'd greatly from his neglect in due accounting: and I mention it as a lesson to those young men who may be employ'd in managing, that they should always render accounts and make remittances with great clearness and punctuality. The character of observing such conduct is the most powerful of all recommendations to new employments and increase of business.[1]

Benjamin Franklin (1737)

Records of business transactions stated in terms of money were used by even the earliest known civilizations, although the early records were crude and lacked systematic arrangement. Modern financial record keeping had its beginnings more than seven centuries ago when cities such as Venice and Genoa became great centers of commerce. The growth of commerce was naturally accompanied by a need for effective business records.

Luca Paciolo, like his contemporary, Leonardo da Vinci, was one of those "all purpose" men during the Golden Age of the Renaissance. The same acute perception that allowed him to make significant and original contributions in mathematics allowed him to discern many of the secrets of successful businesses. One of the most salient observations Paciolo made concerned the methods utilized in keeping records. He attached such importance to this that he included a treatise on the subject in perhaps his most famous work, *Summa de Arithmetica, Geometria,*

Proportioni et Proportionalita, published in Venice in 1494. The basic record keeping system detailed by Paciolo has remained essentially unchanged for almost 500 years and his suggestions on how to succeed in business, such as, "He who does business without knowing all about it sees his money go like flies," and "Frequent accounting makes for lasting friendship,"[2] are as applicable today as in the 15th century.

CRUCIAL FUNDAMENTALS

Financial record systems are based on keeping track of the property of the business. Furthermore, it is not sufficient just to keep track of the property. It is equally important to distinguish between the property that creditors have a right to and the property belonging to the owners. Succinctly stated, the basic relationship is:

ASSETS = LIABILITIES + CAPITAL

where

ASSETS	Represent all the property of the business (Inventory, Desks, Chairs, Cash, Equipment, Accounts Receivable, Supplies, etc.)
LIABILITIES	Represent creditors' rights to some of the firm's property (various Accounts Payable, Notes Payable and other items on which the business still owes money).
CAPITAL	Represents the owners' rights to the remainder of the company's property (consisting typically of Common Stock that is issued to owners as a measure of property contributed by the owners to start or expand the business, and Retained Earnings, that consist of property generated for the owners by the successful and profitable operation of the business). In this context, capital does not have the dictionary meaning "a stock of accumulated goods denoted to the production of other goods."

Consequently, the basic property relationship may be stated as follows:

$$\begin{matrix} \text{Property} \\ \text{of the Business} \end{matrix} = \begin{matrix} \text{Creditors' Rights} \\ \text{to the Property} \end{matrix} + \begin{matrix} \text{Owners' Rights} \\ \text{to the Property} \end{matrix}$$

Another way of stating this relationship is:

$$\begin{matrix} \text{What} \\ \text{a Business Has} \end{matrix} = \begin{matrix} \text{That which the} \\ \text{Creditors Contribute} \end{matrix} + \begin{matrix} \text{That which the} \\ \text{Owners Contribute} \end{matrix}$$

Each of the three terms in the accounting equation can consist of numerous subdivisions. Some of the commonly recognized subdivisions or accounts are as follows:

ASSETS	LIABILITIES	CAPITAL
Cash	Accounts Payable	Common Stock
Accounts Receivable	Taxes Payable	Retained Earnings
Inventory	Notes Payable	
Equipment		
Accumulated Depreciation		

How to Deal with Increases and Decreases in Business Property

Efforts to devise a simple, straightforward system for recording changes in the property relationship previously expressed resulted in the recognition of transactions and the use of a simple mechanical procedure to keep track of them.

TRANSACTIONS Refer to activities which affect the property of a business and thus change the basic property equation. Transactions are characterized by the giving up of one thing to get another—a trading of one thing for another. For example, a business may exchange cash for equipment; inventory for an account receivable (their promise to pay us); or, purchase supplies in exchange for an account payable (our promise to pay them). Also, as far as the company records are concerned, what is given up is always equal to what is received.

Obviously then, recording a transaction requires a notation of what is given up and what is received, (i.e., recording a transaction requires the noting of two changes) every time a change in property occurs and an entry is made in the record system. Hence, the terminology, "double entry record systems."

The simple mechanical procedure utilized is bilateral recording (i.e., left or right) in each of the three major categories: ASSETS, LIABILITIES and CAPITAL. Whether a right or left entry is utilized depends upon whether an increase or a decrease is being recorded in a particular account. The practice is as follows:

$$\text{ASSETS} \quad = \quad \text{LIABILITIES} \quad + \quad \text{CAPITAL}$$

LEFT	RIGHT	LEFT	RIGHT	LEFT	RIGHT
(Increases)	(Decreases)	(Decreases)	(Increases)	(Decreases)	(Increases)

It is important to observe the relationship between left-side and right-side entries depending upon which side of the = (equal) sign you are recording an entry. In other words, increases in company property are recorded on the left side of an asset account, increases in money owed (creditors' rights) are recorded on the right side of a liability account and increases in property belonging to the business owners (owners' rights) are recorded on the right side of a capital account. Just the opposite is true of decreases in each of these categories. One of the beauties of this system is that, at all times

$$\frac{\text{Sum of All}}{\text{Left Side Entries}} = \frac{\text{Sum of All}}{\text{Right Side Entries}}$$

This creates a convenient relationship that permits an interim check for accuracy of the recording work at any time during the process. If you are not sure that an entry has been made correctly, stop and add up all the left sides and then all the right sides. The two totals should be equal.

Keeping Score in the Business Game

The business game is a property game. The basic objective is to increase property (assets) just as much as possible. The game should be played in a manner that causes the bulk of the property to end up belonging to the owners (capital) and not the creditors (liabilities). The expanded version of the property equation (shown in Exhibit 12-1) will be helpful in understanding how some of the game plays are recorded.

Types of Plays in the Business Game

Football, chess and bridge all have plays contributing to their winning objectives. So does business. Plays or activities in the business game have been referred to as transactions. Reference to the preceding expanded form of the property equation will be helpful in considering some of the various kinds of plays that can occur as shown in the following illustrations.

EXHIBIT 12-1
ILLUSTRATION DESCRIBING HOW TO RECORD INCREASES AND
DECREASES AFFECTING BUSINESS PROPERTY

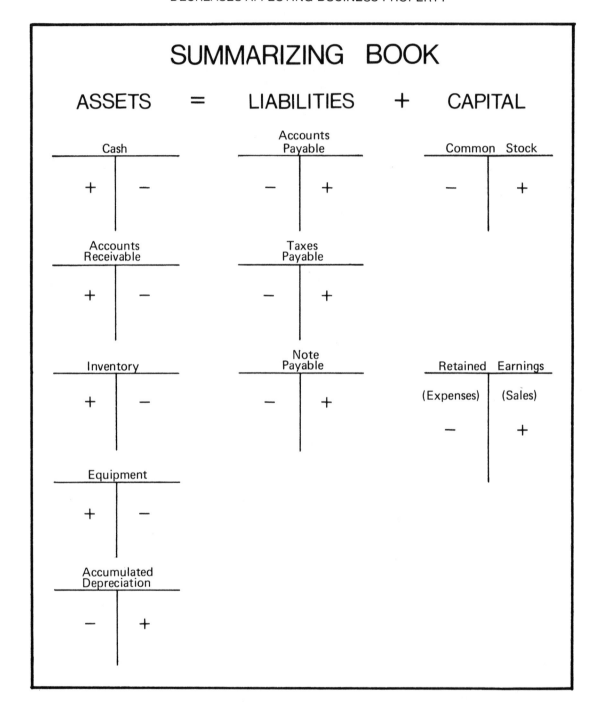

Sell $5,000 of Common Stock: The owners agree to contribute property to the business. It seems pretty clear that the two accounts affected by this transaction are Cash and Common Stock. Referring to the basic property relationship, it is seen that the increase in company cash due to the increase in issued stock is recorded with a left-side and a right-side entry, respectively, as follows:

	Left Side	Right Side
Cash	5,000	
Common Stock		5,000

Purchase $1,200 of Equipment on Credit: A creditor agrees to contribute property to the business. In this play, the company's properties (assets) have increased and the creditors' rights to the property (liabilities) have also increased. Referring to the expanded form of the basic property relationship, Assets = Liabilities + Capital, one notes that the asset Equipment increases with a left-side entry and owing money to a supplier for the Equipment is represented by a Note Payable that increases with a right-side entry in a liability account. The transaction would be recorded as follows:

	Left Side	Right Side
Equipment	1,200	
Note Payable		1,200

Acquire $1,000 of Inventory on Credit: Before the sale of tangible items can be completed, inventory must be acquired. Subsequently, a product is shipped and a sale is recognized. When inventory is acquired, one asset of the company, Inventory, increases. Increases in an asset result in a left-side entry. If one does not, at the time of receipt of inventory, give the supplier money, then the resulting promise to pay at a future date increases the Accounts Payable. Since Accounts Payable is a liability account, an increase would be recorded on the right side as follows:

	Left Side	Right Side
Inventory	1,000	
Accounts Payable		1,000

Make a $600 Sale on Credit: The business makes a sale on credit; hence, the customer contributes property to the benefit of the owners but does not contribute cash.

In this transaction, a promise to pay by a customer has been obtained and constitutes an increase in Accounts Receivable. However, it may not be clear as to where the sale should be recorded. Consider the capital account, Retained Earnings. This is where increases and decreases in the owners' rights to the company property, resulting from the daily operations of the business, are recorded. Sales increase the owners' property and, hence, increase Retained Earnings. Expenses decrease the owners' property and decrease Retained Earnings.

	Left Side	Right Side
Accounts Receivable	600	
Retained Earnings (Sale)		600

Recognizing an Expense which Reduces Inventory: Suppose the preceding sale involved items held in Inventory costing $160. This sale would result in the reduction of an asset, a right-side entry in Inventory. The expense of doing business associated with the "using-up" of materials in Inventory would result in a left-side entry involving Retained Earnings as follows:

	Left Side	Right Side
Retained Earnings (Materials Expense)	160	
Inventory		160

Recognize that $250 in Taxes Is Owed: Sometimes, the government decides to claim some of the property of the business to the detriment of the owners. Assume that the company incurs a tax. The tax may be considered an actual expense of the business. Also, the company wishes to acknowledge its obligations to pay. Expenses decrease Retained Earnings and, therefore, require a left-side entry, while the newly incurred promise to pay increases the company liabilities and requires a right-side entry. The entry in this case would be:

	Left Side	Right Side
Retained Earnings (Tax Expense)	250	
Taxes Payable		250

Pay $100 for Labor: Labor totaling $100 is paid for in cash. Clearly, Cash would decrease with a right-side entry. Labor represents a class of expense that in this case would decrease Retained Earnings on the left side as follows:

	Left Side	Right Side
Retained Earnings (Labor Expense)	100	
Cash		100

Make a $50 Monthly Payment on the Equipment Note: Suppose that at some time during the month, a $50 payment is made on the Equipment note. If $40 goes to reducing the amount of the note, then this liability is reduced with a left-side entry. If the other $10 is for interest on the unpaid balance of the note, that would represent a cost of doing business during the current period resulting in an expense. This expense would be recorded with a left-side entry in Retained Earnings.

Finally, Cash would be reduced by this payment. The resulting decrease in this asset would be handled with a right-side entry. The complete transaction would be recorded as follows:

	Left Side	Right Side
Note Payable	40	
Retained Earnings (Interest Expense)	10	
Cash		50

Recognize $25 in Equipment Depreciation: Business assets generally decrease in value over time. Spoilage, rust and obsolescence are the culprits that initiate this process. Some assets, such as furniture and manufacturing equipment, have a useful life greater than one year. Instead of expensing such an asset in its entirety when it is acquired, it is usually expensed a little bit each month over its useful life. This process of recognizing the using up of a long life asset gradually over its useful life is called depreciation. Generally, one would like to keep a running tally of all the depreciation that has accumulated to date (on assets that have not already been completely depreciated).

Since depreciation expense decreases Retained Earnings by a left-side entry, it may be straightforwardly entered. The account in which past and current depreciation are recorded is called Accumulated Depreciation. It is a contra-asset account, which means that the rules you have learned about assets are reversed in this account. An illustration follows:

Assets		Contra Assets	
Left side	Right Side	Left Side	Right Side
(increases)	(decreases)	(decreases)	(increases)

Therefore, recording an increase in Accumulated Depreciation results in a right-side entry as follows:

	Left Side	Right Side
Retained Earnings (Depreciation Expense)	25	
Accumulated Depreciation		25

Receive $200 from Customer as Payment on Account: Property of one kind is often exchanged for different property of equal value with no resulting change in either the owners' or the creditors' property. The receipt of a check, obviously, increases Cash and is recorded with a left-side entry. Payment by a customer on an Account Receivable decreases this asset and is recorded on the right side.

	Left Side	Right Side
Cash	200	
Accounts Receivable		200

Make a $150 Deposit on Taxes Owed: Deliver part of the property owed to the government and reduce this payable on the books. Making a tax deposit will decrease Cash and likewise decrease the amount of taxes owed.

	Left Side	Right Side
Taxes Payable	150	
Cash		150

The preceding illustrations constitute a sufficient number of transactions to demonstrate how a basic financial record system is used to keep score.

THE RECORDING BOOK

To create a basic financial record system, a procedure must first be established that systematically funnels all of a business firm's little pieces of paper, representing transactions, into one central place. The transactions should then be logged in chronological order—i. e., whatever happens first is recorded first. Logging in the transactions is usually done with a Recording Book, a book of original entry in the records system. As one might anticipate, this book is designed to facilitate easy recording of left-side/right-side transactions, and might be as simply organized as the one shown below:

Recording Book

Description of Transactions	Left Side Entries	Right Side Entries

To illustrate the process of making entries in the recording book, consider the preceding series of typical transactions. The Recording Book would appear as seen in Exhibit 12-2.

As an illustration, assume that these randomly selected occurrences are the only transactions that have taken place in a business. It is now easy to draw up financial statements demonstrating the basic process for far more complicated cases.

THE SUMMARIZING BOOK

The first step is to summarize all of the transactions of this period. This is accomplished by transferring and grouping the left-side and right-side entries of the Recording Book in a Summarizing Book. Consult the immediately preceding Recording Book to verify that the grouping process has been correctly carried out in the Summarizing Book shown in Exhibit 12-3.

EXHIBIT 12-2
ILLUSTRATION OF THE FORM OF A RECORDING BOOK

RECORDING BOOK

Description	Left Side	Right Side
Cash	5,000	
Common Stock		5,000
Equipment	1,200	
Note Payable		1,200
Inventory	1,000	
Accounts Payable		1,000
Accounts Receivable	600	
Retained Earnings (Sale)		600
Retained Earnings (Materials Expense)	160	
Inventory		160
Retained Earnings (Tax Expense)	250	
Taxes Payable		250
Retained Earnings (Labor Expense)	100	
Cash		100
Note Payable	40	
Retained Earnings (Interest Expense)	10	
Cash		50
Retained Earnings (Depreciation Expense)	25	
Accumulated Depreciation		25
Cash	200	
Accounts Receivable		200
Taxes Payable	150	
Cash		150

EXHIBIT 12-3
ILLUSTRATION OF THE FORM OF A SUMMARIZING BOOK

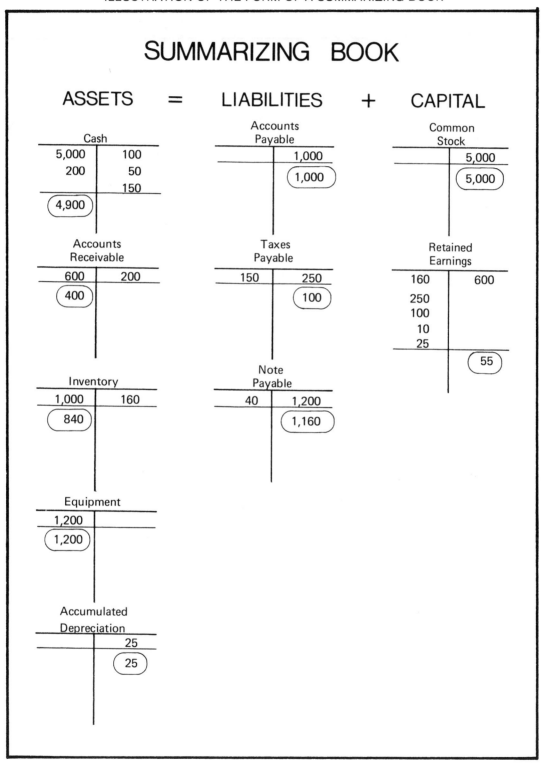

HOW A BALANCE SHEET IS DERIVED

If the balance (number circled) in each summarized account of the Summarizing Book is listed on a sheet of paper in an orderly fashion, the result would be a Balance Sheet and, in this case, would simply appear as illustrated in Exhibit 12-4.

A Balance Sheet is the instrument commonly utilized to display and to report a firm's property and the ownership of that property. This financial statement is an integral part of conversations with the financial community. In addition, a balance sheet must be filed annually with the taxing authorities. A Balance Sheet reflects the cumulative effects of all the transactions in the history of the company as of a certain point in time (i.e., the balance sheet date).

EXHIBIT 12-4
ILLUSTRATION OF THE FORM OF A BALANCE SHEET

BALANCE SHEET

ASSETS

Cash		$ 4,900
Accounts Receivable		400
Inventory		840
Equipment	1,200	
Less Accumulated Depreciation	25	1,175
Total Assets		7,315

LIABILITIES

Accounts Payable	1,000
Taxes Payable	100
Note Payable	1,160
Total Liabilities	2,260

CAPITAL

Common Stock	5,000
Retained Earnings	55
Total Capital	5,055
Total Liabilities + Capital	$ 7,315

We may draw up another fundamental financial statement by listing the flows into (increases) and out of (decreases) the Retained Earnings account. Inflows are called Revenues and outflows are called Expenses. The difference between the two for a given period of time is called Profit (if inflows exceed outflows) or Loss (if outflows exceed inflows). Hence, the name Profit and Loss Statement, P & L, or simply Income Statement.

HOW AN INCOME STATEMENT IS DERIVED

"First, I assume," said Paciolo, "that each businessman is working toward an end and that he makes use of every effort to satisfy this end. The end or objective of every business is to make a lawful and satisfactory profit, so that he can remain in business."[3] As mentioned in the previous section, the Income Statement is utilized to determine and measure a business' profit.

Referring to the Summarizing Book, the following simple Income Statement is a summary from the Retained Earnings account and is obtained by listing the inflows (revenues) and the outflows (expenses) in an orderly manner as portrayed in Exhibit 12-5. The Income Statement is for a particular period of time such as a month or a year.

For a more complex business, the Income Statement might show all the following items:

Item	Description
REVENUES	Represent the sales that were made and are recorded at the time the goods are shipped.
EXPENSES	
Direct Materials	Refers to those specific materials that were used to make the product actually sold.
Direct Labor	Refers to that labor expended in making the product which was actually sold.
Manufacturing Overhead	Refers to those indirect costs incurred in making the product actually sold.
Cost of Goods Sold	Is the sum of Direct Materials, Direct Labor and Manufacturing Overhead. It refers to the total direct costs of a business or the costs associated with producing the product delivered to a customer.
Gross Profit	Is the difference between total sales and Cost of Goods Sold. It is the profit of the basic business—the business without the organizational burden.
General & Administrative	Refers to those indirect organizational costs required to support the overall business (the receptionist's salary, the president's telephone costs, company stationery, legal fees, etc.)
Marketing	Refers to those costs incurred in promoting the company or its products (advertising, sales brochures, market surveys, etc.)

These categories describe the general case. A labor-oriented service business would, for example, merely omit the Direct Materials and Manufacturing Overhead to have its Income Statement categories. A retail business would have Direct Materials, Direct Labor and Manufacturing Overhead combined in Cost of Goods Sold and would also list General and Administrative as well as Marketing to have its outline of Income Statement categories.

EXHIBIT 12-5
ILLUSTRATION OF THE FORM OF AN INCOME STATEMENT

INCOME STATEMENT

REVENUES

Sale	$ 600
Total Sales	600

EXPENSES

Materials	160
Labor	100
Cost of Goods Sold	260
Gross Profit	340
General & Administrative	
Interest	10
Depreciation	25
Taxes	250
Total Expenses	285
Profit	$ 55

HOW A CASH FLOW STATEMENT IS DERIVED

Paciolo observed "There are three things necessary to one who wishes to operate a business successfully. The most important is cash . . ."[4] The movement of cash is monitored and measured with a cash flow statement.

Referring once again to the Summarizing Book, the simple Cash Flow Statement of Exhibit 12-6 is produced from the Cash Account by listing the inflows (Receipts) and the outflows (Disbursements) in an orderly manner.

As in the case of the Income Statement, a more realistic business might have a Cash Flow Statement with the following representative categories of Receipts and Disbursements:

RECEIPTS
  Sales (Cash)
  Collections (of Accounts Receivable)
  Common Stock
  Loans (Received)

EXHIBIT 12-6
ILLUSTRATION OF THE FORM OF A CASH FLOW STATEMENT

CASH FLOW STATEMENT

RECEIPTS

Sales (Cash)	$ —
Common Stock	5,000
Collections (of Accounts Receivable)	200
Total Receipts	5,200

DISBURSEMENTS

Labor	100
Note Repayment (including Interest)	50
Tax Deposit	150
Total Disbursements	300
Net Cash Flow*	4,900

---

*If there had been a previous balance in the cash account, as would normally be the case, Net Cash Flow would not be the same as the cash balance on the Balance Sheet.

DISBURSEMENTS
Direct Materials
Direct Labor
Manufacturing Overhead
General & Administrative
Marketing
Tax Deposits
Capital Equipment
Loan Repayments

Direct Materials, Direct Labor, Manufacturing Overhead, General & Administrative, Marketing and Tax Deposits are categories shown on the Cash Flow Statement that relate to the same items that appeared on the generalized Income Statement previously discussed. The difference is that on the Income Statement they indicate when something was utilized or used up and on the Cash Flow Statement, they indicate when something was actually paid for.

EXHIBIT 12-7
GENERALIZED DIAGRAM OF THE ACCOUNTING PROCESS

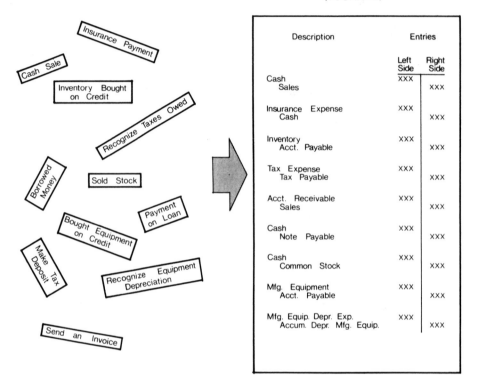

TRANSACTIONS

Business Activities Occur Which
Result in Transactions

RECORDING BOOK
(JOURNAL)

Chronological Listing of Transactions

EXHIBIT 12-7 (CONTINUED)
GENERALIZED DIAGRAM OF THE ACCOUNTING PROCESS

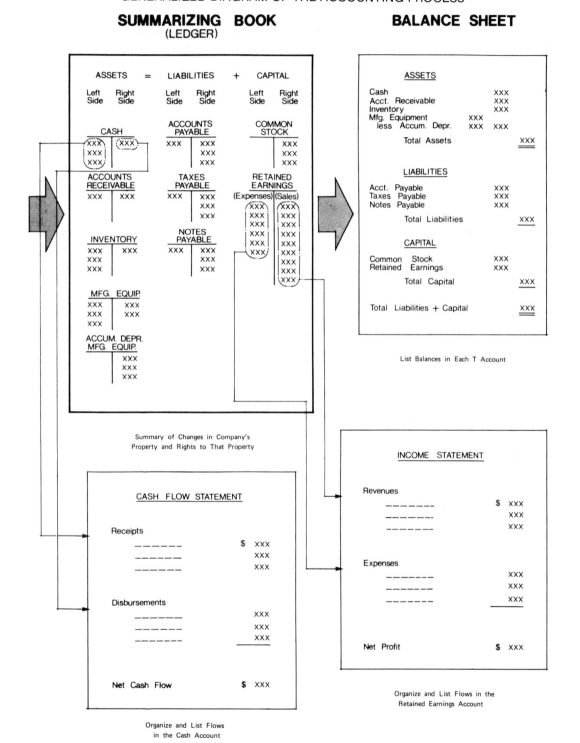

SUMMARIZING BOOK
(LEDGER)

BALANCE SHEET

Summary of Changes in Company's
Property and Rights to That Property

List Balances in Each T Account

Organize and List Flows
in the Cash Account

Organize and List Flows in the
Retained Earnings Account

Two new categories appear on the Cash Flow Statement. Capital Equipment represents equipment purchased and is listed when the check is written. Loan Repayments indicate checks written to pay both principal and interest due on notes payable.

DIFFERENCE BETWEEN INCOME AND CASH FLOW

It should be apparent at this point that there is a dramatic difference between the Income Statement and the Cash Flow Statement. The former is compiled from the Retained Earnings Account and the latter is compiled from the Cash Account. Furthermore, the Income Statement has no provision for handling placements of Common Stock, acquisitions of Loans and purchases of Equipment. On the other hand, the Cash Flow Statement does not report non-cash transactions such as Depreciation.

RELATIONSHIP TO ACCOUNTING

The word "account" has been used numerous times thus far. Is there any doubt why this whole subject matter is called accounting? Also, you may be surprised at this point to realize how much accounting you understand. For example, did you realize that

DEBIT   Is merely the left side of any account?

CREDIT   Is merely the right side of any account?

JOURNAL   Is what was simply referred to as the Recording Book?

LEDGER   Is what was logically called the Summarizing Book?

POSTING   Is simply the process of transferring transactions from the Recording Book to the Summarizing Book?

It is also worthwhile to note that you have working knowledge of terms such as Asset, Liability, Capital, Accounts Receivable, Accumulated Depreciation, Contra Asset, Accounts Payable, Retained Earnings, Balance Sheet, Cash Flow Statement and Income Statement.

THE ACCOUNTING PROCESS

The process that began with the Recording Book, progressed to the Summarizing Book and concluded with a Balance Sheet, is the Accounting Process. The Income Statement and Cash Flow Statement are by-products of the process. This process is graphically illustrated in Exhibit 12-7.

From the manager's perspective, this process may be described functionally in three steps.

- Get all the little pieces of paper (documenting transactions) coming to one central location.

- List the transactions chronologically (in a Journal) so that management can access the information rapidly.

- Rearrange the information (in a Ledger) so that management can use it (in the form of financial statements) to get answers to management questions.

THE SUPERFICIALITY PITFALL

One of the unfortunate but frequent pitfalls that owner-managers find themselves a victim of is superficiality. The superficiality pitfall manifests itself as a shallow understanding of the numbers that describe the way money operates in their business.

There seem to be a couple of common reasons why owner-managers are superficial regarding these numbers. Many seem to have a fear that they won't understand the accounting process when it is explained to them, so why try. It almost appears to be a lack of self-confidence. Some of these managers even seem to be intimidated by the numbers.

Another reason for superficiality is the common feeling that "numbers and accounting stuff" are clerical duties. "As president, I hire bookkeepers to take care of that. If you want to know something about the numbers of my business, then go see my accountant." It is very easy for the busy owner-manager to develop the attitude, "I don't have time to waste with those numbers. I have a company to run." This attitude is a "calling card" of the closely held business on the verge of serious trouble.

The superficiality pitfall is often characterized by receiving a set of monthly financial statements, spending five minutes glancing over them, perhaps routing a copy to the banker or a key supplier and then filing them away. It also appears as listening to what others say (especially, successful peers) without considering if it makes sense.

An effective strategy for dealing with the superficiality pitfall is to THINK. This means use your own brain; scheme; "Grind your headbone"; figure out things for yourself. Thomas Watson, the founder of IBM, made the word, "think," a motto for his company. It is absolutely amazing the extent to which the marketplace is full of misinformation. Experts give advice outside their area of expertise. Successful peers try to impress you with what they are doing that often comes out in the form of a recommendation for you to follow suit. The repeating of hearsay and rumors abounds. Suppliers promulgate recommendations, carry out studies and research and profess expertise that often appears as quality knowledge and advice but is usually geared to only one thing—making a sale and separating you from your money. In addition, employees filter and flavor management information to make themselves look good. To survive and prosper, an owner-manager must think.

One does not have to be an accountant or financial expert to comprehend the numbers arrayed in financial statements and one cannot be an effective president without understanding them. The fundamental principles outlined in this chapter combined with a knowledge of the peculiarities of your particular business are adequate background for most owner-managers. The remaining ingredient is a strong commitment not to treat one's numbers superficially.

NOTES FOR CHAPTER 12

[1]Benjamin Franklin, *Autobiography of Benjamin Franklin*, (New York: Harper & Brothers, Publishers, 1956).

[2]R. Gene Brown and Kenneth S. Johnston, *Paciolo on Accounting*, (New York: McGraw-Hill Book Company, Inc., 1963).

[3]Ibid.

[4]Ibid.

13

Successful Financing
Techniques for Closely Held Companies

Two of the most common and most important sources of financing for the owner-manager are banks and venture capital investors. This chapter focuses primarily on improving the owner-manager's ability to secure bank loans and venture capital. Brief comments will also be made regarding public offerings.

BANK FINANCING

Virtually every owner-manager, at one time or another, utilizes bank financing. Many of these individuals feel that communicating with the banker is difficult. Owner-managers often do not receive the financing they desire, nor the repayment method they prefer, nor the term of repayment they request. Failure to understand how a bank works, how to select a bank that can best serve their needs and how to choose the right banker contribute to the owner-manager's frustration and lack of a satisfactory banking relationship. Failure to know what kind of loan to ask for and then how to make an effective oral and written presentation to the bank also contribute to less than desirable banking relationships. To improve the chances of securing favorable bank financing, it is helpful to consider each of the following areas.

How a Bank Works

A bank is a business. Like all businesses, it must make a reasonable profit in order to survive. While banks may provide a wide diversity of services (checking accounts, savings accounts, certificates of deposit, trust services, etc.), their principal business is the effective and profitable lending of depositors' money. It is important for the owner-manager to understand that it is not the bank's money that is being loaned. It is the money of the depositors that is being loaned. That money includes your grandmother's life savings. Many types of individuals who absolutely cannot afford to have someone speculate with their savings are included in the bank's depositors.

A loan applicant's primary contact with a bank is the loan officer. Loan officers, typically, have a ceiling on the size of any loan they individually approve. This amount is determined by bank policy and will vary depending upon the size of the bank, the experience of the particular loan officer, the loan officer's seniority in the bank's organization and general operating conditions within the bank. Loans larger than the individual loan officer's limit must go before the loan committee that meets periodically. Here, the loan application is discussed. The loan officer advocating the loan may be invited to make any relevant recommendations and presentations before the loan committee. One of the important things to remember here is that for a sizeable loan, your loan officer must go before a committee of peers and superiors and strongly support your loan. A competent loan officer will not go before the loan committee recommending your financing proposal unless convinced it is sound.

It is also helpful to understand that banks are highly regulated institutions. Banks are either federally chartered or state chartered. State and/or federal regulators appear from time to time and make unannounced audits. Banks must meet rigid standards regarding the quality of loans they make. Banks are subject to statutory loan limits and reserve requirements. For reasons beyond their control, banks are frequently unable to grant a loan applicant's request.

Federal regulation and supervision come primarily from three sources: the Federal Reserve, the Comptroller of the Currency and the Federal Deposit Insurance Corporation (FDIC). State supervision comes from the state bank supervisory authorities of each of the individual states. These regulatory bodies devise and enforce many stringent operating ratios and performance criteria on the banking system. Banks must operate within rigid guidelines that relate loans to total deposits, total bank assets and bank capital.

One point frequently misunderstood by owner-managers has to do with the duration of loans typically made by commercial banks. Commercial banks, unlike savings and loan institutions, are interested in short-term financing: Commercial banks prefer 30-day notes, 60-day notes, 90-day notes and one-year notes. Three to five years begins to be considered long term by most commercial banks. This does not mean that they will not lend beyond five years; it means that they, typically, do not lend beyond this period.

It is also helpful to understand that lending money and extending credit is not an exact science even to a banker. Fundamental principles on which credit is based have changed little over the years. The lender must make basic judgments about a borrower's willingness and ability to pay. One way to think about the criteria behind the credit granting judgment is to consider what the bankers refer to as the four "C's" of credit.

The first "C" of credit is *character*. Probably the most essential of all judgments is the evaluation of the borrower's integrity, reliability and moral character. Most of the information regarding character comes from the borrower. The quality and extent of information provided by the individual seeking a loan will reflect upon that person's honesty and sense of responsibility. From the bank's point of view, the past record of the borrower is a good basis for predicting future performance.

The second "C" of credit is *capacity*. This has to do with the ability of the borrower to repay debt. This quality includes a judgment about management itself. Past financial performance, experience, physical and mental ability, age, energy, dedication and determination are all a part of the consideration of capacity.

The third "C" of credit is *capital*." This quality focuses on how much of the owner's money is at stake in relationship to that provided by creditors. Banks have learned that borrowers are much more inclined to struggle through periods of adversity if they have a significant amount of their own money at stake. It is this capital criterion that causes bankers to look at the debt to equity ratio of a particular business. It is not unusual for bankers to require that total liabilities of the borrower's business not exceed twice the equity (net worth) of the business. Another thought involving the capital consideration is that it provides a cushion in the event of adversity. An unanticipated reversal in the business does not necessarily threaten the ability to repay debt if there is adequate capital present.

The fourth "C" of credit is *collateral*. Collateral is often taken to offset a weakness in one of the other "C's." Banks want to be able to look to alternative sources of repayment in the event that capacity becomes inadequate. From the standpoint of the bank, collateral will not make a bad loan good, but it will make a good loan better. In an effort to guarantee repayment, don't be surprised if the bank requests collateral having a current value of more than twice the loan amount. The presence of high quality collateral can easily make the critical difference in a credit judgment by the bank.

How to Select a Bank

Many owner-managers mistakenly believe that all banks make all types of loans. Individual banks, like any other type of business, have a particular product line and a particular market segment that they serve. To prevent inroads by a competitor, a bank must serve its geographical territory. Typically, this is within some reasonable radius of the bank's physical location. One of the first steps in finding a bank is to investigate those institutions within a reasonable geographical distance of your business.

Since individual banks have their own internal policies regarding the type of loans they are willing to make and the conditions under which they are willing to make them, it is helpful when selecting a bank to inquire about the bank's formal loan policy. The Community Reinvestment Act of 1978 requires that a bank make information regarding the principal types of credit the bank is currently extending to the community it serves available upon request. To understand some of the types of internal policy governing the lending of money, consider the following samples of statements from various banks' loan policies.

Usually, there is a general statement regarding policy as follows:[1]

The management of the bank believes that sound local loans are one of the most satisfactory and profitable means of employing the bank's funds available for investment, and the bank, therefore, desires to make all the sound loans that its resources permit and opportunity affords. The Board of Directors recognizes that the lending of money by commercial banks is a business that necessarily includes some business risks, and the management of the bank is willing to undertake such reasonable risks. Some losses are to be expected in any lending program, and a reserve of one-half of one percent of the face amount of loans outstanding will be maintained as a reserve for loan losses.

Bank loan policies will definitely have statements regarding the types of loans that are considered desirable.

An example of this type of statement follows:[2]

Loans of the following types are considered desirable by this bank, provided each such loan meets the tests of a sound, prudent loan.

- Loans to business concerns on a short-term basis, against a satisfactory balance sheet and earnings statement, usually for a term of not more than ninety days.
- Loans to business concerns secured by a chattel mortgage on marketable business equipment, such loans to be amortized over a period of not more than eighteen months.
- Loans to wholesale companies against assignments of accounts receivable on a notification basis.

Banks will, typically, make very definite statements about loans that are not considered desirable. An example of this type of loan policy statement follows:

The loans of the following types are *not* considered desirable loans, and would be declined unless specifically approved by the VP Credit Administration, Senior Credit Committee or Chief Executive Officer for reasons which appear to justify policy exemptions:[3]

- Loans to a business enterprise where the loan cannot be repaid within a reasonable period except by borrowing elsewhere or by liquidating the business.
- Loans to a new enterprise if the repayment of the loan is wholly dependent on the profitable operation of the enterprise.
- Loans to parties whose integrity or honesty is questionable.
- Loans secured by real property out of the Bank's recognized trade area as defined periodically by the Board of Directors or the Chief Executive Officer.
- Interim construction loans except in cases where the improvements are being supervised by an architect and/or a contractor having financial responsibility and where the borrower has produced a satisfactory written takeout commitment.
- Loans to be paid from the proceeds of the settlement of an estate unless these loans are fully collateralized or guaranteed by the estate, and approved by Bank counsel.
- Loans secured by stock in a closely held corporation which has no ready market.
- Loans for speculative purposes, such as purchasing securities or excessive inventory accumulation, or investing in land without well-defined plans for its useful development are not suitable and should be declined.
- Loans secured by junior positions in real estate equities.
- Direct loans to non-depositors or to applicants maintaining substantial banking elsewhere unless the extension of such loans is designed to transfer to this bank that banking or a significant share of that banking to adequately compensate the Bank for the credit extension.

Different bank officers will be authorized to make loans up to a given amount. Individuals who are authorized and the amounts each may approve are, typically, a statement in loan policy. An example of this sort of statement follows:[4]

The officers of the bank shall have authority to make loans up to the amount indicated by their respective names, without the approval of any committee, provided such loans are in accordance with the policies and principles herein expressed. Loans to any person, firm or corporation in excess of the limits indicated must be approved by the Officers' Loan Committee, or as the Directors have provided.

	Unsecured	Secured
Bill Adams, President	$50,000	$50,000
John Doe, Vice President	50,000	50,000
Tom Roe, Vice President	25,000	25,000
Harvey Jones, Assistant Vice President	15,000	25,000
Mark Smith, Assistant Vice President	10,000	25,000
Sandra Davis, Assistant Cashier	5,000	15,000
Marvin Clark, Assistant Cashier	2,500	5,000

Bank loan policies will also have statements regarding collateral and interest rates. An example of a policy statement concerning these two items is presented in the statements that follow:[5]

All loans shall have an ample margin of safety between the advance and the current market value of collateral. When insurance on the collateral or on the life of the borrower is warranted, it shall be obtained and, periodically, reviewed by the loan officer handling the loan or the authorized personnel appointed by the VP Credit Administration. Suggested interest rates, which should not be construed to be maximum rates, may be issued from time to time. Charges and fees must be considered in light of the effective annual percentage rate, a combination of the interest rate and such charges, which cannot exceed the legally permitted rate for the State.

Since banks must have money in order to make money, it is no surprise that they encourage borrowers to also be depositors. An example of such a statement in a bank loan policy is presented as follows:[6]

> The Bank's ability to make loans is dependent upon the Bank's deposit totals. Borrowers should be encouraged to increase their deposit relationships whenever possible.

When shopping for a bank, it is helpful to talk with customers, suppliers and other owner-managers in regard to which banks are providing what kind of service. The annual reports prepared by banks also represent a source of information regarding the banks' programs, activities and general operating character.

There are a number of publications that provide information regarding banks. Polk's *World Bank Directory* from R.L. Polk and Company may be very helpful. Moody's *Bank and Finance Manual*, published by Moody's Investors Service, Inc. is also a valuable reference.

When shopping for a bank, seek out those institutions that offer the products in which you are interested and that have a reputation for cooperation and high levels of professionalism and service.

How to Select a Banker

There is an old saying, "You don't do business with a bank. You do business with a banker." For the most part, this is true. In times of financial adversity, the willingness of the banker to back you can make the difference between surviving or not.

Individual bankers become experienced in the granting of certain types of loans to certain types of businesses. One of the first prerequisites to selecting a banker is to find one who has experience in dealing with your type of business. A banker who is accustomed to making loans to retail businesses may not understand the problems of a high technology manufacturer. A banker who understands the high technology manufacturer may not comprehend the needs of an oil exploration business.

As pointed out in the preceding section on bank loan policy, individuals at different levels in the bank are authorized to approve loans in varying amounts. An assistant vice president can approve a larger loan than an assistant cashier. Likewise, the president of the bank can approve a larger loan than an assistant vice president. It is helpful, therefore, to interact with the highest level officer possible. When your loan goes before the loan committee, judgment is passed by a group of people who do not understand you nearly as well as your individual loan officer. It would be nice if that individual had enough authority to approve your loan without taking it to the loan committee.

When interviewing bankers, try to find one with whom you communicate easily. If you have a problem in communicating with your banker when times are good, the problem will be dramatically magnified when times are bad. Sometimes, common outside interests, such as golf, tennis and hunting can provide an indirect basis of communication and understanding. It may be helpful to try to locate a banker of similar age and educational background. Personalities should be compatible and feelings of trust and confidence should exist between borrower and banker.

Bankers, especially in larger banks, are often very fluid. They are transferred to different departments in the bank, get promoted or decide to go to work for a different bank. It is extremely inconvenient during a period of financial adversity to have your banker disappear. It is wise to get to know your banker well enough that you can formulate a personal opinion as to whether or not that individual is likely to remain in the present position.

When establishing a working relationship with your banker, there are a couple of important points to remember. First, the way to embarrass a banker is to have the regulatory examiner come through the bank, audit the bank's loan portfolio and discover a number of substandard loans, including yours, with the banker's name on them. One of the most common ways that a loan gets classified by the examiner as substandard is to observe that the borrower is not making loan payments on time. Make your loan payments exactly on time. Second, a banker gets fired by making too many loans that go bad. If a given banker has loans go bad exceeding .004 to .006 of that banker's individual portfolio, then, we have a candidate for dismissal. Never do anything that is likely to embarrass your banker or put that individual in a position that can result in dismissal from the bank.

What Kind of Loan Should You Ask for?

There is a fundamental principle owner-managers frequently violate. That principle is using long-term debt to finance long-term assets and short-term debt to finance short-term assets. A 90-day note at the bank may be excellent for Christmas inventory. It is not appropriate, however, for financing a piece of manufacturing equipment having a useful life of 10 years. While owner-managers recognize that fixed assets, such as a building, should be financed with long-term debt, there is one area where short-term financing of long-term needs repeatedly occurs.

Long-term growth in the business is accompanied by the need for long-term financing. This phenomenon was pointed out in Chapter 1. A business that is growing aggressively each year would be wise to seek debt financing that does not have to be repaid in fewer than five years. Commercial banks, as was previously pointed out, are short-term lenders. Three to five years is frequently long-term to these banks. This dilemma is a common source of friction between the owner-manager and the banker.

Many owner-managers think that the simple solution to growth financing is an endless line of credit. Most (working capital) lines of credit, however, are to be paid off at least once during the year. The growing company is a continual consumer of cash and is seldom, if ever, able to repay debt used to finance growth. Retained earnings and external capital infusions from the owners must accompany the growth of the business. The bank should not in general be viewed as a source of permanent long-term capital.

The bank may be able to assist in longer term financing needs if the U.S. Small Business Administration becomes involved through one of its assistance programs.

WHAT THE U.S. SMALL BUSINESS ADMINISTRATION (SBA) CAN DO FOR YOU

For the business that needs money and cannot borrow it on reasonable terms from conventional lenders, the U.S. Small Business Administration (SBA) offers a broad range of loan programs. The Agency may either participate with a bank or another lender in a loan, or guarantee up to 90% of a loan that a bank or other lender agrees to make. Only if the bank or other lender cannot provide funds under either of these methods, SBA by law can consider lending the entire amount as a direct Government loan, if the funds are available. However, the demand for direct loans traditionally exceeds SBA's supply of direct loan monies, and as a result, most of SBA's loans are made in cooperation with banks. SBA loans may be used for:[7]

- Business construction, expansion or conversion
- The purchase of machinery, equipment, facilities, supplies or materials
- Working capital

Regular Business Loans

Under Section 7 (a) of the Small Business Act as amended, SBA is authorized to make regular business loans to small firms on a direct, participation or guaranteed basis.

Economic Opportunity Loans

The Agency grants Economic Opportunity Loans to help persons who are socially or economically disadvantaged own their own businesses. Both prospective and established small firms are eligible for these loans.

Local Development Company Loans

Local Development Companies made up of local citizens whose primary purpose is to improve their area's economy through assisting small business concerns may apply for SBA loans to help buy land, build new factories and shopping centers, acquire machinery and equipment, and expand or convert existing facilities, provided that the project will assist at least one small business. Local Development Companies must provide a reasonable share of the cost of the project to be financed, usually 20% of the total amount.

State Development Company Loans

State Development Companies that are organized by a specific act of a state legislature to assist statewide business growth and development, including small business growth, may apply for SBA State Development Company Loans, the monies from which are then used to supply small business concerns within the state with long-term loans and equity capital.

Pool Loans

Pool Loans are made to corporations formed and capitalized by groups of small business companies for the purchase of raw materials, equipment, inventory or supplies to be used in their individual businesses. These loans may also be used to obtain the benefits of research and development or establish research and development facilities.

Revolving Line of Credit Guarantees

A small firm that cannot obtain a line of credit from a bank in order to fulfill construction or other contracts may apply to SBA for a Revolving Line of Credit Guarantee. The Agency can guarantee the credit extended by the bank for a continuous period of up to 18 months.

Displaced Business Loans

Small firms suffering substantial economic injury because they are displaced by Federally aided renewal or other construction projects are eligible to apply for SBA Displaced Business Loans to help relocate or re-establish. Reasonable upgrading of the business while it is being re-established is permitted.

Handicapped Assistance Loans

Physically handicapped small business owners and public and private non-profit organizations that employ and operate in the interests of the physically handicapped persons are eligible for Handicapped Assistance Loans.

Physical Damage Natural Disaster Recovery Loans

When the President or the Administrator of SBA declares a specific geographical area as a disaster area resulting from a natural disaster, such as a hurricane, a widespread fire, a tornado, flooding, or an earthquake, homeowners, renters and the owners of small and large businesses within the disaster area may apply to SBA for home, personal property and business Disaster Recovery Loans to repair or replace their damaged or destroyed property.

Economic Injury Natural Disaster Loans

When the President, the Secretary of Agriculture or the Administrator of the SBA declares a specific geographical area a disaster area as a result of a natural disaster, the owners of small businesses that have suffered economic losses as a result of the disaster may apply to SBA for Economic Injury Disaster Loans for working capital and funds to pay financial obligations that the owners could have met if the disaster had not occurred.

Product Disaster Loans

SBA makes Product Disaster Loans to small firms that have suffered substantial economic injury because they cannot process or market a product for human consumption because of disease or toxicity resulting from either natural or undetermined causes.

Base Closing Economic Injury Loans

Base Closing Economic Injury Loans are made to small firms that have suffered or will suffer substantial economic injury as a result of the closing of a major Federal military installation or a severe reduction in the scope and size of operations of a major military installation. These loans can be used to help a small business continue in business at its existing location, re-establish its business, purchase a new business or establish a new business.

Strategic Arms Economic Injury Loans

SBA is authorized to make these loans to assist or refinance the existing indebtedness of any small business concern directly or indirectly affected by a significant reduction in scope or amount of Federal support for any project as a result of any international agreement limiting the development of strategic arms or the installation of strategic arms facilities.

Emergency Energy Shortage Loans

These loans were authorized by amendments made to the Small Business Act, as amended in August, 1974. Such loans may be made to small businesses that are suffering economic injury as a result of shortages of fuel, electrical energy or energy-producing resources or shortages of raw or processed materials resulting from shortages of energy.

Regulatory Economic Injury Loans

Small firms that must make changes in their equipment, facilities or operations because of new Federal laws and regulations, and any ensuing state or local laws and regulations, are eligible for SBA Regulatory Economic Injury Loans, if the Agency determines that the concerns are likely to suffer substantial economic injury without such loans. Examples of Federal regulations and laws that have required major changes in small firms are: the Federal Coal Mine and Safety Act of 1969, the Egg Products Act, the Wholesome Poultry Products Act, the Wholesome Meat Products Act of 1967, the Occupational Safety and Health Act of 1970, the Clean Air Act of 1970 and the Federal Water Pollution Control Act of 1974.

Surety Bonds

SBA is committed to making the bonding process accessible to small and emerging contractors who, for whatever reasons, find bonding unavailable to them. The Agency is authorized to guarantee to a qualified surety up to 90% of losses incurred under bid, payment or performance bonds issued to contractors on contracts valued up to $1 million. The contracts may be for construction, supplies or services provided by either a prime or subcontractor for Governmental or non-Governmental work.

Who is eligible for SBA loan assistance? The criteria may change from time to time reflecting national goals and objectives. One recent statement of eligibility follows:[8]

For business loan purposes, SBA defines a small business as one that is independently owned and operated, not dominant in its field and meets employment or sales standards developed by the Agency. For most industries, these standards are as follows:

MANUFACTURING—Number of employees may range up to 1,500, depending on the industry in which the applicant is primarily engaged.
WHOLESALING—Small if yearly sales are not over $9.5 to $22 million, depending on the industry.
SERVICES—Annual receipts not exceeding $2 to $8 million, depending on the industry in which the applicant is primarily engaged.
RETAILING—Small if annual sales or receipts are not over $2 to $7.5 million, depending on the industry.
CONSTRUCTION—General construction: average annual receipts not exceeding $9.5 million for three most recently completed fiscal years. Special trade construction: average annual receipts not exceeding $1 or $2 million for three most recently completed fiscal years, depending on the industry.
AGRICULTURE—Annual receipts not exceeding $275,000.

Ask the nearest SBA field office which standard applies to your type of business.
If you are interested in contacting a field office of the SBA, they are located in each of the following cities:[9]

SBA Field Offices

Agana, GU	Boston, MA
Albany, NY	Buffalo, NY
Albuquerque, NM	Camden, NJ
Anchorage, AK	Casper, WY
Atlanta, GA	Cleveland, OH
Augusta, ME	Columbia, SC
Baltimore, MD	Columbus, OH
Biloxi, MS	Concord, NH
Birmingham, AL	Coral Gables, FL
Boise, ID	Corpus Christi, TX

Dallas, TX
Denver, CO
Des Moines, IA
Detroit, MI
Eau Claire, WI
Elmira, NY
El Paso, TX
Fairbanks, AK
Fargo, ND
Fresno, CA
Greenville, NC
Harrisburg, PA
Hartford, CT
Hato Rey, PR
Helena, MT
Holyoke, MA
Honolulu, HI
Houston, TX
Indianapolis, IN
Jackson, MS
Jacksonville, FL
Jericho, NY
Kansas City, MO
Knoxville, TN
Las Vegas, NE
Little Rock, AR
Los Angeles, CA
Louisville, KY
Lower Rio Grande Valley, TX
Lubbock, TX
Madison, WI
Marquette, MI
Marshall, TX
Memphis, TN
Milwaukee, WI

Minneapolis, MN
Montpelier, VT
Nashville, TN
Newark, NJ
New Orleans, LA
Oklahoma City, OK
Omaha, NE
Philadelphia, PA
Phoenix, AZ
Pittsburgh, PA
Portland, OR
Providence, RI
Rapid City, SD
Reno, NE
Richmond, VA
Rochester, NY
St. Louis, MO
Sacramento, CA
Salt Lake City, UT
San Antonio, TX
San Diego, CA
San Francisco, CA
Seattle, WA
Shreveport, LA
Sioux Falls, SD
Spokane, WA
Springfield, IL
St. Thomas, VI
Syracuse, NY
Tampa, FL
Washington, DC
West Palm Beach, FL
Wichita, KS
Wilkes-Barre, PA
Wilmington, DE

WHAT THE SBA CANNOT DO FOR YOU

The Small Business Administration cannot lend money in the following situations:[10]

- If the company can get money on reasonable terms:

1. From a financial institution.
2. By selling assets that it does not need in order to grow.
3. By the owner's using, without undue personal hardship, his personal credit or resources of his partners or principal stockholders.
4. By selling a portion of ownership in the company through a public offering or a private placing of its securities.
5. From other Government agencies that provide credit specifically for the applicant's type of business or for the purpose of the required financing.
6. From other known sources of credit.

- If the direct or indirect purpose or result of granting a loan would be to:
    1. Pay off a creditor or creditors of the applicant who are inadequately secured and in a position to sustain a loss.
    2. Provide funds for distribution or payment to the owner, partners or shareholders.
    3. Replenish working capital funds previously used to pay the owner, partners or shareholders.

- If the applicant's purpose in applying for a loan is to effect a change in ownership of the business; however, under certain circumstances, loans may be authorized for this purpose, if the result would be to aid in the sound development of a small business or to keep it in operation.

- If the loan would provide for free funds for speculation in any kind of property, real or personal, tangible or intangible.

- If the applicant is a charitable organization, social agency, society, or other non-profit enterprise; however, a loan may be considered for a cooperative if it carries on a business activity and the purpose of the activity is to obtain financial benefit for its members in the operation of their otherwise eligible small business concerns.

- If the purpose of the loan is to finance the construction, acquisition, conversion or operation of recreational or amusement facilities, unless the facilities contribute to health or general well being of the public.

- If the applicant is a newspaper, magazine, radio broadcasting, television broadcasting company or similar enterprise.

- If any of the gross income of the applicant (or of any of its principal owners) is derived from gambling activities.

- If the loan is to provide funds to an enterprise primarily engaged in the business of lending or investments or to provide funds to any otherwise eligible enterprise for the purpose of financing investments not related to or essential to the enterprise.

- If the purpose of the loan is to finance the acquisition, construction, improvement or operation of real property that is, or is to be, held primarily for sale or investment.

- If the effect of granting of the financial assistance will be to encourage monopoly or will be inconsistent with the accepted standards of the American system of free competitive enterprise.

- If the loan would be used to relocate a business for other than sound business purposes.

Checklist for Making a Loan Presentation

There are several important points one would be wise to keep in mind when approaching the banker for a loan.

1. Know what you want—Vagueness about such factors as the amount of money needed, the loan maturity or the type of installment payment creates questions in the banker's mind as to whether you really understand how much is needed, when it is needed and how it is to be paid back. The point is to "have your act together" regarding what you want.

2. Know why you want the loan—Is the purpose of the loan to finance long-term growth? Is this equipment financing? Do you desire a seasonal line of credit? Would you like a factoring arrangement for your receivables? Is mortgage financing more appropriate? All of these questions are appropriately related to understanding exactly why you desire debt financing. If you would like a loan because all of a sudden you have no money, don't expect the banker to be very sympathetic. Remember, the purpose of the loan must be disclosed.

3. Make a good impression personally—Since you must be the one to repay the loan, the banker must develop very positive feelings about the person sitting across the desk. Be straightforward, businesslike and to the point. Don't dodge direct questions. Express self-confidence but don't be so "charged up" that you appear to be out of touch with reality. It is often advisable to adopt a position of asking the banker for suggestions. This indicates you value the banker's judgment. The way you dress, speak and present your thoughts all provide data on the kind of person you are.

4. Be prepared to answer basic questions about your business—Every banker can recite numerous examples of owner-managers who come into their bank requesting large sums of money and who can't answer the most basic questions about the business for which the loan is being sought. Favorite questions a banker likes to ask to see whether you are knowledgeable about your business include:

   a. What is your fiscal year?
   b. What were last year's gross sales?
   c. What are next year's projected gross sales?
   d. What was last year's net profit before taxes and after taxes?
   e. What is next year's projected profit before taxes and after taxes?
   f. What is your gross profit margin?
   g. What is your net profit margin?
   h. What is your average Accounts Receivable collection period?
   i. What is your annual inventory turnover?
   j. What is your trade payables turnover?
   k. Are you discounting your bills?
   l. What are your depreciation methods?
   m. What is the total monthly compensation of officers or partners?

5. Be prepared to leave selected documents and written information with the banker—in addition to your loan officer, other parties in the bank may have to pass judgment on you. Common documents and written information requested

of the borrower include:

a. A projected Income Statement and Cash Flow Statement, monthly for two years (See Exhibits 1-5 and 1-6 for an illustration).

b. A detailed list of any collateral being offered.

c. A detailed list of any co-makers and/or guarantors.

d. A written statement of the purpose and use of proceeds.

e. An Income Statement and Balance Sheet for each of the last three years; a current Income Statement and Balance Sheet for the year to date, signed by an officer of the company.

f. A copy of the last three years' income tax return

g. A detailed schedule of all debts.

h. A detailed schedule of accounts payable.

i. A detailed schedule of aged accounts receivable.

j. A copy of all outstanding leases.

k. A copy of the certificate of incorporation if you have a corporation.

l. A list of all owners, officers, directors or partners with the following information: name, office held, annual compensation and percent of ownership.

m. Brief resume of each principal officer.

n. Brief description of the business operation.

o. Official name of company, address, phone number, all business identification numbers.

p. List of pending lawsuits and dollar amounts.

Characteristics of a Class One, Prime Loan: A Banker's Viewpoint

A banker friend once explained how he rated different loans. Some of the characteristics of what he described as a class one, prime loan are worth repeating.

A prime loan is one that has a floating interest rate above the bank's minimum lending rate. The borrower carries significant balances in the company's checking account, perhaps as much as 20-25% of the amount borrowed. Both of these criteria insure profitability of that loan for the bank.

A prime loan is one in which the borrower maintains current financial statements in the bank's files. Under no circumstances will financial statements be more than one year old. The purpose of the loan will be clearly stated and will conform with bank loan policy. There will be no violations of the terms of the loan agreement and no payments will be past due with a class one, prime loan.

As far as collateral is concerned, appraisals and other reports will be current. If accounts receivable represent the primary collateral, agings of the receivables will be received from the borrower monthly. If inventory is the primary collateral, the bank will conduct periodic audits and will receive a report from the borrower on a monthly basis.

From the bank's point of view, the best loans will have financial statements submitted by the borrower that are audited and have an unqualified opinion stated by the auditing firm.

The general business trends for the borrower of a class one, prime loan will be up steadily and significantly. As far as liquidity is concerned, cash plus receivables will exceed current liabilities. With respect to debt and net worth, the ratio will be better than industry averages.

Both accounts receivable turnover and inventory turnover will exceed the industry averages. With a class one loan, the withdrawals by the officers of the borrowing company will be less than 50% of the net profits after tax. This includes salaries, dividends, bonuses and any other cash benefit. Both the gross profit and the net profit margins will exceed the industry average (the publication, *Annual Statement Studies*, by Robert Morse Associates is useful in establishing industry operating averages). The marketability of any pledged collateral will be high and collateral market value will be 1.5 times the amount of the loan.

While much of the preceding loan lending criteria may vary between banks and between bankers, it is helpful to think about some of the characteristics that cause a bank to consider your business class one, prime.

Why Banks Turn Down Loans: Results of a Survey

Owner-managers who find that their bank failed to approve a loan often wonder why that decision was reached. A survey conducted by *Banker's Magazine* addressed this question to a number of leading lending executives. In order of frequency, with the most frequently given reasons appearing first, the replies to why banks turn down loans were as follows.[11]

1. Capital—insufficient, inadequate.
2. Management—lack of competency, experience.
3. Poor credit record.
4. Loan too speculative.
5. Cash flows—insufficient, questionable.
6. No track record.
7. Too much leverage.
8. Overloaned.
9. Insufficient information.
10. Equity—insufficient.
11. Collateral—insufficient.
12. Use of loan proceeds.
13. Inability to repay.
14. Repayment terms too long.
15. Insufficient income.
16. Customer outside market area.
17. Bank illiquid.
18. Poor financial statements.
19. Lack of capacity to repay.
20. Poor yield.
21. Inability to service debt.
22. Economic conditions—effect on company.
23. Reputation of borrower.
24. Balances inadequate.
25. Lack of profitability.
26. Customer won't accept floating rate.

27. Loan too large for bank.

28. Equity financing confused with debt financing.

29. Prospects poor for long-term relationship.

30. Loan portfolio considerations.

31. Poor business outlook for company.

32-41. Miscellaneous: seasonal repayment; nature of business; split banking relationships; security difficult to sell; poor chance of achieving loan purpose; no plans for emergencies; assets pledged to other banks; no alternatives if loan gets in trouble; inventories high—receivables aging; unwillingness of management to guarantee loan.

Since these are the reasons bankers say they turn down loans, it is helpful to be cognizant of them. This list may provide you with advance warning of weaknesses that could be perceived in your loan application. An attempt to address and correct identified weak areas could enhance your chances of having the desired loan approved.

VENTURE CAPITAL FINANCING

Important sources of financing for the entrepreneur or owner-manager are those individuals and institutions who place their money in high risk situations in the hope of very large returns. The term that has evolved for this type of investment is venture capital. Consider first the venture capital that comes from private sources.

Private Placements:
How to Prepare a Successful Proposal

The term, Private Placement, is derived from the Securities Act of 1933 and its amendments that regulate Public offerings of securities. Securities are broadly defined to mean any documents that represent ownership, partial ownership or a claim against property owned in a business. The law was intended to protect the unwary investor from buying a portion of a business without first fully understanding what it is that is being sold. Buying stock in non-existent gold mines and similar frauds led to the act.

One way to avoid the regulations is not to make a public offering. The alternative has been called a private placement. Find a small number of people with money to invest and convince them of the virtues of the potential investment.

Finding these private individuals without appearing to be making a public offering can cause some difficulty. The recommended way is to talk only to friends, relatives and business associates. They may introduce you to *their* friends, relatives and business associates. Even though you talk to them individually, it doesn't take long to develop a very wide circle of acquaintances, some of whom may have money to invest.

Since these people are individuals with money, they are as different as people of any class or group. What makes them decide to invest in one opportunity and not another can depend upon the most subtle and irrelevant perceptions.

The way to improve your probability of success in getting them to invest can best be described as:

1. Know your audience.

2. Know your subject.

3. Stick to the facts.

A potential investor who has made a fortune in urban rental real estate is not likely to comprehend a story about a new electronic microprocessor component for the automobile after-market. Talk to people who can understand and appreciate what you have to say.

Nothing destroys credibility faster than being unable to answer a question regarding some aspect of your business proposal, except outright lying. One of the greatest virtues in preparing a detailed business plan is in the education it provides to the person preparing it.

Investors have all been burned before. They have heard the tall tales about the greatest investment of a lifetime. Don't tell fairy tales. If the hard cold facts won't justify the investment, maybe it shouldn't be made. Present the facts openly, honestly and with a willingness to accept advice. The investment frequently comes with the advice.

Beware of the Securities Laws

There is a Federal Securities Act and there is a State Securities Act for each state in the union. We are always subject to the Act of the state in which we sell securities. Selling stock or bonds, debentures, warrants or options in two states makes us subject to the Act of each of the two states and the Federal Act simultaneously. A public offering by a large company to individuals in each state in the United States must satisfy the Acts of the Federal government and those of the 50 states simultaneously.

The Acts of these various entities are not the same. They are not even similar in many cases. The basic philosophy behind the Acts fall into two major classifications. They are the philosophy of:

        A. Full Disclosure

        B. Fair, Just and Equitable[12]

The Federal law is based upon A. The staff of the Securities and Exchange Commission will determine whether all pertinent facts and information are being provided to permit an investor to make a reasonable investment decision.

Many state laws are based upon B. In this case, not only must the facts be disclosed, but the security being offered and its price must be deemed to be fair, just and equitable to the buyer. The determination is made by the staff of the state Securities Commission or some regulatory body of the state government with a similar name.

Normally, no problem arises when securities are sold. It is later on when some buyer becomes disgruntled that the trouble arises. Typically, the investor wants the money back. This almost invariably happens when the business can least afford it. But, all the investor has to do to cause trouble is to claim, in the nearest state or Federal Securities Commission office, that the original sale was made in violation of the Act.

Even if no disgruntled investor appears on the scene, the problem will arise if you ever try to have a registered offering under any state Act. At that time, they will review each and every significant transaction and the circumstances surrounding that transaction.

This is one area of business in which it is best to grit your teeth, bear the expense and hire an *experienced* lawyer.

The Golden Rule Pitfall

It is hard to accumulate money. Once accumulated it is very easy to lose. People with enough money available to make an investment in a business are very aware of this phenomenon.

There are many opportunities available to an investor. They range from savings accounts in the bank to Certificates of Deposit to Treasury Bills to tax free Municipal Bonds and so forth on to gold coins and venture capital investments in a new business. When an investor is asked to make an investment in a new or small business venture, that investor is consciously or subconsciously considering the alternative opportunities.

The entrepreneur or owner-manager is always bubbling with self-confidence and, in fact, must be. It is not unusual, however, to have that self-confidence cause a little self-delusion. Investors are in a position that causes them to be cold, objective, realistic and even a little pessimistic. When the entrepreneur is in the position of asking the investor for money, it should be clear that the investor is holding all the cards. The investor doesn't *have* to do anything. Almost invariably the owner-manager *has* to obtain the money.

The entrepreneur's perception of the value of what is being sold, some piece of the business or some portion of future revenues, is quite naturally flavored by self-confidence and broad knowledge of the business and its potential. The entrepreneur, typically, believes that very little needs to be given up in return for the money. It is commonplace to have the investor asking for 60-80% of the business while the entrepreneur is thinking in terms of giving up only 20-30% of the business.

Under these circumstances, the entrepreneur learns venture capital's "Golden Rule," "He who has the gold makes the rules."

Formal and Informal Venture Capital

Venture capital is money invested in a non-proven business. There is, of course, some difference of opinion about what is proven and what is non-proven. Generally, investors view the investment in which there is no absolute guarantee that the investment will be returned with interest or dividends as a venture capital deal.

Real estate seems like a sound, sure investment. At least, the land won't go away and the buildings can be insured against almost all perils. But, investing in the down payment on real estate can be very venturesome. The mortgagor owns the real estate. The mortgagee's equity builds very slowly over the years and all of that is in jeopardy if only a few installment payments go unsatisfied.

A new or small or young business is hardly a proven business. The commonly quoted statistics on the mortality of new businesses, based upon a study by the U.S. Department of Commerce, indicate that 80% of all new businesses will fail within five years of their birth.[13]

Investors in this kind of investment opportunity recognize the risk. They also recognize the high return available if the new or young or small business thrives and grows. Some individuals with substantial pools of money to invest will set aside a small portion of their funds to be risked on venture capital opportunities.

Venture capital is placed informally most of the time. A few individuals who know each other will tend to join together in a venture capital opportunity which strikes the fancy of one of their group. These loops or circuits of private investors keep a very low profile.

A small percentage of the total venture capital available is placed in the hands of formal organizations that specialize in making this kind of investment. They are called venture capital firms. Most often these firms invest the money belonging to a single family, like the J.H. Whitney Co., or a single company, like General Electric Company's investment subsidiary, or a single bank, like the First Dallas Capital Corporation owned by the First National Bank of Dallas.

There are a few venture capital firms that invest on behalf of a larger group of investors. The Heizer Corporation of Chicago is one of the biggest and best known of this kind.

WHERE IS THE VENTURE CAPITAL?

The formal sources of venture capital are reasonably easy to find. There are directories listing them. One source of broad general usefulness is that by Stan Rubel.[14] There is a separate directory for sources in Canada. Another major listing for the United States is published by

Technimetrics, Inc. There are some regional sources, such as those put out by the School of Management at Boston College.

The formal venture capital firms state their principal interests, size of investments they like and their investment philosophy. They are usually happy to receive a copy of a business plan for their review. They will seldom provide an opportunity for an interview or verbal discussion before they have had an opportunity to review a formal, written plan.

The informal sources are hard to find. They learn very quickly that to make the public aware of their existence is to invite every little old inventor within a thousand miles to their office. They are quickly deluged with every hair-brained scheme making its rounds in the country. Consequently, they deny their existence. They keep their group informal enough so that nobody can even suspect that they are a group.

The way to find the informal sources is to be introduced to one of their members by someone they respect. A number of individuals perform this intermediary function. Lawyers and accountants are probably the primary groups. Investment counselors and stockbrokers sometimes fill this role. Occasionally, an insurance broker will have this kind of connection.

Senior bank officers are familiar with the bank's clients who might be venture investors. Often, the bank's officers are among the investors. But, remember that the banker must maintain cordial relations with the bank's clients. If the banker doesn't view a potential investment as almost good enough for the bank, it isn't likely the banker will tell anyone about it.

The likely potential private venture investors are those individuals who have high current income, but no substantial equity-building property. They could be vice presidents in large companies, doctors, lawyers, athletes and show people. They may also be people who have done well on their own recently, like automobile dealers, small business owners, manufacturer's representatives, landlords or the ex-farmer who just sold the farm to a building developer. And, of course, children of families with money are given a chance to try their wings on their own typically when they are in their late 20s.

SBIC'S: WHAT THEY WILL AND WON'T DO

The Small Business Investment Companies or SBIC's are a unique source of venture capital. Their specific objective is to provide financing to small businesses which have difficulty in obtaining bank loans or equity from either the normal venture capital firms or the private placement sources. They are licensed venture capital firms supported by and regulated by the U.S. Small Business Administration under the Small Business Investment Act of 1958. A copy of this Act as amended is available from the nearest office of the Small Business Administration.

A variation on the SBIC is the MESBIC, that is an SBIC organized under Section 301 (d) of the Act. The term MESBIC implies Minority Enterprise Small Business Investment Company. They are provided greater support by the U.S. Government in return for concentrating their investments on businesses owned (at least 50%) by citizens who are socially or economically disadvantaged due to race, sex or other social or economic considerations beyond their control, such as education, financial capacity, geographic or regional economic distress or physical or mental handicap.

The term "small," does not imply very small under the SBIC guidelines. The general guideline is assets of less than $9 million, net worth less than $4 million and net profit after tax of less than $400,000 for each of the past two years. SBIC's and MESBIC's are encouraged to finance start-up ventures. As a practical matter, they spread their risk over a broad range of situations.

During the first few years following passage of the Act by Congress, there were many firms licensed and many did very well. Some became public companies. In 1962, however, the stock market experienced one of its periodic lows and the SBIC's fell into disrepute with investors. Those early years under the Act were accompanied by the growing pains of every new industry. During the decade of the 1960s, Congress improved the provisions, the SBA improved the regulations and the SBIC owners improved the management of the firms.

During the decade of the 1970s, the industry matured and the number of firms began to increase. The SBA report titled, "The 20th Anniversary of the SBIC Program," August 21, 1978, indicated nearly 300 SBIC's and nearly 100 MESBIC's with combined total capital resources of more than a billion dollars.

SBIC's are in the business of making a fair return on their investment. (We refer to both MESBIC and SBIC with the term SBIC.) Like any prudent investor, they want to insure the return of their investment with a profit and they spread their risk as broadly as possible to minimize the effect of a bad investment. They make their profit in two ways: interest on loans and increase in the value of the stock they acquire.

Prudent investment policy also calls for leveraging their investment as much as possible. Typically, an SBIC will consider a financing package that includes a stock purchase and loan by their firm in combination with bank loans guaranteed up to 90% by the Small Business Administration. They will also syndicate with other SBIC's to spread their risk.

The purchase of stock may or may not be immediate. SBIC's have as much freedom and as much imagination as any other investor. They may offer loans in the form of debentures, convertible into stock, or loans with associated warrants to purchase stock at some later date, the price being set at the time of the loan. Interest rates are limited by usury laws but like most financial institutions, they will structure the financing so that their real return is reasonable.

Somehow, the conventional wisdom has evolved to suggest that the SBA and the SBIC's impose undue controls and interfere with management. This is just not true. They ask for, and rightfully expect, good financial control and adequate, timely accounting. What may appear to be imposed control is no more than providing the discipline that any good manager should exercise.

SBIC's are formal venture capital firms. Approaching them and dealing with them should be viewed in the same way as any other formal venture capital firm. Locating them is relatively easy. Their names and addresses are listed in the Directory of Small Business Investment Companies available from the nearest office of the U.S. Small Business Administration. The Directory for MESBIC's will probably be located in the same SBA office. If not, it can be obtained from the U.S. Department of Commerce.[15]

WHAT ARE YOUR CHANCES FOR ACQUIRING VENTURE CAPITAL?

The formal venture capital firms report that they look at 100 proposals to find one worth studying. They study ten to find one worth investing in. Of each 10 they invest in, only one works out to meet the expectations they had at the time of the investment.

A venture capital portfolio containing fewer than 10 investments is like a chip on the roulette tables in Las Vegas. A firm needs 20 to 30 investments before it is investing and not "gambling." When you walk in the door with your proposal, you are one of the next hundred the firm has to look at to find one worth studying. You are one of the next 1000 they have to see before making their next investment.

Don't be discouraged. Just make sure your proposal is worth studying. After all, everybody who ever got money from a venture capital firm walked the same road you are walking and there are lots of people who got the money.

Obtaining money from the informal sources may be easier than from the formal sources once you locate them. Frequently, the investment decision is based upon one individual's gut feeling for you or your idea. That individual can be very helpful in finding the other investors and selling them on the proposition. This is one reason why it is wise to know your audience.

The potential investor probably has a lifetime of experience in one field of endeavor. A discussion about a product or service in that field can be lively and knowledgeable. On the other hand, it is possible to bore a person to tears with the most exciting story in the world. When reading something you don't understand, it puts you to sleep. When listening to a speaker discussing something about which you know nothing, it takes an especially animate personality to keep you from going to sleep. If the potential investor doesn't know anything about the proposal you are discussing, don't be surprised at the drooping eyelids and the glassy stare.

If you want money for a product used in oil well production and service, talk to a potential investor who knows something about oil fields. That won't guarantee that you get the money, but it improves the probability that you will get a hearing.

After all is said and done, the investor is making an emotional decision based upon confidence in the individual asking for the money. You improve your chances when you win that confidence.

Types of Public Offerings

It would be presumptuous to imply that all of the types of public offerings of securities could be fully discussed in a single section of a single chapter in a book. There are many books devoted to the subject. It might be helpful, however, to know just a little about public offerings before you visit a lawyer.

When contemplating selling securities within a single state, it is necessary to complete a registration statement and have it approved by the Securities Commissioner in that state. It is absolutely necessary to obtain the forms on which to file such a statement. It is also absolutely wise, prudent and smart to obtain a copy of the Securities Act of the state with the latest amendments. It may be necessary to ask a lawyer for help in understanding the Act, but a long list of headaches can be avoided by reading it.

If securities are to be sold in two or more states, it will be necessary to obtain the forms from each state and from the Federal Securities and Exchange Commission. Again, it is very advisable to obtain copies of the Acts from those states and the federal government. They are surprisingly short documents. Like most government regulations and legal documents, they are in that language peculiar to the legal profession. With a little effort, however, you'll find they are not much more difficult to read than Shakespeare.

The Federal Securities and Exchange Commission provides for a full-blown registration and for a smaller, less complicated registration usually referred to as the Regulation "A" registration. Both are complex, time consuming and expensive. It is best to employ a lawyer *experienced* in public offerings for guidance under the latest rule changes promulgated by the regulatory agencies.

There is one word of caution to be aware of in any public offering. The offering must be registered with the securities authorities. Many people fail to understand the preciseness of that last sentence and speak of registering their stock. Only the offering is registered. The securities exchanged as a result of that registered offering are public stock. No other stock or securities of the company become public as a result of the registered offering. You register the transaction, not the securities.

It is not necessary to have an underwriter to hold a public offering, but it helps. They find buyers for the securities, that solves one problem, and they have a wealth of experience to help guide the company, its lawyers, its accountants and its prospectus printers through the ritual of registration and public offering.

Pros and Cons of Going Public

Being a company with publicly held stock can be a mixed blessing. Some of the positive aspects result from the ability to determine a value for the company and its stock. Stock options to employees can have a clear identifiable value and if the company is growing and the economy isn't passing through a low period, the management and employees can find a public record of their increasing value.

If the company is growing profitably, it will need capital for expansion. Provided the economy isn't passing through one of its periodic lows, the public may serve as a source of the capital needed.

Having public stock permits stockholders to sell their stock. This is sometimes a tremendous advantage. One of the most troublesome problems for management is having a stockholder who wants to sell stock, for whatever reason, but who holds stock that has never passed through a registration. Founders, private placement investors and venture capital investors usually fall into this class. There are rules for the disposition of such stock provided by the Securities and Exchange Commission, but they are such as to almost require that some stock of the company be publicly held as a result of a prior registration.

On the negative side, being publicly held requires that the registration statement be maintained by periodic reports to the Securities and Exchange Commission. The reports are not complex provided the company keeps scrupulous accounting and stockholder records. The expense of maintaining that degree of timely and detailed records can only be born by a company that can support a substantial General and Administrative staff.

The closely held business management, and owners, give up one of the best things a closely held business has to offer them when it goes public. This might best be termed the perquisites. A publicly held business must act in the best interest of its public stockholders. Sale and leaseback of the company's real estate to the owners and managers may be viewed dimly by public stockholders. Company automobiles and country club memberships may come under vocal scrutiny. The owner-manager who sells a small portion of the company to the public becomes just another stockholder.

The Problem with Taking Other People's Money

People's goals and aspirations change as time goes by. The circumstances in which people find themselves are always changing. No matter how right an investment may be at the time it is made, there will come a time when it is no longer tolerable to some of the investors. If they are unable to get out with an acceptable gain on their investment at the time of their choosing, they will be dissatisfied, if not disgruntled.

Unfortunately, the company does not make the market for securities held by its investors. That market is often unrelated to the company's performance. Even the stock of companies traded on the New York Stock Exchange will rise and fall in value despite a company's continued and consistent excellent performance.

In a thinly traded market, that is, one in which there are not enough shares in the hands of the public to provide a broad and diverse pool of shareholders, there are usually few shares bought and sold during any trading day. There may be no trades for days or weeks. Under those circumstances, the value of the shares is never clear. Also, in that kind of market, a sale of a few shares may depress the price of the stock very unduly. Stockholders with large holdings may find that although they have the legal right to sell their shares, they can't find buyers or if they find buyers, the price may fall to the point that they will lose money on the sale.

When stockholders find themselves thwarted in the market place, they vent their frustrations on the only available audience, the company's management. The staunchest supporters, including friends, relatives and business associates, can become the most ferocious consumers of management time and money.

Management, typically, has a longer-range perspective than investors. This is probably because management is in a position to take action, to make things happen. Investors can only sit idly by waiting for the opportunity to sell at a big profit. Even inaction, never mind adverse reports on the progress of the business, can make investors impatient and uneasy. The result is investor fatigue and frustration.

When you take someone else's money, you become involved in their emotions. The result is much like accepting their love and pledging your troth at the altar.

NOTES FOR CHAPTER 13

[1]William H. Baughn and Charles E. Walker, *The Banker's Handbook*, (Homewood, Illinois: Dow Jones-Irwin, Inc., 1966).

[2]Ibid.

[3]Ibid.

[4]Ibid.

[5]Ibid.

[6]Ibid.

[7]*SBA: What It Does*, U.S. Small Business Administration, 1977.

[8]*SBA: Business Loans*, U.S. Small Business Administration, 1977.

[9]*SBA: What It Does*.

[10]*SBA: Business Loans*.

[11]"Why Banks Turn Down Loans—A Bankers Magazine Survey," *The Banker's Magazine*, pp. 67-70.

[12]James S. Mofsky, *Blue Sky Restrictions on New Business Promotions*, (New York: Matthew Bender, 1971).

[13]Betty Churchill, "Age and Life Expectancy of Business Firms," *Survey of Current Business*, December, 1955.

[14]Stanley M. Rubel, *Guide to Venture Capital Sources*, 3rd. ed. (Chicago: Capital Publishing Corporation, 1974).

[15]Directory: MESBIC's (Section 301(d) Licensees) Office of Minority Business Enterprise, U.S. Department of Commerce, Washington, D. C. 20230.

14

Blueprinting and Administering
Lucrative Expansion Strategies and
Beat - the - Competition Policies

Most successful entrepreneurs mention luck when they describe the experience of building their business. Some observers will claim that they were lucky while others will grant entrepreneurs attributes of the gifted: brilliance, intelligence and education. During the past century, a pattern has been identified to the strategies pursued by many successful managers in business. Whether gifted or lucky, it now appears that there is at least one underlying principle to the strategies of the successful.

The underlying principle may not yet be completely understood, but enough evidence has emerged during recent decades to permit its description with some authority. The principle is identified by many names in the literature, but its conventional identity is the Learning Curve.

THE LEARNING CURVE

The time required to complete a task becomes less and less as you accumulate experience performing the task. Early life experiences confirm this. Learning to walk was such a task. So were the early school tasks of reading, writing and arithmetic. In the beginning, just holding the pencil was a problem. In due time, that was replaced with choosing the right letter to be written. And so the learning progressed until now, as adults, the problem is more one of composition and expression than actual writing.

During the 19th century, the industrial revolution precipitated the creation of many repetitive manufacturing tasks. After the Civil War, Fredrick G. Taylor observed that workers were typically given a task and allowed to complete it in the best way they knew how. Some came up with better methods than others. He claimed that if all the workers were required to perform the task in the manner of the best worker, the overall production efficiency of the business would be greatly improved.

Taylor began making time studies of the many individual motions performed by workers in an attempt to identify the most efficient necessary motions and to eliminate the unnecessary motions. Many startling improvements resulted from Taylor's work. Such simple things as the location of an on-off switch made significant improvements in the time required to perform a repetitive task.

Time studies on manufacturing tasks became normal practice in progressive industries during the late 19th century. By the early 20th century, it was standard practice and sufficient data became available to observe trends in the productiveness of workers doing repetitive tasks.

Miguel A. Reguero[1] reports that the first observation of the pattern of the Learning Curve was made by the base commander of Wright-Patterson Air Force Base in Ohio in 1925. It was publicly reported for the first time in 1936 by T.P.Wright[2] who observed that the direct labor required to construct an aircraft decreased by 20% each time the number of such aircraft produced had doubled.

In 1954, Frank J. Andress[3] published an article in the *Harvard Business Review* speculating on a general theory of learning based upon evidence from the aircraft industry. In 1964, Winifred B. Hirschmann[4] published an article in the same journal providing a more general discussion on the theory and its applicability to industries that appear to have little labor content. In 1968, the staff of the Boston Consulting Group, Inc.[5] published the results of a series of studies relating price decline to accumulated total production across a spectrum of industries. These studies led to conclusions of still greater generality and suggest the existence of an underlying principle.

All production workers observe the phenomenon in their own experience. One owner-manager related a personal experience. At the age of 16, he was employed to operate a stamping press in a soap factory. The press automatically closed its die 96 times per minute. The jaws of the die were fed raw cylinders of soap from a chute. The operator's job was to pick up the raw soap cylinders from a passing conveyor belt and place them in the trough of the chute.

Behind the press, there was a long conveyor belt carrying the finished soap to a group of eight workers who wrapped and packaged the bars. One press kept those eight workers busy.

Needless to say, the press kept its operator fully occupied. Picking up the raw soap cylinders and depositing them in the chute was no great task, but delivering 96 cylinders per minute was. The operator leaned over the 30-inch wide conveyor belt to pick up the soap then turned a full 180 degrees to face the chute. Also, the conveyor was about table height while the chute was shoulder height.

The young operator quickly learned that it was necessary to pick up six cylinders at a time, three in each hand, in order to keep up with the press. At first, this was a formidable task. At the end of the first week, it could be handled. In three weeks, the operator was faster than the machine. The extra time that became available was used to lubricate the press or the dies periodically.

Later, even this work could not fully occupy the operator and conversation developed with the eight workers behind the press. Within two months, the operator had developed a rhythmic, full-body motion that was very similar to a dance step. It was performed with the same inattention to its intricacy as two ballroom dancers engaged in delightful conversation.

Time studies performed on production workers reveal that the time required to perform a repetitive task decreases by an equal percentage each time the worker doubles total accumulated experience performing the task. Surprisingly, the phenomenon continues for as long as the worker continues the task.

If the results of this observation are plotted on a graph, the time to perform the task follows a curve as shown in Exhibit 14-1. If the repetitive task is thought of as resulting in the creation of a unit of some sort, then the curve indicates that the time required to produce the last unit made is less than the time required for any prior unit made.

If the curve in Figure 14-1 is plotted on graph paper having logarithmic scales, log-log paper, the curve becomes a straight line and its slope is a direct measure of the reduction in time required to perform the task each time the total accumulated experience doubles. Exhibit 14-2 is data from Exhibit 14-1 plotted on log-log coordinates.

The horizontal scale suggests the major limitation to progressing down this curve forever.

EXHIBIT 14-1
TIME REQUIRED TO PERFORM A REPETITIVE TASK VS. ACCUMULATED
EXPERIENCE PERFORMING THE TASK

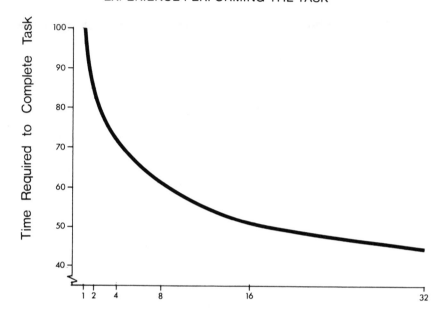

Total Number of Times Task Has Been Performed

EXHIBIT 14-2
DATA FROM EXHIBIT 14-1 PLOTTED ON LOG-LOG COORDINATES

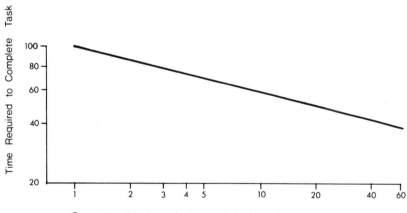

Cumulative Number of Times Task Has Been Performed

When the total accumulated experience is 100, it is not hard to conceive of doubling that experience. When the accumulated experience is 1,000,000, doubling that experience may take considerable time. Eventually, the total past experience will be so great that it will take forever to achieve one more doubling.

THE EXPERIENCE CURVE

The Learning Curve has been recognized and accepted for a long time now. During World War II, government contracts for ships, tanks and airplanes were priced with built-in decreases proportional to the progress of workers down their Learning Curve. Following the war, this progress was routinely anticipated by progressive management.

The results of the studies of price declines with industry experience, published by the Boston Consulting Group, Inc. in 1968, suggested an extension of the Learning Curve concept. These studies demonstrated that the price charged for a product decreased by an equal percentage each time the total accumulated experience for the entire industry doubled. Curves were developed for Germanium Transistors, Silicon Transistors, Germanium Diodes, Silicon Diodes, Integrated Circuits, Crude Oil, Motor Gasoline, Ethylene, Polystryrene, Polyvinylchloride, Primary Aluminum, Primary Magnesium, Titanium Sponge, Monochrome Television Receivers, Free Standing Gas Ranges, Free Standing Electric Ranges, Facial Tissue, Japanese Beer, Electric Power and Refined Cane Sugar. The results were impressive. Price, in constant dollars (taking out the effects of inflation), declined with experience in a consistent and persistent pattern.

The Learning Curve can be observed directly and immediately. The Experience Curve is more subtle. Observing prices over a period of years in constant dollars results in curves with a characteristic shape. When plotted on log-log paper, price, typically, decreases slightly until the number of competitors increases sufficiently that capacity exceeds demand. Then price decreases more rapidly for a sufficient period of time to eliminate the weaker competitors. This is usually referred to as the shakeout. In due time, prices stabilize on a curve that decreases at a rate somewhere between the two other rates. Also, prices tend to stabilize at a level that would have existed had prices been decreased along this final curve since the first time reasonable profit margins were achieved by the first competitor to enter the field.

Exhibit 14-3, "Typical Curve of Price Versus Experience," makes this phenomenon more readily seen. The vertical axis in this figure is measured in price of the last unit sold in constant dollars. The horizontal axis is the cumulative total number of units ever sold. The first part of the curve shows the slow decrease in price while competition builds. The second part of the

EXHIBIT 14-3
TYPICAL CURVE OF PRICE VS. EXPERIENCE PLOTTED ON LOG-LOG
COORDINATES

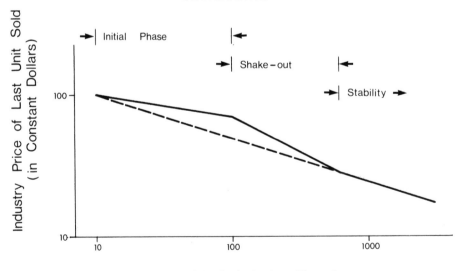

Total Accumulated Industry Experience

curve represents the shakeout. The third part of the curve shows the stable price eventually achieved.

The staff of the Boston Consulting Group hypothesized a fundamental curve underlying this observed behavior. Since price decreases in proportion to accumulated experience, then cost must also decrease in proportion to accumulated experience. If this were not so, there would come a time when the producers would have lowered their price below their cost.

Published financial reports indicate that competitors in stable industries have a profit margin characteristic of their industry. The profit margin stays the same while price decreases in constant dollars. This can only happen if costs decrease in proportion to prices. Cost decreases in proportion to the slope of the price curve when stability is achieved.

This observation results in the conclusion that total cost of a product decreases by a uniform percentage each time accumulated experience in its production is doubled. This is the same phenomenon as the Learning Curve except that it applies to all of the components of cost, not just to the repetitive tasks of individual workers. These components include administration, research and development, marketing, investment and so on. This is the fully allocated cost in constant dollars.

Exhibit 14-4 describes the Experience Curve relationship. The curve is drawn on log-log paper that results in a straight line sloping downward to the right. If the observations made by the Boston Consulting Group hold true for all cases, then this curve is of fundamental importance and has far-reaching implications. It says that, in a competitive marketplace, the cost (in constant dollars) of goods or services will decrease in proportion to the accumulated experience without limit.

EXHIBIT 14-4
THE EXPERIENCE CURVE PLOTTED ON LOG-LOG COORDINATES

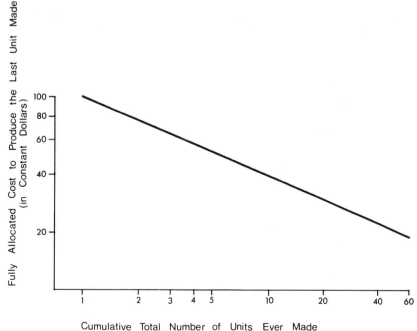

Cumulative Total Number of Units Ever Made

Knowledge of this fundamental relationship and an understanding of its basic precepts provides managers with a powerful tool for competitive strategy. Likewise, it provides investors, including managers, committing to an investment in new or existing product lines, the same strategic tool. Implications for pricing policy, changing market share, investment commitment and reaction to competitor actions become quantifiable. The results of various management decisions may be calculated and compared.

A management that does not maintain a policy of relentless cost reduction will become a weak competitor, susceptible to elimination in a competitive marketplace. Only the imposition of regulation by legislation of the state or elimination of competition by achieving a monopoly can alter this likelihood in the long run.

If prices do not decline along the characteristic curve, profit margins will increase and the entrepreneurial individuals in the population will perceive their opportunity. Being entrepreneurs, they will not sit idly observing opportunity for long. Their competition for a finite market will bring about the shakeout and, in time, the stable price decline.

YOUR BUSINESS IS ON AN EXPERIENCE CURVE

The preceding discussion would be little more than speculation were it not for the evidence supporting the observations. The Boston Consulting Group has published an impressive number of curves for a variety of industries both in the United States and Japan. *The Harvard Business Review* article by Abernathy and Wayne[6] adds an interesting curve for the Ford Motor Company's Model "T" automobile for the period from 1909 to 1923.

More recently, an article in *Business Week*[7] reports the results of a management that accepts the principle and vigorously pursues the strategy it dictates. Texas Instruments Incorporated aggressively pursues the cost reductions implied by the Experience Curve with technology, research and development expenditures, and has dramatic results. The *Business Week* writer suggests that in integrated circuits, Texas Instruments has beaten the Japanese at the low-price end of the product line and Hewlitt-Packard at the high end. Texas Instruments is the dominant competitor in integrated circuits worldwide. It is also the dominant competitor in digital watches and just about the only company still assembling watches in the United States. Texas Instruments has an inhouse video educational program called "Design to Cost." Design cost, for them, is that dictated by the Experience Curve.

Some companies sign contracts for the delivery of large quantities of their products at prices below existing costs. Obviously, they anticipate cost reduction with experience that would make these deliveries profitable when they actually occur at some future date.

The data referred to so far is for substantial products and industries over relatively long time periods. This does not imply that the principle applies only to these examples. If there is such a principle as the Experience Curve, it should apply to many other business endeavors. This appears to be true.

If you have the opportunity to tour the facilities of a growing fast food chain, you may be surprised at the number of time-saving improvements built into the newer outlets as compared to older stores. Observing the floor design and material, the legs of the furniture in old and new McDonald's restaurants will provide evidence of how the effects of the curve manifest themselves. The layout of the cup and plate storage, the bun warmers, the plastic container storage and even the cash registers dramatize time-saving and labor-saving changes that occur with experience.

The effects of the Experience Curve are clearly of fundamental importance to the owner-manager or entrepreneur.

HOW TO DESCRIBE AN EXPERIENCE CURVE

The description thus far has been general. The examples of products of Texas Instruments may seem remote from retail outlets or small manufacturers. How, you may ask, does the principle describe any particular business?

The first clue is found· in the description of what the Experience Curve says: in a *competitive* marketplace, the cost (in constant dollars) of goods or services will decrease indefinitely in proportion to accumulated experience. It is competition that brings about the cost reduction. A curve must be related to the product or service that is in the competition.

What the competitors do provides another clue. What is the collection of activity that can be identified as repetitive? Since the curve represents fully allocated cost, the collection of activities will include the entire array of functions performed by the organization in accomplishing a sale.

Still one other clue is in the reference to competitors. A curve describes the collection of activities that are common to the competitors. One competitor may have logging operations and plywood manufacturing operations while another has plywood manufacturing operations and a cabinet manufacturing plant. An Experience Curve involving these two competitors would describe only the plywood operations.

Businesses have characteristic expense profiles. The profiles are well known and usually readily available. They are typically presented in the form of an Income Statement. Sometimes they are presented in the form of a family of ratios. One source of these profiles is the *Annual Statement Studies* by Robert Morris Associates.[8] Profiles are frequently available from trade associations that gather data from their members and publish it for the industry. Reputable franchisors prepare similar information for their franchisees.

The expense patterns for competitors are similar because each of the competitors needs the same goods and services to produce their own product or service. In a competitive environment, they all seek these goods and services, including labor, in the same marketplace. Although there may be variations in some costs due to geographical location or quantity purchasing, the variations tend to be equalized by transportation costs and the mobility of the population.

A competitor with a labor cost advantage obtained by locating production facilities on the United States-Mexico border will quickly discover competitors' production facilities in a similar location. The first competitor to move to the border location may have obtained a cost advantage that changed the characteristic expense pattern of the business. But the other competitors must quickly change their profile to conform to the more advantageous profile or be threatened with price competition and loss of business.

The Experience Curve phenomenon results from observation of price changes, as competitors continually seek competitive advantage or competitive parity.

Listen to the Sales Pitch

The words that describe an Experience Curve are frequently utilized in the selling process. What does the seller say to induce the buyer to part with hard-earned cash? What words does the buyer accept as evidence for a preference of one product or service over another when satisfying a need or desire?

Individuals who specialize in selling develop a knack for recognizing the words that work. Good, better and best are words of value. A careful listener when the sale is being made will find a long list of key words being used. The key words that produce results depend upon the product or service being offered and the individual who is the potential buyer.

Imagine the conversation in the showroom of an automobile dealership where a customer is looking fondly at a Cadillac. Price is discussed very matter-of-factly. Comfort, color, style, ease of handling and the arrangement of the instrument panel consume a much greater proportion of the discussion.

Imagine this same conversation in a Volkswagen dealership. Price and fuel efficiency consume much more of the discussion while comfort and ease of handling are incidentally mentioned when pointing out the functional nature of the vehicle. Color and style may not even be considered.

Now imagine the same situation with the customer looking at a four year-old Dodge compact. Price, mechanical condition and condition of the tires, paint and upholstery will occupy most of the discussion.

Each of these consumers perceives value in the product being examined. Clearly, price is an important consumer value, but it is less important to the Cadillac customer. Other values, such as comfort, style and prestige are important consumer values to the Cadillac buyer.

This exercise may be repeated for a great variety of selling transactions. A careful listener will find that the key words make up a list of things that the consumer views as being of value. We call these key words consumer values.

Facts and Opinions

There is something else to be learned by listening in at the selling transaction. Claims are made, opinions are offered and statements are expressed with an air of authority. Evidence to support these pronouncements is seldom sought by the buyer or offered by the seller.

Hard evidence may be difficult to deliver as in the instance of a pharmaceutical product. In these cases, reference to proclamations by authority figures is used to support claims. That authority is seldom verified by the buyer. The seller's statements seem to be accepted on the basis of trust. More than that, it appears that the buyer often has already reached some preconceived opinions about the product and the seller merely reinforces those opinions.

Experienced sales people have learned that it helps to be armed with factual evidence to support their sales pitch. What a customer feels about a product, or thinks about it, however, is often more important than factual evidence.

It appears that what makes a consumer part with hard-earned cash is the consumer's perception of value. In the competitive marketplace, these perceived consumer values determine the success of one product or service over another. The words that identify an Experience Curve must then be the words that represent perceived consumer values.

KEY WORDS TO MAKE THE SALE

There are numerous key words utilized at the selling transaction. These words tend to relate to the perceived consumer values previously mentioned.

Perceived Consumer Values

The list that follows is not the complete list nor the total number of different consumer values. This list will provide a clue, however, to recognizing words that may be used to identify an Experience Curve.

Despite the Cadillac buyer's seeming lack of interest in price, a careful observer will find that even among affluent buyers there is a concern for value as measured by price. Even the very rich like to buy at a good price. This word leads the list of perceived consumer values.

Some Perceived Consumer Values		
Price	Uniqueness	Size
Financing	Prestige	Weight
Quality	Status	Color
Reliability	Education	Feel
Durability	Entertainment	Comfort
Convenience	Maintenance Service	Beauty
Efficiency	Resale Value	Safety
Longevity	Delivery Time	Economy
		Taste

Changing Times — Changing Values

There are other distinctive perceived consumer values that are related to what people find to be popular or acceptable words at any given time. During the 1950s, it seemed that all children's toys were passe unless they were educational. More recently, children's toys must be safe. Having toys safe, educational or both is commendable. The significant observation is that the importance of toys being educational was related to a time when the children of the World War II baby boom made an attractive market and a major thrust of American society was being directed at educating their parents.

Recent times may be characterized in large part by rising concern for consumers and overt action by consumer advocates. The emphasis on safety during the selling transaction is a response to people's aroused perception of its value. Clearly, a sales pitch for a product serving our children should be more effective if it includes favorable reference to safety.

Some of the key words observed at the selling transaction change with time. Educational replaced fun when referring to toys. Then, safety replaced educational. Other examples of changing perceived consumer values abound in the marketplace. For instance, automobiles with more and more powerful engines are being replaced by those with more fuel-efficient engines. Heavy autos are being replaced by lighter ones.

Other key words emerge from these observations including:

Pollution Control	Energy Saving
Cholesterol Free	Self-Cleaning
Biodegradable	Disposable
Recycled	Light
Computerized	Natural
Low Tar	Ecologically Safe
Low Fat	Insulated

This observation suggests that there is no closed list of distinctive perceived consumer values that will bring about success in the selling transaction. One must be aware of the current values in society that are important to potential customers.

HOW TO IDENTIFY YOUR EXPERIENCE CURVE

Experience curves relate cost to experience among competitors. The observation of a consistent cost decline with growth in accumulated experience results from the efforts of aggressive competitive producers to out-perform one another. When trying to identify an Experience Curve, the key words used in its description are related to competition.

If a producer has a concept for a new product or service and wants to know whether its cost will follow a new Experience Curve or be on an existing curve, the answer lies in the description of the new product or service in terms of perceived consumer values when compared to its competitors. If the producer wants to initiate a new curve, then the description of the product, service or business concept when compared to the competition must be so different that it is not like the competition.

Consider the product used by typists to correct a mistake. Not many years ago a typed mistake was erased with a hard and abrasive rubber compound. One day, Bette Claire Graham came up with the idea of painting over the error with a liquid that would be indistinguishable from the paper. At the time, one might have asked how this correction fluid compared with an eraser. Here is a product that accomplishes the same goal as its competitor, yet it doesn't erase. It is so different from its competition that it isn't like the competition. The business that evolved from this concept, Liquid Paper Corporation, is a classic example of the advantages of being the first competitor on a new Experience Curve.

The presented lists of perceived consumer values are representative. You can add to the lists from current experience. The important observation is that the list of values is open-ended. New values are added from time to time while others drop from the list or become less important.

To determine whether your product or service can be represented by a new Experience Curve or is following someone else's curve, follow these steps:

1. Describe the product or service concept in terms of perceived consumer values.

2. Compare this description to all competitive products or services.

3. Determine how different the concept is from the competition.

4. If the concept is only better than the competition, it is probably on an existing Experience Curve.

5. If the concept is so different from the competition that it isn't like the competition, then the concept represents a new curve.

Case in Point
(Client File No. 286-H)

Bob is 38 years old. He was raised on a farm and then graduated from college and started a business in his home town. His small fertilizer and farm chemicals business grew and prospered over the years. As he accumulated experience, he gradually became the dominant competitor in his geographical market. Sales were approaching $2 million annually and profits were respectable.

Upon the death of his parents, Bob inherited the sizable family farm, virtually debt free. With this valuable property as collateral, the bank made available an extensive amount of credit. Bob decided to expand. First, he formed a corporation to farm the land (after all, he could provide agricultural chemicals at an attractive price). Next, he formed a corporation to transport farm products and farm chemicals and bought several large tractor/trailer rigs. Since he couldn't keep the big trucks busy all year around, he formed yet another company that engaged in logging operations to provide them with additional hauling business.

Three years later each business except the original fertilizer and farm chemicals company had accumulated large operating losses and the bank refused to lend additional money. Bob was in danger of losing everything.

After considering the message of the experience curve, it became clear that the farming, trucking and logging companies were on someone else's experience curve. Each of these companies was competing with much larger and more experienced competitors. Bob then moved quickly to liquidate all three businesses as well as sell the farm. He was thereby able to clear up all outstanding liabilities.

Today his original agricultural chemicals business is continuing to grow profitably. Several new competitors have tried to "jump on" Bob's experience curve. They have each learned the painful lesson of trying to beat the entrenched, dominant competitor at his own game.

DUPLICATING A GOOD BUSINESS

Experience Curves may be limited by geography and market segmentation. A retail outlet typically deals only with those consumers who visit the store. A small convenience grocery store or a gasoline service station will reach a very small market segment represented by a geographical radius. The radius is determined by things like the density of the population, their affluence, their need for the products or service of the store and, most of all, by the population's access to transportation.

The effective radius of a retail outlet's market is increased by being located in a shopping mall. The number of potential consumers is increased by locating in a densely populated area. The traffic can be increased by locating on or within easy access to major transportation arteries.

Outside of the effective radius of a retail outlet, the establishment is not in competition with another store. Hence, it is commonplace to find a successful retail outlet replicated just far enough away that the radii of the stores do not overlap. Fast food restaurant chains are a prime example, but so are fabric stores, supermarkets and automobile dealerships.

Sometimes, businesses are regional in scope. Potato chips and fried chicken are flavored differently in different regions of the country. The perceived consumer values may be provincial or ethnic.

Market segmentation is another means of isolating an Experience Curve from what might otherwise appear to be an existing curve. An example may be found in axles, tires, batteries, spark plugs and fan belts for motor vehicles. None of the major automobile manufacturers is a competitor in these products (although some own the competitor as an independent subsidiary). Still another example is city buses in which General Motors Coach is the dominant competitor.

DOMINANT COMPETITORS VS. ALL THE OTHERS

There are distinct advantages to being the dominant competitor among a group of competitors whose product or service can be represented by an Experience Curve. For this discussion, we would like to refer to the dominant competitor as the "D" competitor. We would like to consider the second largest competitor as the "S" competitor and allow this competitor to represent all the rest.

Exhibit 14-5 represents an Experience Curve on which the fully allocated cost of the last unit produced (in constant dollars) is reduced 25% each time a competitor's accumulated experience doubles. This 25% reduction in cost with each doubling of experience is commonplace among aggressive competitors.

If two competitors, D and S, enter the marketplace at the same time, but D sells two units each time S sells one unit, then we can look at their relative position at some time later. Suppose

EXHIBIT 14-5
RELATIVE POSITION OF COMPETITORS, D, FOR DOMINANT, AND S, FOR
SECONDARY, ON THEIR COMMON COST CURVE

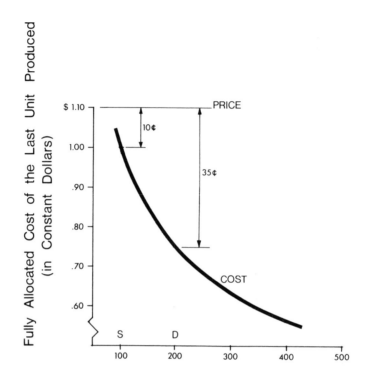

Total Units Made To Date

that when S has produced 100 units, the cost to S is one dollar per unit while they sell for $1.10 in the marketplace. S can make 10¢ per unit.

Since D sells two each time S sells one, D will have made 200 units when S has made 100 and D will be located further down the curve. In fact, D's cost will be 75¢ while the units sell for $1.10 in the marketplace. D can make 35¢ per unit sold.

This condition will continue until the S salesperson meets a customer who is dealing with the D salesperson. Imagine the conversation that ensues. At the head of the list of perceived consumer values is price. The S salesperson can offer a discount of as much as 10¢ per unit. But how will the D salesperson react to that? D's discount can be 11¢ providing D with a profit margin of 24¢. With an 11-cent discount, S will lose one cent per unit sold.

It should be clear that the dominant competitor has an advantage sufficient to control the secondary competitor. There may be enough control that D can determine whether S continues to exist.

Suppose, as another example, D enters the marketplace first and does well enough that S decides to enter the competition. Suppose further that S is a very strong and aggressive competitor who sells one unit each time D sells one unit right from day one in the markeplace (an unlikely situation). We can then look at the relative positions of S and D at some later time.

If D had sold 100 units when S entered the marketplace and S sells one unit each time D sells a unit, then when S has sold 100 units, D will have sold 200. If the cost to S after accumulating experience of 100 units is one dollar and the units sell for $1.10 in the marketplace, Exhibit 14-5 illustrates their relative positions on their Experience Curve. They are in exactly the same position as if they had started together and D outsold S in the marketplace. No matter how long they continue this nose-to-nose competition and success, D will always have lower cost than S, although the magnitude of the advantage may decrease when they have produced many hundreds of units.

HOW TO DOMINATE COMPETITION

If the Experience Curve phenomenon is valid, and there now seems little doubt that it is valid, at least as a fundamental underlying trend, then an S competitor is at a very distinct competitive disadvantage. An S competitor must gain the dominant market share and hold it for long enough to build up cumulative experience equal to the D competitor just to equalize its competitive position. Any business that has attempted to increase market share against a dominant competitor knows how difficult and expensive that task can be. Few competitors succeed in the attempt unless the D competitor allows it to happen.

The clear message of the Experience Curve is "be the dominant competitor in some market." Secondary competitors merely provide the dominant competitor with higher profit margins and elasticity in the marketplace.

If you are a secondary competitor, there are some alternative strategies including:

1. Concentrate all of your resources on a narrow segment of the market where you have the most experience.
2. Enter a market where you have the most cumulative experience.
3. Enter a market that is highly fragmented so that there is no clearly dominant competitor (such as auto repairs).
4. Sell out and do something different.

If there is one admonition resulting from this, it is to dominate some market. In a highly fragmented market, all of the competitors are bunched together on the Experience Curve and none is far enough down the curve to exercise control over price. There is at least a chance that one of them can break out of the pack and make a dash for dominance. A market that already has a dominant competitor is all but inaccessible to a secondary competitor, and then only with diminished margins and the constant threat of retaliation to attempts to increase market share. When the economy makes the market tight, the dominant competitor will retaliate just to maintain sales.

GROWTH AND THE CASH TRAP

As a business thrives and grows, its management is faced with an ever-increasing number of opportunities for new and expanded business. In addition, management is under constant pressure to grow. Growth provides advancement opportunities for capable employees and rewards for managers. Since growth consumes cash, the rewards for managers and owners are seldom in the form of spendable money. These individuals, however, may bask in the delight of owning or controlling a larger asset.

One of the most prevalent reasons for business failure results from seizing opportunities for growth. Growth consumes management time and talent as well as cash. Although the psychic rewards are great and the monetary rewards are possible, the initiation of growth cannot be taken lightly. The Experience Curve has much to say about decisions regarding growth.

The Experience Curve says, "Build on your experience." Acquiring a new business that is unrelated to your present business is starting down someone else's curve and you are clearly an S competitor. Replicating a business in an area that is geographically remote from an existing business has promise. You may be the first on a new curve in your geographic market area.

Starting a new curve by replication is only available when the market for a business is geographically limited. In the case of a retail outlet, the effective radius for the store may be small. That is one reason why franchising works so well in certain kinds of business. Replicating a computer component business that serves a national market would be creating a secondary competitor.

Technology provides a means to compete in markets not restricted geographically. The computer market is replete with examples of new products or new components entering a national market and gaining a dominant position. It is also clear that entering a geographically limited area with a product that can be marketed nationally carries the risk of another competitor's gaining regional dominance outside your limited introductory market area. Later on, it will be difficult for either competitor to enter the other's geographical area.

Marketing new products that use or build upon past experience can often overcome deficiencies in experience with the new product or service. Automobile assembly plants produce several models as different as trucks and automobiles on the same assembly line. The worker who tightens the bolts while mounting wheels on vehicles gains the same experience whether the wheel is on a compact car or a pickup truck. The same is true for the soap-making assembly line whether the bars are bath size or guest size, pink, green, blue or white, and whether the chemical composition of the soap contains sand or milk.

The Experience Curve provides another caution. It takes one good restauranteur to run one restaurant. It takes a manager to run two or more restaurants. Considerable experience as a restauranteur does not necessarily suggest experience in managing multiple restaurant facilities. The record is strewn with examples of the highly successful restaurant that went broke when it opened a second location. The same is true for dress shops, tire stores, furniture stores and so on.

DISSECTING AN EXPERIENCE CURVE

The vertical axis of the graph on which the Experience Curve is plotted is the fully allocated cost, in constant dollars, of the last unit produced. Fully allocated means the cost of everything including accounting, administration, marketing, research and development, capital investment, transportation and all of the functions of a business required to deliver the product or service to a customer.

An Experience Curve is really the total or sum of a family of curves. For simplicity, we might think of them as production, marketing, administration, distribution, service, research and development and investment. Exhibit 14-6, "Components of an Experience Curve," displays such a family of curves. The total cost of the last unit made is the sum of the costs for each component.

There are some interesting observations to be made about this family of curves. Consider the example of a new high technology electronic device developed by a small group of engineers. Initially, the engineers develop the device in their garage or basement, probably with some of the work being done at off hours in their employer's establishment. When the breadboard model proceeds to a prototype and then on to the first few production models, the engineers have little trouble finding buyers for their product. As sales grow, still without much difficulty, the engineers spend their time on the problems of production of the product in greater quantities.

EXHIBIT 14-6
COMPONENTS OF AN EXPERIENCE CURVE PLOTTED ON LOG-LOG
COORDINATES

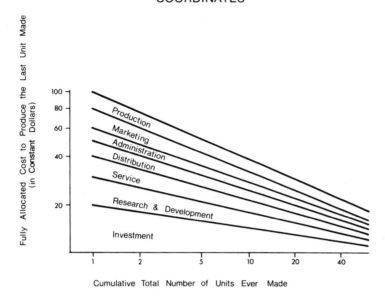

Cumulative Total Number of Units Ever Made

EXHIBIT 14-7
COMPONENTS OF AN EXPERIENCE CURVE DURING PRODUCTION
BUILD-UP PLOTTED ON LOG-LOG COORDINATES

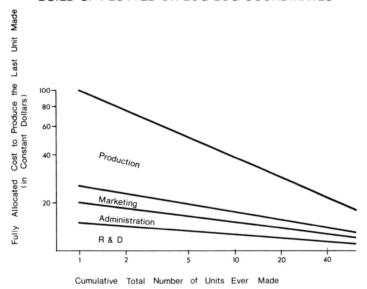

Cumulative Total Number of Units Ever Made

At this point, the Experience Curve components might look like Exhibit 14-7, "Components of Experience Curve During Production Buildup." Research and development, administration and marketing comprise small but noticeable segments, while production makes up the major portion of the segments of cost adding up to the total curve.

Once sales are well established and a major selling effort is needed to maintain sales levels and increase them, the curve and its components may look more like Exhibit 14-8,

EXHIBIT 14-8
COMPONENTS OF AN EXPERIENCE CURVE DURING MARKET
PENETRATION PLOTTED ON LOG-LOG COORDINATES

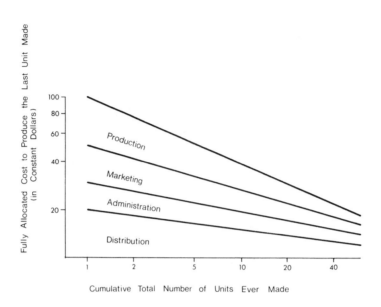

"Components of Experience Curve During Market Penetration." In this representation, production, marketing, administration and distribution become larger portions of the components adding up to the total curve. With further growth in the product, marketing, distribution, service and investment will become larger portions of the whole.

It is not unusual to find that engineers with a new high technology device do very well in the early stages of their growth, only to be replaced in the marketplace by a larger competitor when the sales reach a level that would appear interesting to a larger company. It is often said that the large competitors let the new, small business grow until it has proven that a market exists. Then the big companies step in and take the business away from the smaller competitor.

The Experience Curve suggests that this is not true although the outcome is the same. The curve suggests that the engineers have been accumulating experience in production and they may well be the D competitor in that component of the curve. However, when distribution, selling, service, administration and investment become the major components of the curve, the engineers are S competitors in these areas. Clearly, when investment begins to dominate the components of the curve, the big business has all of the advantages.

In a sense, the curve suggests if you are good at production, join with someone who is good at marketing, distribution and investment, or recognize that you are the S competitor in these areas. As these areas begin to dominate the components of the total cost, you will become the S competitor on the total curve.

A classic example is the company that decides to buy its own 18-wheel tractor-trailers to deliver its products. That is a distinctly different business and to enter it, even if only for the delivery of the company's own products, makes you an S competitor in that component of your Experience Curve. Even in the highly fragmented trucking business, the cluster of S competitors is far down the curve compared to you.

Distinctive Business Functions

The example of the business that buys its own 18-wheelers illustrates another major caution suggested by the Experience Curve. Managing a trucking business with big tractor-trailer equipment is quite different from operating a manufacturing business. Imagine the firm operated by the engineers with the new electronic device. The assembly workers are probably people with considerable finger dexterity, patience and attention to detail. Now imagine the people who load big trucks and who drive the tractor. Management must provide quite different incentives to these two groups. Facilities, labor relations, compensation and even the language of the supervisor must be different. Manufacturing and distribution are two entirely different and distinctive business functions.

The regulatory climate for these functions is so different as to require different legal specialists, audit specialists, labor relations specialists and so on. There are innumerable subtleties to these two functions that are entirely foreign to each other. Experience in managing an electronic assembly line would be almost useless in managing the distribution business with trucks.

A large company that is vertically integrated has accomplished the blending of the distinctive business functions. Typically, the integration is at the very top of the management pyramid where finance, investment and return on investment are the concerns of management. Operations are placed in the hands of subordinates who typically have the title of division president. Divisions are usually decentralized and relatively independent profit centers clustered by distinctive business functions.

The list of distinctive business functions includes:

1. Raw Materials—mining, drilling, logging, farming and ranching.
2. Manufacturing—refining, smelting, machining, assembly and packaging.
3. Distribution—physical distribution, picking things up at one place and delivering them to another place.
4. Sales and Service—the whole range of activities from conception of promotional material to closing the sale. Service may be a separate function in some businesses, although as a business grows it usually supports its sales effort with a repair service.
5. Research and Development—technical people, well educated, producing a single prototype product or experimental evidence of the possiblity of producing a prototype.
6. Administration—paper work people, recordkeepers, data collectors, personnel care and encouragement, training and the myriad of things associated with information systems.
7. Finance—bringing together conceptual contractual arrangements, people with money to invest and people in need of invested money.

These distinctive business functions require considerable experience that is seldom transferable from one function to another. The curve suggests that it may be better to buy the service in a distinctive function other than your own. Otherwise, recognize that you are likely the S competitor on someone else's home ground.

Pitfalls of Economies of Scale

Economies of scale are achieved when, as a result of larger production quantities, you can buy materials in large quantities at a discount, you can justify a machine to replace people or you can construct an assembly plant dedicated to producing a single product. Economies of scale result from jigs, fixtures, specialized tools and machinery, dedicated facilities and a large product or service base over which to spread the cost of these.

Many times managers mistakenly assume that economies of scale result from just being bigger, that is, having larger annual sales. It is not uncommon to find managers taking advantage of opportunities to acquire businesses unrelated to their own assuming that being larger will reduce costs.

The Experience Curve points out that economies of scale are related to producing things in which you already have considerable experience. Doubling sales by jumping into a business in which you have no experience contributes nothing to progress down your existing curve. Furthermore, it makes you an S competitor on the newly acquired curve.

EXPANSION STRATEGY

The Experience Curve has much to say about expanding an existing business. As suggested by Exhibit 14-5, market share may be more important than present profit. Certainly,

EXHIBIT 14-9
D HOLDING TWICE THE MARKET SHARE OF S

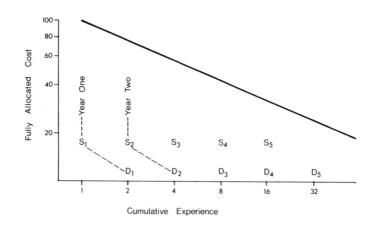

the D competitor is more secure and in the long run establishes the price and the margin to be achieved by the product or service. To do this, however, the dominant competitor must be clearly dominant. Suppose that D needs twice the cumulative experience of S to stabilize price and margin while maintaining the clout to defend against attempts to increase market share by S.

To achieve and maintain twice the cumulative experience, D needs twice the market share of S, the next largest competitor. D must sell two each time S sells one. Exhibit 14-9 shows D holding twice the market share of S.

Achieving greater market share probably requires decreasing price in proportion to cost during the entire history of the competition. This may reduce the immediate profit on sales. On the other hand, it becomes more difficult for secondary competitors to enter the field, never mind increase their market share.

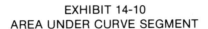

EXHIBIT 14-10
AREA UNDER CURVE SEGMENT

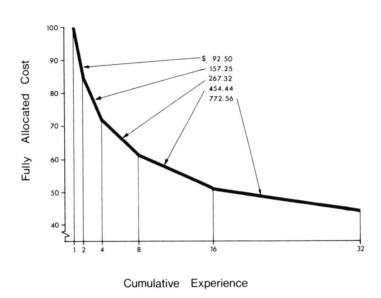

Cumulative Experience

The total sales available from a product or service is proportional to the area under the Experience Curve and the profit available is a reasonable markup on this total cost. In a growing market, the advantage is with the company having a dominant market share. When the market ceases to grow, the advantage is even more likely to go with the dominant market share.

Exhibit 14-10, "Area under Curve Segments," may be helpful in substantiating these observations.

The curve in Exhibit 14-10 shows costs decreasing by 15% with each doubling of experience. The choice of 15% was arbitrary. Decreases of 20-30% are commonplace. If D has twice the market share of S, then when S has sold one, D will have sold two. If they now double their experience, S will make one at a cost of $92.50 and D will make two at a cost of $157.25, or $78.63 each.

Now if S can sell its one at a 10% markup, its price will be $92.50 plus $9.25 or $101.75. Presumably, D can get the same price for its two units. Then S will make a profit of $9.25 per unit and D will make $23.12.

If D decides to ignore S and sell its two units at a 10% markup, its price will be $78.63 plus $7.86 or $86.49. Presumably, S will have to meet that price in order to make a sale. Then D will make a profit of $7.86 while S will lose $6.01 per unit.

We can repeat this exercise for the other end of the curve. When S has sold eight, D has sold 16. If they now double their experience, S will make eight at a cost of $454.44, or $56.81 each, and D will make 16 at a cost of $772.56, or $48.29 each.

If S can sell its eight units at a 10% markup, its price will be $56.81 plus $5.68 or $62.49. If D can sell its 16 units for the same price, then S will make a profit of $5.68 per unit and D will make $14.20 per unit.

If D decides to ignore S and sell its 16 units at a 10% markup, its price will be $48.29 plus $4.83 or $53.12. Presumably, S will have to meet that price in order to make a sale. Then D will make a profit of $4.83 while S will lose $3.69 per unit.

If the previous examples were worked out for a 25% curve, the S competitor would have been wiped out sooner and more soundly. As an alternative, the D competitor could be investing heavily in the next product line out of current profits.

In practice, D usually does not choose to eliminate S. That action risks the wrath of regulatory authorities who do not comprehend the potential opportunities available from a completely free and competitive marketplace. Rather, D will meet the best price S can get and use the difference in profit margins to strengthen its position in the marketplace, provide its employees with better training and greater fringe benefits and mount a strong research and development effort to provide future products and services in which it can be the D competitor.

The conclusion to be drawn from this discussion is that gaining market share is worth more than immediate high profit margins. Margins should be large enough to support the financing of the increase in market share and the related expense of increasing capacity to satisfy the demand. Any margin greater than that threatens larger future gains in profit, the ability to compete and the stability of the business.

PRICING POLICY

The original observations leading to the discovery of the Experience Curve were of product price histories. Exhibit 14-3 shows the usual trend of these observations. Price decreased with experience until a sufficient number of competitors entered the marketplace and caused capacity to exceed demand. Then the rate of price decrease was more rapid until the shakeout was completed. In time, the price stabilized at a decreasing rate somewhere between these two.

When competing with a product that can command a substantial margin, the producers are tempted to maintain the highest margin possible. This pricing strategy has inevitable results as shown by Exhibit 14-3. Producers who understand the Experience Curve accept its validity and adopt a pricing strategy based on the curve. They reduce their price in proportion to their cost from the day they first achieve a reasonable profit margin. This typically accomplishes two results: Rapid market penetration leading to dominant market share and elimination of potential secondary competitors before they enter the marketplace.

The message of the Experience Curve with respect to pricing is to price for profit margin as a reasonable percent of sales, pursue an aggressive cost reduction strategy and maintain constant profit margins. The results in the marketplace are rewarding.

INVESTMENT COMMITMENT

If the message of the Experience Curve is dominate your market and be the competitor with the largest market share, it is crucial for managers to recognize what this implies about investment. Market penetration means greater sales. Maintaining market share in a growing market means producing greater quantities at lower cost. The profit potential is over the life of the product. The investment needed to achieve that potential is immediate and continuing until the growth of the market ceases. Growth consumes cash.

The Experience Curve phenomenon results from learning, specialization, scale and investment. Specialization is achieved when larger quantity production permits breaking work tasks into smaller increments, such as the individual worker tasks on an assembly line. Scale is achieved when larger production quantities can support specialized machinery and equipment. Investment is needed for machinery, equipment, production lines, specialized facilities and to support greater inventories and greater accounts receivable. Pursuing the strategy dictated by the Experience Curve demands a commitment to investment.

Growth in sales and growth in profits seldom provide owners and managers with the cash to satisfy their needs. The business will consume more than it can produce until a dominant market share has been achieved and held for long enough to allow the growth in the market for that product to slow down and stabilize. Only then will the business become a source of cash.

Owners must realize that what they are building is a valuable asset, not a bank balance. If they wish to enjoy the monetary rewards of their deeds, they must sell the asset. With patience, however, and a conservative lifestyle, in time the market growth will slow, the demands for cash by the business will decrease and the owners can then reap the rewards of a growing bank balance and a valuable asset.

NOTES FOR CHAPTER 14

[1]Miguel A. Reguero, *An Economic Study of the Military Airframe Industry*, Wright-Patterson Air Force Base, Ohio, Department of the Air Force, October, 1957, p.213.

[2]T.P. Wright, "Factors Affecting the Cost of Airplanes," *Journal of Aeronautical Science*, February, 1936, pp. 122-128.

[3]Frank J. Andress, "The Learning Curve as a Production Tool," *HBR*, January-February, 1954, pp. 87-97.

[4]Winifred B. Hirschmann, "Profit from the Learning Curve," *HBR*, January-February, 1964, pp. 125-139.

[5]The Boston Consulting Group, Inc., *Perspectives on Experience*, 1968.

[6]William J. Abernathy and Kenneth Wayne, "Limits of the Learning Curve," *HBR*, September-October, 1974, pp. 109-119.

[7]"Texas Instruments Shows U.S. Business How to Survive in the 1980's," *Business Week*, September, 1978, pp. 66-92.

[8]Robert Morris Associates, The National Association of Bank Loan and Credit Officers (sic.), *Annual Statement Studies*. Philadelphia, Pennsylvania: Philadelphia National Bank Building, 19107.

15

Improving Productivity
in Your Closely Held Organization

Price declines in a persistent and consistent pattern with accumulated experience when measured in constant (inflation free) dollars. (See Experience Curve, Chapter 14.) Also, profit margins tend to remain constant in stable industries. For these two observations to be true, it follows that cost must decline with accumulated experience in a persistent and consistent pattern. Stated differently, the quantity of what is produced for sale increases with no increase in the total cost to produce it or, the cost to produce the same quantity decreases. In other words, the ratio of the units of output available for sale divided by the value of the input, or cost, increases in proportion to accumulated experience.

This ratio of output units divided by input value is a measure of Productivity. Since the Learning Curve shown in Exhibit 14-2 and the Experience Curve shown in Exhibit 14-4 are straight lines (on log-log coordinates) that continue for as long as experience is being accumulated, Productivity is capable of increasing in a persistent and consistent pattern as long as experience is being accumulated.

It is not unusual to find that the Experience Curve for an industry shows costs declining 25%, in constant dollars, with each doubling of accumulated experience. This implies a Productivity increase of 33% with each doubling of experience. If a unit cost one dollar at some point in time, it should cost 75¢ when accumulated experience has doubled. The number of units produced for sale per dollar of cost, in constant dollars, is one unit at the beginning of the period considered and 1.33 units per dollar when the experience has doubled (one dollar divided by 75¢).

This Experience Curve is shown in Exhibit 15-1, "An Experience Curve with 25% Cost Reduction per Doubling of Experience on Log-Log Coordinates." Its counterpart Productivity Curve is shown in Exhibit 15-2, "A Productivity Curve Reflecting 25% Cost Reduction per Doubling of Experience on Log-Log Coordinates."

The Learning Curve, as discussed in Chapter 14, describes the increase in efficiency of individual workers performing repetitive tasks. Curves similar to those in Exhibit 15-1 and 15-2 could be drawn for the Productivity of the worker. They would be similar and have the same characteristics. A worker whose Learning Curve shows 15% less time consumed to produce a unit with each doubling of accumulated experience would have a Productivity Curve increasing by nearly 18% with each doubling of experience (one hour divided by .85 hours).

EXHIBIT 15-1
AN EXPERIENCE CURVE WITH 25% COST REDUCTION PER DOUBLING
OF EXPERIENCE ON LOG-LOG COORDINATES

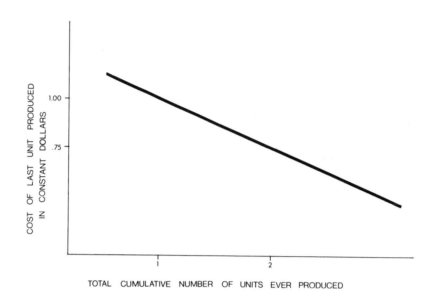

EXHIBIT 15-2
A PRODUCTIVITY CURVE REFLECTING 25% COST REDUCTION PER
DOUBLING OF EXPERIENCE ON LOG-LOG COORDINATES

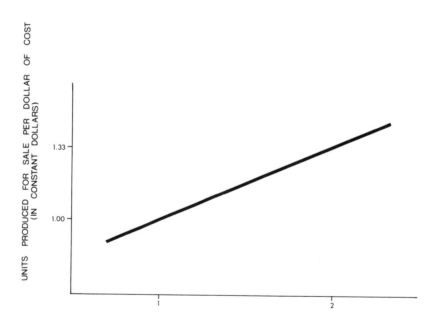

The Learning Curve data and the Experience Curve data available in published studies indicate that this phenomenon is at work at all times as long as there is competition. Not only are these Productivity gains possible, but, they are necessary if one is to avoid becoming the weak competitor who is driven from the marketplace.

ORGANIZATIONAL STRUCTURE AND PRODUCTIVITY

One of the most exciting and satisfying work environments is that of the start-up business that is succeeding and growing rapidly. Productivity is typically high in these fast growth start-ups. A major reason for high productivity is that the entrepreneurs, or the owner-managers, work long, hard hours to make the business succeed. But, the high productivity continues even after the business has had to bring in employees on whom the entrepreneur is dependent for production. There comes a time, however, when the number of employees has increased enough that some organizational structure is necessary. Communication and supervision procedures begin to constrain the activities of the business and a pyramidal management relationship develops.

It is not unusual for a craftsman entrepreneur who produces 100 units per hour on a certain machine to find that three machines with three operators and a foreman produce only 200 units per hour. It frequently appears as though the organizational structure itself consumes time and energy for its sustenance.

In a small organization, everyone can see and talk with everyone else. Activities that require coordination are sensed by the individuals without verbal or written communication. Appreciation for support and assistance are communicated openly both verbally and non-verbally. The people in the group feel participation and recognition.

As the organizational structure grows, the individuals become more and more dependent on written communication and upon communication through other people. The original variety of non-verbal communication diminishes. Further growth increases the number of links in the chains of dependence and communication.

Written communication is amazingly imprecise. What is perfectly clear to the writer often seems like unintelligible hieroglyphics to the reader. Worse, there are no lips, no eyes, no hands, no furrowed brows on the printed page. In addition, the page will not respond to questions.

Communication through other people is equally imprecise. What the listener hears is never exactly what the speaker says. This phenomenon provides the basis for an old parlor game in which someone whispers a short story to the person next to them. The story is then passed from person to person in a whisper. Having passed through four to six participants, the last person hearing the story retells it aloud to the group. Then the first person who whispered the story retells it aloud. The fun in the game is in that the two stories told aloud are so different.

Structure frequently creates a barrier to productivity. In the small organization, everyone knows what is going on. They see the beginning and the end of the process and their position in it. As structure builds, what individuals see is the other individuals physically near them, unrelated to an overall process. Inability to complete a task because of shortage in a needed supply causes frustration. Observing a clutter of finished work not being utilized suggests that it was not needed. Both imply that haste is unnecessary and unappreciated.

SHORT-INTERVAL SCHEDULING

Wasted time comes in little pieces. Short-interval scheduling is a work measurement concept that observes, reports and controls production in short-time intervals. If 25 units are produced from 8 to 9 a.m., 20 from 9 to 10 a.m., 85 from 10 to 11 a.m. and 50 from 11 to 12 noon, the variance warrants an explanation from the supervisor.

A supervisor's job is to provide the workers with a supply of work to be done, guidance and training in how to accomplish it, coordination between this group of workers and the other elements of the business, materials, tools and supplies necessary to do the job. An environment and atmosphere conducive to getting the job done is also required. Observing and recording the output of a group of workers and trying to explain variances focuses the supervisor's attention on that job and provides a visible picture of how things are going. With such a picture in hand, the desire to improve performance is unavoidable.

For the owner-manager, initiating a Short-Interval Scheduling program begins with a picture of the overall production process. It might be described by the three steps:

1. Prepare a floor plan showing the sequence of operations in detail.

2. Write a description of the duties and responsibilities for each section and for key personnel; describe how each operates and name their problems.

3. Decide upon and list all activities for which standards of performance should be established, the time required for such activities and the frequency of measurements to check performance against standards.

A period of time will be consumed by section heads selecting and refining the units to be measured, the frequency of the measurements and the forms on which data are to be recorded. Their interaction with the rest of the management team will refine the information listed above for the owner-manager.

Once management begins to see what production levels are being achieved, these can be put in graphical form for each section and for the whole organization. Reasonable goals for improvement can be determined and shown on the graphs. A sensible presentation of goals may be derived from Learning Curve and Experience Curve knowledge. It is reasonable to expect cost, in constant dollars, to decrease by 20-30% with each doubling of total accumulated experience. This can be shown as a band on a graph. Performance should remain within that band if properly managed.

FINANCIAL IMPACT OF PRODUCTIVITY

Expense ratios, expenses expressed as a percent of sales, are related to revenue. They provide information about whether revenues are sufficient to offset business expenses and provide some return to the investors. Productivity is a ratio that measures efficiency. The efficiency of one competitor compared to another may be concealed while expense ratios for a particular period appear to be satisfactory. In the long run, however, efficiency determines strength and weakness in the marketplace. Improving efficiency builds competitive strength.

Among any group of producers who compete with each other, the most efficient will have the least expense to produce a dollar of sales. The less efficient producers usually establish the price in the marketplace as long as the market is growing and can absorb what is offered for sale by the group. The less efficient producers can only lower price enough to appear competitive, but not so low as to operate at a loss. These producers provide an umbrella over prices of the most efficient producer.

When the group of competitors finds that their goods or services are not being absorbed in the marketplace, the most efficient producer can lower price enough to take part of the market away from the rest of the group. Expense ratios, like Cost of Goods Sold divided by Sales, will then grow for the less efficient producers because revenue, the denominator in the ratio, will decrease while expense, the numerator, remains the same. The producer who increases efficiency in proportion to price decreases, however, can maintain the expense ratios while price declines. If efficiency increases faster than price declines, the efficient producer can have increasing margins, that is, decreasing expense ratios, while price declines.

Productivity and Profit

Productivity of workers may be increased by two factors: (1) the diligence of the workers and (2) the tools provided to assist them in their work. Diligence may imply many things, but certainly attitude and morale. If the workers enjoy what they are doing, they may produce more per hour. If they are unhappy, frustrated or uncomfortable, they may produce less per hour. This can occur with no change in hourly wages paid.

If the Productivity being measured is that of the workers, the ratio may be written with the sales value of what is produced in the numerator and the payroll expense of the workers in the denominator. If sales are defined as R, for revenue, and the workers payroll is defined as L, for labor, then one measure of the Productivity of the workers may be defined as:

$$\text{Productivity} = \frac{R}{L}$$

Improving diligence can increase R with no change in L and result in greater Productivity. Since it is possible for revenue to increase with no change in payroll, profit and profit margins can increase provided all other expenses remain the same. This is easier to understand if the denominator of the ratio is chosen to be labor, L, plus All Other Expense, AOE. Productivity of the business may then be defined by:

$$\text{Productivity} = \frac{R}{L + AOE}$$

If L decreases while R and AOE remain the same, this Productivity will increase. Since profit is the difference between the numerator and the denominator, profit will also increase

$$\text{Profit} = R - (L + AOE)$$

The tools provided to workers to assist them in their work may be viewed as of two kinds. One is represented by jigs, fixtures and machinery. The other is management coordination of the flow of work and the materials needed to accomplish it. Each has its own effect on expense.

If we look at increasing the workers' productivity by providing them with machinery, the expense of the machinery must be considered. Buying jigs, fixtures and machinery requires some investment. The form of this expense and its size depends upon many things. Purchased equipment may be depreciated by several methods. Whichever method is chosen, there will be a depreciation expense. Borrowing the money to buy the equipment will result in an interest expense.

The recurring expenses related to the investment needed to improve worker productivity may be incorporated into the preceding formulas. If the *expense* associated with the investment (not the investment itself) is defined as X, then:

$$\text{Productivity} = \frac{R}{X + L + AOE}$$

It should be clear that to improve productivity by providing equipment, it is necessary that the sum of X plus L must decrease (assuming AOE remains constant). Similarly, profit will increase only if the sum, X plus L, is decreased. It is possible to improve the productivity of the workers tremendously by buying expensive equipment, but if the expense of carrying the investment in the equipment is very high, this can decrease the productivity and profit of the business.

If we look at increasing the workers' productivity by hiring additional personnel to expedite, plan, coordinate and manage the flow of work and the materials needed to accomplish it, the additional expense must be considered. If this additional expense is defined as Y, then:

$$\text{Productivity} = \frac{R}{Y + L + AOE}$$

Once again, the ratio will not improve unless the sum of Y plus L decreases. Also, profit will increase only if the sum, Y + L, is decreased. It is possible to improve the productivity of the workers while decreasing the productivity of the business and its profits.

Productivity and Return on Investment

Improving worker diligence may or may not require investment. Often, the attitude and behavior of supervisors and managers can improve diligence without additional cost to the company. On the other hand, worker frustration, discontent and discomfort may be the result of the work environment. For instance, if the heating or lighting are inadequate, an investment may be necessary to improve the situation.

When providing equipment to help the workers improve their efficiency, there is certainly going to be some investment in machinery and its installation. Likewise, when providing additional personnel to coordinate and manage the flow of work, there will be some investment in the form of additional furniture, phones, services, etc.

The manner in which these investments affect ROI is not easy to see. First, it is necessary to decide what denominator and what numerator are going to be chosen for the ROI measure. Suppose that whatever denominator is selected we define it as INV, and suppose that profit is selected as the numerator. Now assume that the additional investment needed to achieve the increase in the workers' productivity is defined as Z. This is the total investment, not the carrying expense of the investment. Then:

$$\text{ROI} = \frac{R - (X + Y + L + AOE)}{INV + Z}$$

This somewhat imposing formula includes both X, the expense related to investment, and Y, the expense of additional support personnel, to provide an overall picture. There may be increases in Z, actual additional investment, associated with X, with Y or with some combination of X and Y.

Perhaps you can already see why it may not be easy to see how these investments in productivity affect ROI. Presumably, the investment does increase productivity so that the numerator, profit, increases. A small improvement in the sum, X + Y + L, may produce a small or a large improvement in profit depending upon how large L is compared to AOE. If all other expense is large compared to labor payroll, the effect may be small. If AOE is small compared to L, the effect may be large.

In the denominator, the size of Z, the additional investment made to improve productivity, by itself may not be important. Its size compared to INV, the existing investment before making the investment in productivity improvement, is what affects ROI. If Z is small compared to INV, then a small improvement in profits may appear to be a large improvement in ROI. On the other hand, if Z is large compared to INV, it will take a big improvement in productivity and profit to make a small improvement in ROI.

Productivity and Cash Flow

All of the relationships so far, Productivity, Profit and Return on Investment contain terms describing Revenue, Expense and Investment. As we have shown in the early chapters of this book, profit is not cash flow and profit is not cash. Profit is revenue minus expense, either of which may or may not impact a cash flow directly.

In many respects, investment is similar to profit. Investment (depending on the definition utilized) can be made with cash or credit. Cash can be obtained by selling a portion of the company or by borrowing. Credit may be used to lease equipment. Credit may also be used in the form of dragging out payments to suppliers; in effect, borrowing from creditors. Cash may be obtained by decreasing the average level of the accounts receivable. Prior chapters have shown other ways to obtain cash and credit.

It was not easy to see the effect of Productivity on ROI. It is even more difficult to see the effect of Productivity on Cash Flow. It cannot be gleaned from the preceding formulas. The methods of paying for X, Y and Z and the method of obtaining Z must be portrayed in a forecast of profit and cash flow as demonstrated in Chapter 1. Comparing the cash balances resulting from the "before" and "after" X, Y and Z forecasts will demonstrate the effects of Productivity on Cash Flow.

THE SCANLON PLAN: HOW IT WORKS

Ever since Joseph Scanlon made his first contributions toward improving union-management relations, many variations of the unprecedented Scanlon Plan have evolved. The most appropriate application to owner-managed businesses, however, is in the Scanlon Plan as a philosophy of management rather than as a plan.[1] Emerging as a means of surviving the depression of the 1930s, this philosophy strongly emphasized the importance of each employee's function within the organization and the significance of each employee's contribution to the overall success of the company. Joseph Scanlon understood the basic need for work incentives and incorporated a reward system for management and all employees into his concept. Bonuses were determined and distributed according to what degree the company as a whole and the employees as individuals had succeeded in achieving a more efficient level of production.

Among the most valuable aspects of the Scanlon Plan are joint participation and shared remuneration. Joseph Scanlon realized the difficulties associated with stimulating employee interest and participation and, therefore, instituted production committees for all departments. These production committees were composed of both management and union representatives who were elected by the employees of their respective departments. Meeting at least once a month, they studied department schedules, ways of improving production, methods for reducing waste and suggestions submitted by union, employee or management members of the committee. Acceptance or rejection of these suggestions was ultimately the responsibility of management.

Minutes of the production committee's meeting were then distributed to a screening committee that was also comprised of management and union representatives. Three important responsibilities were assigned to this committee:

1. To explore all suggestions submitted by the production committees and to present recommendations to management for final decisions;

2. To study the current market status of the company's product(s) and to discuss any problems associated with the production of the product(s);

3. To review all financial statements for the previous month and to determine the bonus or deficit incurred.

This last function was by far the most important. To determine the bonus or deficit, the Scanlon Plan utilized a formula based upon Productivity. To illustrate, consider the following example.[2]

Choose a base period to serve as a standard. Assume that in the 12 months preceding the determination of the standard, the payroll cost of making each dollar of sales was 40¢. This, then, is a Productivity Norm or a ratio of 40% against which to measure performance in the coming months.

Now suppose sales this month are $100,000. Using the Productivity Norm, the payroll cost should be $40,000. Suppose the actual payroll cost turns out to be $32,000. Then, there has been an $8,000 improvement over the norm.

The company and the employees share this $8,000 according to some previously agreed-upon basis. Suppose, for example, the basis is 50-50. The company would set aside half of the improvement, $4,000, for the employee incentive bonus distribution.

Since, in some months, the difference from the norm may be positive and in other months it may be negative, the company must set up a reserve from this $4,000. Perhaps 20% would seem reasonable for the reserve. Then $800 would be put in the bank and the remaining $3,200 would be distributed to the employees.

The easiest way to distribute this bonus is in proportion to the worker's present salary or wages. If the bonus is $3,200 and the payroll for the month is $32,000, then the bonus is 10% of the employee's normal pay for the month. An employee who would normally receive $800 gross pay for the month would receive $880 gross pay.

Occasionally, some adversity may arise that results in the group not meeting the norm. Suppose that in some month the sales are $100,000 and the actual payroll cost is $44,000. This is $4,000 more than the norm. For this month, there would be no bonus distribution and the company would withdraw $4,000 from the reserve account to cover the cost of payroll in excess of the norm.

If, after a period of time, the reserve account appears to be more than is reasonable, an additional bonus distribution can be made from the reserve account. It would be appropriate for this to occur annually, probably just before Christmas.

A reward system like this provides management with a visible and participative means for stimulating and maintaining employee motivation. In return, the employees benefit from an understanding of how their individual contributions to productivity are reflected in the financial success of their company.

Donnelly Mirrors, Inc.: An Example

Donnelly Mirrors, Inc. is a successful business. Since 1952, the employees, numbering close to 500, have almost doubled the company's productivity rate in the manufacturing of rear-view mirrors for automobiles. Working out of four plants in Holland, Michigan, and another one located near Dublin, Ireland, Donnelly Mirrors, Inc. proudly reported a sales volume of almost $20 million for the year 1976. This non-union company had adopted the Scanlon Plan more than 20 years earlier.

"Concern for people, coupled with managerial expertise, is clearly the most effective means of achieving corporate goals."[3] This statement was the basis on which Donnelly's top-level management worked to establish group incentive. Employees were treated with respect and were urged to contribute any ideas or suggestions essential to upgrading the company. Employee integrity was highly valued by management. Company time clocks were removed, employee time cards were disposed of, and salaries as opposed to hourly rates were introduced. Results were immediate: Absenteeism dropped from 5% to less than 1.5%, tardiness dropped from 6% to below 1% and employee turnover averaged about .5% monthly. The end result was participative management.[4]

As of 1974, Donnelly Mirrors, Inc. had lowered the cost of their product substantially, but had simultaneously increased their profits. Wages had increased by close to one million dollars while costs had been reduced by approximately 1.5 million. The significance of this latter statistic is that 40% of all net cost reductions were transferred to the bonus pool.[5]

The idea of the bonus pool was the most important factor in Donnelly's successful adoption of the Scanlon Plan. From the very beginning, management held the opinion that employees would benefit from the financial rewards resulting from cost savings. Therefore, a method was formulated and implemented that reflected the basic hypothesis that the more a bonus plan absorbed expenses, the greater the savings capability for the future. Their formula was as follows:

> Actual expenses are deducted from gross sales. From 50% of the balance, a portion is set aside as deficit reserve. The remainder becomes the monthly bonus, divided among employees as a bonus percentage on earnings.[6]

In 1970, the employees collectively agreed on a 10% base-salary increase. This meant that the employees had to minimize costs by some $610,000. The outcome was a reduction in costs by $643,000. In 1971, the projected goal was $453,000, but this mark was overshot by $58,000 for a total reduction of $511,000. Subsequently, between the years 1972 and 1974, Donnelly Mirrors, Inc. achieved an overall cost reduction of 24% on its production of rear-view mirrors.[7]

Obviously, such results required extraordinary teamwork and commitment on the part of everyone in the organization. This bonus pool plan was actually one of shared productivity rather than one of shared profits. The distinction is important. All employees were members of departmental work teams whose primary purpose was improving the quality of the product and the rate of productivity only as it related to their particular function. Furthermore, they operated on the premises that when a problem was detected, it must be corrected immediately. If a problem arose that involved another team as well, then both work teams devoted their energies to solving the problem at hand.

Moreover, each team had a "link pin." The "link pin" was the managerial person on the departmental work team who was also a member of the next highest group.[8] It was because of this membership that the original work team felt and actually *was* a part of the whole organization. Such vertical overlapping created an open and responsive communication system while protecting employees against those individuals attempting to control the direction of the company.

Donnelly's teamwork strategy assumed a horizontal dimension, too, that was complementary to the vertical one. This was achieved through the establishment of Employees' Committees that were composed of representatives from four work levels.[9] For example, supervisors had work teams of their own, but each supervisor belonged to an Employee Committee made up of members from other work teams throughout the company. With four hierarchal levels represented, total integration of efforts and ideas was attained and maintained on a company-wide basis. Company strategy was better understood and, therefore, more effective. Company strategy became the dominating factor in the productivity process.

NOTES FOR CHAPTER 15

[1]Douglas McGregor, *The Human Side of Enterprise* (New York: McGraw-Hill Book Company, Inc., 1960), p. 110.

[2]Frederick G. Lesieur, Ed., *The Scanlon Plan, A Frontier in Labor-Management Cooperation* (Boston: The Technology Press of Massachusetts Institute of Technology; New York: John Wiley and Sons, Inc., 1959), p. 131.

[3]Edward M. Glaser, *Productivity Gains Through Work-Life Improvements* (New York: Harcourt, Brace Jovanovich, 1976), p. 48.

[4]Betty Shelton, "Participative Management Bonuses Boost Productivity for Michigan Firm," *Commerce Today*, November 11, 1974, p. 12.

[5]Ibid., p. 12.

[6]Ibid., p. 12.

[7]Glaser, p. 51.

[8]Ibid., p. 49.

[9]Ibid., p. 49.

16

Cashing in the Chips:
Getting Your Hands
on the Net Worth You've Created

Our heritage is the opportunity to fulfill the American dream, to be your own master, to create your own little empire, to own your own home, farm, ranch or its equivalent in the world of commerce. The story is told and retold in various versions of the lives of Horatio Alger, Henry Ford and Andrew Carnegie. Invariably the stories end, like the fairly tales of our early childhood, with the words, "And they lived happily ever after." Owning your own business enterprise is often viewed as the final words in the retelling of the American dream.

Those who have spent careers building their own business know there is more to the story. There comes a time, sooner or later, when the owner-manager is faced with the question of what to do with the business that took so long to build and that contains so much of the owner's soul. If the question is pursued to the point of considering what you can get for the business, and from whom you can get it, the owner-manager is faced with the stark reality that cashing in the chips may be as difficult as creating them.

Few owners seem to fully grasp the fact that profit is not cash. What most of them build is an asset, not a bank account. The asset, however, is like your home. The market changes, the equipment wears out, the neighborhood deteriorates. The asset needs continual renewing. There is no end point where the mortgage is finally paid off and the owner can go fishing.

As the years go by, the owner changes. No matter how young you feel or how well you have preserved your health, middle age is frequently a transition period leading to a more relaxed way of life and a greater desire to satisfy affiliation needs. Spending time on affiliation with family, friends, business associates and social circles requires giving up time at the shop. The question quite naturally arises, "How do I cash in some of these chips?"

A few owner-managers are sufficiently lucky, or perhaps clever, to build the business large enough to be able to afford both owners and professional managers. Most small businesses can support only one or the other. As long as the business can support only one, the owner is the owner-manager.

To the owner-manager, the business is like his own flesh and blood, his child, carefully nurtured, loved, trained, worried over in sickness and in health, forever his no matter what. Some owners find it impossible to turn their business over to someone else even after they have begun drawing their social security checks.

317

At some time before or during middle age, it is wise for the owner-manager to seriously consider some long-range questions about life:

What do I want out of life?

What would I like to be doing five years from now? Ten years from now? Twenty years from now?

What will I do if my children don't want to run the business?

What, besides what I am doing now, would I enjoy doing?

What would I do if for reasons entirely beyond my control I lost the business?

PROS AND CONS OF KEEPING, SELLING, MERGING

As with any suggestion concerning a decision for other people, there is no right or wrong that is suitable for everyone. What an owner-manager should do is be aware of as many options as there is time to learn about. While building and running the business, there isn't much time to consider the various possibilities. Each day is consumed with that day's peculiar brush fires. On the other hand, the sands of time are running. Our own mortality has been demonstrated by the loss of friends, relatives and business associates. A brief look at the options may not be too different from dealing with those brush fires.

Keeping the Business

If your business is doing well, you have a good job and a reasonable salary. More importantly, you have freedom. One of the principal characteristics of individuals who succeed as entrepreneurs and owner-managers is an innate need to control and direct. What this describes is the characteristic of being blessed with, or cursed with, such a strong need to be your own boss that you can't function well in large, structured organizations. It is not a need for power or money; it is purely and simply a *need* for freedom to run your own life.

Most owner-managers work long hours, carry a heavy emotional burden and receive comparatively small current income for their effort. On the other hand, they like it. As long as they are the one deciding to work 16-hour days and six-day weeks, everything is all right. If anyone else told them to work such hours, they would thoroughly enjoy saying no in very colorful language.

The foremost pro for keeping the business is the freedom it provides. Along with that goes salary, prestige and the perquisites of the position. "Perqs" are usually thought of as the car, the dinners, the travel, the club and little favors bestowed by grateful employees. There is another "perq," however, that will be sorely missed when it is gone. We think of it as access to G & A (i.e., accesses to those services and expenditures normally classified in the General & Administrative category of a business' income statement).

Included in the general and administrative expenses of your business is a myriad of little things like the copy machine, postage, typing, an office and a phone. This group of things sometimes includes such things as having someone else pick up the kids at school on a stormy day, find a special gift, conduct a library search and prepare your tax return.

A major concern is the problem of keeping the ship afloat. Unless the business grows to the size where it can afford to hire professional management, the owner-manager is the captain as well as the first, second and third mates. Keeping the ship off the shoals requires someone on the bridge at all time. As the years go by, the skipper grows tired.

Part of the fun, the thrill and the excitement of guiding the business is in that the shoals keep moving. In the words of W.W. Caruth, Jr., "A business is always sailing in uncharted seas." No matter what it was like yesterday, it will be different tomorrow.

To your dismay, you sometimes come awfully close to the shoals. Although it is hard to admit, one day you realize that it is possible to be wrong. Even you might run the ship ashore. When that day arrives, it might be wise to consider staying in the marina and to settle for telling the sailors how to find a fair wind.

Selling the Business

The value of a business is a function of both tangible and intangible assets. It is difficult to make those assets provide cash just to meet the payroll. They seldom provide more than enough to meet short-range needs. Selling part of the business might provide the owner with a little extra. A minority interest in a business, however, is valued by the marketplace at a substantial discount. Generally, the best price available for the business is for the entire business as a single package.

Selling the business provides one very satisfying result. It demonstrates the successful completion of the overall task. You can only verify the achievements of success by completion of the full cycle of the investment that includes the sale and profit taking.

Successfully selling the business permits choosing a lifestyle more suitable to your age and station in life. It permits planning and executing a career path. Frequently, by the time the business is in a condition such that it can be sold, the owner-manager perceives something more interesting to do. It may be a different business or it may be running a school for the handicapped. It could be, and frequently is, advising others who aspire to emulate you.

Selling has another favorable result. It permits crystallizing plans for children and relatives, such as establishing trust funds for education of children and retirement for parents.

Owner-managers tend to feel that the reward will be there when it is needed. It is not necessary to worry about that now. The problem of the moment is building the business. Unfortunately, the reward is not waiting for us to say when we want it. That reward is as elusive as most of the solutions to many day-to-day problems.

There are negative aspects to selling a business. You may or may not still have a job. Even if the terms of the sale include a management contract, the job will become quite different. That principal characteristic of the entrepreneur, the need for freedom, is very likely to be frustrated by a structured environment. After all, the new owner has feelings about how things ought to be done. Furthermore, the new owner has the power to see that they are done that way. Despite the best of intentions, the entrepreneurial personality may end up in an untenable situation.

Those subconscious feelings of the business being your flesh and blood can cause pain and anguish when new owners impose even the slightest alteration in what you know is best for your organization. Those feelings of anguish can be swallowed for a while, but in time, the medicine is worse than the disease. The owner-manager who is a strong leader has trouble with the relationship. In a survey of venture capital companies in 1975, we found that very few entrepreneurs survive as managers in the portfolio companies of professional venture capital firms.

Merging the Business

Joining with a larger company has many glittering attractions. The financial strength of the bigger company becomes available to ease negotiations with bankers, suppliers, landlords and all of those people who question your balance sheet. Stalled plans for growth and expansion can be pressed forward. Management expertise that was too expensive to employ is probably available from the staff of the larger company.

The position of the owner-manager is often a lonely one. There is no one with whom to share problems or concerns. The president must always appear self-confident and fully in control regardless of any inner doubts, fears or uncertainties. Merger provides someone to whom the buck can be passed.

A potential advantage in merger is the possibility of exchanging stock for stock. This transaction is not taxable until some of the acquired stock is actually sold. The new security is probably more readily marketable. Hopefully, the new stock received will appreciate in value so that when it is finally sold, the realizable return is handsome.

There are no guarantees, of course. One very successful company merged with Penn-Central just before that giant had to admit its inadequacies.

Merging has some of the disadvantages of selling. It is, in fact, selling. Those management experts who become available to help the newly acquired business will provide advice and counsel. They will also represent the power of the new owner. It should not be too surprising if their advice sounds like direction. The owner-manager should recognize that seeking the advice of the acquiring company's staff may lead them to the natural conclusion that they are superior. That posture, together with their staff position in the acquiring company, can lead to a parent-child relationship that is untenable.

Many of us fall into the trap of not listening openly to suggestions, advice and counsel. This behavior is often referred to as the "not invented here" syndrome. Staff experts in the acquiring company are often afflicted with this disease.

As a rule, the chief executives of merging companies have a healthy respect for each other and are able to function well together when in direct communication. Problems usually develop at the next level or two down from the chief. For instance, the group insurance cost could be reduced by including the employees of both companies in the group. Who can argue against reducing costs? But whose employees are folded into which group? And so it goes with stationery, travel services, legal and audit help, expense forms, personnel records and on and on.

Despite the best intentions of the parties to the merger, things change. The boss now has a boss. Favored employees, like relatives and old-timers, are subject to cold, objective evaluation. There may no longer be a need for multiple officers in multiple offices with multiple secretaries.

Think in terms of mergor and mergee. The mergor is looking for an increase in earnings per share and has no personal ties to the employees of the mergee. Interpersonal relationships developed over years have little meaning to strangers. It takes time to develop loyalty, trust and understanding. Often this is developed through sharing adversity. The mergor needs an increase in earnings per share long before such relationships can be developed. The mergee is a vehicle for increasing earnings per share. The honeymoon in a merger marriage is often a brief one.

Having strewn some pessimism on the merger option, we want to quickly add that for some owner-managers the relationship is a very happy one. The probability of success in merger seems to lie in the personality of the entrepreneur being acquired. The head of the mergee becomes a senior employee of the mergor. The position has great merit if it can be accepted gracefully.

NEGOTIATING A DEAL

You can't make a good deal unless you know what you want. Sometimes a person has to do a little dealing just to find out what one might aspire to.

An owner-manager can draw up a list of reasons for wanting to sell or merge. It might be wiser to begin with a list that describes what the manager wants to do or to be. The business is an asset that may be used as a vehicle to achieve an objective. The first order of business is to establish one or more objectives and rank them according to their desirability.

There is nothing wrong with listing such objectives as, be a ski bum or be a golf nut. Whatever the list, it permits some organized investigation into what it takes to be a ski bum or a golf nut. It would also be helpful to find out what it is like to be one of those. Talk to some people who have done it. Treat it like planning a new business or new product line. What is sold and how it is sold could be altered dramatically by one's personal objectives. How about swapping the business for a ski lodge in Colorado?

KNOW THE VALUE OF WHAT YOU ARE SELLING

If there is ever a time when good accounting records are needed, it is when trying to value a business. It is not sufficient to call for an audit at the time the value is being determined. A portion of the determination is dependent on historical data and trends in the performance of the business. Besides, an auditor cannot prepare a clean statement without having certified the taking of inventory at two points in time, normally at the beginning and the end of the fiscal year being reported.

Accounting is not an exact science. Audits are prepared according to generally accepted accounting principles applied on a consistent basis over the years. Within that generally accepted practice there exists a very broad range of subjective decision making and estimating. Good records for the past five years and reasonable projections for the next three years are extremely useful tools for placing a value on the business. These records, however, must be consistent and they must be complete.

There is no single method for valuing a business. In fact, there are several values for any business. For instance, the net worth (i.e., total assets minus total liabilities) on the books may differ from the liquidation value. On the other hand, the going price may be a multiple of annual after-tax profits.

The value of a business, or the price that might be asked for it, must be viewed from the perspective of the buyer. To the buyer, it is an investment, one of many investment opportunities. These opportunities have varying degrees of certainty of the investment being returned and varying degrees of certainty of returning a profit in addition to the investment. Since there is a relatively free and diverse market for investors, the value of any particular business can be identified within a range that makes it competitive with other investment opportunities.

Valuing a business has been the subject of many books offered by major publishers. Unfortunately, many of the books are written in language that requires a lawyer and an accountant to interpret. They are worth reading, however, because they provide a basis for discussion with these experts, if nothing more. It is much cheaper to wade through three or four books to pick up some of the language than to have the lawyers and accountants provide that education. We suggest you include among those you read the *Business Valuation Handbook* by Desmond and Kelley from Valuation Press, Inc., Llano, California.

Without going into detail, the following might be helpful in beginning to grasp the methods used to value a business. No single method gives *the* value. Calculating the value by several methods establishes a range of values. This provides the seller with a realistic concept of what is reasonable and a basis upon which to justify a quoted price. The following are only four of many methods available.

As an aside, owner-managers who make this series of evaluations annually find their operating objectives fall into much sharper focus.

Book Value

The Balance Sheet reports Assets, Liabilities and Capital (Stockholders Equity). Book Value is Total Assets minus Total Liabilities.

The values shown on the books for Assets can vary quite widely depending upon the accounting conventions used and the accuracy of the record keeping. A prudent buyer will examine the assets, item by item, and place a market value on them. Some inventory may be obsolete or just not moving in the marketplace. Some equipment may be worth more than the depreciated value on the books. Each item in both Assets and Liabilities should be realistically valued and the book value adjusted to find a more realistic current market value for what is owned by the business and what is owed by the business.

Return On Investment

This method is based on the concept that in a particular market environment any annual stream of earnings can be related to an investment such that the return on investment (ROI) is reasonable. For example, if the net profit for a business over the last three to five years had averaged $30,000 and if 20% appeared to be a reasonable ROI then a value of $150,000 for the business (i.e. $30,000 divided by .20) would result. This assumes that the stream of earnings will continue into the future.

The crux of the matter, using this method, is selection of the return on investment percentage to be used. Since risk and return are typically related, the more risky the investment the larger the percentage rate the buyer will want to use, hence the smaller the investment. Closely held businesses are more risky than certificates of deposit, treasury bills and NYSE corporate bonds. Consequently, the percentage rate (often called capitalization rate) is likely to be larger. Rates of 15% to 30% are not uncommon.

To get the best price for your business using the ROI method, consistent and predictable earnings are essential. The closely held business that makes a profit *every other year* is unlikely to be very highly valued.

Price Earnings Ratio

This term is frequently used when valuing a business, but it has limited value for the closely held company. Still, it may provide a basis for evaluation if the closely held company has publicly held counterparts.

The terminology describes a ratio found by first determining the annual after-tax profits of a publicly held company and, second, by dividing this by the total number of shares of stock outstanding. The result is earnings per share (EPS). Third, the price at which these shares are trading in the public market is determined. This price per share divided by the earnings per share is the price earnings (P/E) ratio. This method, therefore, values the business based on a multiple of earnings.

The ratio is valid for widely owned, frequently traded, publicly held stocks. It is one of many indicators used by analysts when studying the performance of a company's stock in the marketplace.

Since the stock of a closely held company is not widely owned and frequently traded, there is no highly reliable data to determine the ratio. If, however, there are public companies that are like, or are similar to, the company being valued, then, their P/E ratio may be assumed to be a reasonable ratio for valuing the business. For instance, if similar companies have a P/E ratio of 10, then, one possible value of the company is 10 times its most recent annual after-tax profits. The seller of a stock might argue for a high price based upon that P/E ratio times the pro forma (projected) profits.

There is a multitude of ifs and buts surrounding this method. It is hoped that enough has been said to indicate the benefits and limitations of the method.

The Going Rate

Many kinds of businesses are bought and sold based upon some formula that has become customary in the marketplace. These prices may have little justification other than that everyone who buys and sells uses them. Some small businesses sell for book value. Others may sell for three times the profit excluding owner's salary. Still others may sell for 1.5 times annual sales. Bankers, accountants and lawyers who practice in business cases are sources of information regarding the going price for various types of small businesses. The going rate is usually relevant to small proprietorships. Sometimes, however, these customs arise with larger entities.

THE TIME TO SELL IS WHEN YOU DON'T WANT TO

The best deals are made when you aren't under excessive pressure to make them. If the deal *must* be made, you may have to take what is offered. It is difficult to make a good deal unless you are prepared to get up and walk away from the negotiating table.

When the business is doing well and seems to have excellent prospects for profitable growth, there are almost always parties interested in buying it. This is probably the very time when the owner-manager has the least interest in selling. In fact, approaches by potential buyers are typically dismissed.

When the business is having trouble, or perhaps when its prospects for the future seem less than exciting, it is normal for the owner-manager to have thoughts of selling. A cold, objective observer will recognize this thought as the owner's wish to palm the "dog" off on some other fool.

Needless to say, potential buyers are seldom fools. They recognize a real deal when they see one and would like to buy in at pennies on the dollar. When a business' prospects for the future are less than exciting, the buyer finds it easy to walk away from the deal. The result can be protracted negotiations with little real progress toward resolution.

Perhaps the owner-manager would be wise to consider that the buyer is paying for the present business as well as for the future prospects for the business. It is not only the business that is being sold. It is the glowing prospect for future profits that is on the block. Once the prospect vanishes, so does a portion of the value of the asset.

All of this suggests that consideration of cashing in your chips should be a fundamental part of plans to build the business in the first place. Overtures by potential buyers should never be dismissed out-of-hand. The most desirable position is one where the business has long-range potential for profitable growth and a superior past performance documented by good records. The time to sell is when an excellent offer comes along and there is not the slightest desire to accept it. Those two conditions constitute the ingredients of an irresistible offer. Furthermore, under these conditions, you don't have to accept the offer.

HOW TO FIND A BUYER

One of the first steps in finding a buyer is knowing what is for sale. Also, a buyer will ask why the business is for sale. Previous sections in this chapter have dealt with these two points.

Assuming that your personal objectives are clear and your understanding of the value of the asset is thorough, then there is a question of how to find a potential buyer.

The *Wall Street Journal* carries advertisements every day with businesses for sale. Daily newspapers typically carry a business opportunities section in their classified ads. Although some use this approach, others consider it undesirable.

Many professionals dealing with businesses are aware of buyers and sellers. These include commercial loan officers and trust officers in banks, accountants, lawyers, management consultants, the vice president of corporate finance in your stockbroker's office and many of the brokers themselves. Surprisingly, physicians, dentists, commercial real estate company officers and insurance agents with commercial accounts are often aware of potential buyers and sellers.

When considering a merger, there are some preliminary steps that might be helpful. Try making a list of companies that could really do something with your business. Include in the list both friends and foes, competitors and the competitors of your competitors. Add to that list companies that have products, channels of distribution and other resources that could significantly increase the competitive position and future prospects of your business.

Select from this list combinations that seem to make the most sense. Then, familiarize yourself with those potential merger partners. A display of knowledge of their business is likely to be complimentary to the merger candidates' management. Becoming knowledgeable about their business will also provide a better insight into the desirability of the merger and the list of characters in the play.

Libraries often contain public information on your identified merger prospects. Ask your stockbroker for any studies by the research departments of the brokerage houses. The big eight accounting firms also have research studies and data that are frequently available. Check with trade associations. You may consider calling a few of the merger candidates' customers and suppliers, their bankers, their landlords and their chambers of commerce. If possible, talk to officers, not subordinates, in these organizations.

If you have the time, forecast the next three years income statements and balance sheets for your business, for a merger candidate's business and then with your business as part of theirs. Don't worry that you have to make some gross assumptions to prepare the combined forecast. Their accountants can make adjustments to your forecast if necessary. If the combined forecast comes out favorable to their future earnings per share, you can anticipate management's attention and respect.

Business brokers are an avenue to finding a buyer. There are a few large firms in the business of finding buyers and sellers and there are plenty of small firms attempting the same thing. Among the smaller firms there are, unfortunately, many who do not provide a professional service. Beware of glowing promises that sound like guarantees. It takes time and energy, to say nothing of expertise, patience, diligence and hard work, to bring a buyer and a seller to an agreement. Check out the business broker as you would a potential merger partner. Firms of this kind are listed in the Yellow Pages under Business Brokers. Niederhoffer, Cross & Zeckhauser, Inc., 505 Park Avenue, N.Y., N.Y., 10022, is a firm that specializes in mergers for closely held businesses in the one to $50 million annual sales range.

Brokers get paid for their services. Commissions amounting to 5% are common. Ask about the commission schedule, and who pays it, near the beginning of the first discussion with a broker. Ask again as the relationship proceeds. Be sure the price is clearly understood by all parties. Ask the question, "Percentage of what?" Inquire as to how it is calculated. Reputable brokers are clear and open about their commissions and they earn them. A finder's fee, on the other hand, may be a legally enforceable obligation, but it is sometimes frightfully difficult to justify.

DEALS THAT CAN BE MADE

The variety of possible deals is as numerous as the humans making them. There is almost no limit to the ingenuity brought to the deal-making table.

The constraints on deals are important to consider if only because they, at least, can be identified. Most deals are structured to make them advantageous under the Internal Revenue Service rules in force at the time. Also, rules of the accounting profession may influence valuations and tax treatments. In addition, the Securities and Exchange Commission may constrain the kind of securities changing hands and their subsequent disposition.

The age and financial condition of the seller may strongly influence the IRS rules selected as most advantageous to the deal. Family relationships may also become a factor. All of these: age, condition, family, IRS rules, SEC rules and accounting rules change with time so that what may be a reasonable deal today could be a poor one tomorrow.

The way out of this seeming dilemma is to go back to the clear objectives of the owner-manager coupled with a clear identity of and valuation of what is being sold. The assistance of lawyers and accountants *experienced* in mergers and acquisitions is worth the price charged. These professionals are typically partners in large legal and audit firms. They have specialists within their own organizations to help them do what is best for you. Don't let your divorce lawyer or the person who prepared your income tax form handle the deal just because you are friends and have developed a trusting relationship. This is a time when you can risk losing the friend but you can't afford less than the best.

Even after the best advice has been obtained and the opinion of the experts has been rendered, *you* must make the decision as to what is best for you.

Case in Point

(Client File No. 367-R)

Mark is a farmer. At middle age he had no intention of selling his land. He had decided, however, that if someone offered enough cash he might consider getting out of the agriculture business.

One day both he and the bankruptcy judge across the road were offered an irresistible price for their properties by a large real estate development syndicate. The judge, being financially sophisticated, negotiated a payout to be extended over 15 years. This would permit a reduction in income taxes and net him, over the 15 years, a very substantial improvement in after-tax gain on the property. Mark, being inexperienced and uneducated in these matters, demanded cash on the barrel head now or no deal. No amount of persuasion could convince Mark that he would actually receive more money by taking payment over an extended period of time. Thus, the deal was closed and our farmer paid the IRS.

Three years later the real estate syndicate found itself in the unfortunate circumstances of appearing in the judge's bankruptcy court. Among other things, the syndicate managers had to explain that the real estate taxes had not been paid for three years on the ranch that the judge was going to get back. The reason for their being in these circumstances was discovery that the rural area where the ranch was located could not be developed economically for many years to come. It was, alas, just farm land.

Mark, the farmer, bought his farm back at farm land prices and lived happily ever after.

Under identical circumstances two different individuals made dramatically different "sell out" deals. Even if the story had turned out differently it is important to recognize that ultimately *you* must decide what is right for you.

SO YOU'VE GOT YOUR CHIPS

Owner-managers are notoriously poor investors in anything other than themselves. While building the business, fighting the brush fires and grabbing a little recreation on the run, there is seldom time to relax and study the world of investment. Besides, it really doesn't mean much unless you have a pool of money to invest.

Money in the form of cash is as big a problem to manage as the asset that was converted cash. The world is overpopulated with advisors and counselors looking for someone else's money to invest. Their fees represent a very small percentage of the total pool of money being invested. Unfortunately, so do the gains. The net gains from investments often shrink to zero or to losses by the time lawyers', accountants' and brokers' fees are included in the expense side of the tax return.

Rule Number 1 for the owner-manager who has acquired a pool of capital is, "There is no need to put it to work immediately." Certificates of Deposit, Treasury Bills and Municipal Bonds will provide net income without the aid of professionals while you think about how to invest the capital.

Rule Number 2 is, "Don't place all your capital in one investment." Entrepreneurs and owner-managers do well when they control and direct their own destiny. They usually do not fare as well when they place their destiny in the hands of other people. Investing is a passive role in someone else's affairs. It may be desirable to put the newly acquired capital into an investment that satisfies the owner-manager's personal objectives, such as in swapping the business for an ocean marina.

Rule Number 3 is, "Don't turn your back on the investment and forget it." Investing is as demanding of your time and energy as any other management pursuit. It may be more relaxed than running a business if the investments are safe and long term, like Certificates of Deposit. That kind of investment also provides a lower return. Investing in the stock market is much more like running a business. The commodities market is even more demanding.

Rule Number 4 is, "It is more rewarding to preserve the capital than risk it." There is no need to sleep restlessly when you own a pool of capital. The slightest feeling of concern for the safety of your capital is a call for action. Invest it in something that removes the concern. If you perceive little or no risk of losing the pool of capital, perhaps the investment is right for you.

Rule Number 5 is, "Listen to advice, but don't just accept it." Advisors don't have to be right. They just have to be helpful. When advising yourself, you aren't trying to be helpful, you are trying to be right. Despite the best of intentions on the part of professional advisors, they are still only trying to be helpful.

Before rushing into investments with newly acquired chips, consider the "time value of money," something financial institutions like banks understand very well. A little interest on a lot of money is itself a lot of money. A dollar becomes two dollars in about fourteen years compounded at 5%, seven years at 10% and five years at 15%. (See Chapter 10 for a discussion of compounding.)

Chapter 9 contains Exhibit 9-9, "An Exponential Curve." This is the same type of curve that describes the compounded value of money. Value increases by a percentage with time. The pre-conditions are that the principal to which the interest is applied is preserved intact and that the earned interest is added to the principal as it is earned.

Chapter 14 discusses dominant and secondary competitors on their Experience Curve. Exhibit 14-6 displays the components of such a curve. The components are described as Distinctive Business Functions. One of these distinctive functions was investment. Isn't it interesting that having succeeded in building the business and cashing it in for chips makes you a secondary competitor on somebody else's Experience Curve?

Our heritage is the opportunity to fulfill the American dream. Cashing in the chips provides new opportunities. Fulfillment of the dream is another problem. You have to know what the dream is for you. Then use the available opportunities to fulfill your dream.

Appendix

Asset Guideline Classes and Periods,
Asset Depreciation Ranges, and Annual Asset Guideline
Repair Allowance Percentages

Asset Guideline Classes and Periods, Asset Depreciation Ranges, and Annual Asset Guideline Repair Allowance Percentages

Asset Guide Line Class	Description of assets included	Asset depreciation range (in years)			Annual asset guideline repair allowance percentage
		Lower limit	Asset guideline period	Upper limit	

SPECIFIC DEPRECIABLE ASSETS USED IN ALL BUSINESS ACTIVITIES, EXCEPT AS NOTED:

00.11	**Office Furniture, Fixtures, and Equipment:** Includes furniture and fixtures that are not a structural component of a building. Includes such assets as desks, files, safes, and communications equipment. Does not include communications equipment that is included in other CLADR classes	8	10	12	2
00.12	**Information Systems:** Includes computers and their peripheral equipment used in administering normal business transactions and the maintenance of business records, their retrieval and analysis. Information systems are defined as: 1) Computers: A computer is an electronically activated device capable of accepting information, applying prescribed processes to the information, and supplying the results of these processes with or without human intervention. It usually consists of a central processing unit containing extensive storage, logic, arithmetic, and control capabilities. Excluded from this category are adding machines, electronic desk calculators, etc. 2) Peripheral equipment consists of the auxiliary machines which may be placed under control of the central processing unit. Non limiting examples are: Card readers, card punches, magnetic tape feeds, high speed printers, optical character readers, tape cassettes, mass storage units, paper tape equipment, keypunches, data entry devices, teleprinters, terminals, tape drives, disc drives, disc files, disc packs, visual image projector tubes, card sorters, plotters, and collators. Peripheral equipment may be used on-line or off-line. Does not include equipment that is an integral part of other capital equipment and which is included in other CLADR classes of economic activity, i.e., computers used primarily for process or production control, switching and channeling	5	6	7	7.5
00.13	**Data Handling Equipment, except Computers:** Includes only typewriters, calculators, adding and accounting machines, copiers, and duplicating equipment	5	6	7	15
00.21	**Airplanes (airframes and engines),** except those used in commercial or contract carrying of passengers or freight, and all helicopters (airframes and engines)	5	6	7	14
00.22	**Automobiles, Taxis**	2.5	3	3.5	16.5
00.23	**Busses**	7	9	11	11.5
00.241	**Light General Purpose Trucks:** Includes trucks for use over the road (actual unloaded weight less than 13,000 pounds)	3	4	5	16.5
00.242	**Heavy General Purpose Trucks:** Includes heavy general purpose trucks, concrete ready-mix truckers, and ore trucks, for use over the road (actual unloaded weight 13,000 pounds or more)	5	6	7	10
00.25	**Railroad Cars and Locomotives,** except those owned by railroad transportation companies	12	15	18	8
00.26	**Tractor Units For Use Over-The-Road**	3	4	5	16.5
00.27	**Trailers and Trailer-Mounted Containers**	5	6	7	10
00.28	**Vessels, Barges, Tugs, and Similar Water Transportation Equipment,** except those used in marine contract construction	14.5	18	21.5	6
00.3	**Land Improvements:** Includes improvements directly to or added to land, whether such improvements are section 1245 property or section 1250 property, provided such improvements are depreciable. Examples of such assets might include sidewalks, roads, canals, waterways, drainage facilities, sewers, wharves and docks, bridges, fences, landscaping shrubbery, or radio and television transmitting towers. Does not include land improvements that are explicitly included in any other class, and buildings and structural components as defined in section 1.48-1(e) of the regulations. Excludes public utility initial clearing and grading land improvements as specific in Rev. Rul. 72-403, 1072-2 C.B. 102.	20			

Asset Guideline Classes and Periods, Asset Depreciation Ranges, and Annual Asset Guideline Repair Allowance Percentages

Asset Guide Line Class	Description of assets included	Asset depreciation range (in years)			Annual asset guideline repair allowance percentage
		Lower limit	Asset guideline period	Upper limit	
00.4	**Industrial Steam and Electric Generation and/or Distribution Systems:** Includes assets, whether such assets are section 1245 property or 1259 property, providing such assets are depreciable, used in the production and/or distribution of electricity with rated total capacity in excess of 500 Kilowatts and/or assets used in the production and/or distribution of steam with rated total capacity in excess of 12,500 pounds per hour, for use by the taxpayer in his industrial manufacturing process or plant activity and not ordinarily available for sale to others. Does not include buildings and structural components as defined in section 1.48-1(e) of the regulations. Assets used to generate and/or distribute electricity or steam of the type described above of lesser rated capacity are not excluded but are included in the appropriate manufacturing equipment classes elsewhere specified. Steam and chemical recovery boiler systems used for the recovery and regeneration of chemicals used in manufacturing, with rated capacity in excess of that described above, with specifically related distribution and return systems are not included but are included in appropriate manufacturing equipment classes elsewhere specified. An example of an excluded steam and recovery boiler system is that used in the pulp and paper manufacturing industry	22.5	28	33.5	2.5

DEPRECIABLE ASSETS USED IN THE FOLLOWING ACTIVITIES:

0.01	**Agriculture** Includes machinery and equipment, grain bins, and fences but no other land improvements, that are used in the production of crops or plants, vines, and trees; livestock; the operation of farm dairies, nurseries, greenhouses, sod farms, mushroom cellars, cranberry bogs, apiaries, and fur farms; the performance of agricultural, animal husbandry, and horticultural services	8	10	12	11
01.11	**Cotton Ginning Assets**	9.5	12	14.5	5.5
01.21	**Cattle, Breeding or Dairy**	5.5	7	8.5	
01.22	**Horses, Breeding or Work**	8	10	12	
01.23	**Hogs, Breeding**	2.5	3	3.5	
01.24	**Sheep and Goats, Breeding**	4	5	6	
01.3	**Farm Buildings**	20	25	30	5
10.0	**Mining:** Includes assets used in the mining and quarrying of metallic and nonmetallic minerals (including sand, gravel, stone, and clay) and the milling, benefication and other primary preparation of such materials	8	10	12	6.5
13.1	**Drilling of Oil and Gas Wells:** Includes assets used in the drilling of on-shore oil and gas wells and the provisions of geophysical and other exploration services; and the provision of such oil and gas field services as chemical treatment, plugging and abandoning of wells and cementing or perforating well casings. Does not include assets used in the performance of any of these activities and services by integrating petroleum and natural gas producers for their own account	5	6	7	10
13.2	**Exploration for and Production of Petroleum and Natural Gas Deposits:** Includes assets used by petroleum and natural gas producers for driling of wells and production of petroleum and natural gas, including gathering pipelines and related storage facilities	11	14	17	4.5
13.3	**Petroleum Refining:** Includes assets used for the distillation, fractionation, and catalytic cracking of crude petroleum into gasoline and its other components	13	16	19	7

Asset Guideline Classes and Periods, Asset Depreciation Ranges, and Annual Asset Guideline Repair Allowance Percentages

Asset Guide Line Class	Description of assets included	Asset depreciation range (in years)			Annual asset guideline repair allowance percentage
		Lower limit	Asset guideline period	Upper limit	
13.4	**Marketing of Petroleum and Petroleum Products:** Includes assets used in marketing petroleum and petroleum products, such as related storage facilities and complete service stations, but not including any of these facilities related to petroleum and natural gas trunk pipelines	13	16	19	4
15.1	**Contract Construction Other than Marine:** Includes assets used by general building, special trade, and heavy construction contractors. Does not include assets used by companies in performing construction services for their own account	4	5	6	12.5
15.2	**Marine Contract Construction:** Includes assets used by general building, special trade, and heavy construction contractors predominantly in marine construction work. Does not include assets used by companies in performing marine construction services for their own account except for floating, self-propelled, and other drilling platforms and support vessels used in offshore drilling for oil and gas which are included whether used for their own account or others	9.5	12	14.5	5
20.1	**Manufacture of Grain Mill Products:** Includes assets used in the production of flours, cereals, livestock feeds, and other grain and grain mill products	13.5	17	20.5	6
20.2	**Manufacture of Sugar and Sugar Products:** Includes assets used in the production of raw sugar, syrup, or finished sugar from sugar cane or sugar beets	14.5	18	21.5	4.5
20.3	**Manufacture of Vegetable Oils and Vegetable Oil Products:** Includes assets used in the production of oil from vegetable materials and the manufacture of related vegetable oil products	14.5	18	21.5	3.5
20.4	**Manufacture of Other Food and Kindred Products:** Includes assets used in the production of foods and beverages not included in classes 20.1, 20.2 and 20.3	9.5	12	14.5	5.5
20.5	**Manufacture of Food and Beverages—Special Handling Devices:** Includes assets defined as specialized materials handling devices such as returnable pallets, palletized containers, and fish processing equipment including boxes, baskets, carts, and flaking trays used in activities as defined in classes 20.1, 20.2, 20.3, 20.4. Does not include general purpose small tools such as wrenches and drills, both hand and power-driven, and other general purpose equipment such as conveyors, transfer equipment and materials handling devices	3	4	5	20
21.0	**Manufacture of Tobacco and Tobacco Products:** Includes assets used in the production of cigarettes, cigars, smoking and chewing tobacco, snuff, and other tobacco products	12	15	18	5
22.1	**Manufacture of Knitted Goods:** Includes assets used in the production of knitted and netted fabrics and lace. Assets used in yarn preparation, bleaching, dyeing, printing, and other similar finishing processes, texturing, and packaging, are elsewhere classified	6	7.5	9	7
22.2	**Manufacture of Yarn, Thread, and Woven Fabric:** Includes assets used in the production of spun yarns including the preparing, blending, spinning, and twisting of fibers into yarns and threads, the preparation of yarns such as twisting, warping, and winding, the production of covered elastic yarn and thread, cordage, woven fabric, tire fabric, braided fabric, twisted jute for packing, mattresses, pads, sheets, and industrial belts, and the processing of textile mill waste to recover fibers, flocks, and shoddies. Assets used to manufacture carpets, man-made fibers, and nonwovens, and assets used in texturing, bleaching, dyeing, printing, and other similar finishing processes, are elsewhere classified	9	11	13	16
22.3	**Manufacture of Carpets, and Dyeing, Finishing, and Packaging of Textile Products:** Includes assets used in the production of carpets, rugs, mats, woven carpet backing, chenille, and other tufted products, and assets used in the joining together of backing with carpet yarn or fabric. Includes assets used in washing, scouring, bleaching, dyeing printing, drying, and similar finishing processes applied to textile fabrics, yarns, threads, and other textile goods. Includes assets used in the production and packaging of textile products, other than apparel, by creasing, forming, trimming, cutting, and sewing, such as the preparation of carpet and fabric samples, or similar joining together processes				

Asset Guideline Classes and Periods, Asset Depreciation Ranges, and Annual Asset Guideline Repair Allowance Percentages

Asset Guide Line Class	Description of assets included	Asset depreciation range (in years)			Annual asset guideline repair allowance percentage
		Lower limit	Asset guideline period	Upper limit	
	(other than the production of scrim reinforced paper products and laminated paper products) such as the sewing and folding of hosiery and panty hose, the creasing, folding, trimming, and cutting of fabrics to produce nonwoven products, such as disposable diapers and sanitary products. Assets used in the manufacture of nonwoven carpet backing, and hard surface floor covering such as tile, rubber, and cork, are elsewhere classified	7	9	11	15
22.4	**Manufacture of Textured Yarns:** Includes assets used in the processing of yarns to impart bulk and/or stretch properties to the yarn. The principal machines involved are falsetwist, draw, beam-to-beam, and suffer box texturing equipment and related high-speed twisters and winders. Assets, as described above, which are used to further process man-made fibers are elsewhere classified when located in the same plant in an integrated operation with man-made fiber producing assets. Assets used to manufacture man-made fibers and assets used in bleaching, dyeing, printing, and other similar finishing processes, are elsewhere classified	6.5	8	9.5	7
22.5	**Manufacture of Nonwoven Fabrics:** Includes assets used in the production of nonwoven fabrics, felt goods including felt hats, padding, batting, wadding, oakum, and fillings, from new materials and from textile mill waste. Nonwoven fabrics are defined as fabrics (other than reinforced and laminated composites consisting of nonwovens and other products) manufactured by bonding natural and/or synthetic fibers and/or filaments by means of induced mechanical interlocking, fluid entanglement, chemical adhesion, thermal or solvent reaction, or by combination thereof other than natural hydration bonding as occurs with natural cellulose fibers. Such means include resin bonding, web bonding, and melt bonding. Specifically includes assets used to make flocked and needle punched products other than carpets and rugs. Assets, as described above, which are used to manufacture nonwovens are elsewhere classified when located in the same plant in an integrated operation with man-made fiber producing assets. Assets used to manufacture man-made fibers and assets used in bleaching, dyeing, printing, and other similar finishing processes, are elsewhere classified	8	10	12	15
23.0	**Manufacture of Apparel and Other Finished Products:** Includes assets used in the production of clothing and fabricated textile products by the cutting and sewing of woven fabrics, other textile products, and furs; but does not include assets used in the manufacture of apparel from rubber and leather	7	9	11	7
24.1	**Cutting of Timber:** Includes logging machinery and equipment and roadbuilding equipment used by logging and sawmill operators and pulp manufacturers for their own account	5	6	7	10
24.2	**Sawing of Dimensional Stock from Logs:** Includes machinery and equipment installed in permanent or well-established sawmills.	8	10	12	6.5
24.3	**Sawing of Dimensional Stock from Logs:** Includes machinery and equipment installed in sawmills characterized by temporary foundations and a lack or minimum amount, of lumber-handling, drying, and residue disposal equipment and facilities	5	6	7	10
24.4	**Manufacture of Wood Products, and Furniture:** Includes assets used in the production of plywood, hardboard, flooring, veneers, furniture, and other wood products, including the treatment of poles and timber	8	10	12	6.5
26.1	**Manufacture of Pulp and Paper:** Includes assets for pulp materials handling and storage, pulp mill processing, bleach processing, paper and paperboard manufacturing, and on-line finishing. Includes pollution control assets and all land improvements associated with the factory site or production process such as effluent ponds and canals, provided such improvements are depreciable but does not include buildings and structural components as defined in section 1 48-1(e)(1) of the regulations. Includes steam and chemical recovery boiler systems, with any rated capacity, used for the recovery and regeneration of chemicals used in manufacturing. Does not include assets used either in pulpwood logging, or in the manufacture of hardboard	10.5	13	15.5	10
26.2	**Manufacture of Converted Paper, Paperboard, and Pulp Products:** Includes assets used for modification, or remanufacture of paper and pulp into converted products, such as paper coated off the paper machine, paper bags, paper boxes, cartons and envelopes. Does not include assets used for manufacture of non-wovens that are elsewhere classified	8	10	12	15

Asset Guideline Classes and Periods, Asset Depreciation Ranges, and Annual Asset Guideline Repair Allowance Percentages

Asset Guide Line Class	Description of assets included	Asset depreciation range (in years)			Annual asset guideline repair allowance percentage
		Lower limit	Asset guideline period	Upper limit	
27.0	**Printing, Publishing, and Allied Industries:** Includes assets used in printing by one or more processes, such as letterpress, lithography, gravure, or screen; the performance of services for the printing trade, such as book-binding, typesetting, engraving, photoengraving and electrotyping; and the publication of newspapers, books, and periodicals	9	11	13	5.5
28.0	**Manufacture of Chemicals of Allied Products:** Includes assets used in the manufacture of basic chemicals such as acids, alkalies, salts, and organic and inorganic chemicals; chemical products to be used in further manufacture, such as synthetic fibers and plastics materials, including petrochemical processing beyond that which is ordinarily a part of petroleum refining; and finished chemical products, such as pharmaceuticals, cosmetics, soaps, fertilizers, paints and varnishes, explosives, and compressed and liquified gases. Does not include assets used in the manufacture of finished rubber and plastic products or in the production of natural gas products, butane, propane and byproducts of natural gas production plants	9	11	13	5.5
30.1	**Manufacture of Rubber Products:** Includes assets used for the production of products from natural, synthetic, or reclaimed rubber, gutta percha, balata, or gutta siak, such as tires, tubes, rubber footwear, mechanical rubber goods, heels and soles, flooring, and rubber sundries; and in the recapping, retreading, and rebuilding of tires	11	14	17	5
30.11	**Manufacture of Rubber Products—Special Tools and Devices:** Includes assets defined as special tools, such as jigs, dies, mandrels, molds, lasts patterns, specialty containers, pallets, shells, and tire molds, and accessory parts such as rings and insert plates used in activities as defined in class 30.1. Does not include tire building drums and accessory parts and general purpose small tools such as wrenches and drills, both power and hand-driven, and other general purpose equipment such as conveyors and transfer equipment	3	4	5	
30.2	**Manufacture of Finished Plastic Products:** Includes assets used in the manufacture of plastic products and the molding of primary plastics for the trade. Does not include assets used in the manufacture of basic plastics materials nor the manufacture of phonograph records	9	11	13	5.5
30.21	**Manufacture of Finished Plastic Products—Special Tools:** Includes assets defined as special tools, such as jigs, dies, fixtures, molds, patterns, gauges, and specialty transfer and shipping devices, used in activities as defined in class 30.2. Special tools are specifically designed for the production or processing of particular parts and have no significant utilitarian value and cannot be adapted to further or different use after changes or improvements are made in the model design of the particular part produced by the special tools. Does not include general purpose small tools, such as wrenches and drills, both hand and power-driven, and other general purpose equipment such as conveyors, transfer equipment, and materials handling devices ...	3	3.5	4	5.5
31.0	**Manufacture of Leather and Leather Products:** Includes assets used in the tanning, currying, and finishing of hides and skins; the processing of fur pelts; and the manufacture of finished leather products, such as footwear, belting, apparel, and luggage	9	11	13	5.5
32.1	**Manufacture of Glass Products:** Includes assets used in the production of flat, blown, or pressed products of glass, such as float and window glass, glass containers, glassware and fiberglass. Does not include assets used in the manufacture of lenses	11	14	17	12
32.11	**Manufacture of Glass Products—Special Tools:** Includes assets defined as special tools such as molds, patterns, pallets, and specialty transfer and shipping devices such as steel racks to transport automotive glass, used in activities as defined in class 32.1. Special tools are specifically designed for the production or processing of particular parts and have no significant utilitarian value and cannot be adapted to further or different use after changes or improvements are made in the model design of the particular part produced by the special tools. Does not include general purpose small tools such as wrenches and drills, both hand and power-driven, and other general purpose equipment such as conveyors, transfer equipment, and materials handling devices	2	2.5	3	10

Asset Guideline Classes and Periods, Asset Depreciation Ranges, and Annual Asset Guideline Repair Allowance Percentages

Asset Guide Line Class	Description of assets included	Asset depreciation range (in years)			Annual asset guideline repair allowance percentage
		Lower limit	Asset guideline period	Upper limit	
32.2	**Manufacture of Cement:** Includes assets used in the production of cement, but does not include any assets used in the manufacture of concrete and concrete products nor in any mining or extraction process	16	20	24	3
32.3	**Manufacture of Other Stone and Clay Products:** Includes assets used in the manufacture of products from materials in the form of clay and stone, such as brick, tile, and pipe; pottery and related products, such as vitreous-china, plumbing fixtures, earthenware and ceramic insulating materials; and also includes assets used in manufacture of concrete and concrete products. Does not include assets used in any mining or extraction process	12	15	18	4.5
33.1	**Mannufacture of Primary Ferrous Metals:** Includes assets used in the smelting and refining of ferrous metals from ore, pig, or scrap, the rolling, drawing, and alloying of ferrous metals; the manufacture of castings, forgings, and other basic products of ferrous metals; and the manufacture of nails, spikes, structural shapes, tubing, wire, and cable	14.5	18	21.5	8
33.11	**Manufacture of Primary Ferrous Metals—Special Tools:** Includes assets defined as special tools such as dies, jigs, molds, patterns, fixtures, gauges, and drawings concerning such special tools used in the activities as defined in class 33.1, manufacture of Primary Ferrous Metals. Special tools are specifically designed for the production or processing of particular products or parts and have no significant utilitarian value and cannot be adapted to further or different use after changes or improvements are made in the model design of the particular part produced by the special tools. Does not include general purpose small tools such as wrenches and drills, both hand and power-driven, and other general purpose equipment such as conveyors, transfer equipment, and materials handling devices. Rolls, mandrels, and refractories are not included in class 33.11 but are included in class 33.1	5	6.5	8	4
33.2	**Manufacture of Primary Nonferrous Metals:** Includes assets used in the smelting, refining, and electrolysis of nonferrous metals from ore, pig, or scrap, the rolling, drawing, and alloying of nonferrous metals; the manufacture of castings, forgings, and other basic products of nonferrous metals; and the manufacture of nails, spikes, structural shapes, tubing, wire, and cable	11	14	17	4.5
33.21	**Manufacture of Primary Nonferrous Metals—Special Tools:** Includes assets defined as special tools such as dies, jigs, molds, patterns, fixtures, gauges, and drawings concerning such special tools used in the activities as defined in class 33.2, Manufacture of Primary Nonferrous Metals. Special tools are specifically designed for the production or processing of particular products or parts and have no significant utilitarian value and cannot be adapted to further or different use after changes or improvements are made in the model design of the particular part produced by the special tools. Does not include general purpose small tools such as wrenches and drills, both hand and power-driven, and other general purpose equipment such as conveyors, transfer equipment, and materials handling devices. Rolls, mandrels, and refractories are not included in class 33.21 but are included in class 33.2	5	6.5	8	4
34.0	**Manufacture of Fabricated Metal Products:** Includes assets used in the production of metal cans, tinware, nonelectric heating apparatus, fabricated structural metal products, metal stampings, and other ferrous and nonferrous metal and wire products not elsewhere classified	9.5	12	14.5	6
34.01	**Manufacture of Fabricated Metal Products—Special Tools:** Includes assets defined as special tools such as dies, jigs, molds, patterns, fixtures, gauges, and returnable containers and drawings concerning such special tools used in the activities as defined in class 34.0. Special tools are specifically designed for the production or processing of particular machine components, products, or parts, and have no significant utilitarian value and cannot be adapted to further or different use after changes or improvements are made in the model design of the particular part produced by the special tools. Does not include general purpose small tools such as wrenches and drills, both hand and powerdriven, and other general purpose equipment such as conveyors, transfer equipment, and materials handling devices	2.5	3	3.5	3.5

Asset Guideline Classes and Periods, Asset Depreciation Ranges, and Annual Asset Guideline Repair Allowance Percentages

Asset Guide Line Class	Description of assets included	Asset depreciation range (in years)			Annual asset guideline repair allowance percentage
		Lower limit	Asset guideline period	Upper limit	
35.1	**Manufacture of Metalworking Machinery:** Includes assets used in the production of metal cutting and forming machines, special dies, tools, jigs, and fixtures, and machine tool accessories	9.5	12	14.5	5.5
35.11	**Manufacture of Metalworking Machinery—Special Tools:** Includes assets defined as special tools, such as jigs, dies, fixtures, molds, patterns, gauges, and specialty transfer and shipping devices, used in activities as defined in class 35.1. Special tools are specifically designed for the production or processing of particular machine components and have no significant utilitarian value and cannot be adapted to further or different use after changes or improvements are made in the model design of the particular part produced by the special tools. Does not include general purpose small tools such as wrenches and drills, both hand and power-driven, and other general purpose equipment such as conveyors, transfer equipment, and materials handling devices	5	6	7	12.5
35.2	**Manufacture of Other Machines:** Includes assets used in the production of such machinery as engines and turbines; farm machinery, construction, and mining machinery; general and special industrial machines including office machines and nonelectronic computing equipment; miscellaneous machines except electrical equipment and transportation equipment	9.5	12	14.5	5.5
35.21	**Manufacture of Other Machines—Special Tools:** Includes assets defined as special tools, such as jigs, dies, fixtures, molds, patterns, gauges, and specialty transfer and shipping devices, used in activities as defined in class 35.2. Special tools are specifically designed for the production or processing of particular machine components and have no significant utilitarian value and cannot be adapted to further or different use after changes or improvements are made in the model design of the particular part produced by the special tools. Does not include general purpose small tools such as wrenches and drills, both hand and power-driven, and other general purpose equipment such as conveyors, transfer equipment, and materials handling devices	5	6.5	8	12.5
36.1	**Manufacture of Electrical Equipment:** Includes assets used in the production of machinery, apparatus, and supplies for the generation, storage, transmission, transformation, and utilization of electrical energy such as; electric test and distributing equipment, electrical industrial apparatus, household appliances, electric lighting and wiring equipment; electronic components and accessories, phonograph records, storage batteries and ignition systems	9.5	12	14.5	5.5
36.11	**Manufacture of Electrical Equipment Special Tools:** Includes assets defined as special tools such as jigs, dies, molds, patterns, fixtures, gauges, returnable containers, and specialty transfer devices used in activities as defined in class 36.1. Special tools are specifically designed for the production or processing of particular machine components, products or parts, and have no significant utilitarian value and cannot be adapted to further or different use after changes or improvements are made in the model design of the particular part produced by the special tools. Does not include general purpose small tools such as wrenches and drills, both hand and power-driven, and other general purpose equipment such as conveyors, transfer equipment, and materials handling devices	4	5	6	
36.2	**Manufacture of Electronic Products:** Includes assets used in the production of electronic detection, guidance, control, radiation, computation, test, and navigation equipment or the components thereof including airborne application. Also includes assets used in the manufacture of electronic airborne communication equipment or the components thereof. Does not include the assets of manufacturers engaged only in the purchase and assembly of components	6.5	8	9.5	7.5
37.11	**Manufacture of Motor Vehicles:** Includes assets used in the manufacture and assembly of finished automobiles, trucks, trailers, motor homes, and buses. Does not include assets used in mining, printing and publishing, production of primary metals, electricity, or steam, or the manufacture of glass, industrial chemicals, batteries, or rubber products, which are classified elsewhere. Includes assets used in manufacturing activities elsewhere classified other than those excluded above, where such activities are incidental to and an integral part of the manufacture and assembly of finished motor vehicles such as the manufacture of parts and subassemblies of fabricated metal products, electrical equipment, textiles, plastics,				

Asset Guideline Classes and Periods, Asset Depreciation Ranges, and Annual Asset Guideline Repair Allowance Percentages

Asset Guide Line Class	Description of assets included	Asset depreciation range (in years)			Annual asset guideline repair allowance percentage
		Lower limit	Asset guideline period	Upper limit	
	leather, and foundry and forging operations. Does not include any assets not classified in manufacturing activity classes, e.g., does not include assets classified in asset guideline classes 00.11 through 00.4. Activities will be considered incidental to the manufacture and assembly of finished motor vehicles only if 75 percent or more of the value of the products produced under one roof are used for the manufacture and assembly of finished motor vehicles. Parts that are produced as a normal replacement stock complement in connection with the manufacture and assembly of finished motor vehicles are considered used for the manufacture and assembly of finished motor vehicles. Does not include assets used in the manufacture of component parts if these assets are used by taxpayer not engaged in the assembly of finished motor vehicles	9.5	12	14.5	9.5
37.12	**Manufacture of Motor Vehicles—Special Tools:** Includes assets defined as special tools, such as jigs, dies, fixtures, molds, patterns, gauges, and specialty transfer and shipping devices, owned by manufacturers of finished motor vehicles and used in qualified activities as defined in class 37.11. Special tools are specifically designed for the production or processing of particular motor vehicle components and have no significant utilitarian value, and cannot be adapted to further or different use, after changes or improvements are made in the model design of the particular part produced by the special tools. Does not include general purpose small tools such as wrenches and drills, both hand and power-driven, and other general purpose equipment such as conveyors, transfer equipment, and materials handling devices.	2.5	3	3.5	12.5
37.2	**Manufacture of Aerospace Products:** Includes assets used in the manufacture and assembly of airborne vehicles and their component parts including hydraulic, pneumatic, electrical, and mechanical systems. Does not include assets used in the production of electronic airborne detection, guidance, control, radiation, computation, test, navigation, and communication equipment or the components thereof	8	12	12	7.5
37.31	**Ship and Boat Building Machinery and Equipment:** Includes assets used in the manufacture and repair of ships, boats, caissons, marine drilling rigs, and special fabrications not included in asset guideline classes 37.32 and 37.33. Specifically includes all manufacturing and repairing machinery and equipment, including machinery and equipment used in the operation of assets including assets guideline class 37.32. Excludes buildings and their structural components	9.5	12	14.5	8.5
37.32	**Ship and Boat Building Dry Docks and Land Improvements:** Includes assets used in the manufacture and repair of ships, boats, caissons, marine drilling rigs, and special fabrications not included in asset guideline classes 37.31 and 37.33. Specifically includes floating and fixed dry docks, ship basins, graving docks, shipways, piers, and all other land improvements such as water, sewer, and electric systems. Excludes buildings and their structural components	13	16	19	2.5
37.33	**Ship and Boat Building—Special Tools:** Includes assets defined as special tools such as dies, jigs, molds, patterns, fixtures, gauges, and drawings concerning such special tools used in the activities defined in classes 37.31 and 37.32. Special tools are specifically designed for the production or processing of particular machine components, products, or parts, and have no significant utilitarian value and cannot be adapted to further or different use after changes or improvements are made in the model design of the particular part produced by the special tools. Does not include general purpose small tools such as wrenches and drills, both hand and power-driven, and other general purpose equipment such as conveyors, transfer equipment, and materials handling devices	5	6.5	8	0.5
37.41	**Manufacture of Locomotives:** Includes assets used in building or rebuilding railroad locomotives (including mining and industrial locomotives). Does not include assets of railroad transportation companies or assets of companies which manufacture components of locomotives but do not manufacture finished locomotives	9	11.5	14	7.5
37.42	**Manufacture of Railroad Cars:** Includes assets used in building or rebuilding railroad freight or passenger cars (including rail transit cars). Does not include assets of railroad transportation companies or assets of companies which manufacture components of railroad cars but do not manufacture finished railroad cars	9.5	12	14.5	5.5

Asset Guideline Classes and Periods, Asset Depreciation Ranges, and Annual Asset Guideline Repair Allowance Percentages

Asset Guide Line Class	Description of assets included	Asset depreciation range (in years)			Annual asset guideline repair allowance percentage
		Lower limit	Asset guideline period	Upper limit	
38.0	**Manufacture of Professional, Scientific, and Controlling Instruments:** Includes assets used in the manufacture of mechanical measuring, engineering, laboratory and scientific research instruments, optical instruments and lenses; surgical, medical, and dental instruments, equipment and supplies; ophthalmic goods, photographic equipment and supplies; and watches and clocks	9.5	12	14.5	5.5
39.0	**Manufacture of Athletic, Jewelry and Other Goods:** Includes assets used in the production of jewelry; musical instruments; toys and sporting goods; motion picture and television films and tapes; and pens, pencils, office and art supplies, brooms, brushes, caskets, etc.	9.5	12	14.5	5.5
	Railroad Transportation: Classes with the prefix 40 include the assets identified below that are used in the commercial and contract carrying of passengers and freight by rail. Assets of electrified railroads will be classified in a manner corresponding to that set forth below for railroads not independently operated as electric lines. Excludes the assets included in classes with the prefix beginning 00.1 and 00.2 above, and also excludes any nondepreciable assets included in Interstate Commerce Commission accounts enumerated for this class.				
40.1	**Railroad Machinery and Equipment:** Includes assets classified in the following Interstate Commerce Commission accounts: Roadway Accounts: (16) Station and office buildings (freight handling machinery and equipment only) (25) TOFC/COFC terminals (freight handling machinery and equipment only) (26) Communication systems (27) Signals and interlockers (37) Roadway machines (44) Shop machinery Equipment Accounts: (52) Locomotives (53) Freight train cars (54) Passenger train cars (57) Work equipment	11	14	17	10.5
40.2	**Railroad Structures and Similar Improvements:** Includes assets classified in the following Interstate Commerce Commission road accounts: (6) Bridges, trestles, and culverts (7) Elevated structures (13) Fences, snowsheds, and signs (16) Station and office buildings (stations and other operating structures only) (17) Roadway buildings (18) Water stations (19) Fuel stations (20) Shops and enginehouses (25) TOFC/COFC terminals (operating structures only) (31) Power transmission systems (35) Miscellaneous structures (39) Public improvements construction	24	30	36	5
40.3	**Railroad Wharves and Docks:** Includes assets classified in the following Interstate Commerce accounts: (23) Wharves and docks (24) Coal and ore warves	16	20	24	5.5
40.51	**Railroad Hydraulic Electric Generating Equipment**	40	50	60	1.5
40.52	**Railroad Nuclear Electric Generating Equipment**	16	20	24	3
40.53	**Railroad Steam Electric Generating Equipment**	22.5	28	33.5	2.5
40.54	**Railroad Steam, Compressed Air, and Other Power Plan Equipment**	22.5	28	33.5	7.5
41.0	**Motor Transport-Passengers:** Include assets used in the urban and interurban commercial and contract carrying of passengers by road, except the transportation assets included in classes with the prefix 00.2	6.5	8	9.5	11.5

APPENDIX

Asset Guideline Classes and Periods, Asset Depreciation Ranges, and Annual Asset Guideline Repair Allowance Percentages

Asset Guide Line Class	Description of assets included	Asset depreciation range (in years)			Annual asset guideline repair allowance percentage
		Lower limit	Asset guideline period	Upper limit	
42.0	**Motor Transport-Freight:** Includes assets used in the commercial and contract carrying of freight by road, except the transportation assets included in classes with the prefix 00.2	6.5	8	9.5	11
44.0	**Water Transportation:** Includes assets used in the commercial and contract carrying of freight and passengers by water except the transportation assets included in classes with prefix 00.2. Includes all related land improvements	16	20	24	8
45.0	**Air Transport:** Includes assets (except helicopters) used in commercial and contract carrying of passengers and freight by air. For purposes of section 1.167 (a)-11(d)(2)(iv)(a) of the regulations, expenditures for "repair, maintenance, rehabilitation, or improvement" shall consist of direct maintenance expenses (irrespective of airworthiness provisions or charges) as defined by Civil Aeronautics Board uniform accounts 5200, maintenance burden (exclusive of expenses pertaining to maintenance buildings and improvements) as defined by Civil Aeronautics Board uniform accounts 5300, and expenditures which are not "excluded additions" as defined by section 1.167(a)-11(d)(2)(vi) of the regulations and which would be charged to property and equipment accounts in the Civil Aeronautics Board uniform system of accounts	9.5	12	14.5	15
45.1	**Air Transport (restricted)** Includes each asset described in the description of class 45.0 which was held by the taxpayer on April 15, 1976, or is acquired by the taxpayer pursuant to a contract which was, on April 15, 1976, and at all times thereafter, binding on the taxpayer. This criterion of classification based on binding contract concept is to be applied in the same manner as under the general rules expressed in section 49(b)(1), (4), (5), and (8) of the Code	5	6	7	15
46.0	**Pipeline Transportation:** Includes assets used in the private, commercial, and contract carrying of petroleum, gas, and other products by means of pipes and conveyors. The trunk lines and related storage facilities of integrated petroleum and natural gas producers are included in this class. Excludes initial clearing and grading land improvements as specified in Rev. Rul. 72-403, 1972-2 C.B. 102, but includes all other related land improvements	17.5	22	26.5	3
	Telephone Communications: Includes the assets identified below and that are used in the provision of commercial and contract telephonic services such as:				
48.11	**Telephone Central Office Buildings:** Includes assets intended to house central office equipment, as defined in Federal Communications Commission Part 31 Account No. 212 whether section 1245 or section 1250 property	36	45	54	1.5
48.12	**Telephone Central Office Equipment:** Includes central office switching and related equipment as defined in Federal Communications Commission Part 31 Account No. 221	16	20	24	6
48.13	**Telephone Station Equipment:** Includes such station apparatus and connections as teletypewriters, telephones, booths, private exchanges, and comparable equipment as defined in Federal Communications Commission Part 31 Account Nos. 231, 232, and 234	8	10	12	10
48.14	**Telephone Distribution Plant:** Includes such assets as pole lines, cable, aerial wire, underground conduits, and comparable equipment, and related land improvements as defined in Federal Communications Commission Part 31 Account Nos. 241, 242.1, 242.2, 242.3, 242.4, 243, and 244	28	35	42	2
48.2	**Radio and Television Broadcastings:** Includes assets used in radio and television broadcasting, except transmitting towers	5	6	7	10
	Telegraph, Ocean Cable, and Satellite Communications (TOCSC) Includes communications-related assets used to provide domestic and international radio-telegraph, wire-telegraph, ocean-cable, and satellite communications services; also includes related land improvements.				

Asset Guideline Classes and Periods, Asset Depreciation Ranges, and Annual Asset Guideline Repair Allowance Percentages

Asset Guide Line Class	Description of assets included	Asset depreciation range (in years)			Annual asset guideline repair allowance percentage
		Lower limit	Asset guideline period	Upper limit	
48.31	**TOCSC-Electric Power Generating and Distribution Systems:** Includes assets used in the provision of electric power by generation, modulation, rectification, channelization, control, and distribution. Does not include these assets when they are installed on customer's premises	15	19	23	
48.32	**TOCSC-High Frequency Radio and Microwave Systems:** Includes assets such as transmitters and receivers, antenna supporting structures, antennas, transmission lines from equipment to antenna, transmitter cooling systems, and control and amplification equipment. Does not include cable and long-line systems	10.5	13	15.5	
48.33	**TOCSC-Cable and Long-line Systems:** Includes assets such as transmission lines, pole lines, ocean cables, buried cable and conduit, repeaters, repeater stations, and other related assets. Does not include high frequency radio or microwave systems	21	26.4	32	
48.34	**TOCSC-Central Office Control Equipment:** Includes assets for general control, switching, and monitoring of communications signals including electromechanical switching and channeling apparatus, multiplexing equipment, patching and monitoring facilities, in-house cabling, teleprinter equipment, and associated site improvements	13	16.5	20	
48.35	**TOCSC-Computerized Switching, Channeling, and Associated Control Equipment:** Includes central office switching computers, interfacing computers, other associated specialized control equipment, and site improvements	8.5	10.5	12.5	
48.36	**TOCSC-Satellite Ground Segment Property:** Includes assets such as fixed earth station equipment, antennas, satellite communications equipment, and interface equipment used in satellite communications. Does not include general purpose equipment or equipment used in satellite space segment property	8	10	12	
48.37	**TOCSC-Satellite Space Segment Property:** Includes satellites and equipment used for telemetry, tracking, control, and monitoring when used in satellite communications	6.5	8	9.5	
48.38	**TOCSC-Equipment Installed on Customer's Premises:** Includes assets installed on customer's premises, such as computers, terminal equipment, power generation and distribution systems, private switching center, teleprinters, facsimile equipment, and other associated and related equipment	8	10	12	
48.39	**TOCSC-Support and Service Equipment:** Includes assets used to support but not engage in communications. Includes store, warehouse, and shop tools, and test and laboratory assets	11	13.5	16	
	Cable Television (CATV): Includes communications-related assets used to provide cable television (community antenna television services). Does not include assets used to provide subscribers with two-way communications services.				
48.41	**CATV-Headend:** Includes assets such as towers, antennas, preamplifiers, converters, modulation equipment, and program non-duplication system. Does not include headend buildings and program origination assets	9	11	13	5
48.42	**CATV-Subscriber Connection and Distribution Systems:** Includes assets such as trunk and feeder cable, connecting hardware, amplifiers, power equipment, passive devices, directional taps, pedestals, pressure taps, drop cables, matching transformers, multiple set connector equipment, and converters	8	10	12	5
48.43	**CATV-Program Origination:** Includes assets such as cameras, film chains, video tape recorders, lighting, and remote location equipment excluding vehicles. Does not include buildings and their structural components	7	9	11	9
48.44	**CATV-Service and Test:** Includes assets such as oscilloscopes, field strength meters, spectrum analyzers, and cable testing equipment, but does not include vehicles		8.5	10	2.5

Asset Guideline Classes and Periods, Asset Depreciation Ranges, and Annual Asset Guideline Repair Allowance Percentages

Asset Guide Line Class	Description of assets included	Asset depreciation range (in years)			Annual asset guideline repair allowance percentage
		Lower limit	Asset guideline period	Upper limit	
48.45	**CATV-Microwave Systems:** Includes assets such as towers, antennas, transmitting and receiving equipment, and broad band microwave assets if used in the provision of cable television services. Does not include assets used in the provision of common carrier services	7.5	9.5	11.5	2
	Electric, Gas, Water and Steam, Utility Services: Includes assets used in the production, transmission and distribution of electricity, gas, steam, or water for sale, including related land improvements.				
49.11	**Electric Utility Hydraulic Production Plant:** Includes assets used in the hydraulic power production of electricity for sale, including related land improvements, such as dams, flumes, canals, and waterways	40	50	60	1.5
49.12	**Electric Utility Nuclear Production Plant:** Includes assets used in the nuclear power production of electricity for sale and related land improvements. Does not include nuclear fuel assemblies	16	20	24	3
49.121	**Electric Utility Nuclear Fuel Assemblies:** Includes initial core and replacement core nuclear fuel assemblies (i.e., the composite of fabricated nuclear fuel and container) when used in a boiling water, pressurized water, or high temperature gas reactor used in the production of electricity. Does not include nuclear fuel assemblies used in breeder reactors	4	5	6	
49.13	**Electric Utility Steam Production Plant:** Includes assets used in the steam power production of electricity for sale, combustion turbines operated in a combined cycle with a conventional steam unit and related land improvements	22.5	28	33.5	5
49.14	**Electric Utility Transmission and Distribution Plant:** Includes assets used in the transmission and distribution of electricity for sale and related land improvements. Excludes initial clearing and grading land improvements as specified in Rev. Rul. 72-403, 1972-2 C.B. 102	24	30	36	4.5
49.15	**Electric Utility Combusion Turbine Production Plant:** Includes assets used in the production of electricity for sale by the use of such prime movers as jet engines, combustion turbines, diesel engines, gasoline engines, and other internal combustion engines, their associated power turbines and/or generators, and related land improvements. Does not include combustion turbines operated in a combined cycle with a conventional steam unit	16	20	24	4
49.21	**Gas Utility Distribution Facilities:** Including gas water heaters and gas conversion equipment installed by utility on customers' premises on a rental basis	28	35	42	2
49.221	**Gas Utility Manufactured Gas Production Plants:** Includes assets used in the manufacture of gas having chemical and/or physical properties which do not permit complete interchangeability with domestic natural gas	24	30	36	2
49.222	**Gas Utility Substitute Natural Gas (SNG) Production Plant (naptha or lighter hydrocarbon feedstocks):** Includes assets used in the catalytic conversion of feedstocks of naptha or lighter hydrocarbons to a gaseous fuel which is completely interchangeable with domestic natural gas	11	14	17	4.5
49.223	**Substitute Natural Gas-Coal Gasification:** Includes assets used in the manufacture and production of pipeline quality gas from coal using the basic Lurgi process with advanced methanation. Includes all process plant equipment and structures used in this coal gasification process and all utility assets such as cooling systems, water supply with treatment facilities, and assets used in the production and distribution of electricity and steam for use by the taxpayer in a gasification plant and attendant coal mining site processes but not for assets used in the production and distribution of electricity and steam for sale to others. Also includes all other related land improvements. Does not include assets used in the direct mining and treatment of coal prior to the gasification process itself.	14.5	18	21.5	15
49.23	**Natural Gas Production Plant**	11	14	17	4.5
49.24	**Gas Utility Truck Pipelines and Related Storage Facilities:** Excludes initial clearing and grading land improvements as specified in Rev. Rul. 72-403	17.5	22	26.5	3

Asset Guideline Classes and Periods, Asset Depreciation Ranges, and Annual Asset Guideline Repair Allowance Percentages

Asset Guide Line Class	Description of assets included	Asset depreciation range (in years)			Annual asset guideline repair allowance percentage
		Lower limit	Asset guideline period	Upper limit	
49.25	**Liquefied Natural Gas Plant:** Includes assets used in the liquefaction, storage, and regasification of natural gas including loading and unloading connections, instrumentation equipment and controls, pumps, vaporizers and odorizers, tanks, and related land improvements. Also includes pipeline interconnections with gas transmission lines and distribution systems and marine terminal facilities	17.5	22	26.5	4.5
49.3	**Water Utilities:** Includes assets used in the gathering, treatment, and commercial distribution of water	40	50	60	1.5
49.4	**Central Steam Utility Production and Distribution:** Includes assets used in the production and distribution of steam for sale	22.5	28	33.5	2.5
50.0	**Wholesale and Retail Trade:** Includes assets used in carrying out the activities of purchasing, assembling, storing, sorting, grading, and selling of goods at both the wholesale and retail level. Also includes assets used in such activities as the operation of restaurants, cafes, coin-operated dispensing machines, and in brokerage of scrap metal	8	10	12	6.5
50.1	**Wholesale and Retail Trade Service Assets:** Includes assets such as glassware, silverware (including kitchen utensils), crockery (usually china) and linens (generally napkins, tablecloths and towels) used in qualified activities as defined in class 50.0	2	2.5	3	
70.2	**Personal and Professional Services:** Includes assets used in the provision of personal services such as those offered by hotels and motels, laundry and dry cleaning establishments, beauty and barber shops, photographic studios and mortuaries. Includes assets used in the provision of professional services such as those offered by doctors, dentists, lawyers, accountants, architects, engineers, and veterinarians. Includes assets used in the provision of repair and maintenance services and those assets used in providing fire and burglary protection services. Includes equipment for facilities used by cemetery organizations, new agencies, teletype wire services, frozen food lockers, and research laboratories	8	10	12	6.5
70.21	**Personal and Professional Services Service Assets:** Includes assets such as glassware, silverware, crockery, and linens (generally sheets, pillowcases and bath towels) used in qualified activities as defined in class 70.2	2	2.5	3	
79.0	**Recreation:** Includes assets used in the provision of entertainment services on payment of a fee or admission charge, as in the operation of bowling alleys, billiard and pool establishments, theaters, concert halls, and miniature golf courses. Does not include amusement and theme parks and assets which consist primarily of specialized land improvements or structures such as golf courses, sports stadia, race tracks, ski slopes, and buildings which house the assets used in entertainment services	8	10	12	6.5
80.0	**Theme and Amusement Parks:** Includes assets used in the provision of rides, attractions, and amusements in activities defined as theme and amusement parks, and includes appurtenance associated with a ride, attraction, amusement or theme setting within the park such as ticket booths, facades, shop interiors, and props, special purpose structures, and buildings other than warehouses, administration buildings, hotels, and motels. Includes all land improvements for or in support of park activities (e.g. parking lots, sidewalks, waterways, bridges, fences, landscaping, etc.), and support functions (e.g. food and beverage retailing, souvenir vending and other nonlodging accommodations) if owned by the park and provided exclusively for the benefit of park patrons. Theme and amusement parks are defined as combinations of amusements, rides, and attractions which are permanently situated on park land and open to the public for the price of admission. This guideline class is a composite of all assets used in this industry except transportation equipment (general purpose trucks, cars, airplanes, etc., which are included in asset guideline classes with the prefix 00.2), assets used in the provision of administrative services (asset guideline classes with the prefix 00.1), and warehouses, administration buildings, hotels and motels	10	12.5	15	12.5

Index

A

Accelerated depreciation, 132, 167-168
Accounting:
  depreciation, 117-118
  terms, 260
Accounting maneuvers, taxation, 177-180
Accounts payable:
  decision tree, 95, 96
  delaying payment, 114-115
  evaluating discount, 96-113
    annualized interest rate, 97
    borrowing from bank, 103
    change cost of supplier financing, 104-107
    company almost went broke, 98-103
    compensating balances, 112-113
    fallacies of conventional approach, 98
    late payment penalty, 111-112
    liquidity pitfall, 98
    real cost of bank financing, 112-113
    reverse discount strategy, 107-111
  financial considerations, 95-113
  improve cash flow, 115
  non-financial considerations, 114
Accounts receivable:
  collection agencies, 71
  consolidation of customers, 63-64
  discounts, 63-64
  diversification of customers, 62-63
  different collection schedules, 54-59
    accelerating collections, 55, 56, 57
    comparison of operating results, 57-59
    slower collections, 54-55
    typical situation, 54
  factoring, 68-69
  form letters, 64-65
  get customers' money faster, 60-67
  intimate information about customer, 69
  invoicing procedures, 67-68
  late penalties, 64
  legal action, 71-71
  sales personnel as collectors, 65
  screening new accounts, 61-62
  special agreements, 70-71
  top management intervention, 69-70
  tricks, 65-67

Accrual method, 177, 178
Accumulated retained earnings tax, 200
Administration, 301
Advertising, image, 182
Agencies, collection, 71
Agreements, special 70-71
Agriculture, small business, 271
Annualized interest rate, 97
Annual Statement Studies, 276, 291
Assets, 246, 247

B

Balance sheet:
  diagram, 258
  FIFO pays off on, 144
  how derived, 254-255
  LIFO and FIFO, 142
Bank and Finance Manual, 267
Banker's Magazine, 276
Base Closing Economic Injury Loans, 270
Basis, 119
Benevolence, 185
Bonds:
  municipal, 198, 278
  surety, 271
Book value, 321-322
Borrowing from bank, 103, 112-113
Business:
  book value, 321-322
  cashing in, 317-326
  distinctive functions, 301
  duplicating, 295
  existence, 232, 233
  Experience Curve, 290
  finding buyer, 323-324
  hierarchy of needs, 232-233
  investments after cashing in, 326
  keeping, 318-319
  merging, 319-320
  owner-manager, failure, 239-243 (*see also* Failure)
  people nature, 241
  price earnings ratio, 322
  profile, 210-212